THE LIVING WORLD OF HISTORY

The Living World
OF
HISTORY

TEXT BY
Gareth H. Browning

London   COLLINS   Glasgow

First printed in this edition 1963
This Impression 1970

I.S.B.N. 000 100103-5

CONTENTS

CONTENTS

CONTENTS

*The publishers are indebted to the City Art Gallery, Leeds, for permission to
reproduce as an endpaper design, Lady Butler's famous painting of*
The Charge of the Scots Greys *at the Battle of Waterloo*

THE COMING OF MAN

Man appeared on the earth by instalments. It is very generally accepted by scientists that all plants and animals, including human beings, have developed, or " evolved ", from earlier and simpler forms. Because of certain physical and chemical resemblances, biologists include man, the apes, monkeys and lemurs in one animal group, known as Primates. They believe, though many people scorn the idea, that man and the apes have descended from a common remote ancestor.

At a time that may be as much as half a million or a million years ago, vast areas of the earth were shivering in the grip of the Ice Age. In the northern hemisphere, half Europe, including Britain as far south as the Thames, became covered by an advancing ice sheet. The movement of ice occurred not once but four times. In between, as the ice retreated, there were very long periods when the climate became temperate again.

FOSSIL REMAINS

It is to the Ice Age, and to an even remoter epoch, that the earliest fossil evidences of evolving man are assigned. The earlier physical remains combine, in varying degrees, characteristics of both ape and man; and it is often hard to decide whether a particular creature should be described as an ape with some man-like features (a man-ape), or a man with some ape-like features (an ape-man). This is seen extensively in the numerous fossils (whose finding began in Bechuanaland, in Africa, in 1924) of a group which has been given the name of *Australopithecidae* (the southern apes). The fossils suggest that they belonged to creatures who stood and walked erect—a momentous advance in man's evolu-

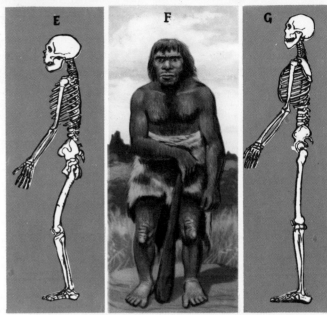

E. *Skeleton found in the Dordogne area of France.* F. *Scientific reconstruction of living man on basis of skeleton.* G. *Compare skeleton of Australian aborigine.*

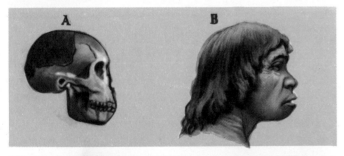
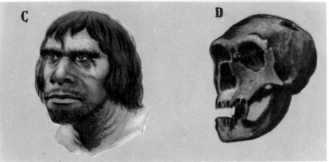

A. *and* B. *Skull and reconstructed living model of Piltdown man, now exposed as a fraud.* C. *and* D. *Skull and reconstructed living model of* Homo Neanderthalensis.

tionary progress. The period of this group was reckoned at some 750,000 years ago. The *Australopithecidae* do not appear to have reached the stage of making tools, though doubtless they made use of any implements, such as sticks and long animal bones, that came to hand. However, as recently as 1959 some surprises occurred when, in Tanganyika, an almost complete skull was unearthed which is thought to date back another million years. And nearby lay some very crude stone tools. Now the *making*, far more than the mere *using*, of tools has been a decisive step towards man's ultimate supremacy in the age-long struggle for existence. This points to an increasing capacity for thought and planning of the implements. The Tanganyika finds, therefore, show that the primitive I.Q. was definitely on the rise $1\frac{3}{4}$ million years ago.

Going back in the story to 1891, what were then generally accepted as the oldest physical fossils in man's ancestry were found in Java. Their owner was christened *Pithecanthropus erectus* (erect ape-man), for he, too, had abandoned progress on all-fours. He may have lived more than half a million years ago. *Pithecanthropus pekinensis* (ape-man of Peking) whose remains were discovered from 1927 onwards, existed at roughly the same period and was very closely related to *Pithecanthropus erectus*. He could make stone tools and had stumbled·on the priceless secret of producing fire. Discoveries begun in 1856 in the River Neander valley (the Neanderthal), Germany, revealed the skull cap bones and implements of another creature who was well on the way to becoming wholly a man. He and his kind may have begun to shamble over the earth from 200,000 to 100,000 years ago. The erect ape-man, the ape-man of Peking and Neanderthal man, together with other primitive

Long ago Europe was thinly populated by an aboriginal race who lived mainly by hunting. Palaeolithic man threw stones to ward off attacks by animal or man.

beings, developed a way of life, or culture, which archaeologists call the Palaeolithic or Old Stone Age.

HOMO SAPIENS

It is not certain whether these extinct beings are man's direct ancestors, but the skeletons found in 1868 at Cro-Magnon, France, are much more advanced. They were those of men of our own type—*Homo sapiens* (intelligent man). These people and their successors are thought to have drifted into Europe from Africa or Asia from at least 25,000 years ago. They were an accomplished folk, and carved life-like images of wild horses and monstrously fat women. They drew and painted astonishingly vivid pictures of reindeer, bison and other animals on the smooth walls of their cave dwellings. Twenty-five thousand years is nothing in the vast time-span of evolution, but other finds made in 1935, on Britain's own doorstep, further enlarged the horizons of Modern Man. A chance discovery at Swanscombe, Kent, revealed early implements and parts of the skull of a man who was probably very similar to *Homo Sapiens*. The deposits in which this fossil lay dated back at least 100,000 years. At

Dating back to Palaeolithic times, early man left on the walls of caves a remarkable pictorial record of his activities, his prowess as a hunter and the animals he hunted. These cave paintings were executed about 12,000 years ago.

present, that is as far back as we can trace the footsteps of Modern Man.

NEW STONE AGE

From the period of Cro-Magnon man, progress in the conditions of life began to speed up. Gradually it reached a stage of culture called the Neolithic or New Stone Age. Formerly, in the Old Stone Age, man had sharpened his tools merely by chipping. By now he had learned to produce a better edge to produce superior tools by grinding and polishing. Furthermore, men were learning agriculture, domesticating sheep and cattle, and making pottery. Settled life led to the growth of large village communities living in huts or pit-dwellings or, as in Egypt, in brick houses. Some of them, like the earliest phase of Maiden Castle, Dorset, were situated on hill tops. A most interesting type is that of the Swiss lake dwellings—wooden houses raised above the water on piles. The New Stone Age culture first appeared in the Near East from about 6,000 B.C. and reached western Europe about 2,500 B.C.

THE BRONZE AGE

About 2,000 B.C. a great leap forward, again appearing

The discovery of metals gave a new impetus to civilisation, enabling early man to fashion tools and implements. At first only the more malleable materials such as copper and tin were worked.

first in the Near East, was made. At first man learned how to produce copper, and then an alloy of copper and tin called bronze, which is much harder than copper and enabled him to fashion a greater variety of superior tools and implements. This was the bronze age and it came to Britain in about 1,800 B.C.

THE IRON AGE

After bronze came iron. The invaluable metal had long been in limited use in the progressive Near East, but it was not until about 1,000 B.C. that it spread over Europe. Invaders—most probably Celtic peoples—brought the gift to Britain some 500 years later. The iron age opened up a period of new inventions and immense progress in social, industrial and artistic life.

Meantime, from 4,000 B.C. onwards, the first great organised civilisations—Sumeria, Egypt, Assyria and Babylon—had arisen, and recorded history had begun. Europe, however, still lagged behind, only slowly responding to the stimulating impulses received from the Orient.

CRADLE-LANDS OF CIVILISATION

During the fourth millenium B.C., while Europe was still living in the middle phase of the Stone Age, the earliest civilisations were born in the Near and Middle East.

The valleys of the Nile in Egypt and of the Tigris and Euphrates in Mesopotamia, where the rivers annually flooded and renewed the soil, offered attractively fertile settling places to early man. In time, the first groups of settlers grew into teeming communities: they further irrigated the land; they built splendid cities; great empires arose, with priests and kings and a cultured society; efficient administrative systems were developed; the arts and crafts flourished; and manufacturers and commerce brought wealth and luxury.

In Egypt, the primitive inhabitants of the Old Stone Age gave place, about 5,000 B.C., to a blend of peoples who, by the end of the fourth millenium B.C., had built up a thriving civilisation.

The fortunate tourist who takes a steamship trip up the Nile may gaze upon the massive remains of pyramids, temples and tombs that date back to 5,000 years ago. The gigantic pyramids are the tombs of Egypt's god-kings, the Pharaohs. The great pyramid of Cheops at Gizeh stands 450 feet high and, it is said, employed the labour of 100,000 men for twenty years. Further upstream, the astonished tourist beholds works no less overpowering in their sheer magnitude. The ruins of the great city of Thebes and the vast temple of Karnak suggest giants' work rather than man's. In the immense colonnaded hall of the temple are sculptured columns seventy feet in height. Still further south, at Abu Simbel, the colossal rock statues of Rameses II are nearly as tall.

In Egypt's palmy days, industry, foreign commerce, and successful wars poured untold wealth into the coffers of the Pharaohs and the nobles. Their magnificent palaces and houses, of sun-dried brick or stone, were sumptuously equipped with richly inlaid furniture, beautiful tapestries, and the handiwork of accomplished sculptors, painters, goldsmiths, jewellers and glaziers.

Ancient Egypt is like a bright pupil who walks off with a whole batch of first and second prizes. By 3,800 B.C., her people were working copper mines to provide metal (instead of stone) for their weapons and tools. Their sailing ships and their use of stone in building are the earliest on record. They may be the creators, before 1,500 B.C., of the first known alphabet, in which each sign represents a single letter. They made the first materials for true writing—at all events in the Western world: reeds for pens; a mixture of water, vegetable gum and soot for ink; and strips of the reed called *papyrus* for paper.

When the 30th dynasty of the Pharaohs came to an end in the mid-fourth century B.C., it had endured for nearly 3,000 years.

THE SUMERIANS

In Mesopotamia we stand in the battle-area of a succession of rising and falling kingdoms. The first of them, Sumeria, may well be even older than Egypt. Excavations at Ur (the biblical Ur of the Chaldees, Abraham's reputed birthplace) have uncovered treasures of tomb and temple architecture, sculpture, gold and copper work, and jewellery that tell of a rich and splendid civilisation that flourished about 3,500 B.C., and began at least 500 years earlier.

By about 3,500 B.C., the Sumerians were using picture writing. Writing began by drawing pictures to represent objects and ideas. The Sumerians later modified their pictures into standardised signs for words or syllables. They invented the " cuneiform " style of writing. It was done on

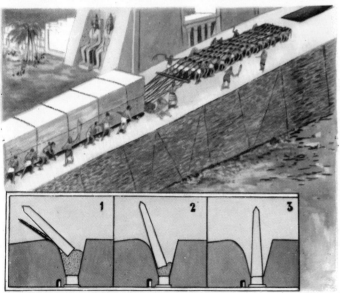

The three inset pictures demonstrate the method the ancient Egyptians used to erect an obelisk. The same system was used to build the Pyramids.

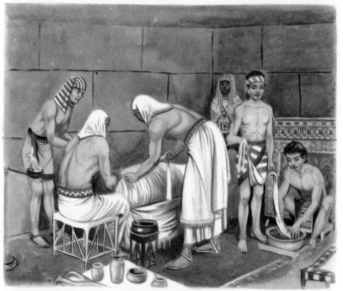

Embalming was practised by many ancient peoples, including the Egyptians. The internal organs are removed from the body and preserved in special jars.

11

The Assyrians built magnificent palaces, the walls of which were adorned with images of winged lions with human heads.

soft clay tablets with a blunt-ended reed which made cuneiform (wedge-shaped) impressions. The clay tablets were afterwards hardened by baking.

About 2,550 B.C., the Sumerians were conquered by the first of a series of Semitic peoples, the race which included the Jews. One of these peoples, the Amorites, had a famous king, Hammurabi, who established the first Babylonian Empire before 2,000 B.C. His most enduring monument is his extraordinarily comprehensive code of laws, which were based on the Sumerian code. By this time bronze was superseding copper.

THE ASSYRIAN TIGER

The Assyrians, with their big noses, square-cut black beards and long, closely-curled hair, next come actively into the story. These shaggy-headed people were a cruel, fighting breed, ferocious as tigers. They came into frequent conflict with the spirited Hittites, a non-Semitic people who ruled over much of Asia Minor and Syria between 2,000 and 1,200 B.C. That the Hittites enjoyed an advanced civilisation is shown by their picture-writing, historical records and highly organised administration. In the 8th and 7th centuries B.C., during a second spell of power, the Assyrian archers, spearmen, and charioteers, using *iron* weapons now, carried the terror of their name to the Aegean Sea and Lower Egypt. But the Assyrians were more than savage men of war. The magnificent palaces and temples in and near far-famed Nineveh show that they were great builders, sculptors and librarians too.

In 612 B.C., the Assyrian tiger was pulled down and the Babylonian Empire of the Chaldeans set up. Its best-remembered emperor was Nebuchadnezzar who, in 586 B.C., carried off the Jews into captivity in Babylon. Nebuchadnezzar rebuilt Babylon and filled it with splendid palaces and temples.

MEDES AND PERSIANS

The Chaldean empire was very short-lived. Tribes belonging to another race, the vigorous Aryans or Indo-Europeans (to which we and the European peoples mostly belong) thrust in and, in 539 B.C., overthrew Babylon. These tribes were the Medes and Persians under the brilliant Cyrus the Persian.

By 525 B.C., the new Persian Empire had made an amazing expansion. It extended from Egypt to Asia Minor and away eastward to the distant borders of India. It was the largest empire the East had ever seen. Persia borrowed from the arts, as well as annexing the territories, of the conquered peoples.

But, two hundred years later, the all-conquering Alexander the Great was on the march. Following on the annihilation of the Persian armies in 331 B.C., the last of the oriental empires passed into the hands of a European master.

Meantime other chapters in the story of early civilisation had been written or begun.

THE AEGEAN CIVILISATION

The island of Crete was the brilliant centre of the widespread Aegean civilisation. From its earliest beginnings it endured for at least 3,000 years, until perhaps 1,400 B.C., when the splendid Cretan capital, Knossos, was sacked and burned. Sixty years ago, excavations begun amid the ruins of the vast and magnificent palace of the legendary King Minos astonished the world. For there were found the evidences of a richly cultured, pleasure-loving, and luxurious society. It was the first-known advanced non-Oriental civilisation, though it was one which had early been influenced by Egypt.

The Cretans were enterprising overseas traders and their downfall brought great advantages to another maritime people. The harbour-towns of the Semitic Phoenicians, Tyre, Sidon and others, were strung out along the coast of Syria. From perhaps before 2,000 B.C., the Phoenicians were carrying their costly merchandise around the Mediterranean. Their North African colony of Carthage, founded before 800 B.C., became the world's greatest maritime state. Though Alexander the Great added the Syrian towns to his string of scalps, Carthage lived to fight to the death—its own—with the Romans in the third and second centuries B.C. Phoenician traders voyaged as far as the Scilly Isles in quest of tin. In one of their bold explorations they are said to have circumnavigated Africa. The alphabet which they developed is the foundation of the Greek and all subsequent European alphabets, including our own.

The three " orders " of Greek architecture, from left to right : Doric, Ionic and Corinthian, named after the Greek tribes who built in these styles.

ANCIENT CHINA

China is a unique country. It is the oldest surviving civilisation; yet it still stands forth as a great power of incalculable import to the world. During its history it has been several times reduced to its last gasp, but always the sick patient has rallied. Its career, indeed, has been a wave-like succession of rises, downfalls and recoveries. China, apparently, is indestructible. The country is larger than the United States of America. Its teeming people are rapidly absorbing Western ideas. And one of them is the grinding and autocratic system of Communism. China stands to-day in the forefront of history.

The Chinese, who belong to the Mongolian race, are fascinating and puzzling, and often a forbidding people. Their oriental make-up is a bewildering compound of superstition and culture, courtesy and pride, simplicity and guile, refinement and callous cruelty.

EARLY SETTLEMENTS

It seems that, more than 4,000—perhaps 5,000—years ago, the direct ancestors of the modern Chinese were settled in two richly fertile regions. One region is in the north, where the Huang-ho (the Yellow River) makes a great bend. The other, lying to the east, forms the immense North China Plain. The people lived in pit dwellings, in caves, in Peter-Pan-like tree-shelters, or in houses raised on piles above the flood waters. They grew grain and reared pigs, dogs, sheep and goats, cattle and horses. As time went on they made roads, invented wheeled vehicles, built boats, shaped pottery and bred silkworms—one of their most profitable future industries. The first pictorial characters of the written language were designed.

Two model emperors are celebrated in ancient tradition as the bright ornaments of the " Golden Age " of peace and prosperity: the " Emperor " Yao (from 2357 B.C.) and Shun.

Another revered sovereign was Yu, who is said to have stemmed a legendary Noah's Ark flood that threatened to turn all those who survived into fishes.

THE SHANG DYNASTY

Actually, it is not until we arrive at the Shang dynasty, or line of rulers,(say from 1523 to 1027 B.C.) that we get a clear and reliable glimpse of the advancing Chinese civilisation. Excavations and discoveries have revealed much of the vigorous life of the Shang capital, near Anyang, about the fourteenth century B.C. The earth-walled city contained the palace of the priest-king and other handsome timbered residences. Amongst the finds were richly decorated pottery, superb bronze vessels, carved and inlaid work and beautiful marble sculptures. The nobles fought and hunted from horsed chariots. The archers used the curly-shaped " reflex " bow, whose penetrating power far exceeded that of the later English longbow.

The most exciting finds were the " oracle bones ". These were mostly pieces of animal bones and tortoise shells, and they were inscribed with questions addressed to the Shang gods and deceased ancestors. The questions were written in the current picture-language and the pictures or " characters " —of buildings, animals, hunting, ploughs and so on—threw a flood of light on the life of the times.

The Shangs, it appears, had a fairly extensive literature. Their books were inscribed, or rather painted, with brush and ink—on narrow strips of wood or bamboo fastened together with cords.

Religion was based on Nature worship, but intimately bound up with the worship of ancestors. The Chinese believed that the universe was regulated by a supreme law which they called the Tao, " the Way ". In harmony with the Tao were the Nature gods—such as the forces of sun,

In China, irrigation and drainage were necessary to fertilise marshy land and, at the same time, stem the disastrous river flooding.
Emperor Yu, of the first millenium B.C., is reputed to have supervised such a scheme of irrigation.

rain, wind, rivers, and mountains, the soil and the grain. Among them Tien, the sky or " Heaven ", became supreme. To an agricultural people these forces were, of course, of fateful and terrifying power. The Shang kings were reverenced as mediators between the higher Nature powers and the people.

Chinese ancestor worship began early in history and only later developed its full range. Each household had its own minor, and often somewhat impish gods—the spirits of the hearth and the courtyard and many others. The family tie was like a bond of steel binding together in harmony, self-sacrifice, courtesy, loyalty and obedience, all the members of the household, which commonly included several generations. The father's power was almost unlimited. And it actually increased with his death, when he became a spirit. The ancestral spirits had to be honoured with regular sacrifices to secure their blessings; otherwise woe betide the family. The importance of the family system cannot be over-emphasised. Indeed China itself was not so much a nation as a collection of families which, together, formed one Great Family under the fatherhood of the sacred emperor.

THE CHOU DYNASTY

The Shangs were followed by the Chous, whose dynasty lasted for the immense period of some 800 years—perhaps from 1027 to 256 B.C. The newcomers carried their arms southwards across the Yangtze-Kiang River and set up a strong feudal system of vassal States. By the fifth century, however, the vassals had got out of hand and China came to consist of about a dozen politically disunited rival kingdoms. A Dark Age began, one of ferocious warfare and brutal anarchy that scarred the land for 260 long years. Before it finished the Chou dynasty was finished too.

Chou times were good times—for the hereditary feudal nobles. They were a cultured, chivalrous and luxury-loving ruling class. Their children were educated for war and peace, particularly in the elaborately polite and ceremonious code of manners which has always distinguished the Chinese. The country peasants were less fortunate. They were serfs, fit only to work and fight and pay taxes in grain and other produce. And here we come to China's ever-recurring weak-

Confucius, China's great philosopher, was born in the year 551 B.C. A man of culture, with a passion for learning and literature, he founded a way of life.

ness—a discontented peasantry who formed nine-tenths of the population. Time after time they rose in savage revolt and wreaked their vengeance in orgies of bloodshed and destruction.

SOCIAL UPHEAVAL

At the end of the Chou period, feudalism was crumbling away. The old class divisions, based on the nobles' monopoly of land, were breaking up. Traders and merchants were amassing wealth in hard cash and rising in the social scale. Changed methods of warfare, too, diminished the prestige of the nobles and increased that of the peasants.

There was as well a different outlook on religion. Men began to feel that the Tao and Heaven demanded good moral conduct, not just ritual sacrifices. The priest-king came to be accepted as the adopted " Son of Heaven ". He ruled by divine right—so long as he ruled justly. Yet, during the Dark Age, there was a grievous decline in public morals, in piety and honour and loyalty to the throne and the family.

One of the unique features of Chinese history is the rise of the " scholar-class ". They appear in an early form, from the sixth to the third centuries B.C. (which includes the Dark Age), as " the Wandering Scholars ". At that time many of them became very active in spreading ideas of reform and enlightenment. The best known was Confucius, who lived from 551 to 479 B.C. He was a man of highly cultured mind with a passion for learning and teaching. He collected the country's ancient literature with its glowing accounts of the happy conditions of the past, and made it the text-book of his teachings. His message was " Return to the ways of the Golden Age and all will be well again ". He sought to revive and extend the neglected code of family life. And he attached supreme importance, as a wholesome discipline, to a restoration of the half-forgotten religious rites and ceremonies. His system is not actually a religious creed; it is a code of morality pleasing to Heaven for practical daily life. The great teacher's labours bore little immediate fruit. That was to come later.

The Chou period embraced the great age of Chinese philosophy. It also included the classical age of literature, comprising the works of the early sages and moralists, historians and poets. These came to be cherished as a treasury of ancient wisdom and the true source of instruction for all succeeding times.

THE CH'IN DYNSATY

After the Chous came the Ch'in. A reunited China arose, stretching now from southern Manchuria to the lower Yangtze River valley and from Tibet to the eastern sea-coast. Its creator took the proud title of Shih Huang Ti, " the First Emperor ", and proceeded to make himself an emperor indeed. He destroyed the power of the hereditary feudal nobles and ruled as an absolute despot. He ruthlessly burned the ancient writings to make his subjects stop thinking too much about the Golden Age. He completed the Great Wall of China, one of the constructional wonders of the ancient world. His aim was to keep out the untamable barbarians of the Mongolian steppes—then known as the Hsiung Nu—who from the earliest times had continually harassed the northern frontiers. His dynasty fell in 207 B.C. and the Han line that succeeded it ushered in one of the most brilliant epochs of China's history. In war, in commerce, in the splendour of court life, the empire became universally famous. Sculpture, architecture and other arts and crafts flourished. Literature expanded. Paper was invented in 105 B.C., a thousand years in

Confucius taught that respect for one's family was of prime importance. Social order was based on virtue, brotherhood and justice. Eventually, Confucius collected many followers, and disciples followed the master wherever he went.

advance of Europe. In the conquests of Wu Ti, " the Warlike Emperor ", who reigned from 140 B.C. for fifty-three years, China touched hands with the Western world. Northern Korea was occupied and the emperor's sway extended southwards to Annam and westwards to the gateways of Persia and India. Later, Pan Chao, a government clerk turned soldier carried the Chinese arms to the Caspian Sea. The advance into Central Asia opened the great Silk Road. Along this highway China—which alone possessed the secret of producing the finest silks—carried on her oldest and richest commercial traffic with Rome and the West.

REVIVAL IN LITERATURE AND RELIGION

Meantime important social changes were occurring. With the ending of feudalism and the virtual passing away of the nobility, a new upper class of gentry, not of noble blood, gradually took shape. Through their growing monopoly of classical education they became the recognised " scholar class ". Unlike their forerunners, however, in this as in other respects, they were not " Wandering Scholars ". It was mainly from them that the officials who administered the government of the State—the Civil Service—were increasingly recruited. The teachings of Confucius were now coming into favour. Much of the old classical literature, so closely associated with his name, was recovered; and its works furnished—and continued to do so down to recent times— the principal text-books for the Civil Service examinations. The sound moral principles which these taught were valued far more than general knowledge in qualifying the students for high office. The scholars became the stronghold of the Confucian learning and the Confucian creed. And that creed (though frequently changing and suffering periods of disfavour) formed the dominant code of the educated classes and, in a measure, an established state religion, for two thousand years.

Another religion—Taoism—now came to the fore. In its earlier form its followers had sought happiness by the renouncing of the restless world of action and passively accepting the simple, harmonious life of Nature as regulated by the Tao. Such notions have little attraction for

Westerners, but to the mystical Chinese temperament they made a compelling appeal. Later, however, Taoism became hopelessly entangled with really fantastic beliefs and also with popular magic and other hocus-pocus. In the end a mixed and debased form of the creed became mainly a religion for the ignorant masses.

In A.D. 220 the Han line was overwhelmed by an avalanche of calamities: civil wars, peasant risings and barbarian invasions. Its end marks the conclusion of a constructive phase in China's institutions. We may summarise the position in this way. The Chinese people were made up of the peasant class, the artisans, craftsmen and traders, merchants and manufacturers, the big farmers and the scholar class. The nobility of birth had faded out. Supreme over all stood the emperor, the sacred Son of Heaven. Parliament was an unknown institution. Three " religions " were practised: Confucianism, Taoism, and the recently arrived Buddhism which we shall come to presently. The family, with its ancestor-worship, was the dominating factor in the life of the community. A common culture, based on ancient history and custom, language, literature and religion, bound the people together and proudly distinguished them from all " barbarian " races—meaning the rest of the world. Now the Chinese are the most conservative of people. They have always shown a fixed and devoted attachment to their ancient ways of life. The pattern of their customs and institutions, laid down by the third century A.D., remained fundamentally unchanged till modern times.

FOUNDING OF THE SUI DYNASTY

A woeful "Age of Confusion " followed the great dynasty's crash. Its foreign conquests fell away. Violence and insecurity reigned at home. The empire split into warring kingdoms. Then the Hsiung Nu descended and, by 316, seized all the country north of the Yangtze-Kiang valley. The imperial court, with the scholars, fled across the river and transferred the standard of empire and the torch of civilisation to a new capital, Nanking. Unhappy China was torn in two. But, in 589, a Chinese prime minister, Yang Chien, once more brought north and south together and founded the Sui dynasty.

Work was started on the Great Wall of China in 215 B.C. Although intended as a complete defence against the fierce Mongols, it did not succeed in saving China from the invasion of Jenghiz Khan.

It was during the Age of Confusion that Buddhism which had previously arrived from India, established its hold. In China, however, it was a transformed creed. New and adored figures were introduced who, in their compassion for humanity, were always at hand to help sufferers along an easier road to salvation. The invading Buddhist creed, with its new promises of divine aid and comfort in this world and a heaven of bliss hereafter, was widely and eagerly adopted side by side with Confucianism and Taoism. The strangely accommodating Chinese attitude to religion is quite incomprehensible to the Western mind. In practice the three different creeds overlapped, each borrowing from the others.

The Sui dynasty was overthrown in 618 by one of China's great characters Li Shih-min (also known as T'ai Tsung) who made the new T'ang line glorious. His strong arm mastered all Inner Mongolia, recovered control of much of Central Asia and the Silk Road and restored the empire's prestige abroad. He renewed the shattered administration and modified the harsh laws that oppressed the peasantry. He was an ardent Confucianist and his reforms were decisive in advancing the scholars towards the control of the Civil Service. In the course of time that control was to be of momentous consequence. The scholars became the ruling and most highly honoured class in the State, an aristocracy of learning. Right down to modern times they served as guardians of the ancient culture that united and sustained the spirit of the Chinese community during the numerous storms and stresses of their history.

Soon after Li Shih-min's death in 649, an unheard-of event took place; a female grasped the reins of power. The empress Wu, the wife of the dead emperor's timid and lazy second son, was a dominating and unscrupulous woman. But she had talent and intelligence and she ruled with vigour and efficiency.

The empress's grandson, Hsuang Tsung, who mounted the throne in 713, carried the great upsurge of China's fortunes to new heights of fame. During the T'ang period, and especially under Hsuang Tsung, while Europe lay under the shadow of the Dark Ages, China's achievements made her the hub and centre of civilisation. Her poetry and prose, painting, sculpture and music, pottery and porcelain created an age of unparalleled artistic splendour. People of all nations, including Christian missionaries, flocked to Ch'ang-an, the western capital, which might claim to be the most brilliantly civilised metropolis in the world.

THE SUNG DYNASTY

But, true to its wave-like habit, the empire took another downward plunge. Its military power was broken by successive defeats. Its foreign possessions were again lost. Civil war blazed out. Military adventurers seized power in the provinces. The frontiers were overrun. A terrible peasant revolt raged for nine years. In 907, the T'ang dynasty crashed and the country became an agglomeration of independent States. At last, in 960, by the effort of a group of army officers, General Chao Kuang-yin was forced on to the imperial throne and thus established the Sung dynasty. But the Sung emperors were no warriors. They lost two northern regions to the barbarians, and finally a half-savage tribe, the Nuchens from Manchuria, pressed southwards and crossed the Yangtze-Kiang. In 1141, the emperor had to cede to the barbarian " Chin " dynasty almost the whole of the north and agree to pay tribute. Once again China was rent in twain.

Throughout her long history, China was plagued by constant invasions; first from the nomads of Central Asia, then from the all-conquering hordes of Jenghiz Khan.

The Sung court settled at Hangchow in the south. Dominated by its scholar-officials, its tastes were all for peaceful culture and refinement. Printing had reached its final stage in the making of movable type of single letters—four centuries ahead of Europe—and a flood of printed books stimulated education and learning. Painting, scholarly literature and philosophy reached their maturity. From this time onwards Chinese civilisation and culture made few noteworthy advances beyond their existing high level. The fixed native distrust of change was the gravest defect of the ruling scholar-class. Their blind veneration for the ancient institutions blocked the path to all new and progressive ideas. The Sung period witnessed a great expansion of maritime commerce; but the Silk Road was blocked and China lost all contact with the Western world.

JENGHIZ KHAN

The thirteenth century brought the most calamitous barbarian invasion the country had ever suffered. The all-conquering Tartar or Mongolian Jenghiz Khan and his descendants swept down from the north like a tidal wave and the empires of the Chin and the Sung were completely submerged. In 1279, Jenghiz's grandson Kublai Khan was emperor of all China. The ancient civilisation received a staggering blow; its people suffered untold misery and degradation.

Yet there were compensations: under the rule of the Mongol " Yuan " dynasty a system of imperial highways, with an efficient postal service, linked China with Persia and Russia. The country was reopened to the outside world and merchants, missionaries, craftsmen and others streamed in. The commerce of the Silk Road revived. New foods and medicines were introduced. It was during the reign of Kublai that Marco Polo, the famous Venetian traveller, made his famous journey to the great Khan's magnificent new capital of Peking and, on his return, whetted the appetite of Europe for a share of China's boundless wealth and commerce.

But the Mongol empire soon fell apart and the Yuan dynasty lasted only eighty-nine years.

THE GLORY THAT WAS GREECE

Greece is a miracle of history. There seems no other way of describing it. Its people were the first primitive Europeans to come fully under the spotlight of history; yet, at an early date, and in an astonishingly brief period, they scaled the very peaks of cultured and civilised life.

From perhaps about the 16th century B.C., Greek-speaking Aryan tribes were rolling down from the north. By about 1,000 B.C. they had spread over the region of the Aegean Sea—Greece, the Aegean Islands and the neighbouring coast of Asia Minor. There they had blundered into an advanced civilisation—the Aegean—whose splendours must have made their jaws drop. The invaders subdued their cultured predecessors, but gratefully absorbed much of their culture.

We learn a lot about the life of part of this period from two of the world's greatest epic poems, the *Iliad* and *Odyssey* of the blind bard Homer. Boys and girls who have not yet read English translations of these vivid and fascinating stories of heroic war and adventure about the twelfth century B.C., are to be envied. They have a treat in store.

The Greeks of historic times were men of quick, inquiring minds, eager for knowledge and not less for glory and adventure, whether as warriors, pirates, athletes or otherwise. Proud and free in spirit, they were definitely live wires. Their fertile imaginations coloured all things in heaven and earth with the poetry and beauty of lovely legendary lore. Their supreme god Zeus and his bright company of lesser deities were idealised men and women with human forms and interests.

BEGINNINGS OF DEMOCRACY

The mountainous character of Greece led the tribes to settle in the form of tiny, independent, and largely isolated city-states. At first these were ruled by kings, then sometimes by nobles and "tyrants". Finally there appeared a political system hitherto unknown to history, the system of democracy, or the rule of "the people", a term which excluded slaves and aliens. Foremost among the cities that developed it was Athens, whose effervescent citizens were in truth forward in most activities. In marked contrast were the Spartans: a grave, grim and forbidding people who organised their State on harsh, military and communistic lines.

The Greeks became skilful mariners, active traders and systematic colonists. By the mid-sixth century B.C., the Mediterranean and Black Seas were girdled with their settlements.

In the sixth and fifth centuries B.C., the little city-states came under the long shadow of the mighty Persian empire. It was a crisis in their history that threatened their cherished liberties with the suffocating oppression of Oriental despotism. In the David and Goliath contest that presently ensued, it was Athens that slung most of the pebbles. And the triumph was as astonishing as David's. In the epoch-making land and sea battles of Marathon, Salamis and Plataea, dating from 490 to 479 B.C., the multitudinous Persian hosts and fleets of Darius and Xerxes suffered humiliating defeat and disaster.

Under the exhilaration of the amazing victory the artistic genius of Athens broke into glorious flower. Dramas that are still world-famous were produced. Under the inspiration of its brilliant magistrate Pericles, the city was adorned with superb masterpieces of architecture and sculpture.

Unhappily the triumph went to Athens' head. She established dominion over some of the Aegean islands and Asian city-states and sometimes used her power oppressively. Resentment and envy produced their fatal consequences. In 431 B.C., the Peloponnesian War between Athens and Sparta and their respective allies flamed out. Alas for gifted and enlightened Athens! When the conflict ended after twenty-seven years she was smitten to her knees.

The ensuing years are filled largely with wrangles that were an habitual weakness of the Greek States. On this disturbed scene descended Philip, king of the half-civilised Greek people of Macedon. In 338 B.C., the battle of Chaeronea made him master of Greece and diverted its history into a new channel.

The lasting glory of the Golden Age of Greece (the fifth and fourth centuries B.C.), of which Athens is the epitome, springs from the Greek thirst for knowledge and ideal beauty. In pursuit of these goals the Greeks achieved superlative triumphs in architecture and sculpture, in literature, science and philosophy. Greece owed much to the Egyptian and Aegean civilisations, but what she borrowed she transformed and vitalised by her soaring genius. The names of her most illustrious sons remain stars of the first magnitude to-day: Aristotle, Socrates, and Plato in science or philosophy; Ictinus in architecture; Pheidias in sculpture; Aeschylus, Sophocles, Euripides and Aristophanes in tragedy and comedy; Herodotus and Thucydides in history; and many others. The genius of classical Greece lighted lamps of ennobling thought and artistic refinement that have illuminated the world ever since.

From the top of the Acropolis in Athens, the golden statue of Athene looked out over the hills of Attica.

THE HEBREWS

The Hebrews—or Jews as we commonly call them to-day—have played a unique part in world history. First and foremost, of course, is the fact that one of them was Jesus Christ. Then, in developing their notions of God, they have been an education to mankind. Finally, they have shown that centuries of persecution and exile are powerless to stifle their exclusive sense of racial and religious fellowship.

The Hebrews belong to the Semitic race. In their early days they were rough shepherds wandering with their flocks over the Arabian desert. In that arid waste their longing eyes were ever fixed on Canaan, the land flowing with milk and honey, which was promised by the God of Abraham to the patriarch and his children. *Genesis* and *Exodus* tell us that Abraham reached the goal, only to die there, and that Moses led the children of Israel out of bondage in Egypt.

Probably the Hebrews did not invade Canaan in force until between 1,400 and 1,200 B.C. They found the Canaanites a people well advanced in civilisation, living in walled towns and carrying on a flourishing trade with their neighbours. It was a very long time before they were subdued. Meantime, the two peoples intermarried and the Hebrews were considerably influenced by the Canaanite civilisation and religious practices. Presently some unwelcome neighbours broke in on the scene. The Philistines, a highly civilised and warlike people, settled in the south-west of Palestine and proceeded to make themselves a constant nuisance.

The upshot of a long period of defeat and oppression from various quarters was that the Hebrews sought unity and strength by setting up a monarchy.

The first king, Saul, who began to reign about 1,025 B.C., won many victories over the Philistines, but in the end they routed him and drove him to his death. He was succeeded by David, who brought his people such success and happiness

Over 1,000 years before the birth of Christ, the Jewish people left Egypt on their mass exodus to the Promised Land. With them went the Ark of the Covenant, containing the laws of their people.

that later generations venerated him as their ideal king. After his death came his son Solomon in all his glory. But the Hebrews found the glory rather expensive. The king's luxurious living and extravagant building projects had to be paid for. The people murmured and, after Solomon's death in about 937 B.C., the tiny kingdom split into two tinier kingdoms: the wealthy and civilised Israel in the north and the poor and backward Judah in the south.

Family quarrels are usually uncommonly bitter and there was continual wrangling between the brother kingdoms. Then the long arm of the Assyrian empire reached out over Palestine and in 722 and 715 B.C. put an end to the bickering.

Israel as a kingdom was blotted out. Judah survived; but, when the Assyrians gave place to the Chaldeans, Nebuchadnezzar, in 586 B.C., destroyed Jerusalem and carried off large numbers of the unhappy Hebrews to Babylon. And there they remained for at least fifty years till the Chaldeans went down in their turn and their Persian conqueror, Cyrus, set the exiles free to return home.

They had not spent *all* their time weeping by the waters of Babylon. They had acquired a great deal of the polished civilisation of their masters. And they had completed the process of religious education which their race had been undergoing through the long centuries of suffering and subjection. In their early desert days their god Yahveh (Jehovah) had been to them a fierce tribal god of war. Adversity and affliction and the burning ardour of their inspired prophets—Amos, Hosea, Isaiah and many others—had taught them a loftier conception of divinity. Other nations were still sunk in the superstitious worship of a multitude of tyrannous and arbitrary deities. But the Hebrews had risen to the idea of one universal and righteous god and loving father whose children must serve him, not merely by burnt offerings, but in the virtue of their lives. This transforming truth was their sublime contribution to the moral and spiritual advancement of mankind.

The returned exiles and their successors over a long period rebuilt Jerusalem and its temple and set up the rule of the high priests in place of the old monarchy. They assembled the ancient Hebrew writings and divided them into three parts: a code of laws which constitutes the religion of the Jews; the works of the prophets; and a body of sacred songs—the Book of Psalms—for use in the temple services, together with other writings. In Christian times all these writings were collected and became the Bible of the Jews and the Old Testament of the Christians.

Time brought new taskmasters. The Romans engulfed Palestine, and in A.D. 70 a fanatical Jewish revolt brought new calamities. The Emperor Vespasian's son, Titus, laid Jerusalem in ruins and destroyed the Temple. The Sanhedrin (the Jewish national council) and the high priesthood were abolished. Long before these disastrous days the Jews had been dispersing from their homeland. In 132-35, during the Emperor Hadrian's reign, the suppression of another revolt completed their national destruction. Judea was practically depopulated and the Jews barred from Jerusalem. In the ensuing centuries the scattered exiles were everywhere alternately tolerated or persecuted. The eighteenth century brought relief, and in the twentieth a new promise dawned. In 1948, the republic of Israel (in south-west Palestine) was proclaimed. There, two million Jews (one sixth of their total world population) are vigorously carving out a national home. But they face the bitter hostility of the neighbouring Arabs and no one can foretell what will be the outcome.

ALEXANDER THE GREAT

Some men are born lucky; others are born geniuses. Alexander was both. He was lucky in his father, King Philip of Macedon, and in his tutor, Aristotle.

The Macedonians were Greeks, but coarse and uncultivated Greeks—rough diamonds. King Philip, however, had a profound respect for the splendid Greek, or " Hellenic ", culture of the south. (The Greeks called themselves " Hellenes " and their country " Hellas "). He moulded his boorish subjects into a nation. And he organised his fighting men into a professional army whose power centred on a massed body of spearmen—the renowned Macedonian phalanx—operating in conjunction with cavalry. Alexander's tutor, Aristotle, still ranks as the foremost intellect of classical Greece. Between father and tutor the young prince grew up with a passionate admiration for Hellenic culture and for the Greek heroes of old.

HIS MISSION

Before his death in 336 B.C., King Philip had made himself master of Greece and designed a tremendously ambitious project. The Greeks' old-time enemy, the vast, oppressive Persian Empire, was settling into decline. Philip planned to lead the Greeks and Macedonians against it. When Alexander, a recklessly brave and high-spirited youth of twenty, succeeded his father he eagerly adopted his mission.

The breathless years that followed his setting forth in 334 B.C., were to show whether he had genius as well as luck. The first indication came at the river Granicus, where he scattered the Persian host. Next, he liberated the Greek cities in Asia Minor from the Persian yoke. In the battle of Issus, he routed Darius III and sent him scuttling across the Euphrates. Marching southward, he stormed Tyre and captured all the other Phoenician seaports along the Syrian coast, then strolled on to gather ancient Egypt into his hands.

Having conquered the empire of Darius, Alexander the Great received homage from the governors and viceroys of the ancient Persian provinces.

A trifling march of a thousand miles or so took his victorious troops across the Tigris towards Arbela. There he finally crushed Darius, who was later murdered by his own officers. Babylon and Susa fell to the young champion of Hellas and soon he entered the royal city of Persepolis in triumph, like a Macedonian St. George who had slain the Persian dragon.

But there were still illimitable regions to be subdued. For four years Alexander led his armies northwards and eastwards till at length they crossed the remote frontiers of India. There the murmurings of his weary troops brought him reluctantly to a halt. In 324 B.C., he was back in Susa. A calculation of his mileage from the map is an entertaining pastime that yields some staggering figures.

DIVINE STATUS

Our young hero is said to have sighed for more worlds to conquer. But, according to some authorities at least, he was something more than a military genius with a thirst for glory; he was a great administrator and a man of vision. His ambition, it is said, was to create a world-wide empire in which Greeks and Orientals should enjoy equality and the benefits of Hellenic civilisation. So he adopted many Oriental practices and appointed Persians to high rank. Furthermore, he married a Persian lady, Roxana, the loveliest maiden in Asia, and later took two more Persian wives, at the same time inducing large numbers of his officers and men to follow his example. His policy, and perhaps his immense vanity, led him into some strange and despotic courses and aroused violent discontent among his own people. The Pharaohs of Egypt had always been accounted divine. Alexander encouraged his people to accord him the honours of a god.

But by now he had fought his last battle. In 323 B.C. he suddenly fell sick and died. He was barely thirty-three and his crowded reign had lasted but thirteen years.

His swiftly-won empire fell apart, to be divided among his self-seeking generals and their successors: the line of Antigonus in Europe, of Seleucus in Asia, of Ptolemy in Egypt. These monarchs more or less preserved their sway and upheld Greek civilisation till the oncoming tide of Roman power swept them away.

Alexander's supreme achievement was not so much his dazzling military conquests as the immeasurable consequences that flowed from them. During what is called " the Hellenistic Age " of some three hundred years following Alexander's death, the clear light of Greek civilisation and culture was spread afar over the old empires of Egypt, Mesopotamia and beyond. Everywhere the language and institutions, the art, learning and inspiration of Greece took root. The magnificent city of Alexandria in Egypt, in particular, became a renowned centre of learning and literature, as it was of commerce. There, mathematics (Euclid taught in Alexandria), astronomy, grammar, medical science and other studies made important advances. Meantime, in Europe, the Greek cities, quarrelling as usual among themselves, chafed under the Macedonian monarchy and declined in power and commerce. Yet Athens remained renowned as the home of philosophy.

THE GRANDEUR THAT WAS ROME

The Romans liked to believe that they were descended from the semi-divine Trojan hero Aeneas, about whom we read in Homer's *Iliad*. We, however, have to accept them as a number of undistinguished primitive tribes who settled in Latium about 1,000 B.C. and formed the village communities on the Seven Hills above the Tiber that were the humble forerunners of the great city of Rome. Much of their early story is legendary, but it seems that, for a period ending about 510 B.C., they were subject to Etruscan kings. The Etruscans had developed an astonishingly advanced civilisation and the crude Romans took many improving lessons from them before they threw them out.

THE NEW REPUBLIC

Having become their own masters in a new republic they proceeded to make themselves other people's masters. By the early third century B.C., they were supreme in Italy. Character, statesmanship and military efficiency were their " secret weapons ", for they were a sober, sagacious and disciplined people. They made steady soldiers and industrious peasant-farmers, and they were strictly attentive to the duties they owed to their gods and their families.

During this period of expansion the republic hammered out its system of constitutional government. The hammering involved a long struggle between the nobles, or *patricians*, and the people, or *plebeians*. The principal officials of the republic, elected annually, were the two consuls, who acted as joint-presidents or chief magistrates, and the tribunes, who stood for the people. In theory, the people assembled in the forum or market-place enjoyed sovereign rights. But in practice, as time went on, the controls of the government machine passed largely into the hands of the Senate. This august body was composed of nobles and distinguished public servants and it formed an ideal combination of wisdom, experience and staunch patriotism.

Rome could not rival Carthage at sea, so a storm-wrecked Carthaginian ship supplied the hard-pressed Romans with a model to copy.

Hannibal, the Carthaginian soldier and enemy of Rome, is best remembered for his journey over the Alps. Undertaken to avoid the enemy on the coast, this march was followed by many victories before his final defeat by Scipio at Zama.

CARTHAGE

Secure at home, the Romans were now faced with a threat from overseas. The great Phoenician colony of Carthage had established a mighty empire in north Africa, Spain, Sicily, Corsica and Sardinia. As the supreme power in the western Mediterranean it threatened not merely Rome's commercial growth but its very existence. A life-and-death conflict was inevitable. The first grim struggle covered twenty-three years, from 264 to 241 B.C. The Romans had to learn how to build and man a formidable war-fleet. They learned the lesson so well that they finally sent the Carthaginian navy to the bottom. The second conflict raged from 218 to 201 B.C. It was a war of giants.

The brilliant Carthaginian general, Hannibal, conceived the audacious plan of marching overland through Spain and Gaul and across the Alps and so right into the heart of Italy. And he carried it out. But he met his match later, in his own country, when he faced the Roman general Scipio. The final stroke in the struggle with Carthage was delivered in 146 B.C.: when the city itself was razed to the ground. Meantime Rome had virtually made herself mistress of Macedonia, Greece, Asia Minor and Egypt. In somewhat over a century she had become the supreme power in the civilised world of the Mediterranean.

REPUBLIC IN DECLINE

But success spoiled her. The riches, the hosts of slaves, and the unsettling foreign ideas of conduct that poured into Italy from the conquered provinces, undermined the simple, manly virtues of the stern old Roman character. The peasant-farmers began to lose their little holdings to the proprietors of vast estates, who worked them with slave labour. In the overcrowded cities, idleness, luxury and vice spread like a pestilence. The provinces were oppressed by

Gnaeus Pompey, distinguished Roman general, was born in 106 B.C., and died in 48 B.C. As Caesar's influence soared, Pompey's declined until he was eventually defeated in battle at Pharsalus in Greece.

committed suicide, effectively removed Antony and left Augustus master of the Roman world.

Thenceforth, though he prudently preserved the time-honoured forms of the republican institutions, he was virtually emperor. He reorganised the State's defences, its finances and administration, its provincial government, even its morals. Augustus and his successors were to show that the empire, unlike the republic, could rule. The new era falls within the Golden Age of Latin literature which produced two of the world's greatest poets, Virgil and Horace. Livy and other great writers also flourished about this time.

ROME AT ITS ZENITH

The two centuries from the reign of Augustus—during which Britain, Thrace and other regions were absorbed—exhibit the Roman Empire in all its grandeur. While the legions defended the frontiers, the provinces basked in the sunlight of the Roman peace. Roman law and justice,

After the death of Pompey, Caesar became undisputed master of Rome and was elected dictator for life. He incurred the hatred of those Romans who desired a Republic, and a conspiracy organised by Brutus and Cassius led to his death.

extortionate governors. Bitter class struggles arose, between poor and rich, people and Senate. Civil wars flared up. Rome was torn by party strife. Most bodeful evil of all, the self-seeking leaders of the warring factions raised professional armies whose loyalties were given to them instead of to the State. The fabric of the republic was shaken. And Rome had proved unequal to the duty of governing the world she had conquered.

Yet the periods of successful war and subsequent decay were a fruitful time in the quieter fields of art and letters. The Romans were a practical rather than an artistic people. But closer contact with the splendours of ancient Greek culture aroused in their educated classes a passion for all things Greek—literature and philosophy, architecture and sculpture, language and education. Rome became the western heir of Greek civilisation.

THE RISE OF CAESAR

Political events moved towards a crisis midway in the first century B.C. Two towering historical figures stood face to face: the illustrious general Pompey "the Great", who was allied to the aristocratic party; and Julius Caesar, who was resolved on curing the sickness of the State by any means. Caesar had already added Gaul to the republic in his masterly campaigns of 58-51 B.C., besides paying Britain a couple of visits. In 48 B.C., Pompey went down before him; later, in Alexandria, he was murdered. Caesar was made a dictator for life.

What was the great soldier-statesman's ultimate ambition? Was it to destroy the republic and set himself up as king? That at least is what the ardent defenders of the ancient constitution feared. They determined to thwart the design. In 44 B.C., the "patriots" led by Brutus and Cassius hatched a dark conspiracy: Caesar was stabbed to death in the Senate house at Rome.

MASTER OF ROME

With the assassination of the one man capable of restoring peace and order, chaos set in again. Caesar's adopted son Octavian (afterwards called Augustus), a youth wise beyond his eighteen years, stepped forward to carry on the work of reform which Caesar had begun. He found a dangerous rival in Mark Antony, Caesar's former supporter; but the sea-fight of Actium in 31 B.C., after which Antony and Cleopatra

The Roman emperor Augustus restored order in Rome and to protect his own person he had nine cohorts of picked soldiers, named " Praetorians ".

Roman security and order, Roman roads, the Latin language and the Greco-Roman culture linked them together in a common citizenship. Roman cities gave them paved streets, fine houses, town-halls and market-places, public baths, shops and inns, amphitheatres for public shows, and all the other pleasures of a rich and civilised social life. To one people, however, the period brought disaster— the Hebrews, or Jews were exiled from their own land when it was overrun by the Romans. In Britain too the Roman advance, with the massacre of the Druids in Mona and the suppression of Boadicea's rebellion at Camulodunum, brought destruction and tumult before it finally brought peace, law and reform to the island.

THE EMPIRE IN DECLINE

But the good times could not last for ever and, before the third century A.D. opened, the sunlight of the Roman peace was becoming overclouded. From republican days the fierce barbarian hordes beyond the frontiers had been knocking on the gates and sometimes bursting through. To conciliate these marauders, they had been permitted to settle large colonies within the imperial borders. From the early third century, with the decline of the population of Italy, the frontier defences were entrusted almost entirely to aliens. There were other signs of the growing weakness of the empire: further barbarian irruptions, civil disorders and provincial insurrections. Rival armies set up their own chosen emperors. The Roman peace had ended. Agriculture decayed. Commerce was ruined. Ground down by increasing taxation and compulsory public service, men's sense of patriotism and civic duty slackened.

CHRISTIANITY ACCEPTED

In the fourth century, two memorable events occurred. Christianity had long been extending its footing. Now it won over the Emperor Constantine. By an edict of 313 it was made a freely permitted faith. At the death of Constantine in 337, it had become the foremost creed. The Emperor Theodosius, who reigned from 379 to 395, established it as the official religion of the empire. The other event was the

The momentous meeting between Pope Leo I and Attila, King of the Huns, took place on the banks of the Mincio. Attila's army was on the march, plundering and devastating Italy, and Leo I is remembered as the Pope who saved the city of Rome from the " scourge of God ".

transfer of the seat of empire from Rome to Byzantium, where, in 330, Constantine completed the new city which he named Constantinople. No one could have foreseen that this was the prelude to the establishment of the Roman Empire of the East that was destined to outlast the Empire in the West by nearly a thousand years.

The century brought no cure for the maladies of the West. The barbarian pressure steadily increased. When the decisive clash came it was like a combat between an enfeebled giant and a pack of ravenous wolves. From 378 onwards, the fierce-eyed, fair-haired German hordes swarmed across the Rhine and the Danube and swept over the helpless provinces. In 410, Rome was sacked. In the mid-century came the terrible Attila and his Huns in a carnival of butchery. In 476, the last emperor in the West was dethroned. German kings reigned in Italy, Gaul, Spain and North Africa. Britain was overrun by Picts from the north and Saxon pirates from the south.

SURVIVAL OF CULTURE

But, though the body of the Western Empire was torn apart, its ghost lived on. The invaders themselves, many of them already Christians and partly Romanised, stood in awe of the majestic institution and regarded it as indestructible. So Roman law and administration, the Latin language in various forms and dialects, and something of the Roman way of life survived the deluge. In the course of time the spoken Latin developed into the French, Spanish, Italian and Portuguese of to-day. But learning was submerged, save some elements of Latin literature and education that were kept afloat by the life-belt thrown out by the Church.

The Church had by this time become a powerful organisation, in civil as well as spiritual affairs. The bishops were men of education and political experience. They now took over much of the authority of the fallen emperors. The ignorant and superstitious Germans looked to them for worldly counsel and spiritual guidance. Thus it became the Church's mission to carry on the ancient Roman traditions and to fit the barbarians for the part they were thenceforth to play in a world they had turned upside down.

On the site of the ancient city of Byzantium, Constantine the Great built the new capital of the Roman Empire— Constantinople.

JULIUS CAESAR

Caius Julius Caesar would have made his mark on events in any circumstances. As it was, he proved himself one who, in Shakespeare's language, did " bestride the narrow world like a Colossus ". The Rome of his period—he was born about 101 B.C.—gave ample scope for the exercise of his genius. The whole frame of the republic was shaken by a political struggle as furious as the legendary Greek Wars of the Titans, in which the combatants hurled rocks, islands and thunderbolts at each other. Rome ruled in the Mediterranean from Spain to Asia Minor. But it seemed that she could not rule herself.

The republic's triumphs in the Carthaginian wars had brought her untold riches, a flood of cheap slave labour and demoralising foreign standards of conduct, and these had sadly undermined the fine old Roman character. The peasant-farmers were being deprived of their lands. Idleness and vice spread in the cities. Political party-leaders walked the streets of Rome attended by bodyguards of armed ruffians. In the forum, the assemblies of the citizens—composed largely of the dregs of the populace—degenerated into savage fights with clubs and daggers. Public affairs were decided by beating up, and not infrequently murdering, one's political opponents. Worse still, the authority of the State was menaced by self-seeking politicians in command of armies whose oaths of loyalty had been sworn, not to the republic but to their general.

At the time of Caesar's birth the contest lay between two factions operating both within and without the Senate. One, the " Senatorial " party, stood for conserving the predominance of the Senate, as a body of experienced statesmen, in the government of the republic. The other, the " Popular " party, championed the rights and interests of the citizens. Some of their leaders were, in fact, sincere reformers; but others, less honest, sought popular support merely as an instrument for advancing their personal ambitions.

CAESAR—THE ARISTOCRAT

Caesar was of noble birth, his family claiming descent from no less a hero than Aeneas, the legendary founder of Rome, who himself was a fabled son of Venus, the goddess of Love. The young aristocrat might, therefore, be expected to attach himself to the Senatorial party. Yet, when he threw himself into the exciting and perilous political fray, it was with the Populars that he found his best opportunities in the quest for fame.

From early days, this keen-eyed and distinguished youth had felt an inward consciousness of great powers and stirring ambitions. In later life he declared that he must be first. And he wept with mortification because Alexander the Great had conquered so many nations at an age when he himself had achieved nothing memorable. Indeed his climb up the ladder of fame was discouragingly slow, for he lacked political influence. He loved pleasure and fine clothes and he spent money—mostly borrowed—like water to make himself known. His main assets in public life were his irresistible charm of manner and his winning tongue, and he made the most of them.

He set himself to court the favour of the people. From early times the citizens had possessed the right of electing the two annual consuls (the chief magistrates), the tribunes (the people's representatives) and other State officials and of passing laws and settling public affairs. In practice, however, such business was, for a long period, largely controlled by the Senate. Now, in the Popular movement, the citizens were reasserting their ancient powers. Caesar, like other shrewd political adventurers, realised that, if he won over the people, he could pull the strings and make the figures work to his own advantage.

CAESAR—THE SOLDIER

By the time he was thirty he had so far progressed in his design as to make himself a recognised figure of public importance. He had seen military service in Asia Minor and won the Civic Crown—a decoration comparable with our Victoria Cross—for saving the life of a fellow-soldier. He had advertised himself by his great oratorical gifts. He had been chosen for the first of the series of civil and military offices which he was destined to secure. And, incidentally, he had undergone the experience of being captured by pirates. The misadventure did not disturb him in the least. While waiting for his ransom money to arrive (he insisted on the pirates' demanding a really high price) the prisoner treated his savage captors with arrogant contempt and warned them that, once released, he would speedily return and crucify the lot. Which, according to the story, he did.

During the next dozen years Caesar's progress up the ladder accelerated. He became closely associated with two public men who for long had been the leading figures in the party struggles and contests for personal power—Crassus and Pompey. Crassus, a soldier-financier, was the richest

Gaius Julius Caesar, statesman, soldier and writer ; when captured by pirates it seems that he composed verses to while away the time.

23

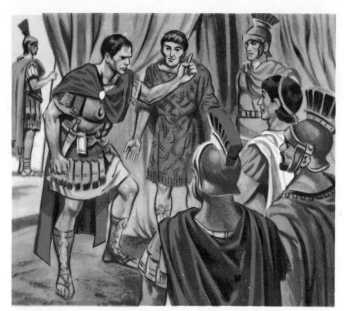

Versatile in war, politics, letters and oratory, Caesar was a man of burning ambitions, and by his bravery and example was an inspiration to his soldiers.

man in Rome, and it is mainly his money that brings him into the story. Caesar had plunged himself up to the ears in debt by the theatrical entertainments, gladiatorial combats and public feasts of unparalleled magnificence with which he had dazzled the city populace. Crassus opened his money-bags and refilled his new friend's empty purse. Pompey "the Great" was a far more resplendent figure. He was Rome's most illustrious general, distinguishing himself before his thirtieth birthday, and having won glorious triumphs for the republic, by land and sea, in North Africa and Asia Minor.

Caesar exerted himself to make use of these influential leaders. They in turn recognised the use they might make of him. His hold over the people would be invaluable in the serving out of the plums of the State pie. The Senate had recently antagonised the pair by opposing certain of their plans and this unwise policy drove them straight into the arms of Caesar. It was accordingly, by means of Crassus's money, Pompey's prestige and his own reputation in the forum, that Caesar climbed the higher rungs of the ladder. The series of elections to public offices continued steadily and Caesar took his seat in the Senate. As High Priest (such offices in the State religion were commonly held by " laymen " and not by professional priests) he acquired great prestige. As governor of Further Spain he got his first regular military command. The Senatorial party watched with increasing alarm the rising star of this golden-tongued favourite of the people.

THE TRIUMVIRATE

They had full reason for their anxiety. Caesar and his friends had been putting their heads together. In 60 B.C., the trio—the Triumvirate as they are known to history, the Three-headed Monster as a Roman writer called them—concluded a secret alliance for securing the biggest of the plums from the State pie. The outcome of the compact, as later renewed, marked a crisis in the fortunes of Rome. Caesar mounted to the top of the ladder. He was elected as one of the consuls for 59 B.C. and made governor of the provinces of Illyria (at the head of the Adriatic Sea), Cis-

alpine Gaul (northern Italy) and Transalpine Gaul (southern France), with the command of a large army. Pompey and Crassus were named as consuls for 55 B.C., with the governor-ship of Spain for the former, Syria for the latter and an army for each. It was the old story of political adventurers, backed by their legions, threatening the authority of the State. Personal influence and popular support had virtually placed the republic under the control of a trio of powerful and self-seeking careerists.

THE MILITARY GENIUS

In 58 B.C., while the unscrupulous pact was being given effect, Caesar passed into Gaul. He was then known only as a popular politician. Soon he was to electrify Rome with the revelation of a military genius that ranked him with the supreme generals of history. He quickly found reasons for intervening in the affairs of the immense and little-known country lying beyond the bounds of the Roman provinces. The inhabitants of those regions were, in the main, partly-civilised Celts, with German admixtures. They were fierce and fear-less fighters, full worthy of the Roman steel, but fatally lacking in military organisation, discipline and unity.

In Caesar's eight years of campaigning, his snap decisions and lightning tactics repeatedly confounded the enemy hosts. His personal bravery and hardihood set the example to his legions and aroused in their hearts a devotion amounting almost to adoration. When they faltered, he himself led them in the charge or shamed them into superhuman exertions. His record is distinguished, and sometimes stained, by the storming of eight hundred enemy positions, the slaughter or atrocious butchery of a million " barbarians " heroically fighting for their freedom, and the enslavement of a million more.

CONQUESTS IN THE WEST

At this appalling cost to the vanquished, Caesar brought all Gaul—comprising modern France and the Low Countries up to the Rhine—under the Roman yoke, besides conducting two expeditions into Britain (in 55 B.C. and again the following year), and, the first Roman to do so, leading an army across the Rhine into Germany. His *De Bello Gallico* tells most of the story and does so in a lucid, vigorous and elegant style which showed that he excelled in letters as he did in oratory and war. It is by his Gallic conquests and his statesmanlike peacetime settlement of the conquered pro-vince's affairs that the victor made his most enduring contri-bution to history. He carried the gifts of Roman civilisation to the North Sea and the Rhine. And he fashioned the mould in which the future of France was shaped.

During these years the angry strife of parties had con-tinued to rack Rome. Caesar's name was now on every tongue. But, while many were intoxicated by his triumphs, others dreaded the use he might make of his swollen power. The Romans were passionately devoted to their free republi-can constitution, despite its faults. Some, indeed, were regretfully beginning to wonder whether lasting harmony and order could ever be restored save by submitting to a strong unifying monarchy. Yet, ever since, some 450 years before, the people had driven out the last of their royal tyrants and established the republic, the very name of king had been detested.

DISSOLUTION OF THE TRIUMVIRATE

But what of the Triumvirate? It had dissolved. Crassus

After the decisive defeat of Pompey's army at Pharsalus, Caesar pursued the defeated general to Egypt. There, becoming enamoured of Cleopatra, dethroned queen of Egypt, he went to war on her behalf for the restoration of her rights.

had fallen in battle against the Parthians. Pompey felt himself overshadowed by Caesar's military laurels. He had always been a man of indecision, reminding one of the Roman god Janus whose two heads looked opposite ways. Pompey's looks were divided between his principles and his ambitions. Though sincerely attached to the republic, he wanted to be the first man in it. But so did Caesar. Thus the former allies became rivals and Pompey was drawn towards the powerful party in the Senate who hated Caesar and were actively seeking to bring him low.

CROSSING THE RUBICON

In 50 B.C., Caesar lay encamped in Cisalpine Gaul. Ahead of him lay the little river Rubicon, forming the boundary between his province and Italy. He must not cross it, for the laws forbade any proconsul to enter Italy in arms. In Rome his enemies were bringing charges against him. Pompey was called upon to save Italy from invasion. In January, 49 B.C., the Senate passed a resolution requiring Caesar to lay down his arms on pain of outlawry. But Caesar knew that, if he obeyed, his power would be gone and his life perhaps imperilled. How much farther his thoughts travelled we can but guess. In the general anarchy that prevailed in Rome the pillars of the constitution had already collapsed. Someone must set them up again—in one form or another. Should it be himself? Caesar realised that on his decision his own fate and that of the republic depended. For long he hesitated in an agony of doubt. And then he took the fatal step. He crossed the Rubicon. The die was cast. He was making history again.

PUBLIC ACCLAIM

Pompey, dismayed by his rival's swift advance, abandoned Rome, and Caesar entered the city in triumph. Pompey fled first to Brundisium and thence in 49 B.C. to Greece. Caesar followed and at Pharsalus in 48 B.C., Rome's two greatest living generals met in a decisive clash of arms. Pompey's army was completely destroyed; its leader once more took flight. He reached Egypt, and there he was murdered as he stepped ashore. By 45 B.C., Caesar had crushed Pompey's followers in Spain and North Africa and,

after becoming enslaved by the charms of Cleopatra, the recently dethroned Queen of Egypt, effectively asserted Rome's suzerainty over her country. When Rome appointed the conqueror dictator, eventually for life, and loaded him with public honours, it was only a recognition of the fact that the republic lay at his feet.

THE AGE OF REFORM

Caesar used his autocratic powers in executing or planning many immense and statesmanlike projects—social, economic, political and administrative—for restoring the health of the sick republic. He even found time for instituting a reform of the calendar, which had come to be about nine weeks ahead of the sun. The Julian calendar, slightly revised by Pope Gregory in 1582, is still in use to-day. Caesar allowed the old republican institutions to continue in name; but he made it plain to all that the real authority was concentrated in his hands.

The belief grew that he was aiming at a throne and, whatever the truth may have been, many of his words and acts gave colour to the notion. The " patriots ", Brutus, whom Caesar loved and trusted, and Cassius, he of Shakespeare's " lean and hungry look", headed a band of conspirators, mainly aristocrats, in a plot against the " tyrant " in the sacred name of Liberty. A soothsayer bade him " Beware the Ides (15th) of March ", but Caesar disdainfully ignored the warning.

THE FATEFUL IDES OF MARCH

On that ill-omened day, in 44 B.C., Rome's master sat in his gilded chair in the Senate. The conspirators crowded round him with their daggers and Caesar fell, his body pierced with three-and-twenty wounds. And, looking down on his prostrate form, stood the statue of that other murdered leader, his rival Pompey. Thus perished the one, strong, soldier-statesman who might have re-erected the ruined pillars of the State. But the autocratic policy he had chosen —perhaps because he judged that no other would serve at that time—pointed to the extinction of the Roman's cherished republican liberties, and they were not yet ready to pay that price.

THE BEGINNING OF BYZANTIUM

The imperial city of Byzantium did not exactly arise at the wave of a fairy wand, but it was conjured up at the bidding of a single individual. We can all remember how we used to enjoy building toy houses with boxes of bricks. The Roman Emperor, Constantine the Great, was luckier: he could build a real city. He created it for religious and military reasons. He had recently been converted from paganism and was making Christianity the State religion; so he probably felt that Rome, with its pagan traditions, was unsuited to be the centre of a Christian empire. The site of the new capital was chosen for strategic reasons. The boundaries of the empire extended from Britain to Asia Minor, and the old Greek town of Byzantium on the Bosphorus stood in an almost impregnable position as a halfway house between Europe and Asia. So there, in 330, the emperor completed his magnificent metropolis with its splendid palaces and churches, its law courts, public baths and monuments. He called it Constantinople, " the city of Constantine ", but the old name Byzantium still continued in use.

EAST ROMAN EMPIRE

The transfer of the seat of government from Rome to Constantinople had one momentous result. It began the permanent separation of the empire into its eastern and western parts. It was, however, still regarded as one indivisible whole. Those were troubled times. The empire had grown old and decayed and its frontiers were being continually battered by barbarian hordes. Within 150 years of the birth of Constantinople the western empire had dissolved and German kings were installed there, though they acknowledged the nominal supremacy of the eastern emperor. The east—Macedonia, Greece, Asia Minor, Syria and Egypt—escaped that fate and waxed strong and prosperous.

Then, in 527, it produced its most famous emperor. Justinian wins our sympathy at once. His eager spirit, thirst-ing for fame, found so many things to do, and he felt confident he could do them. Unfortunately he attempted too much at once and without reckoning the cost. He recovered North Africa, Sicily, Italy and part of southern Spain. He continued a centuries-old war against the Sassanid Persian Empire. He overhauled the confused mass of Roman law and handed on a wise, humane and practical system to posterity for its lasting benefit. (Its elements still operate in the law codes of most of the countries of Europe and in Scotland). He spent money lavishly on building projects. His Church of St. Sophia in Constantinople is one of the loveliest triumphs of architecture.

Hardly less famous than Justinian himself is his bright-eyed young empress Theodora. The story of the emperor's marriage is that of the Prince and the Beggar-maid over again. Theodora is said to have been a bear-keeper's daughter. As a child she was an actress; as a grown woman she acquired an evil reputation. But she was beautiful and intelligent and brave of heart. Justinian adored her and the two ruled the empire together.

If Constantine could have returned to earth in after-times he would have been proud of his new capital. For many centuries Constantinople was the world's leading city. It was the centre of a highly civilised society. It gloried in the possession of the treasures of Greek literature. And it produced a distinctive " Byzantine " type of sumptuously rich art and architecture.

EAST AND WEST

From its situation, the culture of the eastern empire became a mingling of Greek and Asiatic. In the West, the common language was Latin, in the East, Greek. Byzantine society was brilliant, but over-refined, unwholesome and unprogressive. The atmosphere of the court was oriental, with the emperor ruling autocratically and controlling the Church. The supreme service performed by the Byzantine empire was that it formed a stronghold of Christian European civilisation, a home where the imperial Roman traditions and the ancient Greek culture were preserved through the Middle Ages. Though repeatedly diminished and abased, it stood for a thousand years as an immovable bulwark against the barbarian and oriental foes who successively assailed it from every quarter.

Meantime, the half-century following the death of Justinian in 565 demonstrated that the empire's resources had been unwisely dissipated by that impetuous monarch. His wars in Italy had made that fair country a desert and Rome a city of the dead. In 568, the savage Lombards were able to seize the north, which still bears their name. Slav and Bulgarian marauders poured into the Balkans and created the racial mixture that has since made the region one of Europe's most dangerous political storm-centres. The renewal of the Persian war began with a sequence of disasters. And finally the weakened empire had to face a new and formidable menace from an unexpected quarter. The Arab Moslems were on the war-path and a spectacular career of conquest had begun.

After revolting against the usurper Theodosius II and marching upon Constantinople, Leo III (The Isaurian), had himself consecrated emperor by the Patriarch of Constantinople.

BEFORE AND AFTER CHARLEMAGNE

The most renowned of the barbarian German tribes who overran the western Roman Empire in the fifth century were the fair-haired, mighty-limbed Franks who have given France its name. One of their leaders, the murderous Clovis (an early form of the name Louis), founded a kingdom in northern Gaul, made Paris his capital, turned Christian and reigned from 481 to 511. Within fifty years of his death his successors ruled over most of present-day France, Belgium and the Netherlands and a good slice of western Germany. The Romanised population was helpless before them. But a great deal of the Roman institutions, language, and way of life survived the barbarian deluge, and the Church took the newcomers in hand and strove to tame the wildness of their blood. This was especially true in Gaul.

DEFENCE OF LEARNING

The civilising work of the Church was effected extensively through the monasteries, which had been founded in increasing numbers from the fourth century onwards. The cloistered monks laboured for humanity as well as for their monasteries. They toiled in the fields, learning and teaching improved husbandry. They helped to preserve the light of Latin learning, and they tended the poor and sick. They went forth as missionaries to the heathen—including the Saxons in England and Germany.

UNIFICATION OF THE FRANKS

The death of Clovis ushered in nearly two centuries of division and chronic disorder in the Frankish realm, till Charlemagne's ancestors took matters in hand. Incidentally, Charlemagne's grandfather, Charles Martel, made 732 a memorable year in European annals. The Moslems, who were then masters of Spain, surged into France with a great host. But Charles smashed their armies and destroyed their hopes of further conquests in the desperate but decisive battle of Poitiers.

Charles' son, Pepin the Short, followed up this achievement with two historic performances of his own. In 751, he had set aside Clovis' failing "Merovingian" dynasty and founded the "Carolingian" line. Three years later he got the Pope to confirm his usurpation. In return he presented the Papacy with certain districts in central Italy which he had captured from the barbarous Lombards. Thus the Pope, besides being the spiritual head of Western Christendom, became a territorial prince as ruler of the Papal States.

CHARLEMAGNE

From these vigorous ancestors sprang the most illustrious hero of the Dark Ages, Charles the Great, or Charlemagne. He reigned over the reunited kingdom from 771 to 814 and he made it his aim to bring all the German peoples into one great Christian empire. For this lofty ambition he was well fitted by nature. He was bold and statesmanlike, tireless and swift, genial and hearty. His commanding figure and keen blue eyes, his lively spirit and simple tastes made him the idol of his warriors. He became a figure of legend, the hero of incredible adventures.

His sword never rusted. He extinguished the Lombard kingdom; drove the Moslems from the buffer province he created south of the Pyrenees; and hounded the pagan Saxons till he had subdued them and forced them to accept Christianity. He completed the work of bringing Germany under Frankish rule and advanced his power deep into Central Europe.

But the peak of his glory was scaled in Rome. The Roman Emperor in Constantinople, who reigned over the East and,

The Franks, generally tall people with fair or reddish hair, crossed the Rhine and settled in Gaul. Here we see Frankish prisoners before the Roman consul, Aurelian.

Illiterate and pagan, the Merovingians availed themselves of the services of Latin-speaking monks for court proceedings.

After the meeting between Pope Stephen II and Pepin the Short, a bargain was struck whereby Pepin agreed to help the Pope against the Lombards ; in return the Pope recrowned Pepin and gave him the title, " Patrician of the Romans ".

On Christmas day in the year 800 in the basilica of St. Peter's in Rome, Pope Leo III laid the imperial crown on the head of Charlemagne. Thus was born the Holy Roman Empire, destined to last for more than a thousand years.

nominally, over the West, had been dethroned. In 800, the Pope crowned Charlemagne emperor in his place. It was a significant ceremony though it added nothing to Charlemagne's effective power. The line of Eastern Emperors continued as before and the Empire became definitely divided. But it showed how ineradicably the Roman imperial tradition had survived the centuries of barbarian conquest in the West.

REVIVAL OF EDUCATION

Charlemagne was zealous in the cause of education. Latin learning had been almost submerged, and now the Emperor laboured to rescue it for the service of the Church, finding his right-hand man in the brilliant Northumbrian scholar Alcuin. Like many of Charlemagne's priests (such as St. Winfrith, or Boniface), Alcuin was educated in Armagh, then a centre of learning in Western Europe. Schools were founded for brushing up the clergy's faulty Latin and for instructing his own and his nobles' children.

Charlemagne led his army over the Mt. Cenis Pass to Susa where he overpowered the army of the king of the Lombards.

Charlemagne stands out as a monumental figure with a sword in one hand, a torch in the other. Before his coming, Western Europe was engulfed in anarchy and ignorance. The royal Christian warrior brought a semblance of order out of chaos, giving a measure of reality to his vision of a Christian State in which all the diverse peoples of the West should be knit together after the civilised Roman pattern.

But there was only one Charlemagne. After his day his empire broke up into separate realms whose forms dimly foreshadowed the outlines of the future in France, Germany, the Netherlands, Switzerland and Italy. Foreign invaders —Moslems, Northmen and others—continually plagued the land. Darkness and chaos once again prevailed.

THE RISE OF FEUDALISM

The tumult and insecurity of the times gave a great impetus to " feudalism ". Under the Feudal System, as it developed, large estates were granted by the king to the dukes and counts, the bishops and abbots, who attended his court. These " vassals " did homage and swore fidelity to the king and undertook to support him in war and to discharge other dues and services. The nobles and ecclesiastics in turn granted parts of their estates to their leading men on similar terms. The peasants, or "villeins", on the farms and manors became the serfs of their lords. The basic idea was that each lord undertook to protect his vassal in return for his services. It was largely through their vassals that the Frankish kings exercised their powers over the more distant provinces.

The Feudal System of land-holding, in various forms, spread over western Europe and prevailed throughout most of the Middle Ages, shaping the pattern of government and social life.

As time went on, the Frankish kings' control over their powerful vassals progressively weakened and the great nobles increasingly asserted their freedom. When the Carolingian dynasty ended in 987, France had become a collection of more or less independent States and the effective royal domain had shrunk to a belt of territory in the north with Paris and Orleans as its principal towns.

THE PROPHET OF ALLAH

History is full of surprises. In the sixth century A.D., Arabia was a country of little account in the world. Its peoples were a picturesque conglomeration of scattered tribes much given to robbing and murdering each other in fierce family and tribal feuds. Crude pagan gods and idols were the objects of their worship, though contacts with the Jewish and Christian religions were beginning to enlighten their minds. Mecca, one of its chief cities however had some importance in the Middle East. A hallowed place from earliest times, it was too the meeting-place for men of many races, lying as it did at one end of a great caravan route. It was in this city about the year 570 that Mohammed was born—an event which was to have undreamed of consequences. The child came of a good but poor family and, being orphaned at the age of six, he was brought up by an uncle. Young Mohammed learned the ways of the roving desert Bedouins and often travelled far afield with the trading caravans. A promising young business man, he was at some time introduced by his uncle into the service of a rich widow whom he later married.

MEDITATION AND VISIONS

But it was soon apparent that Mohammed was not merely a successful merchant. He was one who pondered on deep moral and spiritual problems. He fell into trances during which, he declared, the teachings of the one true religion were revealed to him. There was no god but Allah, and he, Mohammed, was his prophet. In many respects his notions of God coincided with those of the Jews and Christians. His revelations were written down or memorised and, after his death, collected in the Koran, which forms the Mohammedan Bible whose text the Moslem children learn by heart. Mohammed first delivered his message secretly to a chosen few—members of his family and one friend. When, later, he came out into the open at Mecca, many scoffed at him as a crazy impostor.

Derision turned to open opposition as gradually Mohammed gathered adherents. Mecca rose up against him and in 622 he had to flee for his life to Medina. His flight, or *Hegira*, marks the year One in the Mohammedan or Moslem calendar. Not only did he become the virtual ruler of the city in that first year, he also turned warrior and for several years the country was torn by the bitter struggles of the opposing factions of his supporters and his opponents. But, while the contests raged, his fame and authority continued to spread. His fiery eloquence drew multitudes to his side. His teachings were of a character to stir the imagination of the Arabs. The tribesmen thrilled or quaked at his revelations of the joys of paradise, the terrors of the impending day of judgement and the awful pains of hell. At the same time their hot-blooded temperament was schooled by a wholesome discipline: submission to the will of Allah (Islam, or "submission," is the Mohammedans' name for their faith); regular daily prayers; fasts, pilgrimages and almsgiving; abstinence from wine. At length, in 631, he returned to Mecca at the head of a victorious army and, at his death in 632, the once despised teacher had become generally accepted by the Arabs as a divinely inspired prophet and leader. And he had drawn the unruly tribes together in the inspiring fellowship of a single, fighting creed.

THE ARAB EXPANSION

History had sprung one of its surprises, but this was only a beginning. Under the rule of the Caliphs, or "successors" of the Prophet, the Mediterranean world was about to receive the shock of its life. The Arab camel and horse swept out of their desert homes to proclaim the name of Allah in foreign lands. The mission was one that was all the more to the wild tribesmen's taste because it meant war and the spoils of war and the certainty of paradise for those who died fighting. Within thirty years, their fanatical zeal and superb fighting spirit had wrested Syria, Egypt and part of North Africa from the enfeebled Eastern Roman Empire and overwhelmed Persia. Some fifty years later, in the west, they had conquered the remainder of North Africa and overrun Spain (*see* "Spain and the Moors") and, in the East, subdued western Turkestan and crossed the Indus. Between 669 and 718, they repeatedly hurled themselves against Constantinople. The inspiration of a new exhilarating creed had brought about a shattering explosion of the pent up vitality of the Arabian tribes. At the dawn of the eighth century it must have seemed to Europe that the Moslems' spectacular career of conquest was irresistible. Yet the time was at hand when their triumphant progress was to be halted, their deadly two-pronged advance foiled. In the West, in 732, their confident hosts of cavalry, irrupting out of Spain, were decisively and finally defeated by the Frankish sovereign Charles Martel, the grandfather of Charlemagne, in the long and fiercely contested battle of Poitiers. And meanwhile, in 718, their furious assault on the walls of Constantinople met with a repulse that may well have been even more fateful for the destinies of Christian Europe. The war with the Roman Empire flamed or flickered on through the next three centuries. But the tide of Arab conquest had almost reached the flood, and the vast empire it had won broke up into separate States. Finally, in the eleventh century, it succumbed to another rising power, the brutal Seljuk Turks, who had adopted the Islamic creed.

Meantime history, like a skilled conjurer, was producing more rabbits from its hat. A Moslem civilisation developed that matched in splendour the Arab achievement in war. The arrogant conquerors had shown remarkable tolerance to Christians and other "infidels." Those who submitted to the yoke were permitted, if they wished, to follow their own despised faith on payment of regular tribute. None the less, immense numbers embraced Mohammedanism, and the Arab language and creed spread over the whole empire.

It was this Moslem world—composed of various nationalities reaching from beyond Persia to Spain—that, under the influence of Greek, Persian and other ancient civilisations, turned to the cultivation of literature, art and science. From the mid-eighth century Baghdad became the centre of a brilliant culture that placed the Moslems in the forefront of learning. Contrasted with the intellectual ignorance then overshadowing western Europe, their achievement stands out like a beacon casting its rays into a world of darkness.

THOSE AMAZING NORTHMEN

Northmen, Vikings, Danes: call them what you will, they were an astounding and a terrible breed. For two centuries or more they paralysed Europe. "From the fury of the Northmen, O Lord, deliver us" became a regular supplication in the Church Litany. In their quieter hours they were farmers, fishers, hunters and traders. But poverty, overcrowding, incurable restlessness and other causes impelled the bolder spirits to issue forth from their bleak haunts in Denmark, Norway and Sweden and seek plunder and new homes in richer lands.

Their exploits and their superb poems and sagas, which were collected and written down in later times, tell us vividly of their characters and habits. The Northmen were fearless and hardy, shrewd, cruel and treacherous. They were men of blood and men of the sea. Of their generous allowance of gods, the one-eyed Odin, the bloodthirsty god of war, and Thor, the thunder and lightning god, ranked highest. Odin dwelt in Valhalla, to which all who fell in battle were transported, to revel eternally in the joys of fighting, gluttony and song.

It was from the late eighth century onwards that these fiery barbarians erupted over Europe, like some volcano belching fire and smoke and deadly lava streams. To go a-viking became a national pastime. And they had the vessels for it. Their dragon-prowed " long ships " were swift, efficient and beautifully built. They carried 20-foot oars and a square sail, and there was no other craft afloat that could match them. Moreover, their shallow draught enabled the crews to penetrate by river deep into enemy country. There the warriors would scramble ashore, round up the local horses and scour the countryside. Their first targets were the abbeys and monasteries with their treasures of gold and silver, precious stones and rich fabrics.

East and west both beckoned. Swedish merchants traded and raided down the Volga and the Dnieper to the Caspian and Black Seas. About the mid-ninth century they settled at Novgorod and Kiev and the latter town became a centre from which they ruled the simple Slav inhabitants in the first known organised State in Russia. The supreme lure of the merchant-adventurers, however, was the fabulously wealthy city of " Middlegarth "—Constantinople—for whose glittering treasures they thirsted. But their thirst was never slaked, for the city resisted all their onslaughts.

VIKING MARAUDERS

The western field of operations was distinctly more lively. Beginning in earnest in 793, the pirates raided at will in England, the northern and western coasts and islands of Scotland, the Isle of Man and Ireland; the sacred Isle of Iona was repeatedly sacked. Ireland became encompassed as by a plague of hornets. On the Continent the marauders boldly ravaged the Frankish realms of Charlemagne and his successors. Their ships swept up the Rhine and the Elbe into Germany and the Low Countries, up the Somme, the Seine, the Loire and the Garonne into France. Antwerp, Rouen, Hamburg, Paris, Orleans and many other fair towns were brutally pillaged, razed to the ground or held to ransom amid scenes of hideous butchery. One fleet went buccaneering round Spain, Northern Africa and Southern France and right on to Italy. Plot all these forays on the map and you will see that they practically made a ring round Central and Western Europe.

The lava flood of settlement and conquest covered half England till Alfred the Great stayed it at the battle of Ethandune, but at length it finally engulfed the entire land in the time of the Viking king Sweyn and his son, Canute. In France, Rollo or Rolf the Ganger, in 911, won a settlement that later expanded into the duchy of Normandy. Farther afield, from about 874, the Northmen made settlements in Iceland. Late in the tenth century they sailed on to Greenland's icy mountains. A few years after, they even set foot temporarily in North America, five hundred years before the days of Columbus.

VIKING BUILDERS

Despite their vigorous character, the Northmen abroad could never preserve their identity as a race. Sloughing off their barbarian skins, but retaining their fighting and enterprising spirit, they adopted the Christian faith, and the language and civilisation of the countries in which they settled. In Normandy they became Frenchmen, in England Englishmen. And their work was not all destructive. Normandy best shows their capabilities. There they created a powerful, well-governed feudal State whose organisation demonstrated to disordered Europe their genius for law and administration. They became builders of massive cathedrals and abbeys. In the eleventh century, Norman knights carved out for themselves a brilliant and luxurious kingdom in southern Italy and Sicily. And, of course, there was that little English adventure in 1066. But by this time the true Viking outburst had spent itself. The volcano was exhausted.

Viking leaders were buried fully armed, stretched out in the centre of their warships. Some of these burial ships have been discovered.

SPAIN AND THE MOORS

Geography and history have combined to give the Spanish peninsula a distinctive character. It is shut off from the rest of Europe by the mighty mountain barrier of the Pyrenees; and, judging from its physical characteristics in general, the country seems to be in two minds whether it belongs to Europe at all or to Africa. Furthermore, the Spanish peoples, alone among the greater countries of western Europe, lived for centuries under the rule of Mohammedan invaders from across the Straits of Gibraltar. The marks of that unforgettable experience have never been erased.

When the western Roman empire was dissolved by the German barbarians in the fifth century, it was the Vandals and associated tribes who ran amok over Spain. But the Vandals were soon displaced by the West Goths, who established a monarchy and reigned till 711. As in Gaul, the new barbarian masters extensively adopted the Latin speech and institutions of the Romanised inhabitants. They had already become Christians and passed under the civilising influence of the Church.

Spain's " unforgettable experience " began with the overthrow of the West Gothic royal line. After the death of Mohammed in 632, the Arab horsemen swept out of their desert homes to proclaim the name of Allah in foreign lands. They were finally to win an empire that extended from beyond Persia to Spain. It was in 711 that a number of these fanatical warriors, with an army of savage Berbers from North Africa (a people they had conquered and converted to the Moslem faith), crossed over and began the conquest of Spain. Within seven years that conquest was virtually complete.

The Arabs—who were a ruling minority of the invaders—proved to be, on the whole, tolerant masters. They intermarried with their new subjects. They allowed the Jews—a very numerous body—and Christians to adhere to their own creeds, subject to the payment of tribute. Their coming relieved the Jews from Christian persecution and the peasants from serfdom. Large numbers of the population adopted the Moslem creed and customs. The Arabs brought with them a brilliant civilisation and culture—completely outshining that of western Europe. Cordoba, their beautiful capital, became a city of oriental luxury and splendour. It was adorned with stately palaces and delightful gardens, hundreds of beautiful mosques and public baths, and a thriving university.

Agriculture, industry and commerce, art and science—chemistry, mathematics, astronomy—and education were all advanced. From Spain during the Moslem period much of the forgotten philosophy and learning of ancient Greece was restored to the countries of the West. The European manufacture of paper—an inestimable boon to learning, since parchment was scarce and costly—was begun. The "Arabic" numerals we use to-day began to supplant the unmanageable Roman symbols.

The Arab emirs who governed Spain soon threw off the authority of the Caliphs, who ruled the whole Moslem empire from Damascus. In the tenth century they established their own caliphate of Cordoba. But in the early eleventh century the long period of their dominion was suddenly broken. A remarkable revolution occurred which divided the Arabs against themselves. It was the golden opportunity of the Christian States which had been developing in the north and maintaining a ceaseless but unco-ordinated struggle with the alien infidels. Of these, two in particular—Castile, " the land of castles ", and Aragon—were to shape the map of Spain. The famous crusade of liberation known as the Reconquest now began in earnest and brought forth one of Spain's greatest heroes—El Cid. In 1085, the Castilian horsemen, the *caballeros*, conquered Toledo. In 1118, the Aragonese took Santiago.

But alas for the Christians' high hopes! Fortune now played them a sorry trick. During the eleventh and twelfth centuries two fresh waves of Mohammedan Berbers, who had previously thrown off the yoke of their hated Arab masters, poured into the country from North Africa. The Christians were checked. But the Arab emirs were completely overthrown.

The Christian advance against the " Moors ", as we usually term all the Mohammedans in Spain, was presently resumed. It was a long and doubtful tug-of-war. Not until 1212, when Castile, Aragon, the little Pyrenean kingdom of Navarre, and Portugal (which had become an independent kingdom in 1143) had sunk their differences for the occasion and joined forces, was the decisive victory won. In the succeeding half-century the victors rode from triumph to triumph. The Aragonese gained Valencia. Cordoba, Seville, Cadiz, and Murcia fell to the Castilians. By 1266, all that remained to the Moors was the kingdom of Granada. And there, surprisingly, the bitter 500-years' conflict rested for more than two centuries. The separate kingdoms became too deeply engrossed in their own private interests and animosities to carry it to earlier completion. As for any movement towards drawing the discordant States together in a united community, that, too, had to wait two hundred years for even a partial achievement.

In the campaign against the Moors, the victorious banners of Castile and Leon were in the streets of liberated Toledo.

EARLY INVADERS
Britain under the Romans and the Anglo-Saxons

Probably the two best-remembered dates in British history are 55 B.C. and A.D. 1066, and both record a foreign invasion.

At the first date Rome was the all-powerful centre of European civilisation. Her dominions embraced a great part of the Continent, together with vast regions in Asia and Africa bordering the Mediterranean Sea. Britain was a barbarous and almost unknown island lying beyond the outer edge of the civilised world. Actually it was still very much as Nature had made it, a country of grassy uplands, wild mountain ranges, desolate wastes, marshy river valleys, and trackless virgin forests.

The inhabitants mostly belonged to the Celtic race, an intelligent and artistic, but relatively primitive people. The British Celts, more especially those living in the south-eastern parts of the island, possessed masterly skill and excellent taste in pottery, metal-work, ornamental enamelling, spinning, and weaving. In the main, they lived in squalid, isolated, upland huts and villages or hill-top fortress encampments.

About this time the famous Roman proconsul Julius Caesar was engaged in quelling the tribes of northern Gaul. During his operations he discovered that the Gauls were constantly receiving help from their kindred across the Channel and he resolved to go over and investigate. Thus it came about that, in 55 B.C., the first clear page of the book of British history was written. Caesar's " investigations " led to some decidedly spirited clashes between his legions and the warlike and mettlesome islanders. He eventually brought the local tribes to sue for peace; but, as the campaigning season was then getting short, he withdrew from the island and planned to return in greater force the next year.

The second expedition duly followed, like an echo of the first. As before, the irregular native hordes of horse and foot and nimble charioteers stood little chance against the disciplined and powerfully equipped Roman legions, and Caesar finally brought their king Cassivelaunus to submission. But further trouble in Gaul called him away before he could secure or extend his conquests.

ROMAN CONQUERORS

As things turned out, the reprieve thus granted lasted for nearly a century. Then, in A.D. 43, the Emperor Claudius decided to end it. Third time's lucky, as we know, and the Roman generals proved it now. Within eight years or so, after overcoming the stubborn resistance of the dauntless British chief Caractacus, who was eventually betrayed into their hands, they carried their victorious arms to a line crossing the country between Lincoln and the region of Chester, though Wales remained unconquered.

The year 60 set in train some explosive events, beginning with a mighty bang in the isle of Mona (Anglesey). This was the headquarters of the Druids, the pagan priests, medicine-men and magicians whose influence was a major factor in the Britons' resistance. The Roman governor, Suetonius Paulinus, stormed the sacred groves and smoked out and massacred the whole concourse of long-bearded, white-robed priests, half-demented women, and warriors assembled there.

But in the hour of triumph staggering news came in. The east was aflame with revolt. Boudicca (Boadicea), the warrior-queen of the Iceni tribe, had descended like a black tempest on the Roman colony at Camulodunum (Colchester) and ruthlessly butchered the inhabitants. She cut to pieces a relieving force and set Londinium (London) aflame.

Of course there could be but one end to such goings on. The dangerous revolt was suppressed and a terrible vengeance

The arrival of the Romans seems to have been responsible for the disappearance of the Druids in Anglesey, Scotland and Ireland.

New towns, forts and roads were the result of the improving influence of the Roman occupation of Britain.

exacted. Then the tide of conquest flowed on again. By A.D. 81, under a new and distinguished governor, Agricola, the territories of Wales, northern England and the Caledonian Lowlands had all been engulfed. Next, the " eagles ", the imperial standards, were borne onwards into the Highlands of " Caledonia ", and in 84, somewhere beyond the Firth of Tay, Agricola scattered a Caledonian host in the great battle of Mons Graupius.

But this was barren and profitless country and the half-naked Caledonians, or Picts as they were called later, proved an untamable pest to the invaders. The Highlands were never subdued by Roman arms and even the Lowlands proved difficult to hold down. Accordingly, the real boundary of the new province of Britannia was fixed along a line stretching from the Solway Firth to the Tyne. There, following a visit by the globe-trotting Emperor Hadrian in 120, an immense and massive 74-mile-long barrier, " Hadrian's Wall ", was erected and set at regular intervals with forts for the defending garrison's occupation. Some twenty years later another wall of much simpler construction, "Antonine's Wall ", was erected between the Firths of Clyde and Forth, enclosing the Lowlands, but it was afterwards abandoned.

The first coming of the Romans ushered in a " school term " of some 350 years for Britannia, more particularly the south and east and midlands. The glory of Rome lies more in its civilising achievements than in its military triumphs, and the Britons now began to enjoy the improving advantages of firm government, just laws, peace and security, art and learning, and social refinement. New towns were laid out, with all manner of comforts and conveniences, after the Roman plan. Country life, too, was transformed for the native country squires of the day, who luxuriated in pleasant " villas ", or landed estates, containing spacious and elegant residences. The famous Roman roads improved communications and government administration and encouraged the island's briskly increasing industry and commerce. Roman habits of life, Roman food and dress, Roman art and ideas, and even to a considerable extent the Roman Latin language were increasingly adopted. The rough Britons, in fact, though in widely varying degrees, were given a polish. More promising than all else, Christianity established a footing in the island.

This summer season of security and progress suffered many

stormy interruptions before it drew to its catastrophic close. Following on earlier Caledonian raids, the province was repeatedly assailed, from the late third century onwards, by swarms of plundering barbarians: Saxons and others from over the North Sea, Picts in the north, Scots from Ireland, which in that period was their home. The fourth century saw the protective arm of Rome manifestly weakening, and in about 387, a major calamity occurred: Hadrian's Wall was abandoned. In 410, the Roman emperor notified the Britons that they must now defend themselves. The truth was the whole empire in the West, which had long been sinking into decline, was staggering under the pressure of other barbarian hordes. Later, when it fell to pieces, one of those pieces was Britannia.

The known story of the change-over from Roman Britain to Anglo-Saxon England is like an interrupted cinema film. Detached episodes appear and disappear. Figures come and go. From time to time the screen goes tantalisingly black. But, briefly, this seems to be the tale. About the middle of the fifth century Britain had come under the supremacy of a native chief named Vortigern. To repel the inroads of the Picts and Scots this crack-brained ruler called in a band of piratical Jutes, a tribe associated with the Saxons, and gave them a base in Kent. It was about as crazy as inviting a wolf into the sheepfold to guard the sheep.

What followed was almost a foregone conclusion. Not only the obliging Jutes, but their friends the Angles and Saxons as well, descended joyfully on the island in successive swarms. And this time they had come to stay. Devastation and slaughter marked their path. The Britons who did not make off in time were slain or kept on as slaves or dependants. For a century and a half the conquest continued, till by the early seventh century the greater part of what is now England had been over-run and roughly shaped into a number of separate kingdoms. The polished Britons had been polished off, those still remaining free having fled to the mountains and wastes of the west.

It was during the first half of this period that history or legend, but probably both, placed the most romantic of British heroes—King Arthur of the Round Table.

A Roman magistrate administering justice amongst villagers. Among subject peoples, the Romans gave proof of great tolerance and a spirit of civilisation.

The invaders, then, had mastered most of England, which means that the English had mastered it; for the newcomers were the Teutonic ancestors of the English people. (The native Welsh and Highland Scots are of Celtic descent). They gave the country its name: " England " is "Angle-land ". Their wild blood now flows in British veins. Their language forms the groundwork of English speech. What Rome had done for Britain they mostly destroyed, and with them the story of England begins.

The "Anglo-Saxons ", or " Saxons ", as the invaders are commonly called, belonged to a group of uncivilised Teutonic tribes settled mainly in the southern portion of the Danish peninsula and the neighbouring North Sea districts. They were a fierce and hardy set of heathens, and the most adventurous of them were dare-devil pirates and about as restful in their habits as a Chinese cracker. Their chief deities were Woden (the Northman's Odin) the god of war, Thor, a thunder and lightning god, Tiw, a more ancient war-god, and Frig, a goddess—much needed, one would say—of love. Surprisingly we are continually naming them still: Tuesday is Tiw's day, Wednesday, Woden's day, Thursday, Thor's day and Friday, Frig's day.

In the newly formed Saxon kingdoms in England the king's personal followers and companions-in-arms (" thanes " as they came to be called) formed his barbaric court. Many were rewarded with gifts of land, where they set up house and became the local lords with their own groups of followers. The leading members of the king's court formed his Council of Wise Men, or Witan, whom he consulted on State affairs. The mass of the people, the ceorls (churls), were the farmers, craftsmen and common soldiers of the realm. Though free and independent village smallholders, they rendered dues of farm produce and labour services to the king or the local lord. These sturdy fellows were proud of their rights as citizens. They settled their own village affairs and disputes in their tun-moots or meetings. They, or their representatives, dealt with more important public and legal business in the higher folk-moots and (in a later period perhaps) hundred-moots. These assemblies may be a little dull to read about to-day, yet they are of deep significance. They show the early bent of the Saxon people for self-government and the popular administration of justice. And the struggle for the exercise of those rights, through a national parliament and independent courts of law, was destined to be one of the outstanding themes of subsequent English history.

SAXON LAW

The Saxons' primitive criminal laws would have made a modern magistrate's hair stand on end. Injuries were considered to be personal wrongs rather than public offences. They were atoned for (when they were not avenged in a more satisfying blood-feud) by a queer system of money compensation based on the social position of the victim. To kill a ceorl might cost you a " wergild " of 200 shillings, a thane 1,200 shillings. When a case was tried the accused had to clear himself by a prescribed tally of " oath-helpers ". These supporters testified, not to the facts of the case, as you would suppose, but to the excellent general character of their friend. And the value of their oaths, like the wergild, was reckoned in accordance with their social standing. Particular offences, however, were tried by " ordeal ". In the ordeal by fire the accused had to grasp a red-hot iron bar. If the resulting wound was not clean three days afterwards he was adjudged guilty. Heaven had given a sign.

St. Augustine was the founder of the Christian church in southern England and was the first Archbishop of Canterbury.

The turning point in the lives of these barbarians was the coming of Christianity. The Church had risen to European power and influence on the break-up of the Roman Empire. It became the guardian of the spiritual welfare and of the crumbling civilisation of the West. So it was that, in 597, Augustine and his little band of monks landed in Kent to bring the pagan Saxons into the Christian fold. Soon the kings of Kent, Essex and East Anglia, with thousands of their subjects were won over. But King Edwin of Northumbria hesitated. At length a zealous priest named Paulinus convinced him that his recent miraculous escape from a poisoned dagger-stroke, and a smashing victory over his chief enemy Wessex, were the gifts of the Christian God. Thereupon, in 627, he and his people enthusiastically accepted baptism. Even so, the new faith was stamped out after Edwin's death and it was the Scots who finally restored it.

Happily for the Saxons, the Christian Church of Roman times had survived among the Britons in the West. These Celtic Christians hated their barbarian conquerors too bitterly to work for their conversion. Yet they were destined to be the starting point of a movement which, reaching out in a wide circle, was to redeem more of heathen Britain than the Roman mission itself. As the Saxon conquest spread westwards, the Celtic church had been gradually cut off from contact with the Church at Rome and thenceforth sustained the faith by its own constant endeavours.

In 397, St. Ninian, the first-known apostle of Scotland, had established a primitive monastery at Whithorn in Galloway. About 432, St. Patrick, who was probably born in South Scotland, sailed across from Wales to Ireland to convert the pagan natives. From an early date the Scots who inhabited Northern Ireland began to cross over to, and settle in what is now Argyllshire and the neighbouring islands of the West of Scotland. (Eventually they gave their name to the whole country). In 563, St. Columba, a member of the race, made the same voyage with far-reaching results. Establishing a monastery on the little rocky island of Iona, he laboured tirelessly for the salvation of the Picts. Iona became the centre of the Celtic Church. And it was from there, in 635, that the sweet and gentle Aidan set out to found a monastery on Lindisfarne (now called Holy Island), and it was he who eventually recovered the lost sheep of Northumbria.

SYNOD OF WHITBY

The central question of authority and obedience to a religious "rule" was settled at the momentous Synod of Whitby, in 664. The party favouring autonomy for the British churches, trained by Irish and Scottish missionaries, included Hilda, the great Abbess of Whitby's Benedictine nunnery. However, those who favoured submitting to one universal Church order, emanating from Rome, won the day.

Before the seventh century ended, the remaining kingdoms of Mercia, Wessex and Sussex were gathered in. So Woden's defences fell and the Saxons were received into the Christian family of European peoples and into the Roman Church.

THE WIND OF CHANGE

In the work of the Church throughout Europe, the monasteries played a conspicuous part. The dedication of the monks to a strictly regulated life of piety, good works, and learned study made these holy men the most fruitful labourers in the Lord's vineyard. Many monasteries, therefore, as well as churches and schools, were established in the newly-won island. The influence of the Church spread over every aspect of life. The bishops and other great prelates were men of wide learning and political experience, and as time went on they became members of the nobility and of the Witan.

The seed thus sown produced an astonishing harvest, cultural as well as religious. Besides other arts and studies, a new native literature arose. The humble herdsman Caedmon, in the late seventh century, poured out his inspired religious poetry. The lovable and venerable Bede, who lived from 673 to 735, became one of the foremost scholars of Europe. The once despised island—or, more precisely, Northumbria—actually became, with Armagh in Ireland, a shining light in that dark period of European culture.

The Saxons' great failing, however, was their disunion. From the beginning the kingdoms had mostly been fighting each other in a sort of Island Championship contest. The continual warfare produced many social evils. By the early ninth century the thanes and their followers were becoming a lordly class of professional soldiers. The ceorls were declining in importance as fighting men and sinking into servitude to their lords.

There were other changes too. The Church, grown rich and powerful, was showing signs of laxity and worldliness.

Wessex, under its redoubtable King Egbert, had come out top in the championship struggle and claimed (though not very effectively) supremacy over all its rivals. The idea of island unity was becoming more familiar; but the various kingdoms were still distracted by their old aggressive spirit of independence, their local loyalties and rivalries. They were soon to get a sharp lesson on the subject.

A warning rap on the knuckles had come in 793, when a fleet of savage freebooters sacked the monastery of Lindisfarne. Some forty years later the buccaneers started a widespread succession of vicious stabs that persisted for thirty years. History was repeating itself.

The marauders were the pagan Danes, Northmen or Vikings, bold, ruthless men who ravaged the land in their search for booty. It was no consolation to the afflicted Saxons that the pirate bands were closely akin to them in blood and language.

In 865, an immense Danish army landed in Kent and thereafter for over four years roved to and fro, north and east, looting, killing and destroying at will. The devastated kingdoms, lacking unity, went down like ninepins, till at last Wessex was left standing practically alone. In 870, the exultant Danes threw themselves on this last island bulwark. But, in the ensuing battle of Ashdown in Berkshire, they got their first sound thrashing and the young Prince Alfred won his spurs.

Nonetheless, in 871, Alfred, now King of Wessex, was driven to "buy peace" to gain a breathing space. But six years later, after the Danes had had another try, he completely turned the tables on them and forced them to sue for peace and quit Wessex. But alas: he did not allow for the perfidy of Guthrum, their leader. In the early January of 878, when Wessex was absorbed in the prolonged merry-making of Christmas-tide, the Danes stole down by night like a fox on the poultry yard. Taken utterly unprepared, Wessex collapsed. Alfred, with a small band of faithful companions, took refuge in the dreary swamps and woodlands of Somerset. The heathen conquest seemed complete.

Yet the broken king did not despair. He waited—and planned—and hoped on. And the time came when, from his dismal retreat in Athelney, he was able to issue the rallying call to his afflicted people. At Ethandune, on the edge of

Alfred, fleeing from the Danes, had to retreat through the marshes to the fort at Athelney.

For administrative purposes, Saxon kings divided their kingdoms into districts, each district administered by a royal reeve. Popular government and justice were meted out by the hundred courts, fixed sums being laid down for each type of offence.

Salisbury Plain, the two armies met in the shock of battle. And it was Alfred's hour. Victory, dazzlingly complete and decisive, crowned his arms.

The terms exacted by the Treaty of Wedmore from the beaten foe seem disappointingly lenient. A line running irregularly from Chester to the east of London was eventually fixed as the boundary between Dane and Saxon. It meant, in effect, that Alfred left the north-eastern half of the country to the invaders. (The region in which Danish law prevailed was afterwards known as " the Danelaw "). But Wessex was exhausted, and the Danes, many of whom by now had settled down peaceably in the north and east, were far too strong ever to be destroyed. Alfred had prevented the complete conquest of the island. He had also required Guthrum to accept Christianity. His hope was that in time the two peoples would learn to settle down together in Christian peace and concord. Alfred's triumph brought him the overlordship of western Mercia, including London. But there was a greater gain. He began to be looked up to as the one hope and leader of all the Saxon race.

The Viking threat was renewed in 892. But Alfred was ready for the invaders and, after four years of campaigning, he utterly broke their spirit.

THE ARTS OF PEACE

Between campaigns, and up to his death about 899, the wise and sympathetic king devoted himself to repairing the ravages of war and the decay of social and religious life. He tried to revive the fallen monasteries. He introduced ambitious schemes of widespread education. His translations of useful Latin works gave our great English prose literature its first real start in life. He issued new laws and reformed the administration of justice in the interests of the poor. He is the only English sovereign who has been honoured with the title of " the Great ".

Alfred's successors during the next seventy-six years did him credit. His resolute son Edward the Elder not only recovered the Danelaw but became the acknowledged overlord of the British princes in Wales and the British kingdom of Strathclyde in the north-west and claimed overlordship of that of the Scots, who now possessed the Highlands. His strong-armed son Athelstan stoutly maintained his title of

" King of all Britain ". And that Edgar, who reigned from 959 to 975, sustained his supremacy is pleasingly demonstrated by the well-known story of how he was once rowed on the river Dee by eight kings and princes as a token of their vassalage—surely one of the most remarkable " eights " in boating history. Edgar is further remembered for his co-operation with the saintly Dunstan in continuing Alfred's efforts to re-invigorate the monasteries. Their decline was a real loss to the country's moral and religious life, and the labours of Dunstan and other notable churchmen fired the Church anew with zeal and earnestness.

ETHELRED THE UNREADY

But now the period of strong kings ended and the growth of national unity was checked. In 978, Ethelred the Redeless —*rede* means counsel—began his long and luckless reign. His utter incapacity for kingship was a positive invitation to further Danish invaders. While Denmark and Norway were now united kingdoms with a strongly organised Viking community, England had only a feeble Ethelred, instead of a resolute Alfred, to hearten her resistance. Over a period of more than thirty years, the Danes under Olaf Tryggvason, King Sweyn, and other Viking commanders, sailed over in ever-increasing numbers to raid and run, to stay and bulldoze over the face of unhappy England, and finally to conquer. Had there been more captains like the king's stalwart son Edmund Ironside the end of the sorry tale would have been less tragic. But there was only a worthless king and a nobility divided by mutual jealousies and often faithless to the national cause.

The faint-hearted Ethelred soon resorted to the contemptible plan of buying off the enemy with a tribute of " Danegeld ", instead of facing them squarely as Alfred had done. Naturally, the Danes took the bribe and then returned for more. Meanwhile the ravaging of the island continued. The bewildered English people lost heart. In 1013, the king's flight to Normandy (he had married, as his second wife, the Duke of Normandy's sister, Emma, some years earlier) was but one sign that the country's ill-concerted resistance was futile. So the unbelievable happened. England lay prostrate beneath the heel of King Sweyn and his Northmen.

Fortunately for the vanquished, Sweyn's son, Canute,

accepted as king in 1016, was a Christian and one whose rule, though stern, proved wise and just. And perhaps he was not really such a prig as the dreary moral tale, about his *not* ruling the waves, would make out. As it happened, the break in the native dynasty was brief. On the death of Canute, in 1035, and of the two sons who succeeded him, the Witan, in 1042, elected Edward, a son of Ethelred and Emma of Normandy, to the throne.

Edward was a truly saintly man—he was called " the Confessor " for that reason; but he made a feeble and un-satisfactory king. He had been brought up in Normandy and was almost a complete stranger to his subjects. Not surprisingly, he favoured his Norman friends, giving them lands and titles and high offices in Church and State. And, not less surprisingly, these unwise favours aroused rankling jealousy and discontent among the Saxon and Danish nobles.

The most powerful members of the nobility were the great earls. They dominated the Witan. They possessed boundless estates. The ceorls on their lands, many of them now become practically serfs, were their men. They were the liege lords of the lesser country thanes who, in the hard times of war, sought their protection. They commanded the local *fyrd*, or militia. They often controlled the shire-courts which, with the decline of the cumbrous *folk-moots*, were now the principal centres of county justice, taxation and administration. At this time many of the earldoms, often covering several shires, were concentrated in the hands of a few rival families, and the latter's immense resources made them dangerously powerful subjects of the king. Family rivalry was now to divide the nation at a time when unity was becoming its most insistent need.

In the early years of Edward the Confessor's reign the most dominating, and the most grasping, of these families was that of Godwin, Earl of Wessex, whose lands embraced more than half of England. His nearest rivals were the houses of Mercia and Northumbria. In 1051, Godwin's flat defiance of the king's orders, after having almost plunged the country into civil war, led to his banishment. Yet, eventually, his military strength and his popularity as the enemy of the king's hated Norman favourites, prevailed. His family was restored to favour and many of the intruding Normans were sent packing. The great earl's death in 1053 brought his son Harold to the centre of the stage in an anxious hour of the country's fortunes. In the coming years the question of the succession to the throne was in everyone's mind. The nearest male heir, Edgar Atheling, grandson of Edmund Ironside, was only a child. Harold Hardrada, King of Norway, was known to be a claimant. But, most dangerous threat of all, Duke William of Normandy was closely watching events in England and preparing to shape them to his own ends.

The Normans, or Northmen, were of the same breed as the Danes. In 911, they had planted themselves in north-western France as vassals of the French king. Since then they had shed their barbarian ways and become more civilised and wholly French in language and social customs. The present duke was a cold-hearted and ruthlessly masterful character. He was King Edward's cousin. He asserted that Edward had promised him the succession. And when, in 1064, Harold Godwin had fallen into his hands after being shipwrecked off the French coast, he claimed to have exacted from his captive a solemn oath, to support his claims. Actually the choice of a future king rested with the Witan; but it was unfortunate for Harold's reputation that, in the event, he had placed himself in the discreditable position of an oath-breaker.

REBELLION

Harold, a man of forceful character and military talent, was himself a strong favourite for the kingship, but he was not of royal English blood. Nevertheless, when Edward died in 1066, he was the man of the hour and the Witan raised him to the vacant throne. His sovereignty was quickly challenged. Northumbria had previously risen against its earl, Harold's brother Tostig, and called in Morcar, brother of Edwin, Earl of Mercia, the long-standing rivals of Harold's house. Morcar's appointment had been confirmed by the court and Tostig had gone off in a sullen rage. Now he leagued himself with the King of Norway, who descended on the Northumbrian coast with a powerful fleet. Harold hurried north and, in the desperately fought battle of Stamford Bridge, slew both his brother and the Norwegian king and destroyed their army and their hopes for ever.

Three days later Duke William landed—he himself in fact stumbled—on the shores of Pevensey Bay. Harold made a forced march south. But no levies came from Edwin and Morcar and it was with an incomplete army that he faced the Normans in the epoch-making battle of Hastings. The fate of England trembled in the balance throughout the livelong day. But, when Harold fell, his eye pierced by an arrow, England fell too. So, within fifty odd years, she had twice bowed the knee to a foreign invader, each time paying the price of her seemingly incurable disunity.

Whether in the long run the Norman Conquest was a blessing or a curse modern historians are undecided. But William and his successors gave England a strong, unifying government, an ordered system of law and an efficient admi-nistration of the country's affairs. A quarrelsome people were schooled in self-discipline. And a new and vigorous strain was infused into the native blood. All the elements of the English race—Saxon, Dane and Norman—were now assembled. Only time was needed to blend them in the composite nation that was to play such a mighty part on the larger stage of world-history.

The Battle of Hastings, in which King Harold of England was slain, was a decisive victory for William the Conqueror; from then onwards there was little serious opposition to his rule.

THE NORMAN CONQUEST

In 1066 the battle of Hastings had plunged the proud and independent English people into the depths of defeat and humiliation. This is the story of how they climbed out again.

William the Conqueror's Normans had won because they were up-to-date in the practice of war. In particular, they had developed the cavalry arm, the mail-clad mounted knights. The old-fashioned English still preferred to fight mainly on their own two feet. And the Normans had learned how to keep what they won. They built castles everywhere. From these strongholds the garrison could hold down all the neighbouring countryside. England became peppered with the hated structures.

To the English, the Conquest was an overwhelming disaster. Their homeland became the spoils of war of the harsh and arrogant victors. The nobility lost their lands, political power, prestige—almost everything. The village ceorls (" villeins " as many of them were now commonly termed) passed under the heavy yoke of alien masters who spoke an alien tongue. The confiscated estates of the aristocracy were parcelled out among the Conqueror's Norman and other French barons. The principal offices in Church and State were filled by the foreigners. Yet the fundamental English laws and institutions survived under Norman control. The Great Council, composed of the king's household officials and the great barons and churchmen, carried on the tradition of the English Witan in the government of the State. The old shire-courts and hundred-courts continued to conduct the business of local justice, finance, and administration.

The feature that above all others gave England a new look was the feudal system. Many of its elements were already in existence in England, but William made feudalism the social and military framework of his realm. On receiving their grants of land, or manors, from the king, the great barons became his sworn vassals, engaging themselves to fight for him, with a specified number of knights, in time of war. The barons, in turn, granted parts of their manors to lesser barons and others of their followers on similar terms. The king thus bound the great barons—and likewise the land-holding bishops and abbots—to his service by the sacred oaths of fealty and homage, and the barons and churchmen did the same with their followers. But William was astute. To curb his warlike vassals' power over *their* vassals, he made the latter swear an additional oath of fealty to him direct.

In 1085 William ordered a record to be made of all the land of England. Like any shrewd business man, he wanted to know exactly what he possessed and what revenue he could extract from it. The resulting Domesday Book survives as a priceless record of eleventh century England and an impressive testimony to the painstaking efficiency of Norman officialdom.

William I died in 1087, unloved and unhonoured. But his English subjects acknowledged that his iron rule had at least brought a welcome spell of calm weather into their stormy voyage through history. He left Normandy to his eldest son, Robert, England to his next son, William.

William II, whose oppressive reign lasted till 1100, and his younger brother Henry who succeeded him, were as unlovable as their father. William, with his tubby figure and ruddy complexion (hence his nickname Rufus, " the Red "), was ungainly in appearance and odious in character. Henry's disposition was little more pleasing, but he proved a very capable ruler.

Both brothers devoted much of their time to continental plots and wars for filching Normandy from Robert. The barons, having estates in both countries, were divided in their allegiance, and the grasping and autocratic royal rule further weakened their loyalty. Several rebellions flamed up and the manner in which they were extinguished is very

William I, the Conqueror, gave instructions for a complete survey to be made of his English lands. The results of this survey are preserved in the Domesday Book.

The Saxon people had a strong sense of justice. The village people settled their own grievances in tun-moots, higher courts being folk-moots and hundred-moots.

significant and not a little amusing. Both Willam and Henry turned for support to the despised " dogs of Saxons ". And the Saxon dogs responded with enthusiasm. They bared their teeth so menacingly that the barons were cowed. Plainly the English had learned to appreciate the blessings of peace. Henry went even farther to win the people's affections. He married Matilda, a daughter of the King of Scots and a descendant of Alfred the Great. William's misdeeds were dramatically ended when he was slain by an arrow—whether accidentally or by design no one can say—in the New Forest.

The struggle for Normandy ended in King Henry's favour in 1106. It was small gain to the English. Their interests suffered through the king's constant preoccupation with continental wars and politics. Nevertheless Henry did much to promote justice for his subjects. Indeed he came down so ferociously on wrongdoers (other than himself) that he gained the resounding title of " the Lion of Justice ". Specially trained men were sent to preside over the shire-courts as his officers and to carry the royal justice there, besides organising and collecting the royal revenues. And he kept everyone on his toes by despatching inquisitorial justices " in eyre " (a contraction of Latin *in itinere*, " on a journey,") round the shires for the same purposes.

DICTATORIAL BARONS

Henry gave England thirty years of peace. But, when the Lion of Justice finally ceased roaring in 1135, there was to be precious little more of that boon for many years to come. Henry's only son had been drowned at sea, leaving a daughter, Matilda, as his heiress. The idea of female rule was wholly repugnant in those days and the barons took Stephen of Blois, a son of William I's daughter Adela, for their king.

And then the troubles started. Stephen was a " mild man and soft ". Soon he and the haughty, unpopular Matilda were at each other's throats. The ensuing civil war brought out all that was basest in the character of the Norman barons, their ruffianly violence, their greed and faithlessness. With a few exceptions each fought only for his own interests. In the appalling free-for-all fight that desolated the country, men said that " Christ and his saints slept ". The groaning victims yearned for the strong arm of another Henry. The very name of " baron " became hateful.

Relief came at last. In 1153 the vicious quarrel was settled. Stephen was to retain the crown for his life and Matilda's son Henry, by Geoffrey of Anjou, was to succeed him. Only a year later Stephen died.

THE PLANTAGENETS

Henry II was the first of the Plantagenet line, so named from the Anjou family device of a sprig of broom, in Latin called *planta genista*. The powerfully-built young monarch with the keen grey eyes was a determined and frequently alarming character. His uncontrollable storms of rage were frightful to behold. He was a restless and tireless worker, as highly charged with energy as an electric battery. At his accession he was already a mighty continental potentate; for, through his parents and his wife Eleanor of Aquitaine, he was lord of vast dominions in western France. Later, the King of Scots, who now ruled the whole of Scotland, became his man, and some inconclusive operations in Ireland begun by his lieutenant Richard Clare, Earl of Pembroke (" Strongbow "), gave him the (very sketchy) overlordship of that island. Thus his "Angevin " empire came to embrace half of France and the greater part of the British Isles.

The energetic king resolutely swept away the disorders of Stephen's ruinous reign and fettered the unruly barons' mischievous powers. In 1181, he fastened another shackle on them. In the Assize of Arms he remodelled the old Saxon fyrd by requiring every man of military age to furnish himself with arms and equipment. Rebellious barons and foreign foes alike might take notice that the king had a national militia at his call. Meantime, for many years, his abundant energy was employed in advancing his power in his French possessions by war, diplomacy and family marriages.

LAW REFORM

But all these activities by no means exhausted the battery. The tireless king turned to overhauling the damaged judicial and administrative machinery of his island kingdom and strengthening his control over it. He revolutionised the processes of the law and raised the administrative system to a high pitch of efficiency.

In systematising the visits of the justices in eyre he took a bold leap forward. The Assize of Clarendon of 1166 pro-

In 1099, during the First Crusade, Jerusalem was recaptured for the Christians. The Third Crusade, in which Richard I took part, was the most spectacular of all the Crusades in the Holy Land.

vided that, when the justices visited a district, a select body of men should come forward and testify against the local criminals. Furthermore, in certain " civil " cases, the cause was actually tried by a jury. These practices marked the beginning of the end of the barbarous old Saxon trials by ordeal, and the Norman wager of battle, and their slow and gradual replacement by the rational method of trial by jury as practised to-day. Trial by jury means a fair hearing in open court. It accords with the primitive Saxon bent for impartial popular justice, of which it is the supreme safeguard. Henry's reforms had some notable long-range consequences. As time went slowly on, the decisions pronounced in the royal courts, in the counties and at Westminster, superseded the old, muddled and conflicting provincial laws and customs and built up the Common Law of the land. The growth of the Common Law, in turn, tended to iron out ancient local differences and so to foster a sense of national unity.

DEMANDS OF THE CHURCH

But now the story of successful achievement takes another turn. From the time of the Norman Conquest the Church had been advancing immense claims to authority in Europe. As the spiritual power responsible for men's eternal salvation, it insisted on its supremacy over the rulers of Christendom. Kings and princes were vassals of the pope. They owed him homage. They must obey his " bulls " and other decrees. To enforce its authority the Church possessed two powers of tremendous weight: the interdict, and excommunication. The Church held the Keys of Heaven. Its rites were the only roads to salvation. If a country was placed under interdict, its churches were closed, their regular services suspended. If an offender was excommunicated, he was banished from the Christian fold, his soul damned for all eternity, and he was virtually outlawed.

The Church's sweeping claims inevitably led to conflicts between the Papacy and the sovereigns of Europe. One of such disputes arose over the subject of " lay investiture ". The churchmen claimed that they, and not the king or any other " layman ", had the right to appoint bishops and other clerics to office. But there were two sides to the question. Bishops and abbots, as holders of church lands, were the sworn vassals of their king and liable to perform the customary feudal services, not excluding military service. In England, William I and his sons had steadily repudiated the demands of the popes for homage and unqualified obedience. On the investiture question, however, Henry I and Anselm, Archbishop of Canterbury, had made a sensible compromise. Bishops and abbots were to be chosen by the clergy, but they were to pay homage to the king for their lands. And there the vexed question had remained, like a delayed-action bomb.

A TRAGIC FEUD

In Henry II's reign a new storm centre appeared. The Church enjoyed the privilege of trying spiritual causes and cases affecting clerics in its own ecclesiastical courts. The privilege was sometimes shamelessly abused. The punishments imposed on offenders were often absurdly trivial. Henry's ire was roused. In 1162 he had appointed as Archbishop of Canterbury his old friend and companion Thomas Becket. Shortly afterwards he claimed that condemned " criminous clerks " should become subject to punishment in the same way as laymen. Becket opposed him because, to him, the issue was in fact the difficult problem of the respective limits of the spiritual and temporal power.

The old friends indulged in an unhappy slanging match and became bitter enemies.

At length, in 1164, a council drew up the Constitutions of Clarendon which confirmed Henry's claim. For six years the king and his archbishop remained at daggers drawn. Becket's challenging displays of zeal, however sincere and righteous they might be, drove the fiery-tempered Henry to fury. Becket fled to the Continent. The crisis was reached in 1170. The king had his son Henry crowned as his successor by the Archbishop of York, a flagrant violation of the privileges of the Primate of Canterbury. Becket returned to England and boldly excommunicated the officiating bishops. When the news reached Henry in Normandy he saw red.

"Are there none that will rid me of this turbulent priest ? " he cried.

Four of his knights sped straightway to England. And in the sacred precincts of his own cathedral the " turbulent priest ", the Primate of England, was murdered.

All Europe shuddered. Henry was stunned. Overwhelmed by remorse at the consequence of his hasty words, he admitted his fault and sought the Pope's forgiveness. He yielded his claim to execute justice on criminous clerks. He conceded the Pope's right to receive and decide appeals to Rome concerning spiritual questions. So deep was his sense of guilt that he afterwards did penance at the martyred archbishop's tomb by walking there barefoot while the monks scourged his naked shoulders.

Henry's later years were vexed with rebellions, at home and in France, and a Scottish invasion. His wife and sons leagued themselves against him. But the people of England rallied to his side and he overcame all his trials save one, the final stab in the back by his faithless and quarrelsome children. In 1189, his son Richard, hand-in-glove with the French king, brought his ageing father to the shame of utter defeat in France. Lying on his deathbed he learned that his youngest and dearest son John had deserted his side. The revelation broke his heart.

HERO OF THE CRUSADES

It is a sad disappointment to discover that the hero Richard Coeur-de-Lion, who (his brother Henry having died) succeeded his father, was a hero only on crusade. As King Richard I he is of small consequence in English history. Of his ten-year reign he spent only six months in Britain, and his country was no more to him than a treasure chest to be rifled for the payment of his foreign exploits. To finance the Third Crusade for the liberation of Jerusalem from the Moslem Turks, he sold everything he could, including the suzerainty over Scotland which his father had exacted. On his way home through Austria in 1192-3 he fell into the hands of the Emperor Henry VI, and had to dig into the treasure chest again to ransom his royal person.

During his absence his brother John had seized the chance to make a snatch at the throne. But the plot collapsed and Richard, on returning home, contemptuously pardoned the traitor. In 1194, came another dip into the treasure chest and Richard was off again. This time it was to wage war on the French king Philip Augustus, who was aspiring to his continental possessions. Richard never returned. In 1199, his glowing career was ingloriously cut short by an arrow discharged in a trivial siege operation.

The fatal arrow gave England one of the worst of kings. John was wantonly cruel and tyrannical, mean and faithless, vain and intemperate. There was a rival claimant to his French possessions: his nephew Arthur of Brittany, a boy of twelve. The poor lad was foully murdered and John himself stands charged with the hideous crime. The war with Philip continued; but John was as inferior to the lion-hearted Richard in martial genius as he was in physical stature and disaster after disaster attended his campaigns. By 1204, Normandy was lost.

Unrestrained by these reverses, John, in 1205, proceeded to raise up another powerful enemy. The delayed-action bomb of Henry I's reign exploded. John forced the monks of Canterbury to elect his own favourite as archbishop. The Pope quashed the election and consecrated Stephen Langton, an Englishman of high character and learning. John angrily refused to accept him, seized the revenues of Canterbury and drove the monks out of the country. The Pope retaliated by placing the audacious offender under an interdict. John's reply was a general confiscation of the wealth of the clergy. Finally, in 1209, the outraged Pope pronounced on the royal robber the awful sentence of excommunication and later threatened to depose him. It was like a long-range artillery duel between a couple of battleships.

Meantime John was receiving hits from other quarters. His extortionate taxation, his cruelty and high-handed tyranny had roused anger and hatred among all classes. And, as if this were not enough, King Philip was now preparing an invasion. John saw that he must divide his enemies. So, in 1213, he submitted to the Pope. Stephen Langton was accepted as Archbishop of Canterbury. The plunderings from the Church were to be disgorged. And, to cap everything, the king surrendered his kingdom and received it back again as the Pope's vassal. It seems a degrading act; yet what is unthinkable to-day was not considered so then. Vassalage, especially to the Papacy, held no taint of servility. In any case, John's concern was to buy the Pope's support against his encircling foes.

The pardoned sinner's bargain did not avail him much. In 1214, the battle of Bouvines dashed once for all his hopes of recovering his French dominions. When he returned to England little was left to him of his vast foreign empire except Gascony and the Channel Islands. At home the day of reckoning for his misrule awaited him. The barons assembled in arms to enforce their demands for the country's ancient liberties. And in June, 1215, at Runnymede, the beaten king was compelled to set his seal to Magna Carta.

THE GREAT CHARTER

The Great Charter is as conspicuous a monument in English annals as Nelson's Column is in Trafalgar Square. It was used to drive home the fundamental principle that the king was not above the law. By one of its clauses John bound himself not to levy any *scutage* or *aid* (descriptions of money subsidy), except the recognised feudal dues, without the consent of the Common Council of the Realm, consisting of the barons and the great ecclesiastics. No freeman was to be proceeded against except according to the laws; and the king promised that to none would he sell, deny, or defer justice.

The Charter misfired in John's time. Neither side trusted

Saladin, first Ayyubite sultan of Egypt, negotiated a treaty with Richard the Lion Heart, in which Saladin dictated the terms.

At Runnymede, King John was forced to sign the charter of privileges as set out in the Magna Carta.

the other and soon the clash of arms resounded again. The civil war was still raging when John came to his end in 1216, largely as the result of his disgusting gluttony at table. But the future of the Charter was momentous beyond all expectations or intentions. As it stood, it was largely a partisan measure for the benefit of the baronial class. But in the times ahead it became the rallying ground and a battle cry for all the progressive forces of liberty. Its underlying principles expanded like the ripples of a pool until they came to include the doctrines of freedom from all arbitrary taxation, of equal justice for everyone, whether rich or poor, of trial by jury, and of representative parliamentary government, all of which we now take for granted.

HENRY III

With the accession of John's nine-year-old son as Henry III, it was left to a regency and council to sort things out and to end the civil war. But, on attaining the ripe age of nineteen, Henry decided that he was old enough to rule the country himself. The results showed that he would never be old enough, for he was a fickle and feckless creature. His foreign favourites—connections of his mother and his wife—filled the court, and these arrogant fortune-hunters were not interested in the Charter. Extravagance, folly and chronic misrule brought the government into universal contempt. His excessive piety allowed the Pope to levy toll on the revenues of the Church for his own designs, and to fill vacant offices with absentee Italian clerics.

The fierce resentment and opposition of the barons filled the first thirty years of the king's personal rule with continual friction and wrangling.

PROVISIONS OF OXFORD

In 1258, the situation became unendurable. The barons compelled Henry to accept the Provisions of Oxford, which set up a council to control and reform the government. One of the baronial leaders was Simon de Montfort, Earl of Leicester. Simon was a Frenchman, but he had made the English cause his own. He was a man of lofty principles and Christian ideals, and threw himself heart and soul into the struggle. Unhappily, the barons soon began to disagree among themselves and Henry slipped the bridle they had forced on him. In 1263, Simon became the leader of the

barons who still stood by the Provisions of Oxford and were prepared to fight for the national cause.

Henry's son, the Lord Edward, had been strongly influenced by Simon's principles. Both men were firm supporters of the monarchy and of reform. But Simon, the popular champion, placed reform first. Edward, the royal prince, gave priority to the rights of the throne. It was a tragic fate that placed these two on opposite sides of the battlefield. At Lewes, in 1264, Simon won the first round of the contest and both Henry and Edward were made captive.

THE BEGINNING OF PARLIAMENT

Then Simon made history of another sort. From the earliest times the aristocracy—the barons and clerics of the Great Council—had formed the governing class. Of late, however, the door had occasionally been left ajar for the entry of the knights of the shire, who were beginning to change from men of war to country gentlemen devoted to the peaceful duties of county administration. In 1265, Simon held a parliament—the term was then coming into current use—which opened the door still wider. He called in common folk—representatives from the towns—as well. The event is of deep historic interest; for the assembly contained the germs of the fully representative Parliament of to-day.

It was Simon's last notable achievement. When the Lord Edward, having escaped from captivity, faced him again at Evesham, Simon and his party were destroyed. But his work did not perish with him. The victor himself, who became King Edward I in 1272, carried it on.

BIRTHRIGHT OF THE PEOPLE

The country was ready for it. Great social changes were under way. The Charter had become the birthright of all. The common people were coming into notice and even the villeins were casting off something of their servile condition. And these movements were all part of a greater whole. Normans and English had long been drawing together. By the end of the twelfth century the fusion was all but complete. Saxon and Dane and Norman were one people. The English tongue had lived on through the storm of conquest, though French was the language of the aristocracy. The English people had climbed out of the depths of defeat and humiliation.

42

GERMANY AND THE HOLY ROMAN EMPIRE

Germany may be said to have first appeared in history as a separate and wholly Germanic State in 843. In that year, by the Treaty of Verdun, the Frankish empire of Charlemagne was trisected, and the resulting parts foreshadowed the future territories of France, Germany, and Italy. The subjects of Louis, the first king of the budding German State, were a collection of unruly barbarian tribes—Saxons, Bavarians and others—who, while clinging to their own language, had previously been converted from paganism and brought under the improving influences of the Church and civilised government.

Time brought many troubles. Wild Magyars and Slavs continually assailed the kingdom from the east. Rival dukes who, with the spread of the feudal system, became virtually independent, disrupted it from within. Fortunately, in 919, a king appeared, the Saxon Henry the Fowler, whose strong arm set things right—for a while.

Then, in 936, came Otto I, who launched Germany on a new and adventurous course. Otto's arm, stronger even than Henry's, reached out to the east from Poland to Austria. What was of more consequence was the fact that it also grasped northern Italy.

THE HOLY ROMAN EMPIRE

If only we could foresee the consequences of our acts! Otto had made himself the most powerful monarch in Europe. But appetite grows with eating and Otto was still hungry. The ideal of the old Roman Empire, as a civilised community embracing all Christendom under the enlightened rule of Pope and Emperor, still lingered on. To Otto, with Italy already swallowed, it was a tempting banquet and in 962 he sat down to it: the Pope crowned him Emperor. Thus began the so-called Holy Roman Empire that was to

stagger on till 1806. Germany was fully launched on its new Italian course.

Otto's new title brought him no additional dominions outside Germany and Italy. In any case those two fractious kingdoms were in themselves more than he could control. The German monarchy suffered increasingly from two paralysing weaknesses. It was not hereditary, each king being elected by the great nobles and churchmen. Thus no strong family dynasty could ever take root. From this and other causes the

Otto III, Holy Roman Emperor crowned German king in 983, dreamed of restoring the empire to its former glory.

In order to forestall his enemies in a plot to elect a new emperor, Henry IV secretly crossed the Alps to patch up his quarrel with Pope Gregory VII. This timely act saved the throne of Germany for Henry, but did not end the long struggle over investitures.

In an endeavour to force his imperial rights in Italy, Frederick I (Barbarossa or Redbeard), made six expeditions into Italy. The fifth campaign was a failure and he was defeated by the forces of the Lombard League at Legnano on 29th May, 1176.

kingdom tended to break up into innumerable separate "principalities" whose "princes" (actually dukes, counts, margraves, bishops and others) paid scant respect to the crown. When the emperors were absent in Italy the princes seized the happy occasion to advance their own power. But these troubles were minor squalls compared with the gale that sprang up during the reign of Henry IV, a century or so after Emperor Otto's coronation.

CONFLICT BETWEEN CHURCH AND STATE

The Popes, as heads of Christendom, had long been claiming sovereign powers over the kings of Europe. In 1073, the forthright Pope Gregory VII was ardently resolved on asserting those claims to the utmost. The ensuing conflict centred largely around the question of "lay investiture" —who should appoint the bishops and other clerics to office. Henry's predecessors had lavishly endowed their bishops with feudal estates. If, as Gregory demanded, these powerful clerical vassals were in future to be appointed by the Popes, a blow would be struck at the very heart of the royal authority. Henry defied the Pope and the gale began.

It involved a determined conflict between the two mightiest powers in Europe, the supreme head of Christendom and the Roman Emperor, the one standing for the Church, the other for the State. The struggle convulsed the heart of Europe for nearly fifty years and split the peoples of Germany and of Italy into furiously warring factions. Henry deposed the Pope. The Pope deposed and excommunicated Henry. The German princes turned against their king and in 1077 Henry decided to yield. His act of submission is one of the most dramatic episodes in medieval history. In winter when the snow lay deep, he secretly crossed the Alps and made his way to the castle of Canossa in northern Italy. Kneeling barefoot before Gregory, Henry humbly confessed his errors and craved absolution.

THE WONDER OF THE WORLD

Nevertheless the investiture dispute was not settled until 1122, after Henry's death, when a compromise was agreed upon. Even so, the general conflict for supremacy between Church and State raged on with pen and sword.

During the reigns of the Hohenstauffen emperors [Frederick I (1152-90) and Frederick II (1215-50)], the struggle with the Papacy over rights and territories was almost continuous.

Frederick I, Barbarossa (Redbeard), undertook six expeditions to Italy in an attempt to restore his imperial authority. His chief opponents were the rich cities of the Lombard League in alliance with the Papacy. The fight was fierce, with cities razed to the ground and Rome itself occupied by Imperial troops. Frederick could never give the Italian campaigns his undivided attention. Like every emperor, he had to keep his German territories in order. Finally, in 1176, Frederick was defeated by the Lombard League at Legnano. The following year in Venice he recognised the Pope, Alexander III, and reached agreement over their rival claims. In 1190, Barbarossa was drowned in Asia Minor on his way to fight in the Third Crusade.

Frederick II, Barbarossa's grandson and one of the most remarkable and enlightened rulers of the middle ages, was known as *Stupor Mundi*—the Wonder of the World. He was a man of bold ideas and his court was the most cultured of the time.

Frederick II's possessions were more extensive than any of his contemporaries, for they included the kingdom of Sicily (of which Southern Italy was part) as well as the German possessions of the Holy Roman Empire. The Papacy thus found itself threatened by Hohenstauffen territory on all sides and set itself to break the power of the House. Throughout Frederick's reign the conflict took the usual form of bans and excommunications, war and confiscation. While Frederick lived, the huge Hohenstauffen territories were kept together, but after his death political anarchy prevailed. For the remainder of the century, the Papacy was able to reach what was, in many ways, the zenith of its power.

As for Germany, the princes were tired of strong emperors. They had forced the Hohenstauffens, while they were embroiled in Italy, to accept limitations of their power. During the next century they consolidated their independence and never elected as emperor a man strong enough to threaten it. All hope of establishing a strong and united Germany was ruined, and not until the late fifteenth century did the empire, under the Habsburgs, again speak with its former authority in Europe.

THE MAKING OF FRANCE

When the House of Capet succeeded to the throne of France in 987, Hugh, its first king, found himself in the uneasy position of the colonel of a mutinous regiment. His effective power was confined to an area in the north with Paris and Orleans as its chief cities. The remainder of France was composed of a number of feudal States over which Hugh exercised scarcely more authority than Canute did over the waves. Of these the duchy of Normandy was one of the most powerful, and, after its conquest of England in 1066, it naturally became more powerful still. In the following century Henry Plantagenet, Count of Anjou and Duke of Normandy, completely overshadowed the throne. By marrying Eleanor of Aquitaine he acquired the whole of south-western France, and in 1154 he succeeded to the kingdom of England as Henry II.

After 1180, however, the situation changed. The cool-headed and ambitious Philip Augustus took over the command of the regiment. Henry II and, afterwards, his unpleasant son, John, were decisively defeated and, save for the Gascony region, the English were driven out of the country.

Shortly after Philip's death in 1223, the Capetian line acquired a singular lustre: the saintly Louis IX succeeded to the throne. Louis was one of those exceedingly rare sovereigns who, truly Christian at heart, put their principles into practice. Yet he was more than a man of holiness. In war he proved himself an accomplished and fearless knight. Beneath his oak-tree at Vincennes he was a strict dispenser of justice. He died, appropriately, on a crusade and was canonised in 1297 by Pope Boniface VIII.

THE VALOIS DYNASTY

The direct line of the Capets lasted on till 1328, when a

Fired by an ambition to be crowned emperor of the East, Charles VIII, clothed in the imperial insignia, entered Naples with great pomp on 12th May, 1495. A coalition was formed against him and he had to return to France.

younger branch, the Valois, succeeded it. The dynasty that had started from such small beginnings, had achieved great things. The power of most of the big vassal States had been broken and the country largely freed from the English. Now, when France spoke, Europe listened. A strong central administration had been created. The *parlement* of Paris, which was *not* a parliament but a legal institution, administered a common system of justice. Something of the character of a representative parliament was attempted in the States-General. But this assembly was not destined for the great future which the English Parliament enjoyed. In England, the country gentry, the knights of the shire, formed a connecting middle-class between the aristocracy and the townsmen. In France no such unifying link existed. The nobles, clergy and burgesses remained sharply divided classes and rarely acted together. The assembly never won the control over legislation and taxation which gave the English Parliament its power.

Another notable achievement was the mastery gained over the Papacy, which converted that sacred institution into a tool of French ambitions. The Capets had owed much to their close alliance with Rome, but they were no longer prepared to pay the price for it. As the fourteenth century advanced, the papal claims to supremacy over the kings of Europe were, indeed, treated with scant respect by the rising monarchies of the West. And there were signs of a direct challenge to the whole spiritual authority of popes and priests and of some of the fundamental religious doctrines and practices on which their power rested. In England, for example, the reformer John Wycliffe spoke out boldly against the constitution and abuses of the Church.

Under the Valois, France's progress suffered the calamitous check of the Hundred Years' War with England. The crushing defeats dealt her by England at the battles of Crecy, Poitiers and Agincourt all but bled France to death. But in the end, the common suffering and humiliation, the resulting hatred of the English and the universal yearning for peace and order, drew the French people submissively together around their king. Towards the end of the fifteenth century, with the close of the Middle Ages, France stood, like England and Spain, as a strong and united national state.

The period ended with a half-crazy king's wholly crazy adventure. Charles VIII inherited a claim to the kingdom of Naples, which embraced southern Italy. The peninsula was in its customary state of chronic discord and the city of Milan rashly invited Charles to intervene. Charles, dazzled by visions of martial glory, eagerly accepted. In 1494 he set forth and his army marched down the length of Italy in a bloodless triumph. But the brutal conduct of his troops incensed the Italians against him. A coalition was hastily formed and the valiant Charles was lucky to get back to France after a single battle in 1495. The result, which was only a disappointment for Charles, was tragic for Italy. The invasion had revealed her weakness and her wealth to the great powers of Europe. Henceforth, for centuries, she became the victim and the battlefield of their greedy ambition.

THE CRUSADES

There was gloom in Constantinople in 1071. The Eastern Roman Empire's army in Armenia had been destroyed by the savage Seljuk Turks who had superseded the Arabs in western Asia. Asia Minor lay at the Mohammedan victors' feet. Would Constantinople's turn come next? The Emperor Alexius sent a message to the Pope urging him to rally the West to the aid of Christendom, and in 1096 the First Crusade was on.

It did not, however, take quite the form that Alexius had in mind. His aim was to recover the empire's lost provinces. The Crusaders' particular purpose was to liberate Jerusalem from the hands of the hated Saracens, as they called the Moslems. These different viewpoints were a symptom of a long-standing cleavage between Constantinople and Rome. The Eastern Empire, which was *Greek* in spirit, had preserved the continuity of Roman civilisation when it had been broken by the barbarian invaders in the West. For the descendants of those savage interlopers, and the kingdoms they had created under *Latin* influences, the cultured East entertained the utmost contempt. Furthermore, the Greek " Orthodox " Church disdainfully repudiated the spiritual authority of the Pope and differed from the Latin Church in certain of its beliefs and practices. There was resentment in the West and many talked of overthrowing the haughty Greek empire.

But all this apart, the Pope's clarion call roused the West to the heights of rapturous enthusiasm. Regretfully, however, it must be said that the underlying motives were very mixed. Many went for fighting and adventure, for personal gain or to escape from evils at home. But to the finer spirits the redemption of the Holy City and Sepulchre of Our Lord seemed the most sublime of earthly endeavours, the noblest errand of knightly chivalry. So a great multitude of famous knights, and other eager soldiers of the Cross, set forth. Concentrating at Constantinople, they crossed into Asia and,

A priest at Amiens, Peter the Hermit, was a fervent advocate of the First Crusade.

after heavy loss and travail, reached the Holy Land. Their ardour carried all before it. Jerusalem was freed and much of Asia Minor recaptured. The Crusaders set up the kingdom of Jerusalem and three other Frankish States. The military and religious Orders of the Knights Templars and the Knights Hospitallers were founded.

But some years later, the Turks rallied and counter-attacked and the Second Crusade of 1147 failed to hold them. Then a new star arose in the Mohammedan world—Saladin, the superb leader and pattern of eastern chivalry. In 1187, Christendom was shocked to its depths: Jerusalem had fallen. The monarchs of Europe flew to arms. In 1189, Frederick Barbarossa of Germany, Emperor of the Holy Roman Empire, Philip Augustus of France, and England's Richard Coeur-de-lion captained the Third Crusade. But Frederick was drowned while crossing a river and Philip and Richard quarrelled. Richard's dash and fire snatched Cyprus from the Eastern Empire, triumphantly ended the long siege of Acre and captured Jaffa. But he failed before Jerusalem and in the end all that was left to the Christians was Acre, Jaffa and other Syrian ports, and the promise of free access for pilgrims to the Holy Sepulchre.

The Fourth Crusade, of 1202, was a disgrace to all concerned. The animosity between the Greek Empire and the Latin West had been further embittered. Events, and the merchant traders of Venice who supplied the ships, now tempted the nobles of France and Flanders who commanded the new Crusade to execute the old design of overthrowing the Greek emperor. Constantinople was stormed. Baldwin of Flanders, one of the Crusader chiefs, set himself up as emperor. Jerusalem was forgotten. Not until 1261 was the true dynasty restored.

Meantime, in 1212, the pitiful tragedy of the Children's Crusade was enacted. Two boys, Stephen in France and Nicolas in Germany, led out tens of thousands of guileless children to accomplish what their sinful elders had failed to perform. Their story makes the heart sink. Thousands were kidnapped and sold into slavery. Many were drowned in the Mediterranean. Relatively few returned. All they have left us is the legend of the Pied Piper of Hamelin, which grew out of Nicolas's luckless endeavour.

The thirteenth century saw the last ripples of the true Crusading spirit. The Christian footholds in Syria were lost. The noblest of causes had been wrecked by the leaders' rivalries and selfish greed.

Yet the story is not entirely cheerless. Europe's horizon had expanded. A stimulating prospect had opened up, of unfamiliar lands and peoples, their arts and crafts and sciences, their novel ways and ideas. Trade expanded enormously. The Italian cities of Venice, Genoa and Pisa prospered immensely from transporting crusaders and from the traffic in the rich natural products and luxuries of the East which could once again come overland to Europe. The towns on the European trade routes, by which these commodities were distributed, grew in importance. The Crusades may have been a religious failure, but they were a worldly success, for the mind of Europe as well as for its purse.

ENGLAND UNDER ENGLISH KINGS

Reading English history is agreeably like going on a long tramp through ever-changing country. The years are milestones. The outstanding historic events are landmarks on the way. The stretch of road we are about to travel over is beset with them.

King Edward I, who reigned from 1272 to 1307, gives us a good send-off. He was the first truly " English " king since the Norman Conquest, and he ruled a land where Saxons and Normans had become blended in one composite people. As king and man he was a rare character. Tall and erect and sinewy, his length of leg gained him the nickname of " Longshanks ". He was a proud and truly royal prince, a fearless and peerless knight, and altogether a man's man.

RE-ORGANISING THE LAW

Edward had a deep regard for law and order and he is famous as a law-maker. He reorganised the administration of justice. He clarified and supplemented the laws and built up the Common Law anew. He resolutely checked the encroachments of the baronage and the Church on his own and his people's rights.

What crowns his work of peace, however, is the decisive impulse he gave to the growth of Parliament. Simon de Montfort, in his parliament of 1265, had made constitutional history by calling in a number of the common folk (representatives of certain towns) to sit with selected members of the aristocracy (the barons and clerics who formed the old governing class) and the knights of the shire or country gentlemen.

THE " MODEL PARLIAMENT "

Edward was royally insistent on the rights of the Crown, but he had absorbed something of Simon's progressive principles. His just and enlightened mind recognised that his people were becoming more conscious of their nationhood and that they had at least a claim to be consulted on matters touching their own government. So he, too, made constitutional history by going a step further than Simon. To his parliament of 1295 he summoned a full muster of barons, the higher and lower clergy, two knights from each shire and two representatives from every town. The gathering has been well called " the Model Parliament ", because, with its highly representative character, it offered a fit precedent for future assemblies. It is one of the landmarks of our journey.

Two years later another comes in sight. The king's pressing need for war supplies drove him to some desperately highhanded requisitioning and taxation. A universal outcry resulted. The barons, taking to arms, clamoured for a formal confirmation of Magna Carta, plus a declaration that no such taxes or aids should thenceforth be taken without the common consent of the realm. Edward grudgingly gave way and in so doing he, in effect, conceded a general principle of immense significance—that of " no taxation without consent ".

These two events were memorable advances towards our modern Parliament, a body which represents all classes and, by its hold on the national purse, controls the country's government.

" HAMMER OF THE SCOTS "

It was the masterful Edward's ambition to make Great Britain one firmly-united kingdom. He succeeded brilliantly in Wales. The wars of 1277 to 1283 rounded off a conquest that none of his predecessors had succeeded in completing. But he broke his teeth badly over Scotland. There the English Crown had long claimed overlordship, but the Scots

Representative of nobles, Church and people, the Model Parliament of 1295, consisted of two knights from each shire, two burgesses from each borough and town, and numerous officials of the church.

denied its legality and scornfully repudiated the bond. They were then a mixed and divided people, of Pictish, Scots, British, Saxon and Norman stock. Yet, when the English king tried to make good his shadowy claim, they would have none of it. Edward, in 1296, speedily overran their country, but afterwards Scotland produced two glorious national heroes in turn: William Wallace, and Robert Bruce (who was crowned king of Scotland in 1306). The fiery clans were roused and, when the sick and aged " Hammer of the Scots ", as men called him, died in 1307, he left his work undone. It was a great king's one great failure.

His weakling son Edward II was not the man to redeem it. Idle, vain, and thriftless, his tastes were for frivolous pleasures —pitch and toss, for instance—and low company. He was a King Do-Nothing, a sand-castle king. Not until Stirling Castle, the last great Scottish stronghold left in English hands, was imperilled did he really rouse himself.

DEFEAT FOR EDWARD II

In 1314, the rival armies faced each other on the field of Bannockburn. The Scots were greatly inferior in numbers, but their hearts burned with a dour determination to win or die, and in their adored King Robert they possessed a masterly and inspiring leader. And spirit conquered numbers. In the close-locked contest of that fateful day England suffered an unparalled disaster. Her army was routed and put to flight, King Edward himself showing the way. England's claim to overlordship had to be abandoned. Scotland had won a spectacular triumph, which, despite all her continuing internal rivalries, drew her assorted peoples more closely together than ever before. The unappeasable national hatred of " the Southrons " was to be a thorn in England's side for centuries to come.

In home affairs the rule of the inglorious king was like an echo of that of his grandfather, Henry III: greedy and incompetent favourites, chronic misrule, universal discontent, and wrangling barons were the order of the day. A council was set up to muzzle the king, but the slippery monarch recovered his authority. One gain there was. In the repeated disputes between king and barons, Parliament was frequently summoned by both sides, and so it grew in strength by the

exercise of its muscles. Later, events followed a course of their own—a fox-hunting course we might say—with Edward and his new favourites, the Despensers, father and son, as the quarry.

The precious trio had antagonised Edward's French queen Isabella, a lady of powerful and impetuous character. In 1326, Isabella was in Flanders with her fourteen-year-old son Edward and a band of English exiles which included her confederate, Roger Mortimer, a baron of the Welsh marches. The whole party now sailed over to England with the aim of destroying the Despensers. The oppressed people received the queen as their saviour. Soon the hunt was up. The king and his cronies were chased from London to the West. The huntsmen had good sport, for they " killed " twice: first the old fox, father Despenser, then the young fox, the son. Next year Edward was deposed. And shortly afterwards his gaolers in Berkeley Castle barbarously murdered him.

SCOTLAND GAINS INDEPENDENCE

For three years Isabella and Mortimer ruled, or rather misruled, in Edward III's name. Of their many " offences " the most galling was " the Shameful Peace " with Scotland in 1328. Bruce was recognised as king, and England was obliged to relinquish her claim to overlordship. A year later King Robert died and fierce disputes soon distracted his country. Edward—having asserted himself by hanging Mortimer and sending his mother into retirement—took the opportunity to resume England's old designs, but presently another field of glory beckoned him away.

The new field was France, and military glory at any cost was the dashing young king's ruling passion. There were several reasons for a war with France: King Philip's consistent support of Scotland which was hindering Edward's plans of conquest; the whittling away of England's hold on Gascony, the last remnant of Henry II's great French empire; the threat to the highly profitable wool-export trade with Flanders. Hatred of the French was becoming a national passion, so the prospect of war commanded wide support. And, for good measure, Edward trotted out a preposterous claim to the French throne itself by right of descent through his mother. So, in the year 1337, we reach another land-

Although the French had vastly superior numbers of men at the battle of Crecy, the English won a decisive victory. Deployment of men, the long bow and the use of new weapons—bombards—proved their worth in this famous battle of 1346.

Hotly pursued by the Armagnacs, Henry V was forced to make a stand at Agincourt. Largely due to the repetition of the tactical errors made at Crecy, the French, with superior forces, were routed.

mark—the headlong adventure of the Hundred Years' War.

THE HUNDRED YEARS' WAR

A graph showing the course of the contest would exhibit some remarkable ups and downs. The first notable " up " did not appear till 1346, at Crecy. In that astonishing victory England staggered Europe with her newly-developed weapon, the longbow, whose tremendous powers destroyed the long-standing supremacy of the mail-clad knight over the foot-soldier. Next year Edward took Calais, which was to be England's doorway to the Continent for 200 years. In 1356, came the crushing triumph of Poitiers, in which Edward's redoubtable black-armoured son, the Black Prince, roped in the French king among his prisoners. The graph positively rockets up in 1360, when France ceded the vast Duchy of Aquitaine, with Calais and Ponthieu. But then comes a fearful nose-dive. By 1375, Edward held nothing but Calais and a strip of the Gascony coast.

Not until Henry V fired the nation anew was the upward course resumed. In 1415, at Agincourt, the longbow struck again. The year 1420 sees the graph shooting almost off the paper. Under her mad king Charles VI, France was rent by two warring factions, the Armagnacs and the Burgundians. To secure Henry's support against their hated rivals, the Burgundians were ready to sell him the throne. By the Treaty of Troyes Charles agreed that Henry, who was to marry the French king's daughter Catherine, should be regent till Charles' death and afterwards king. It was an amazing achievement. Yet it was only a compact with a faction, and half of the kingdom still remained in the hands of Charles' son, the Dauphin and head of the Armagnacs.

Henry died in August, 1422, two months before Charles. Accordingly, it was his ten-month-old son Henry VI who was proclaimed king of France, his capable Uncle John, Duke of Bedford, being appointed regent. The dauphin was duly acclaimed by his own party as Charles VII; but he was a poor, spiritless creature incapable of enforcing his rights. Then, in 1429, something like a miracle occurred. Joan of Arc, a humble peasant girl, arose with her sublime faith in her divine mission of leading Charles to victory and crowning him at Rheims. All of which, incredible as it seems, she did, only to be captured and burned at the stake two years later. But the flame she had lit in the heart of France blazed on. The Duke of Burgundy changed sides. The Duke of Bedford died. New French tactics and the improved French artillery outmatched the longbow. The graph now plunged headlong as if trying to represent Niagara Falls. By 1453, the English had lost all their gains save Calais. And that was not the full price exacted from her for her unrighteous lust of conquest. We shall come to that later.

THE BLACK DEATH

Meantime we must return to home affairs under Edward III. While red death was staining the fair fields of France a black spectre was stalking over England. In 1348, the fearful pestilence of the Black Death swept across from the Continent. Perhaps one person in every three died. The deadly visitation brought a growing social problem to a crisis. The ancient system of feudal manors worked by servile villeins had for a long time been undergoing various fundamental changes. For one thing, the lords were beginning to hire paid labourers. The appalling ravages of the Black Death, while raising living costs, made labour scarce and dear. The government attempted to fix wages and prices by the Statutes of Labourers passed from 1351 onwards. But the evil was not cured and a stubborn class struggle developed between landlords and workers. The hitherto silent masses were raising their voices.

There were other troubles too. King Edward, the once glorious victor of Crecy, became a frivolous old dotard. The war taxes were crushing. The war had gone all wrong. The corruption at court was scandalous. The Black Prince, England's hope and idol, died in 1376. And long-standing grievances against the Church were becoming deeply embittered.

The Papacy was accused of greed and worldliness, of subjection to French influences and of making excessive demands on the revenues and rights of the Church in England.

Due to the efforts of Joan of Arc, the Siege of Orleans was lifted on 8th May, 1429. Two months later, Charles VII was crowned in the cathedral of Rheims.

A section of the English clergy themselves had forfeited all respect by their pride and luxury, their spiritual indolence and worldly ambition.

WYCLIFFE'S LOLLARDS

John Wycliffe, a learned and earnest priest, one-time Master of Balliol College, Oxford, vigorously took up the mission of purifying the Church. After Edward's death in 1377, he and his disciples, the Lollards, went a stage further. They boldly challenged certain fundamental religious doctrines and practices, condemning them as unwarranted superstitions that falsely exalted priestly power and authority. But in this they were in advance of the times and they suffered acutely for their "heresies". In 1401, Parliament passed a cruel Act condemning heretics to be burned alive. But the movement lingered on underground until the Reformation of the sixteenth century completed its work. Another achievement of the great reformer was the part he took in the first complete translation of the Bible from Latin into English.

Happily, Edward's reign was not all a tale of woe. Parliament had developed its muscles and became recognised as an assembly which must be consulted in the general affairs of the country, especially taxation. Its members were now definitely divided into "Lords" and "Commons", the latter—consisting of the knights of the shire and the town representatives—taking a leading part in public business. Industry and commerce expanded, particularly the manufacture and export of cloth, which was to bring the country untold wealth later. The once despised English tongue was steadily ousting French from the upper circles. And the beginnings of our modern literature brought forth the first poet of the front rank in Geoffrey Chaucer.

After Edward's death, the war in France slumbered uneasily for nearly forty years, though shortly after the accession of Richard II, the Black Prince's son, the French struck back at sea. This was one of many troubles that Richard—a golden-haired, quick-tempered boy of ten—and his regency council had to face. Wycliffe and his Lollards were another; the growing unrest of the peasants a third.

THE PEASANTS' REVOLT

The manorial system was now not only changing but definitely breaking up. Numbers of the villeins were "commuting" their labour services for a money rent. Many were running away. Other peasants were renting land from the lords and setting up as free yeomen farmers. A growing demand arose for the total abolition of the servile state of villeinage, and in 1381 it voiced itself in the violent upheaval of the Peasants' Revolt led by Wat Tyler. The once silent masses were positively shouting now. At a critical moment, Richard—a lad of only fourteen—fearlessly faced an angry mob of insurgents in London, gave ear to their demands and impulsively granted them. His heroism saved the situation and won the people's hearts. Then came the shameful betrayal. The charters of liberty which Richard had so hastily granted were revoked. The landowners in Parliament refused to surrender their ancient rights. The rebellion was crushed. Yet villeinage was doomed. The degrading system was out of date, and within no great time it died a natural death.

Richard's character is a baffling mixture of good and evil. He had to fight his brutal uncle, the Duke of Gloucester, before he could rule as well as reign. For eight years he governed well and wisely—and then suddenly he went clean off the rails. He struck down Gloucester and his other old enemies and rode roughshod over the rights of Parliament and country. But his wild fit of despotism was soon stilled. In 1399, one of his victims, Henry of Lancaster, a descendant of Edward III's fourth son, John of Gaunt, raised the northern barons, forced Richard to abdicate, and claimed the crown. He was not the immediate heir, since Edmund of March, a descendant of Edward's third son, Lionel, Duke of Clarence, ranked before him. But Parliament confirmed Richard's abdication and enthusiastically elected the liberator Henry. (Next year Richard died—in mysterious circumstances.)

These decrees of Parliament give us something to ponder over; they help us to realise Parliament's own line of succession, from the old Saxon Witan and the Norman Great Council. The assembly had exercised, even though under pressure, the powers of dethroning one king and enthroning another. Henry's best title rested on its election. He would have to mind his p's and q's in his future relations with that king-breaking and king-making institution.

Heavy taxes, extra tolls and the breakdown of the feudal system brought about the Peasants' Revolt of 1381. The courage of Richard II in facing the angry mob and granting them their charter of liberties, pacified the peasants.

Henry IV had little joy of his usurpation. He was like a burglar living in constant dread of the householder and the police. The earlier part of his uneasy reign was disturbed by risings and civil wars. His later years were tortured by a horrible, lingering disease that finally, in 1413, carried him off. The star performer in the various risings was the amazing Welshman, Owen Glendower. Henry could do nothing with him. The dashing and resourceful rebel defied him and assumed the title of " Prince of Wales ". In the end it was mainly his son, Henry, the future victor of Agincourt, who wore the Welsh rebel down.

With his throne so insecure it was well that Henry was a man of tact and caution. Parliament found him graciously eager to consult its wishes—and wisely seized the occasion to strengthen its hold on the conduct of public affairs. It was to win the Church's support that Henry approved of the Act condemning heretics to the stake.

Shakespeare has given us an unforgettable picture of Henry's son, the rollicking young Prince Hal, who succeeded his father; but its features are mostly inventions. In any case, when the prince graduated as Henry V, he stood forth as a model—and much less jolly—king. He was just, wise, and pious, but often strait-laced in judgment and savage in conduct. That he was a brilliant general and a superb leader is sufficiently shown by Agincourt. His valour, his frank comradely spirit and personal charm fired his subjects with a passionate hero-worship.

The story of his brief and glorious reign may almost be summed up in the one word " France ". It would have been well for his overstrained country had he allowed the Hundred Years' War to die in its sleep. We have already seen how his splendid genius bore him to the pinnacle of success in the Treaty of Troyes which made him heir to France, how he died in 1422, two months before the throne fell vacant, and how his baby son Henry VI—born to his French wife Catherine—was proclaimed king instead.

Poor little Henry the Sixth! It was an unkind fate that made him a king at all: he would have been far happier as a monk. During the next twenty years—covering the period when the Maid of Orleans was putting new life into France, and England was fighting a losing battle—the lords of the regency council at home were flagrantly mismanaging the country's affairs, while quarrelling among themselves. The government became divided into a war party and a peace party. In 1444, the earl of Suffolk, a prominent member of the latter, arranged a marriage between Henry, then twenty-two years old, with Margaret of Anjou, a niece of the French king. A more ill-assorted couple could scarcely be imagined. Margaret was a little wild-cat and Henry was a gentle lamb. The price paid by Suffolk for the compact was the surrender of Maine and, when the secret came out four years later, a howl of indignation rent the English skies.

At this time the obvious leader of the opposition was Richard, Duke of York. He was a proved and popular soldier and statesman and, what is more significant, he had two possible claims to the throne. On his father's side he was descended from Edmund of York, Edward III's fifth son, and was Henry's heir, in the male line, if the latter died childless. On his mother's side he was descended from Lionel of Clarence, Edward III's third son, and inherited the rights of Edmund of March (now dead) which Henry IV had usurped.

The queen, with Suffolk and another leader of the peace party, the Earl of Somerset, had the trusting young king completely under their thumbs. The continuing abuses of the government and the scandalous mismanagement of the war, which was forfeiting all Henry V's proud triumphs, set the country seething with discontent. To appease the clamour Suffolk was banished. Somerset, however, remained in office and in 1450 the popular anger exploded in the outbreak known as Jack Cade's rebellion.

The year 1453 brought the final humiliation when the English were driven from the Continent save for the bridgehead of Calais. The Hundred Years' War was over and England was now to receive the backwash of the second wave of swollen ambition which Henry V had set in motion. For forty years her leaders and her fighting men had plunged recklessly into the carnage of war and lived the lawless life of the camp, where might was right, plunder plentiful, and human life cheap. They had brought these disturbing habits home with them and infected England. The greater nobles were men of wealth and broad estates. They commanded large companies of armed retainers, wearing their " livery " or distinctive badge, who terrorised the neighbouring countryside like gangs of brigands. These mischievous private armies were now swollen by streams of unruly soldiers returning from France. The usurping House of Lancaster had failed the nation and fallen into contempt. The seeds of civil strife were thus already sown.

THE WARS OF THE ROSES

Two other telling events occurred in 1453. Unhappy Henry became—temporarily—insane; and Margaret gave birth to a son. Richard of York was no longer Henry's heir, though his prior rights on his mother's side still remained. The tension between the opposing parties reached breaking point. In 1455, the first armed clash occurred in the frightful convulsion we call the Wars of the Roses, the suicidal struggle between the Houses of Lancaster and York, whose respective emblems were the red rose and the white. It is another of the great landmarks of our journey.

The war began with the avowed object of liberating the king from his worthless councillors, but the Crown itself was bound to become the ultimate aim. Family relationships and personal hatreds governed the choice of sides. Of the great noble family groups the most powerful was that of the Nevilles, which included the Duke of York, his brother-in-law Richard, Duke of Salisbury, and the latter's famous son Richard, Earl of Warwick. As the contest heated up it became a welter of ferocious blood-feuds. It was a barons' war and the people wisely took little active part in it.

THE " KING-MAKER "

The changes in the fortunes of the day were as swift and erratic as forked lightning. Now York was up, now Lancaster. Somerset, Richard of York, and Salisbury were among the countless slain. The Yorkist claims on the throne passed to Richard's eldest son, Edward of March; and Edward's hopes of enforcing them rested on the powerful Warwick, " the King-maker " as he came to be called. In 1461, Edward, under Warwick's influence, took the crown as Edward IV. Parliament was not consulted: the sword ruled now. And the sword clinched matters when Edward routed Margaret's forces at Towton.

The new king was a handsome and agreeable youth, but with a horrible streak of cruelty in his make-up. He had worked hard and fought hard. Now he gave himself up to pleasure. Soon he began to chafe under Warwick's domination. The king-maker sought to make Edward marry a French

The Battle of Bosworth, in 1485, marked the end of the Wars of the Roses.

bride. But Edward had already deceived and forestalled him. In 1464, he had secretly married the Lady Elizabeth Grey. He now infuriated Warwick further by building up a powerful " Woodville " party from his bride's relatives to balance Warwick's " Neville " party. By 1469, things had come to an open rupture. Warwick leagued himself against the king with the latter's reckless younger brother George, Duke of Clarence. Then he went brazenly over to Queen Margaret's side. Clarence felt himself being double-crossed and began to ponder.

In 1470, however, Warwick and Clarence proclaimed the dethroned Henry as king and forced Edward to fly overseas. But next year he was back again. Clarence deserted to his side and, in the battle of Barnet, Warwick met his match and his end. Margaret's turn soon followed. At Tewkesbury her army was destroyed, her son butchered, and shortly afterwards she herself was captured. (She was ransomed four years later). Then the cold-blooded victor sealed his triumph with the innocent blood of Henry, the last of his line. Assuredly his poor half-witted victim would have been happier as a monk!

Edward had one more offender to send to his account. " False, fleeting, perjured Clarence ", as Shakespeare names him, had been giving trouble for some time with his insolence and intrigues. In 1478, the wrathful Edward caused Parliament to attaint him of treason, and his death soon followed. The popular story said that he was drowned in a butt of malmsey wine. Maybe he was. In 1483, Edward's life of debauchery and self-indulgence ended. Perhaps the best we can say of him is that his court was distinguished by a revival of the peaceful arts, and that it gave its patronage to William Caxton when he set up the first printing press in England in 1476. Edward left two young princes of twelve and nine years, Edward and Richard, to carry on his line.

Immediately on little Edward V's accession, a struggle for power began between his mother's Woodville party and that of his Uncle Richard, Duke of Gloucester, whom the late king had appointed as Protector during Edward V's minority. Uncle Richard scored first by securing possession of the boy-king and lodging him in the Tower of London (which was then both a palace and a fortress) pending his coronation. Richard's subsequent conduct became distinctly suspicious.

He seized and executed several of the king's friends. He induced the queen to surrender her other son, Richard, to his care and sent him to join his brother. He spread abroad the tale that Edward IV's marriage was invalid and that the two princes were consequently illegitimate. When Edward's reign was less than three months old a scratch Parliament was assembled. Its members were greatly disturbed by the way events were shaping. They were anxious to avoid the dangers of having a minor for king. Above all they were mortally afraid of Richard. So they denounced Edward IV's marriage and offered the crown to Richard—who graciously accepted it.

The frightful rumour that now spread abroad sent a shudder of horror through the land. The helpless little princes were said to have been brutally murdered in the Tower. There is no conclusive evidence confirming the story; but it seems probable that the princes were in fact done to death and that the crime was committed, if not on their uncle's orders, then with his knowledge and approval.

But Richard seems to have overreached himself. He became suspicious of all who approached him. He had good reason for his fears. A plan was afoot to depose him in favour of the Lancastrian Henry Tudor, Earl of Richmond, a descendant of one of John of Gaunt's children whose line had hitherto been barred from the succession. And the feud between the houses of York and Lancaster was to be ended by Henry's marriage with the murdered Edward's sister, Elizabeth. (See the article " The Glory of the Tudors ").

The first rising failed; but afterwards misfortune dogged Richard's footsteps. His only son died in 1484. His queen passed away in the following year. Clearly there would be a disputed succession on Richard's death. The king's hold on the country was shaky. The people dreaded a renewal of the Wars of the Roses, and they were weary of the blood-stained House of York. The moment seemed ripe for Henry Tudor to make another bid for the throne. With the assistance of some disgruntled nobles, Henry, who had been in exile in France, landed at Milford Haven with a force composed of foreign mercenaries and some remnants of the Lancastrian party. On 22nd August, 1485, the issue was decided on the field of Market Bosworth. Richard was betrayed on all sides; but, according to an ancient ballad, he died more gloriously than he had ever lived and fell like a soldier, battle-axe in hand. (The name given to him of " Crookback " is misleading, for he was only slightly deformed). So, in the virtual ending of the Wars of the Roses, vengeance descended on the last of the long line of Plantagenet kings. Richard was not the complete villain that Shakespeare made of him for he possessed some praiseworthy qualities. But in the pursuit of his ambitions he was entirely unscrupulous.

We have reached the last signpost on our way. Feudalism is in decay. The military service rendered of old by the barons, in return for their lands, has largely given place to that of paid royal armies. The manors, as we have seen, are breaking up. The villeins are free. The towns have grown in size and importance. The expansion of trade and industry has created a class of prosperous merchants. (Dick Whittington—with or without his cat—was one of them). Altogether, a new order of society has gradually taken shape, filled with a lusty spirit of conscious national unity and pride. And Parliament gives all, save the lowest orders, at least a voice in the government of the State.

As we look up at the forward-pointing signpost, we see that it reads " The Modern Age ". We have virtually come to the end of " The Middle Ages ".

THE RUSSIAN BEAR~CUB

European Russia overwhelms one with its sheer magnitude. The vast plain of which it consists, with its immense forest lands in the north and centre and its rolling, treeless grasslands, or steppes, in the south, is as large as all the other countries of Europe put together. As for the Asiatic provinces, they are three times as big as the European.

In medieval times, while Western Europe was busily developing its social, political and religious institutions, the young Russian Bear away in the East was performing its first cubbish gambols all on its own. Its real history begins in the ninth century with the operations of certain Swedish Northmen, or Vikings, who traded and buccaneered down the Volga and the Dnieper to the Caspian and Black Seas. The barbaric heathen natives of that western region of Russia were Slavs. The Slavs belong to the same Aryan family as the peoples of Western Europe, but they are a dreamy, passionate and indolent race with something Asiatic in their temperament. The Russian Slavs were continually falling out amongst themselves and the story is that they invited the merchant-pirate Rurik to come and settle their disputes. Rurik and his freebooting followers, arriving in 862, did more than that. They made themselves masters of the simple Slavs and set up a dukedom with Novgorod and, afterwards, Kiev as the centre of their rule.

Time went on and Rurik's successors continued to carry on a profitable combination of ruling and trading. In 988, their Duke Vladimir accepted the Greek form of Christianity (which differed from the Roman Church in certain of its doctrines and practices) from Constantinople, the capital of the Eastern Roman Empire. He then enforced it on his people after giving the popular Slav idol Nerun a sound public flogging just to show that he had finished with him.

With the new faith came something of the civilisation and culture of the empire. Kiev became a city of splendid churches and could boast a measure of art and learning. Rurik's later descendants, however, proved as quarrelsome as their Slav subjects. In 1169, Kiev was sacked and ruined and the duchy dissolved into a dozen independent rival units. It was in this divided condition that the country received a staggering blow.

THE GOLDEN HORDE

Before his death, in 1227, the ferocious Tatar or Mongolian Jenghiz Khan had built up an empire such as the world had never before known, reaching right across Asia from the China Sea into Europe. Under his descendants, an immense host of wild Tatar horsemen swept over Russia in a whirlwind of slaughter and destruction and careered on right across the Danube towards Vienna. There, however, they received a check; their terrifying power exhausted itself; and soon Jenghiz's unwieldy empire broke up. But the Tatar stranglehold remained irremovably fixed on hapless Russia. From about 1240, the Golden Horde—so named from the colour and splendours of the tent of its khan, Jenghiz's grandson Batu—established itself in the south and south-east, and from these regions dominated Russia for more than two centuries. The invaders, who presently adopted the Moslem faith, permitted the native principalities to continue in existence with their own religion and customs; but they were all rigorously subjected to tribute and reduced to the lowest depths of servitude and humiliation.

The shame and misery of that era of Tatar tyranny bit into the very soul of Russia. Not in itself alone, but in its attendant consequences, it was an unqualified disaster. A

Roman soldiers and merchants penetrated into Russia as far as the shores of the Caspian Sea and made the first European contact with the people of the steppes.

The Russian princes pay homage to Jenghiz Khan. The Mongols advanced like a scourge through Russia, destroying and killing. Only the death of Jenghiz Khan, in 1227, saved Eastern Europe from Mongolian domination.

Beneath the walls of Byzantium, the fleet of Prince Igor of Kiev is repulsed. Time and again, Greek fire saved the ancient city on the Bosphorus from would-be invaders.

new despotism arose from within to supplement the terror from without and break the people's spirit.

A century after the fall of Kiev, Moscow became the permanent capital of a new State situated in the remote and sparsely inhabited backwoods of central Russia. Its princes or dukes greedily enlarged their domain till a time came when they considered themselves grand dukes of All Russia. A heartening victory over the Tatars, in 1380, increased their prestige and marked the hopeful rising of a new national spirit.

THE FIRST TSAR

But the principal manner in which these Muscovite rulers advanced their power was not by standing up to the national enemy. It was by toadying to them. They offered themselves as the policemen and tribute-collectors of the Golden Horde and called in Tatar armies to help them overcome their rivals.

The marriage between the autocratic Ivan III and Sophia, daughter of Thomas, despot of Morea and claimant to the throne of Constantinople, took place in St. Peter's in Rome. Ivan later took the title of Tsar.

By such base methods, and under Tatar favour, they achieved their supremacy. Cut off from all contact with the freer institutions and liberal ideas of the West, they learned the ways of unbridled oriental despotism from the Moslem khans. Their court became Asiatic in customs and dress. There was another factor in their favour. A terrible calamity shocked Europe when, in 1453, the Turkish army stormed Constantinople. After that event the ruthless, fighting duke, Ivan III, who reigned from 1462 to 1505 and married the last Byzantine emperor's niece, deemed himself the successor to the autocratic imperial dynasty. Afterwards the title of Tsar (which equals Caesar) and the symbol of the double-headed eagle were adopted.

The Church dutifully sanctioned the Muscovite tyranny and endowed the person of the Grand Duke with, as it were, a sacred halo. The Greek Church in Constantinople had always been controlled by the emperor. With its rooted belief in traditional ways and ideas, it was the buttress of autocratic rule and the conscientious foe of all free thought and progress. The ignorant masses must be kept in their place under their proper pastors and masters. This attitude was adopted in Russia and, after the fall of Constantinople, was strengthened by the claim of Moscow to the headship of the Greek Church. Under the unholy alliance of Church and State the people were held in thrall by abject fear and superstition. With all freedom lost, they sank into the condition of serfdom, which was only finally dispelled when the Bolshevik Revolution of 1917 blew the whole system sky-high —only to replace it with another system equally as oppressive as the first.

In the late fourteenth century the Golden Horde in its turn received a staggering blow. Russia was delivered by another invading oriental conqueror, Timur the Lame, or Tamerlane. Aided by this uninvited but welcome contribution, and reinforced for the first time with cannon, the Russians were at length able to throw off the galling yoke and the Golden Horde fell to pieces.

By the time of his death, Ivan III's realm had expanded enormously: westwards beyond Novgorod, northwards to the White Sea and Arctic Ocean and eastwards to the Ural Mountains. The Russian Bear-cub was growing in bulk and sharpening its teeth and claws.

SPAIN UNITED

The solid rectangle of the Spanish peninsula was obviously meant by fate to form a single kingdom. By 1266, after centuries of desperate fighting, the whole of it, except Granada, had been liberated from the Mohammedan Moors. Yet it was not till more than 200 years afterwards that the separate Christian kingdoms, but with Portugal still odd man out, joined hands. The reason was that their peoples were estranged by differences of character and speech, laws and customs and interests. Navarre, situated astride the Pyrenees, had leanings towards France. Aragon, whose people were noted maritime traders, had their eyes fixed on their claims and possessions in Italy and the Mediterranean. Castile, occupying the great central mass of the peninsula, was engrossed in the problems of governing her immensely increased territories. Portugal, shut off by its mountains, looked out to the Atlantic.

Yet, save for Portugal, good sense eventually prevailed. The marriage of Ferdinand of Aragon with Isabella of Castile brought the two principal kingdoms together in 1479. Then, in 1492, the reconquest from the Moors was completed by the subjugation of Granada. And later the Spanish part of Navarre was annexed. The marriage was a turning point in Spain's history, for it quickly raised her to the power and dignity of a great European State.

The royal pair were forceful characters. Ferdinand was ambitious and astute. Isabella was a woman of high moral principles and a resolute Catholic. One of the questions they had to deal with was religion. Large numbers of their subjects were of Jewish or Moorish descent, though many of them had become professed, but rather inconstant, Christians. During the Reconquest the Christians' zeal for the true faith and their corresponding hatred of the " infidels " had gene-

In Spain, religious intolerance reached its peak with the Court of the Inquisition. Thomas Torquemada, the first Inquisitor-General, was convinced that Moors and Jews undermined the religious life of Spain.

rated a spirit of religious persecution that for centuries was to brand Spain with hideous notoriety. The Spaniards have always been fervently Roman Catholic and submissive to clerical influence. There were frequent massacres and forced conversions. In 1480, largely through Isabella's influence, the terrible Spanish Inquisition was instituted and, as a consequence, thousands were tortured and burnt at the stake. These stringent measures were approved by the people, for it was an acknowledged duty of the State to suppress the hated crime of heresy. But the queen was determined to go further. In 1492, the professed Jews were expelled and, in 1502, the eviction of the Moors began, to be completed a century later.

Spain never realised at what cost the purge was effected. The Moors in Granada were a pattern of refined and artistic culture, and both they and the Jews were the most hard-working and enterprising members of the population. Their destruction was as mistaken a policy as the medieval practice of bleeding an invalid in the expectation that new and healthier blood would replace the old. The Spaniards could not make good their loss and their industries suffered a paralysing set-back.

It is refreshing to turn from these horrors to the sensational tidings that were blowing in from the sea. The age of maritime exploration had already been begun, mainly by the enterprising Portuguese. Beyond their original ambition to explore and possess the unknown parts of Africa, two aims spurred them on: to bring heathen peoples into the Christian fold, and to tap the dazzling treasures of the East. Of the latter, glowing accounts had been spread abroad by the famous Venetian traveller Marco Polo who, in 1295, had returned by sea from a wondrous overland journey to

The capture of Granada, the last Moorish stronghold in Europe, was a triumph for Ferdinand and Isabella.

unknown China. Amongst the most coveted of the alluring oriental products were the spices—cloves, nutmegs, pepper, ginger, cinnamon and others. Spices were something more than fancy flavourings in those days. In winter-time people lived much on salted meat—dull fare at the best and positively unwholesome when it did not keep. The pungent spices made it more palatable. Hence the demand was enormous and the dealers' profits were huge. The trade of "The Spice Islands", in particular the Moluccas, in the East Indies, was in the hands of Mohammedan merchants. These brought the precious freight overland to the eastern Mediterranean ports, where it was bought by Venetian, Genoese and other shippers and resold in Europe.

The adventurous Portuguese set themselves steadily to discover a sea-way to the East and by-pass the Moslem trade route. By the mid-fifteenth century they had discovered the Canary Islands, Madeira and the Azores and sighted Cape Verde in West Africa. In 1488, Bartholomew Diaz rounded the Cape of Good Hope. In 1498, Vasco da Gama reached India. In 1512, his successors reached the rich spice islands of the Moluccas. By the middle of the century they were trading with China and Japan. Portugal had looked out to the Atlantic to some purpose.

THE NEW WORLD

Meantime Spain had put in her oar. The Genoese sailor Christopher Columbus reasoned that, if you sailed long enough west, you must come to the east. In 1492, with Isabella's encouragement, he tried out his theory and in the so-called "West Indies" stumbled on the entirely unsuspected New World of America. (The Viking expeditions of 500 years earlier were unknown or forgotten.) To his dying day he thought he had reached the fringes of Asia and that the Spice Islands were not far away.

Spain followed up his discoveries energetically, and rapidly spread her hold in the West Indies and Central and South America. The conquest of Mexico and Peru by Cortez and Pizarro filled the royal coffers with a boundless treasure of gold and silver and precious stones. Meanwhile the Portuguese Cabral had sighted Brazil, in 1500, and claimed it for his king; and Magellan's expedition, sailing under the

A triumphant Columbus returned from the New World. Besides gifts, he brought some Indians for baptism.

The Treaty of Tordesillas between Spain and Portugal was signed on 7th June, 1494, to settle disputes arising from the discovery of the West Indies.

Spanish flag, had made the first circumnavigation of the globe in 1519-1522.

This surge of geographical exploration marked the opening up of the whole world to the spread of European commerce, colonisation and ideas. Its earlier effects were to turn the commercial world about face. Avenues of direct trade were now established across the Atlantic and around Africa. The countries situated on the Western seaboard—first Portugal and Spain, and afterwards France, Holland and England—were in the fortunate position of shopkeepers whose unfrequented back street had unexpectedly become a busy highway. The monopoly enjoyed by Venice and Genoa was shattered.

Ferdinand and Isabella died while the exciting travel film was still unrolling, Isabella in 1504, Ferdinand in 1516. By wedding their daughter Joanna to Philip, son of the Emperor Maximilian, they had geared Spain into the mighty machine of the Austrian Habsburg House, whose dominions eventually embraced most of western Europe. Charles V, the elder son of the marriage, stepped by instalments into this immense empire, beginning with the Netherlands in 1506, and Spain after Ferdinand's death in 1516. But, though Spain belonged to Charles, Charles did not belong to Spain. He was a stranger there, and he used the country's resources primarily to serve the Habsburg dynasty in its combat with France for predominance in Europe. The wealth that poured into Spain from Mexico and Peru was for the most part dissipated in his wars and statecraft.

Towards the end of his life, however, Charles, tiring of his responsibilities, passed them on to his brother Ferdinand and his son Philip. Ferdinand received the German and Austrian titles and domains. Philip, who had lately married Queen Mary of England, in 1556 got Spain and the Americas, together with the Netherlands (in 1555) and the Habsburg possessions in Sicily and northern and southern Italy. Philip II's Spain was rich in men, money and dominions. Her splendidly drilled soldiers, equipped with pikes and firearms, had proved themselves the finest in Europe. The treasure ships from America brought her wealth. Altogether, she had become a commanding power in the world.

THE END OF BYZANTIUM

When the Greek emperors were restored in Byzantium (or, to use its more familiar name, Constantinople) in 1261, they returned to a greatly shrunken empire. The House of Paleologus ruled over little more than Constantinople itself with a belt of territory extending from the Black Sea to the Gulf of Salonika in Europe and a strip of the Asiatic coast opposite. Most of Asia Minor had been wolfed by the Moslem Seljuk Turks and the greater part of the Balkans was held by Bulgarians and Franks. And what *was* left of the empire was as badly shaken as a rider who has taken a toss and landed on his head. A period of quiet convalescence might have restored the sufferer. But unfortunately he was not going to be allowed one.

THE OTTOMAN EMPIRE

In the successive wave-like movements of the Asiatic peoples, the Seljuk Turks were followed by another Turkish clan, named Ottomans, after the founder of their empire, Othman, who died in 1326. Othman's son Orkhan, while continuing his father's conquests in Asia Minor, developed a remarkable military institution. His " janissaries " were Christian children who were wrested from their homes and rigidly trained as Moslem servants of the State. The bulk of them went into the army and, under an iron discipline that suppressed all natural feelings, they became wholly and solely soldiers. One single purpose dominated and inflamed their minds : to fight for their Sultan and the Moslem faith. It was mainly with this extraordinary leaven of iron-hearted zealots that the Ottoman Turks created the empire which, in its diminished extent (and without any more janissaries), has become the Turkish republic of to-day.

Having overthrown the dreaded Golden Horde, Tamerlane in 1395 turned his armies on the Turks commanded by Bayezid, who were then besieging the city of Constantinople (with its Venetian and Genoese defenders).

The extension of that empire to Europe was begun when Suleiman, in 1355, crossed over one moonlit night and established the first Turkish base on Gallipoli. The foothold was quickly enlarged and, not quite so quickly, opposed. The powers of the West, engrossed in their own immediate concerns, looked the other way. It was the peoples nearer the front line—Serbs, Bulgars, Poles, Magyars, Hungarians and others—who, assembled under the King of Serbia, faced the Moslem threat. But the close-fought fight of Kossovo (in modern Yugoslavia) in 1389, saw the Christian array cut to pieces. The jubilant Turks swept on to the Danube. In Asia they reached the Euphrates.

ROUTING OF THE TURKS

Then came an unexpected pause. The same Tamerlane whose innumerable host had disorganised the Golden Horde in Russia, now fell on the Turks in Asia Minor and in 1402 completely overwhelmed them. But the Turks in Europe did not lose heart. From their capital, Adrianople, they went forth to set their lost empire on its feet again. Meantime western Europe had begun to wake up. A great league, which included Hungary, Serbia, Poland, Genoa and Venice, the Pope and the Eastern Emperor, was formed against the growing Moslem menace. The confederated armies found an inspiring champion in the Hungarian leader John Hunyadi. In 1443, the Turks were gloriously routed and set on the run. Unfortunately in the next year, and again four years later when treachery was working in the Christian camp, it was Hunyadi's turn to suffer decisive defeat.

TURKISH CONQUESTS

A few years afterwards the new Sultan Mohammed II reached out to seize the greatest European prize of all. Constantinople, now isolated by the Moslem conquests, had withstood countless assaults for a thousand years past. It had never lowered its flag save after the shameful stab in the back by the Christians of the Fourth Crusade. If Europe had forgotten its rivalries and sent help, then Constantinople would have successfully defied the Turkish siege of 1453. The Emperor Constantine XI defended his historic capital like a hero. But a day came when, with the besiegers' cannon battering the walls, the grim-faced janissaries poured into the doomed city. Constantine, fighting to the last, rushed in among the enemy and perished beneath their scimitars. So Constantinople fell, and the fall of it sent a shudder through Europe. The Turk—an alien in blood and creed—stood in the Imperial City. He stands there still to-day.

The tide of Turkish conquest rolled on. Allah must prevail in Europe and Asia. When the victor of Constantinople died in 1481, Asia Minor and most of the Balkans were in Moslem hands. His successor Selim I conquered Syria, Egypt, and Arabia and made Constantinople—or Istanbul as the Turks renamed it—the centre of the Moslem world. In Europe, during the reign of Suliman the Magnificent, the fearful shambles of the battle of Mohacs, in 1526, destroyed Hungary and brought the Turk to the gates of Vienna. How much farther would he go ?

THE RISE OF A GREAT HOUSE
The story of the Habsburgs

The growth of the House of Habsburg was as tremendous as that of a certain beanstalk we used to read about, but hardly as rapid. Rudolph I, whom the German Electors chose as king in 1273, was an obscure Swiss noble. Charles V, who was crowned in 1520, dominated Europe. During this long interval the Habsburgs steadily built up their territorial possessions, Rudolph's most notable acquisition being Austria, the future centre of their power. Another gain was the imperial throne, that is, the title of Holy Roman Emperor, which, from 1438 became virtually hereditary in the family. But as a source of power it was almost as empty as a blown bird's egg. The empire had long ceased to be Holy. Territorially it was practically equal to "Germany". And the emperor exercised little real authority over the mosaic-like jumble of "principalities", large and small, of which it was composed.

THE HANSEATIC LEAGUE

Among these independent units the most interesting are certain important cities. Civic life was highly developed in Germany, as in medieval Europe generally. Within the city walls stood magnificent town halls, cathedrals and churches, towers and palaces. Manufactures, and commerce between the Mediterranean and the north, flourished along-side art and culture. The Hanseatic League, which included Lubeck, Hamburg, Cologne, Brunswick and numerous other rich and splendid cities, was a powerful organisation that almost monopolised the trade of the Baltic and North Sea. It built warships to protect its commerce and dealt with powerful States on an equal footing. The wealthy German burghers, living sumptuously in their fine houses, were

The League of 1291. Men from the cantons of Uri, Schwyz and Unterwalden formed the " Everlasting League " to protect themselves from possible attack. This league was the nucleus of the Swiss confederation.

The legend of William Tell, and his skill at shooting an apple from his son's head, is closely linked with the origins of the Swiss confederation.

immensely jealous of their liberties and prepared if need be to die in their defence.

There was one striking event of these times that was *not* a gain for the Habsburgs—they suffered a serious setback in Switzerland, whose people they had tried to keep in subjugation. In a world of aristocratic power and privilege, the hardy Swiss nourished in their hearts advanced ideas of freedom from feudal oppression. They rose against the tyranny of the Habsburgs and other local lords. In 1291, they laid the foundations of the present-day confederation by forming a defensive league between three German cantons on the lake of Lucerne. In time, other towns and districts joined them, bringing in French- and Italian-speaking peoples.

DEFEAT OF THE HABSBURGS

The story of the great crossbowman, William Tell, who was forced by an Austrian official to pierce an apple poised on the head of his little son, is well known. It may be a legend, but the uprising that followed and which brought about the crushing defeat of the Habsburg tyrants in 1315, is true. So are the rousing Swiss victories of 1386 and 1388. The disciplined skill and valour of these mountain cowherds and town burghers astonished Europe, and foreign powers eagerly recruited them for their own service. The final phase of a 200-years' struggle ended in 1499, when the confederation virtually won its independence of the Empire, though it was not formally recognised till 1648. Thus the plucky little Swiss became the first people in medieval Europe—apart from the City-States—to show that a country could govern itself quite satisfactorily without the assistance of kings or nobles.

Andrea Doria as a naval captain in command of the Genoese fleet waged incessant warfare against the Turks and Barbary pirates.

The Habsburg Charles V was born with not one, but half a dozen, silver spoons in his mouth. The world-ranging dominions to which he succeeded had been accumulated less by the clash of swords than by the pealing of wedding bells. His grandfather, the Emperor Maximilian, had gained the Netherlands by marrying the heiress Mary of Burgundy. His father, Philip the Handsome, had espoused Joanna, daughter of Ferdinand of Aragon and Isabella of Castile and, as such, future heiress to Spain, the kingdom of Naples (embracing southern Italy) and Sicily and the growing Spanish dominions in the recently discovered New World. And the Habsburg family inheritance already included Austria and other districts, as well as the imperial crown of Germany. Such was the colossal empire that Charles possessed when, at the age of twenty, he was crowned Holy Roman Emperor in 1520. It was an ill-assorted combination of peoples and could only be held together by power. And it was, understandably, viewed with deep misgivings by the rival kings of France and England. Conflict seemed inevitable.

CHANGING TIMES

Charles's reign marks the beginning of the Modern Age in western Europe. The great rival powers of England, France and Spain had taken up their stations. The growth of nationalism and free thought was dissolving the ancient spiritual unity of Christendom under the sovereignty of the Papacy. Education was spreading. The invention of printing in the mid-fifteenth century diffused knowledge and ideas. What was perhaps the most transforming movement in the later life of the European peoples had arisen. We cannot date it. We can only say that, as the Middle Ages wore on into the Modern Age, a profound change came over man's outlook on life. We call it the Renaissance or Rebirth, and indeed that is what it amounted to. Under its quickening influence thoughtful men were everywhere casting off the repressive religious and philosophical dogmas and outworn traditions which for so long had cramped their minds and overshadowed their lives. A spirit of bold and eager inquiry set them searching anew for the truths of religion and science and human relationships. They discovered a fresh joy in the free exercise of thought and imagination and in the beauty of the world of life and art.

THE RENAISSANCE

The change of outlook was stimulated and sustained by the rediscovery of many of the lost or forgotten treasures of classical Greek and Roman literature in the great movement known as the Revival of Learning. It was as exhilarating as the change from schooldays to holidays. In those days the very globe was altering. The Portuguese felt their way round Africa to India. Columbus and Cabot discovered America. Imagine the newspaper headlines if there had been any newspapers then!

In politics a great drama was played out, with all Europe as the stage and Charles V, Francis I of France and Henry VIII of England as its leading characters. Charles was courageous and persevering, but not greatly distinguished in character. Francis, "the gentleman king", was artistic and high-spirited but irresolute. Henry VIII was forceful, shrewd and stubborn and his reign was one of the most eventful in English history. The main contest, between Charles and Francis, was waged in Italy. Francis, by a brilliant feat of arms in 1515, had taken Milan, to which he claimed hereditary right. But Charles, too, claimed the prize as part of his Spanish inheritance and in the battle of Pavia in 1525 his Spanish generals retook it together with Francis himself for good measure. Two years later, when the Pope was intriguing against Charles, his ruffianly troops sacked Rome and imprisoned the Pope. Eventually France gave in and Milan fell under the power of the Empire.

We must pause awhile to glance at Italy, the victim of these alien, ravaging rivals, for that fair but unfortunate country presented a unique spectacle. We have seen how the German towns advanced in prosperity and culture. The Italian city-states of the northern Lombardy plain completely outmatched them in wealth and splendour. Their people seemed possessed of an astonishingly vital energy which expended itself in various intense activities—in industry and commerce, art and learning, and furious contests for supremacy over each other. By the early fifteenth century the dominant powers were Venice, Milan and Florence, each of which

Francis I was no match for the wily Charles V in their struggles for Italy. It was a condition of the Treaty of Madrid (1526) that Francis should marry Charles's sister.

From his lair in Algiers, the corsair Barbarossa (Khair ud-Din), attacked the Spanish fort of Nizza in 1543.

ruled a considerable area of surrounding territory. Like many of the cities they had absorbed, they were in theory democratic communities, but in practice the government, during the passage of time, had fallen into the hands of the leading families. Venice was ruled by a doge, or duke, and a Council of Ten. Milan and Florence were controlled by dictators, or " despots ". Venice prospered through her overseas commerce. Milan excelled in the manufacture of fine armour. Florence flourished above all in banking and commerce.

The most famous of the Italian despots, such as the Viscontis of Milan and the Medicis of Florence, are fascinating subjects for study because of the extraordinary blend of opposite qualities they so often exhibited. On the one hand they were diabolically crafty, cruel and treacherous and utterly devoid of moral scruples. On the other hand they were exquisitely refined and accomplished patrons of art and literature. By their unscrupulous villainies they secured their power. By their artistic qualities they made their cities —with their splendid public buildings, their superb sculpture, metal-work and paintings, their scholarship and literature and the taste and luxury of their court life—the wonder of all observers. In central and southern Italy, Rome and Naples made their rich contributions to the cultural glory of the period.

THE REVIVAL OF LEARNING

It was in the Italy of these times and conditions that the great uplifting movement of the Renaissance and the Revival of Learning first found definite expression. From the mid-fourteenth to the mid-sixteenth centuries her people produced a dazzling company of scholars, philosophers, architects, painters, sculptors and writers whose names are world-famous: Petrarch, Boccaccio, Michelangelo, Botticelli, Leonardo da Vinci, Raphael, Titian, and many more. And it was from Italy that the movement spread its enlightening rays over Europe during the sixteenth and seventeenth centuries.

After the triumph of Charles V over France, northern and southern Italy were held, like a snared bird, in the suffocating grasp of Spain; the light of its culture dimmed; and Italy,

Near the monastery of St. Just in Estremadura, Charles V spent the last years of his life.

which had given so much to Europe, ceased to have any history of its own for well nigh three centuries.

Meantime Charles had other anxieties. The advancing Turks (who had captured Constantinople in 1453) were a growing menace. The emperor now became quite mettlesome. Taking the field in person, he drove the Moslems back in Hungary and in 1535 was acclaimed as the shining champion of Christendom when he crushed completely the dreaded Corsair, Barbarossa, and captured Tunis in North Africa.

After forty years of sovereignty Charles grew sick in body and weary of public life. He abdicated the imperial throne in favour of his brother Ferdinand and retired to a Spanish monastery where, in 1558, he died. He had already shared out his other realms. Ferdinand, who in true Habsburg manner had earlier picked up the crowns of Bohemia and Hungary by marriage, received the Habsburg Austrian inheritance; Charles's son Philip II got the rest. So the great Habsburg empire fell into two parts, the Austrian and the Spanish.

GO WEST ~ GO EAST
The visions of Christopher Columbus

Imagine an era when Europeans had little precise knowledge of the world beyond their own continent and the other countries around the Mediterranean. That was the geographical position about the time, probably 1451, of Columbus's birth. To the west rolled an unknown ocean, " the Sea of Darkness ". Southwards stretched the undefined land-mass of Africa. " The Indies "—which in the widest use of the term might embrace India, the East Indian Islands, China and Japan (or Cathay and Zipangu as men called them)—were indeed renowned for their fabulous riches; but, notwithstanding the reports of Marco Polo and other travellers, they were only vaguely apprehended and out of reach. America and Australia had as yet no place on the map at all.

EARLY EXPLORATION

The world-horizons, however, were approaching an enormous expansion. The great surge of European exploration and discovery was under way. We may summarise it thus. The Portuguese took the lead, with various objectives in view: to convert heathen people; to develop African trade and possessions, and to secure the treasures of the Indies—gold and silver, gems and pearls, fine silks and cottons and, most especially, the pungent products of the Spice Islands. Up to that time, these coveted treasures were brought to the eastern Mediterranean ports along the caravan routes across Central Asia or by the sea-way via the Red Sea and thence overland; and those avenues of trade were controlled by the Moslem Arabs and Ottoman Turks. To by-pass the infidels' monopoly and capture the commerce for themselves, the Portuguese sought a sea-route to the East round Africa. When Columbus was born they had got as far as rounding Cape Verde. Perhaps it was just as well for them that they did not know what a long haul still lay ahead.

Columbus's entry into this restricted world took place at Genoa. From his youth up, the blue-eyed, ruddy-faced, red-headed boy took to the sea during intervals of working in his father's dull wool-weaving business. The adventure of his life befell him in his twenty-fifth year. The accounts of the affair are conflicting—as, indeed, are most of the records of Columbus's early career. According to some versions, however, the Genoese convoy in which he sailed was attacked by French privateers off Cape St. Vincent. Columbus's ship was set on fire; but, with the aid of a floating oar, the young sailor managed to swim to the distant Portuguese shore. Thence he joined his brother Bartholomew in Lisbon. And there he found himself at the very hub of the wheel of exploration and discovery which Prince Henry, " the Navigator ", had kept spinning up to his death in 1460. Merchants and seamen flocked to the bustling city from all the Mediterranean ports; exploration was in the air; and there was much talk about the possibility of finding a shorter and easier route to the Indies by sailing west.

There was nothing new in the idea; it had been discussed for centuries. Most educated men believed that the earth was a sphere, so that by sailing west you must in time—America's existence being unsuspected—reach the east. The hazards and uncertainties of the venture, however, had hitherto discouraged the most hard-bitten of sea-dogs from committing themselves too far on that forbidding waste of waters. The voyages of the Northmen five hundred years earlier were unknown or had been forgotten in southern Europe.

The idea, however—or, rather, a welter of ideas—was now taking possession of a bolder mind. The more Columbus brooded over it the more feasible it seemed. What precisely he hoped to achieve no one—including, probably, himself—could say. He was a deeply religious, as well as (sometimes) a practical, man and his distinctly high-powered imagination was fired and bemused by a confusion of practical and visionary projects. But the salvation of the teeming millions of the East, the quest for unknown lands and a shorter passage to the Indies, and the discovery of gold and spices were doubtless all woven into the colourful pattern of his dreams. The venture became a devouring ambition that would not be denied despite the indifference or contempt which the idea received in many influential quarters. The conviction grew upon him that God had chosen him for some wonderful enterprise.

In the imperfect knowledge of the times his reading, and his calculations, led Columbus into some notable errors. He greatly underestimated the size of the globe and over-estimated the extension eastwards of the Asiatic continent. Through these miscalculations he convinced himself (he was good at believing what he wanted to) that the open ocean crossing, from the Canaries to Japan, would after all be only about 2,400 nautical miles. (Actually the distance in a direct line is four times as long). He thought, moreover, there might be some islands on the way to break the journey. Make a double fold in your map of the world so as to conceal

Christopher Columbus became a sailor at the age of 14.

61

America and you will get an idea of how the position looked to the hopeful investigator. Columbus button-holed high and low in his efforts to procure ships, men and money for what he regarded as a sacred mission.

Meantime he had become an experienced mariner, skilled in navigation. By the time he was thirty-three—if we can trust the records—he had sailed to Iceland, the Azores, Madeira and the Gold Coast. He now approached King John II of Portugal with his plans. The king shook his royal head. Columbus went to Spain. But Queen Isabella and King Ferdinand were engrossed in the conquest of the Moors. For nearly six years he was alternately encouraged and repulsed. When at last his hopes did really spread their wings it was only to see them flutter to earth again, seemingly because the rewards he asked for his exalted enterprise were refused him. His brother Bartholomew had sounded Henry VII of England and Charles VIII of France, without result.

For years now Columbus had met with jeers and insults and suffered ignominy and want. Men thought him half crazy and wholly a bore. He was like a needy " bagman " calling from door to door, trying to sell something that nobody wanted. So, in 1492, he resolved on a new course. Saddling his mule, he set out to try his luck in France. He didn't ride far. Queen Isabella underwent a quick change of mind and sent a messenger post-haste to bring the bagman back. Columbus had found a customer, and on his own terms. It was settled that he should have a fleet. He and his heirs forever were to be Admirals of the Ocean Sea and Viceroys and Governors-General of any new lands discovered. And they were to receive ten per cent. of all gold, spices and other merchandise procured.

VOYAGE TO THE WEST

So, on 30th August, 1492, a little fleet sailed out from Palos, near Cadiz, on the most momentous voyage in the annals of exploration. And what a fleet it was for such an enterprise! The flag-ship, the *Santa Maria*, was of some 100 tons, the *Nina* and the *Pinta* round about half that burden. The crews numbered about ninety men. In the insignificance of its means and the grandeur of its results it recalls the fable of the mouse and the enmeshed lion which the little creature liberated with its tiny teeth.

In under a week the fleet made the Canaries, where, as Columbus knew, they would pick up the trade wind blowing steadily from the east. On 6th September, they weighed anchor again and three days later, like Coleridge's Ancient Mariner, they were " alone on a wide, wide sea ". Plotting your position was not easy in those days. Some idea of latitude could be gained by measuring the angles of sun and stars, but longitude was largely guesswork. Columbus relied mostly on " dead reckoning " of direction, time and speed.

For thirty-three days the ships drove on with never a sight of land, though on several occasions landfalls were imagined by over-eager eyes. The wily Columbus was keeping two logs of his course: a " correct " one for himself and a faked one, understating how far they had left Spain behind, for the benefit of his nervous crew. None-the-less, as the days dragged on, mutinous mutterings arose and Columbus was hard put to it to suppress the faint-hearts who agitated for a return home. In truth the Captain-General himself was becoming a little uneasy. " What about that 2,400 miles ? " He had sailed that distance long ago.

Fortunately, some reassuring signs, such as floating branches of green trees, presently appeared. Then, in the small hours of 12th October, an excited lookout once more raised the rousing cry of " Land! Land! " And this time he spoke true. Next day, Columbus and a company of captains and men were kneeling on the white coral beach of the island which he christened San Salvador, " Holy Saviour ", and offering up thanks to God with tears of joy.

Exhilarated by the thought that they were:
>The first that ever burst
>Into that silent sea,

the discoverers coasted among the neighbouring islands. Their eyes were delighted by the luxuriant fertility and enchanting loveliness of all they saw. Two islands in particular, which Columbus named Juana and Espanola, were explored. The natives proved wholly friendly and guileless—and for the most part naked. The Europeans had their first sight of maize, or Indian corn, yams, sweet potatoes and tobacco-smoking. Far more gratifying, however, were the reports—partly supported by the evidence of their own eyes—received in Espanola, of a fantastic abundance of gold.

Columbus persuaded himself that these unknown islands

Isabella, Queen of Spain, supported Christopher Columbus in his plan to reach the East by sailing west.

were situated on the fringe of Asia in the vicinity of Japan. India and the Spice Islands could not be far off. Well, he had certainly hit the target: he couldn't very well miss, seeing that it stood right across his line of fire. Only, it wasn't the target he had aimed at. The group of islands which he named " the West Indies " lay off the coast of Central America, not Asia. His San Salvador, Juana and Espanola are the Watling's Island (in the Bahamas), Cuba and Hispaniola of to-day. Between them and the East lie the American continent and the Pacific Ocean. Blissfully ignorant of these immensities, Columbus, on 4th January, 1493, set sail for Spain with the glad tidings of his spectacular achievement. To verify his claims he assembled a varied collection of trophies: spices (of a sort), gold, parrots and other tropical birds and a few " Indians " whom he destined for conversion. On 15th March, he dropped anchor at his starting point, Palos.

He was welcomed like a conquering hero. The king and queen received him with flattering graciousness and confirmed his promised honours. He had in fact reached the pinnacle of his fame. But not to rest there. This was only the beginning of his mission. To its completion he dedicated the remainder of his life, and in that span he made three more voyages westwards.

LATER VOYAGES

During his second expedition, in 1493, when he transported several hundred colonists and gentlemen-adventurers, he added the Lesser Antilles, Puerto Rico and Jamaica to his bag of island discoveries. On the third voyage, in 1498, he discovered Trinidad. Then, off Venezuela, though without realising it, he had his first view of the American mainland and sent some boat-loads of his men ashore. But they weren't the first Europeans to set foot on the American continent. Quite apart from the Northmen, Cabot had probably landed in North America the previous year. Columbus thought at first that the place was just another island, though he afterwards changed his opinion. Later in the voyage he had another thought: he had located the Garden of Eden.

These are the high-lights of the picture. The shadows, unhappily, were spreading gloom over the whole canvas.

The court in Spain and the adventurers in the islands were greedy for gold and spices; but the quantities so far forthcoming were woefully short of expectations. The once friendly natives were alienated by the ferocious tyranny of their Spanish masters. Columbus began a systematic slave trade and shipped hundreds of his miserable victims to Spain. However strongly we may condemn his action to-day, as Ferdinand and Isabella did at the time, we have to remember that slavery was then a recognised institution. Yet, even if the souls of the Indians were rescued from heathenism, it is hard to square the enslavement of their bodies with Columbus's " sacred mission ". The trading settlement which Columbus founded was dying of disease, lack of food and loss of heart. The Governor found himself continually in conflict with the proud and hot-blooded Spaniards under his rule. Bitter personal quarrels and open rebellions occurred. A number of the discontented colonists slipped home and spread disquieting reports of the failure of the settlement. It is evident, even allowing for the slanderous element in their complaints, that Columbus, though incomparable as a navigator, was unsuccessful as a Governor. A mystical dreamer was not the man to handle a community of tough and lawless fortune-hunters.

On 12th October, 1492, Rodrigo de Triana, a sailor on board the Pinta *sighted land. This was an island, which Columbus named San Salvador.*

Pinnacles, whether of fame or otherwise, are tricky elevations on which to maintain a footing, and very early Columbus began to slip from renown to disrepute. True, he had discovered some promising islands. But the promise, up till now, had been falsified, and he hadn't as yet found the expected doorway to the dazzling treasures of Zipangu, Cathay and India. In 1495, the Spanish sovereigns sent out an official to report on the deplorable situation. Five years later a royal commissioner superseded Columbus altogether and finally sent him home—in chains.

The unhappy prisoner's wounded spirit found some measure at least of consolation. The people, seeing the plight of their fallen hero, with his sad eyes and noble presence, were filled with indignation. The king and queen received their old favourite sympathetically. But they did not restore his authority. Instead, responding to the restless navigator's plea, they gave him a sort of roving commission to go out again and search for the visionary passage to the Indian Ocean.

FINAL VOYAGE

In 1502, then, he sailed west on his final adventure. Of course he never found the strait: it didn't exist. But in some ways this last voyage, with its incredible perils and hardships, is the most interesting of all. Columbus came so near to discoveries which would have put his geography right that one itches to urge him forward to the final revealing step. As he drove ahead hopefully on his hopeless quest, along the coast of Central America between Honduras and Panama, he passed the point on the Isthmus where the Panama Canal now opens into the Caribbean Sea. If only he had reconnoitred the country a little farther he might have anticipated Balboa by ten years and been the first of Europeans to gaze on the immeasurable expanse of the Pacific Ocean. But the truth was denied him and to the last he held to his conviction that his voyages had brought him to the outskirts of Asia.

In 1504, two and a half years from his setting forth, he returned to Spain. And there, on 20th May, 1506, the great ocean-pathfinder who had discovered a New World and opened up a new empire for Spain ended his life's voyage, a disappointed and discredited man.

THE GLORY OF THE TUDORS

The Tudor period is one of the liveliest in English history. There is scarcely a dull moment and never a dull sovereign. Even the reign of Henry VII—a cold and calculating character who opened the performance in 1485—has a particular distinction. It is in some respects a dividing line between the Middle Ages and the modern era when Europe was being influenced by the development of nationalism, education and free thought of the Renaissance and by the rivalry of the great powers.

FIRST OF THE TUDORS

Henry could trace his descent from Edward III, but his grandfather, Owen Tudor, was a Welshman. His reign began under promising circumstances. The Wars of the Roses had decimated the ranks and broken the power of the old feudal nobility, and England was yearning for peace and settled government. Henry was just the man to give them both. After his coronation he unified the rival houses of York and Lancaster by marrying the Yorkist princess Elizabeth, the eldest daughter of Edward IV. He was determined that the survivors of the nobility should never again recover their power. He took measures to abolish their pernicious private armies of retainers and set up a tribunal, which was to become famous as the Court of Star Chamber, to keep them in order. His chosen ministers were mostly "new men". The fillip he gave to foreign trade and commerce and shipping brought him the support of the wealthy merchants. These, together with the country gentry, the yeomen farmers and others, formed a sort of "middle-class" of growing weight and importance, and it was pre-eminently this class that formed the solid buttress of Henry's throne.

Though the Wars of the Roses were practically over, their embers still smouldered. Some unappeasable Yorkists

Cardinal Wolsey's diplomatic intrigues and failure to obtain a divorce for Henry VIII, lost him the royal favour.

trained a baker's son, Lambert Simnel, to impersonate Edward of Warwick (the son of Richard III's dead brother Clarence) and claim the crown. Then an engaging lad named Perkin Warbeck pretended to be Richard of York, the younger of the two princes who had died in the Tower. But Henry scotched both these plots. In 1492, a threat to Calais—England's one remaining trophy from the Hundred Years' War—brought him into collision with France. Henry, however, did not advance far on the war-path: instead he accepted a subsidy from the French king, Charles VIII. He always ranked the purse above the sword, shrewdly realising that money was power.

The careful king's diplomacy made England a force to be reckoned with in Europe. He married his elder son Arthur to Catherine of Aragon, a younger daughter of the powerful Ferdinand and Isabella of Spain, and, when Arthur died, passed her on to his next son, Henry. He won a brief spell of peace with his ever-troublesome neighbour Scotland by wedding his daughter Margaret to the Stuart king, James IV. Immeasurable consequences were to flow from both these alliances.

In matters of local justice and government, Henry and his successors gave increased scope to the Justices of the Peace. These useful country gentlemen had long been taking over the duties of the declining shire and hundred moots of Saxon origin. The forerunners of these Justices can be traced back to the twelfth century, and in the twentieth they are still actively functioning as local magistrates.

When Henry died in 1509, he had given the country the peace and settled government it needed. But it had been done at a price. He had ruled almost as an autocrat. Parliament, grateful for his blessings, had been content to serve him as a willing agent. This was to be the keynote of Tudor government.

FOUNDER OF THE NAVY

Henry's son, the eighth Henry, was a talented, gay, and handsome prince, but shrewd, secretive and stubbornly self-willed. His people were proud of him and admired him for his fine, masterful spirit and his robust and bluff demeanour. The outstanding event of his early years was the battle of Flodden in 1513, in which the Earl of Surrey, while Henry was in France, shattered the Scots and slew King James IV. Henry's own best services to the country's defences were of the salt-water kind. He was, substantially, the founder of the modern Royal Navy. How England would have fared in Queen Elizabeth's day had she not had her navy is something that does not bear thinking about.

The first half of the reign produced its most spectacular figure in Thomas Wolsey, the butcher's son, who in 1515 became Lord Chancellor of England and a cardinal of the Church. The king's favour allowed him to climb to the peak of power and riches. The political situation abroad gave his subtle brain good exercise. From 1519, Francis I and Charles V were competing for supremacy in Europe. Francis was king of France. Charles was ruler of Germany, Austria, Spain, the New World, the Netherlands and parts of Italy.

Having defied the Pope by divorcing Catherine of Aragon, Henry VIII is given a papal bull of excommunication.

The predominance of either of these mighty rivals would be a grave menace to poor little England, and Wolsey guilefully manoeuvred to preserve the balance of power between them. But his complicated diplomacy achieved little. In the end Francis was crushed and Charles came out on top. Furthermore, in 1527, Charles had sacked Rome and made the Pope a prisoner—a circumstance particularly unwelcome to Henry just then.

THE REFORMATION

Events have brought us to one of the most momentous crises of European history: the Reformation movement that was to split the Catholic faith into the conflicting creeds that still divide Christendom. The Reformation broke out in Germany, where Luther attacked the abuses of the church. The movement was an outgrowth of the critical and inquiring spirit of the Renaissance and it was fanned to a blaze by the abuses—administrative, financial and disciplinary—within the church. The reformers had come to believe that the Bible was the sole guide to the truths of Christianity. Many fundamental doctrines and practices, on which the authority of the church rested, were challenged, including the spiritual supremacy of the Pope. You can read more about it in the article on " The Protestant Reformation ". Originally, Henry VIII had been one of the strongest opponents of the Reformers, and his writings against Luther's teachings in 1521 earned him as a reward from the Pope the title " Defender of the Faith ".

It was in about 1527 that the flames began to get a real hold on England, and, strangely enough, it was through a purely personal concern of the king's. Henry badly wanted a male heir, for all his children by Catherine of Aragon, except Mary, had died. He now said that he had become troubled in mind about the legality of his marriage to his dead brother Arthur's widow. At any rate, he had fallen in love with an attractive young maid-of-honour, Anne Boleyn. So he told Wolsey to get the Pope to dissolve his marriage—which was easier said than done. Catherine was Charles V's aunt, and the Pope was in Charles' pocket. Wolsey's mission was a failure and, in 1529, the great cardinal was dismissed and left to die in ruin and disgrace.

The next seven years showed how lively the Tudor era could be. Self-willed Henry launched an all-out campaign against the disobliging Pope. He caused Parliament to pass a series of Acts which brought the clergy completely under his control, and which acknowledged him as Supreme Head of the Church of England and made it a capital offence to disobey or deny his designs. Those who did so soon began to pay the extreme penalty as the masterful tyrant callously struck them down. Among the many who died for conscience's sake were the noble-minded scholar Sir Thomas More and the saintly Fisher, Bishop of Rochester. Thus Henry boldly snapped the ties which had bound the church in England to Rome for nearly a thousand years.

Meantime, the year 1533 had seen other notable events simply tumbling over each other. Henry secretly married his beloved Anne. Thomas Cranmer, whom he had made Archbishop of Canterbury, held a court which dutifully pronounced Henry's marriage to Catherine void. Anne gave birth to the future Queen Elizabeth. The Pope denounced the marriage.

Henry still had some arrows left in his quiver. Between 1535 and 1539 he dissolved the monasteries and sold their vast estates to laymen. It was a staggering blow. It removed from the English scene one of its most venerable, if sadly declining, institutions. It also created a powerful vested interest in the new religion among those who were fortunate enough to acquire the church lands cheaply. In 1539, the Bible was given to the people in their native tongue by placing copies in the parish churches for all to read.

The breach with Rome, whose consequences were of such profound spiritual significance to all, could not, of course, have been effected through the mere personal quarrel of a wilful king. It needed the co-operation of his more influential subjects, and this he enjoyed in sufficient measure. Resistance to papal encroachments on the revenues and rights of the church was a centuries-old story. A strong and ambitious section of the people was ready at least for a scrap with the Pope. Some were eager to go farther. The influences that inspired Luther's movement of protest were at work. The extreme Protestants were few in number; but they were active. So the king was enabled to forge ahead.

Thomas More, refusing to acknowledge Henry as the spiritual head of England, was executed on 7th July, 1535.

On the death of Henry VIII, his son, Edward VI, aged 9 years, succeeded to the throne.

Henry presently rested on his oars. Like the bulk of his subjects he was still sincerely attached to the basic doctrines of the Catholic Church. It was only from the Pope that he had broken away. So, in 1539, to check the more rampant Protestants who would have made a clean sweep of everything not supported by the Bible, Parliament passed " the Six Articles ". This imposed the severest penalties on any who denied the truth of the six doctrines named. England was left like a ship moored in mid-channel, half-way between Catholicism and Protestantism.

The rest of Henry's matrimonial adventures deserve a short paragraph to themselves. Anne Boleyn was heartlessly executed and Bluebeard Henry took to himself one new wife after another: Jane Seymour, who bore him an heir, the future Edward VI; Anne of Cleves; Catherine Howard (likewise executed); and Catherine Parr—all this within seven years.

Henry died in 1547, a diseased and bloated hulk, his hands red with the blood of his many victims. Under his dominating influence, Parliament had empowered him to regulate the succession, and he bequeathed the crown in this manner: first, to his son Edward; then, should Edward die without an heir, to his daughters Mary and Elizabeth in turn; and finally, if they too left no heirs, to the descendants of his younger sister, another Mary.

EDWARD VI's BRIEF REIGN

Edward was a frail boy of nine years, and the government was conducted by a regency council headed by his uncle Edward Seymour, later Duke of Somerset. The duke was an ardent Protestant and a man of statesmanlike ideals. His first undertaking was praiseworthy but hopeless. Among the political factions which for more than 200 years had riven Scotland there was a pro-English party, the other factions being very much anti-English. Henry VIII had tried to win over his nephew, James V, (son of James IV and Henry VII's daughter Margaret) to the reformed Church by advising James to enrich himself by dissolving the Scottish monasteries. James had refused on the plea that while some monks were bad, most were good! Henry then suggested a marriage between his son, Edward, and James's infant daughter Mary. But the plan, unacceptable to James for political and religious reasons, fell through. Somerset now revived it and backed his endeavours with an army. The battle of Pinkie Cleugh, fought in 1547, was a fruitless English victory. The Scots bundled their infant queen off to France—their constant ally against England—to be wedded to the dauphin, the French king's son.

In the all-important religious question Somerset was more effective. Protestant influence dominated the council and soon Somerset, powerfully supported by Archbishop Cranmer, slipped the moorings by which Henry VIII had kept England in mid-channel and sailed on to the Protestant shore. Parliament repealed the " Six Articles " Act. In 1549, the First Book of Common Prayer, the earliest form of the Anglican Prayer Book, was issued. The reformed faith made increasing headway in the country throughout Edward's reign; but there was one new feature that deeply wounded the feelings of the mass of the nation. With the aim of removing all visible reminders of what was deemed to be popish superstition, the churches were stripped of many of their sacred images and pictures, their richly carved woodwork and glowing stained glass. The services, too, were shorn of much of their former impressive ceremony and colourful ritual.

This brutal and irreverent vandalism combined with another grievance to provoke widespread unrest. Ever since the time of the Black Death landowners had been steadily turning plough-land into sheep-pasture, seizing the common land on which the villagers fed their stock, evicting the occupiers and enclosing the land with hedges. The enormous expansion of the wool and cloth industry made sheep-raising immensely more profitable than corn-growing, and it required fewer labourers. Thus the unfortunate peasants and yeomen tended to lose both land and employment. The sympathetic Somerset tried to remedy the growing economic crisis; but the grasping landlords defeated his efforts.

PLOTS AND COUNTER-PLOTS

They likewise helped to deprive Somerset of his office and his head. Whereupon the unprincipled and self-seeking Earl of Warwick, who in 1551 became Duke of Northumberland, stepped into his shoes. The duke seems to have had no religion worth speaking of, but he committed himself forcefully to the advancing Protestant cause. In 1552, a Second Prayer Book carried the principles of the Reformation much farther than the first. In 1553, Forty-two Articles of Religion defining the English Church doctrine (reduced in Elizabeth I's reign to the present Thirty-Nine) were published and required to be accepted by all.

In the same year the sickly Edward seemed likely to die and self-seeking Northumberland, like other and more sincere Protestants, began to worry about their future. For Mary, who stood next in the succession, was a staunch Roman Catholic. The duke hastily contrived a madcap design. He would ignore the claims of Mary and Elizabeth and enthrone the Lady Jane Grey, a descendant of Henry's younger sister Mary. The far-seeing duke had already married the lady to his son Guildford Dudley. He persuaded, or forced, Edward and the council to accept his plan and only a fortnight later Edward died.

The country soon showed that it had no use for the plan or for Northumberland either. The people rose; Mary won her throne, and the duke lost his head. The luckless Lady Jane, the " Nine Days' Queen ", spared at first, was also later a victim of the tragic politics of the time.

Mary did all and more than the Protestants feared. Her

mind was embittered by many wrongs: the heartless divorce of her mother, the branding of herself in consequence as illegitimate, and twenty years of loneliness, neglect and suspicion. Her creed was a consuming flame within her. She believed passionately that her people's salvation depended on a return to the true faith.

So, within two years, Protestant ministers were replaced by Catholic priests; the old rites and ceremonies were revived; the laws establishing the reformed Church were swept away. Protestants, fearing for their lives, panicked in hundreds to the Continent. Before this furious change in the wind the English ship was driven back hard on the Catholic shore.

Meantime another threat was brewing. The queen's heart was set on marrying the haughty, sour-faced Philip II of Spain, son of the Emperor Charles V and Catholic to the core. Her subjects viewed with dismay the prospect of a succession of Catholic children on the throne. Even staunch Catholics objected to the marriage, fearing that England would become a Spanish dependency. The majority of the people were still Catholics at heart, but they dreaded Spain. Mary, however, was heedless of opposition and, in 1554, the detested marriage took place. Shortly afterwards the Pope's legate, Cardinal Pole, came over and England was received back into the Roman Catholic fold.

" BLOODY MARY "

In 1555, Mary embarked on that course of systematic persecution that has stigmatised her with the name of " Bloody Mary ". During the ensuing three years nearly three hundred Protestant martyrs trod their way to the stake. Of that noble army three at least have earned imperishable glory. " Be of good comfort, Master Ridley ", cried the grand old Bishop Latimer to his fellow-sufferer as the faggots crackled around him. " We shall this day light such a candle by God's grace, in England, as I trust shall never be put out ". And Cranmer, whose hand, in a moment of agitated doubt, had signed a recantation of his principles, now thrust the offending member into the flames and held it there while it blackened and burned. The incredible heroism of it all takes one's breath away.

In 1558, the fanatical queen died. She had thought to stamp out heresy through terror. But the spectacle of her

pitiless inhumanity and of the unshakable constancy of her victims had only inspired the people with an increased sympathy for the sufferers' creed. Mary never understood the English people.

One more wrong she had done them. Her adored Philip had dragged the country into war with France, and, in 1558, Calais, which England had held for over two hundred years, was lost. Well might the queen exclaim, " When I die, Calais will be found written on my heart! "

A NEW ERA

When her half-sister Elizabeth I took her place on the throne England breathed a deep sigh of relief. But it was a thorny path that lay before the young queen. Her kingdom was poor, ill-armed and simmering with religious discord; her title and her country were both threatened. The Emperor Charles V had abdicated. Philip had become King of Spain and Lord of the Netherlands, parts of Italy, and the New World. The contest for European supremacy was now being waged by Spain and France, and each of these powerful rivals was scheming to gain control of England to tip the balance in its favour. But Elizabeth soon proved herself equal to the occasion. She was a comely young woman of twenty-five, bold of heart and quick of intellect, fond of gay pleasures, but withal shrewd and wily.

Although she came to the throne nominally as a Catholic and was crowned as a Catholic, Elizabeth was not herself deeply religious and she disliked extremists of any kind. Her outlook was perhaps affected by the fact that in the eyes of the Catholic Church, Anne Boleyn's marriage was invalid and Elizabeth herself illegitimate. Her immediate need was to close the gulf that was dividing and weakening the nation. So she opened up a middle way, broad and accommodating enough for all except papists and advanced reformers to follow. The Protestant cause was continually waxing stronger and, recognising this, the queen, in 1559, caused Parliament to reverse Mary's return to Roman Catholicism and revive Edward VI's Protestant laws, with some judicious modifications to appease moderate Catholics. Attendance at the reformed church services was made compulsory. The queen's policy was well rewarded. As time passed, the bulk of the nation gradually settled down to the new system, and the

Under Mary I, the persecution of the Protestants went on for nearly four years, about 300 people being put to death.

For years English seamen such as Sir Francis Drake made sailing routes unsafe for Spanish merchantmen.

independent Anglican Church, much as it exists to-day, became firmly established.

THE RISE OF THE PURITANS

Yet two parties, throughout the reign, conscientiously refused to walk in the middle way: the out-and-out Catholics, and the extreme Protestants who felt that the Reformation had not gone far enough. The latter party hated the sight or sound of " popish " priestly vestments, church ornaments and music and various ritual usages. They longed to see the church return to what they believed to be the purity and stark simplicity of the days of the early Apostles: hence their name of " Puritans ". An increasing number of them abhorred the whole order of bishops as unscriptural and wished to replace them with freely elected presbyters, ministers and elders. The majority of the Puritans were followers of John Calvin, the great French reformer on whose teaching the Presbyterian Church was based; and they believed in the grim doctrine of "predestination": that every individual's salvation or damnation was pre-ordained by God.

For a while the discontented Puritans remained loyally in the Anglican Church. But presently numbers of them entirely rejected it and claimed that every church congregation should be a separate and independent unit, electing its own ministers and free from the Crown's control or direction. Elizabeth naturally detested the Puritans, for they disturbed her religious settlement. Moreover, opposition to the Crown in religious affairs was apt to lead to opposition in political affairs. So she vigorously attacked the widely spreading movement, and, for a time, suppressed it. The idea of tolerating different creeds was quite foreign to the spirit of the age. " Bloody Mary's " belief that heresy was a sin to be suppressed was common. Furthermore, with England standing in such peril from the Continental powers, religion and patriotism had become inseparable. There must be one national church and every loyal citizen should conform to it.

In the struggle between the French and Spanish heavy-weights, Spain was in the ascendant. Catholic France had become strongly infected with the Protestantism of the Huguenot sect. The Pope was firmly resolved on recovering England for Catholicism and Philip was his foremost champion.

MARY, QUEEN OF SCOTS

The immediate threat, however, came from France. The old Franco-Scottish alliance had been reinforced by the marriage of the Catholic Mary, Queen of Scots, to the French dauphin. The dauphin had since become King Francis II, and Mary, accordingly, Queen of France. But she also claimed the English Crown, either immediately, or in succession to Elizabeth, as a descendant of Henry VII's daughter Margaret and the Stuart King, James IV.

Scotland's chronic condition of anarchy had been complicated by a new factor. The Reformation movement there had been unsuccessful under James V, but it was brought to a successful conclusion by the great, passionate-hearted leader John Knox and the most powerful lords, amid a welter of religious, financial and political factions. The end was reached after the defeat in 1560, with Elizabeth's assistance, of Mary's French mother, Mary of Guise, who as regent of Scotland represented French influence in the country. In the same year King Francis died and Mary lost her glittering French crown.

Mary was a fascinating and vital creature, destined to live in violent times. Her second husband, Lord Darnley, by whom she had a son, the future James I of England, was killed when his house was blown up and Mary married his probable murderer, the Earl of Bothwell. This was too much for the Scottish nobles, who forced her to abdicate. In 1568, she threw herself in desperation into the hands of her rival, Queen Elizabeth. And there she remained imprisoned for nineteen long years while the contest of the European heavy-weights raged on. Wily Elizabeth skilfully played off one power against the other. France was torn by religious wars. The Netherlands Protestants revolted against Spain. The Pope excommunicated and deposed Elizabeth. There were Catholic insurrections in England and Ireland, and plots were hatched for invading England, " removing " the queen, crowning Mary, and restoring the Catholic faith. At length, in 1587, Mary's alleged complicity in the Babington plot for Elizabeth's assassination brought her to the block.

Comprising 130 vessels, the Spanish Armada sailed to invade England. Outmanœuvred and beset by bad weather, sickness and lack of fresh water and provisions, only 75 ships returned.

Elizabeth I of England sent an army to Scotland, where a large number of Regent Mary's French soldiers were upholding the Catholic cause.

Trade and commerce flourished in the Elizabethan era, and the command of the sea was in the hands of the English, who raided all likely-looking Spanish merchant ships.

Philip, now England's arch-enemy, resolved on a show-down. From the beginning the heretical Elizabeth had been playing cat-and-mouse with him. She was brazenly supporting his rebellious Dutch subjects. Her privateers were boarding his merchant ships. And her audacious sea-captains were challenging his cherished monopoly in the New World. He began to build his Invincible Armada.

England was ready for the death-grapple. She knew what defeat would mean and her people were united in passionate pride and loyalty to an adored queen. Her sailors had become hardy sea-dogs. Hawkins, Raleigh and Drake had scoured the Spanish Main and flouted the hidalgos. " Dragon " Drake, indeed, had sailed round the world. Frobisher and Davis had gone seeking a north-west passage to the East. Gilbert had claimed Newfoundland. Raleigh—though unsuccessfully—had attempted a colony in " Virginia ". Such men as these feared neither Spaniards nor anyone else.

In 1588 the " Invincible " Armada sailed. And the English fleet drummed it up the Channel, shot it to pieces off Grave-lines, and left the elements to finish it off. So England breathed again in triumph and in freedom.

Another country was less fortunate. In 1603, when Good Queen Bess died and the lively Tudor dynasty ended its performance, Ireland was brought into subjection. But the conquest was achieved by ferocious measures that sowed the seeds of many future evils.

" MERRIE ENGLAND "

The eventful Tudor period saw England raised immensely in power and prestige, in conscious national pride, in intellectual and artistic vigour. She was alive to her finger-tips. She had preserved her independence and established her national church. For the time being she was the leading maritime power. New industries were developing. Trade and commerce attained a world-wide range as her ships ploughed the remotest seas, from the Russian north to the Far East and the New World. In 1600, the East India Company was founded. In the field of literature, during Elizabeth's reign, the nation's genius seemed to break into flower. Its joyous energy, in that high tide of the Renaissance, found expression in imperishable works. Spenser, Hooker,

The death of Elizabeth I marked the end of the Tudor line.

Francis Bacon, Marlowe, Ben Jonson and the matchless Shakespeare are but the brightest of its many jewels. In music, Elizabethan England has been called " a nest of singing birds."

Social conditions, too, had changed, though not always for the better. A new aristocracy had taken shape, recruited from the new traders, the " Venturers ", and from those enriched with the confiscated Church lands. Society learned its manners as the crude barons of an earlier day gave place to polished and elegant courtiers. But the poor had become poorer, largely because of the increasing enclosures that robbed them of land and employment. The government tried to grapple with the grave social problem by the Poor Law Act of 1601, which ordained various relief measures, including the finding of work for those who wanted it and workhouses for those who did not. There was a seamy side to " Merrie England ". Elizabeth was to bequeath to James I a legacy of serious and unsolved problems, social, religious, financial and constitutional.

THE PROTESTANT REFORMATION

In the sixteenth century, Western Europe, despite all its political and religious quarrels, had been united for a thousand years on one fundamental matter. Though, in the East, the Orthodox Church had gone its own way, the West was a single Christian community acknowledging the spiritual authority of the Pope. That unity was now to be disrupted. The epoch-making movement that created the schism was an outgrowth of the new free-thinking attitude to life known as the Renaissance. It was a protest against the corruption of popes and priests, a challenge to their claims to power over men's salvation and a demand for a return to the purity and simplicity of the early Church. In the fourteenth century Wycliffe, in England, had denounced the wealth and worldliness, and what he deemed the unscriptural dogmas and spiritual pretensions of the Church, and his protests had been echoed in far-away Bohemia. Wycliffe, however, was before his time; Luther, in the sixteenth century, was not.

RELIGIOUS REFORMER

Martin Luther was a German friar, of peasant stock, but highly educated. He became deeply concerned about the dread question of his own salvation, for he had come to doubt the Church's teachings on the subject of man's redemption. Then one day he thought he had found the answer. Man was born in sin; but, by faith in God and the merits of Our Lord, and by these only, he could be saved. Fasts, pilgrimages, penances and similar "good works" were in themselves of no avail.

A visit to Rome had opened his eyes to the widespread corruption at the Papal court. Soon they were to be opened wider. It was an accepted practice for priests to grant indulgences: the remission of the temporal punishment for actual sins to which the sinner was still liable in this life and in purgatory. In fact, this practice was open to great abuse in the hands of the worldly and unscrupulous, and such indulgences could be openly bought for money.

In 1517, a Dominican friar named John Tetzel came to Wittenberg, where Luther was teaching, with a sheaf of indulgences for sale to raise funds for the rebuilding of St. Peter's in Rome. Luther resolved to expose the scandalous traffic. He composed ninety-five arguments against the practice and nailed them on the church door. Soon his "theses" were copied and printed. All Germany read them and was deeply stirred.

Meantime Luther had travelled far along the road to a definite revolt against the Papacy. He attacked the Pope's supremacy, the spiritual powers of priests, and several of the Church sacraments. The Bible, he declared, was the ultimate guide to the truths of Christianity and every educated man could read that for himself. (Later he himself translated it into German). This, of course, was outright heresy and, in 1520, the Pope issued a bull, or decree, of excommunication against the offender. Luther's reply was to burn it. Next year the Pope called on Charles V to suppress him. Luther, refusing to retract his words, was outlawed.

But neither Pope nor Emperor could silence his passionate and scathing tongue. Germany, divided in its opinions, was harrowed by savage persecutions and devastating civil wars. Eventually, in 1555, nine years after the death of the staunch reformer, religious peace was established for a time by allowing the rulers of the various States into which Germany was divided to decide whether their particular subjects should be Roman Catholics or Lutherans. In the end the South adhered to Rome, the North established the Lutheran Church. From thence the new doctrines spread over Denmark, Norway and Sweden.

CALVINISM

The fires of the German Reformation kindled another

In 1517, the German friar Martin Luther drew up the document known as the 95 Theses against the abuse of indulgences. This was nailed to the door of the Castle church in Wittenberg.

Between the years 1523 and 1532, Luther and some colleagues made the first widely-read translation of the Bible in German. This tremendous service alone entitles him to be called a great religious benefactor for his people.

blaze in Switzerland. It was fanned first by a young priest named Zwingli, later by the more famous French exile John Calvin, a man of reserved, austere manner and keen intellect. Calvin adopted many of Luther's ideas; but the two leaders differed on the question of Holy Communion and their followers never marched together. Calvin believed in the now generally discredited doctrine of predestination—that every man's salvation or damnation was preordained by God—but that it was Man's duty to practise virtue for its own sake. From 1536 to his death in 1564, he laboured in Geneva (which was then just outside Switzerland) to make that city a model Christian community. He laid the basis for the Presbyterian Church, with its simple ceremonies and its elected ministers and elders. Church and State were made one. A gimlet-eyed council scrutinised everyone's conduct and punished offenders. It was like being confined in a straitjacket, or living in church all day and every day. The horrified Pope called it a nest of devils.

SPREAD TO FRANCE

Yet Calvinism suited the temperament of many and spread its doctrines far afield. In France, where its followers were called Huguenots, its fight for existence, from 1562 onwards, drenched the country in blood for forty years. In 1572, on St. Bartholomew's Eve, the crowning horror was perpetrated when thousands of Huguenots were massacred. At last, in 1598, the Edict of Nantes gave the sect a measure of recognition. But in 1685, after years of systematic persecution, the edict was revoked and the betrayed and wretched " heretics " fled the country.

The Reformation followed its own course in England, and Calvinism entrenched itself in the New England colonies, in Holland despite appalling persecution of Protestants, and in Scotland, where the theology of the Kirk was based on it. Christendom, quite apart from the Eastern Orthodox Church, stood ranked under separate banners—Roman Catholic and Protestant. Since then the bitter enmity of the opposing creeds has died down; but the chasm dividing them remains.

THE GREATNESS AND RUIN OF SPAIN

The splendour and greatness of Spain in the sixteenth century were followed by a long decline to the rank of a secondary power. It will be useful to connect up the various links of the chain and study how the latter came to be broken.

SPAIN IN THE ASCENDANT

The first link is the union of Aragon and Castile under Ferdinand and Isabella in 1479. Then comes the final subjugation of the Moors in 1492. The discovering of America by Columbus, in the same year, and the rich conquests that followed brought wealth untold into the royal coffers. In 1496, the marriage of Ferdinand and Isabella's daughter Joanna allied Spain with the great Austrian House of Habsburg; and by 1520 Charles V, the elder son of the marriage, had stepped into the immense Habsburg empire embracing most of western Europe. Finally, Charles divided up his realm and, in 1556, his son Philip II received, as his share, Spain and the American colonies, added to the Netherlands (1555), Sicily and northern and southern Italy. Spain was thus established as a commanding power in Europe.

Yet within half a century her strength was failing. Fortune had showered abundant gifts upon her: fine soldiers, boundless wealth and vast dominions. But one boon she had withheld: good kings and sound statesmen to use them wisely.

Philip's reign continues the old story of the intense rivalry between the Habsburgs (in both Spain and Austria) and France and the bitter struggle between Roman Catholic and Protestant. Philip, a gloomy and suspicious autocrat, backed

The Massacre of St. Bartholomew on 24th August, 1572, was the name given to the massacre of the Huguenots in Paris by Roman Catholic zealots. It was an attempt to crush the French Protestants.

Spanish colonisation of the Americas was confined mostly to the Southern Continent. In North America, the Spanish occupation was confined to the tropical zone, such as the swamplands of Florida.

The "Spanish Main", the mainland and islands bordering the Caribbean, was the scene of many sea battles between rival nations as well as between merchant ships and privateers. Eventually the supremacy of Spanish shipping was crushed and the richly-laden Spanish ships scourged from the sea.

up by the Inquisition and the Jesuits, was the spear-head of the Catholic cause. His life was one long battle for the Roman Church and the House of Habsburg. The wars he waged for their advancement reveal both the might of Spain and the cause of its failure. Philip strove his hardest to stamp out Calvinism and rebellion in the Netherlands, but, by 1609, the Dutch had fought him to a standstill. The truce they secured was only a half-time pause, but the game was as good as won by the home team. England and France, with mixed political and religious motives, had helped the rebels and so Philip had to fight them too. But the English crippled his naval power with the scattering of the Armada in 1588, and the French threw him out of their country ten years later. At the same time he was fighting the Turks at sea. Spain was becoming Europe's football.

THE COST OF WARS

The cost of these lengthy and widespread conflicts was enormous. To meet it, Spain looked to the riches of the Americas and to taxation. But the whole history of the kingdom from Philip's time for a century onwards shows that they were wells which were running dry. Spain herself produced little wealth. The "nobles"—a very comprehensive term—were too proud and too lazy to work. There were no manufacturers. Agriculture was largely unproductive. The expulsion of the Jews, and that of the Moors which was completed in 1609, deprived the country of its most industrious and enterprising citizens. Commerce and industry were throttled by corruption and unwise restrictions and taxes. The fact that, in 1581, Philip annexed Portugal, with its immense possessions in Brazil, Africa, the Azores and the East Indies, didn't seem to help matters. In the end, Spain, as is the fate of spendthrifts, became insolvent.

SPAIN IN THE DESCENDANT

After Philip's death in 1598, Spain slithered downhill with increasing velocity. In the Thirty Years' War her armies suffered heavy defeats, and Holland's struggle for independence, ended in a win. Furthermore, in 1640, Portugal kicked off the traces and set up its own king again

from the House of Braganza, whose descendants continued on the throne till the revolution of 1910 turned them out. Since then, Portugal has been a republic. In 1640, also, revolts broke out in Catalonia and Naples. However, although they came to nothing, altogether it was a calamitous year for Spain.

So was 1665, when the crown was donned by the feeble-minded Charles II, who thought himself bewitched and possessed of a devil. During his reign French and Austrian influences competed for control of the government and, in 1700, the former led the dying king to bequeath his kingdom to the French Louis XIV's grandson Philip, Duke of Anjou. The outcome was the war of the Spanish Succession which convulsed Europe till 1713. Spain's unfortunate part in the conflict brought her pretty well to the bottom of the hill. The rest of the Netherlands, and her possessions in Italy, were stripped from her and given to Austria. Gibraltar—a part of her very homeland—and Minorca were ceded to England together with trading rights in Spain's hitherto jealously guarded American settlements. And Louis' grandson, as Philip V, the first of Spain's Bourbon line, remained king of what was left. This comprised Spain itself, the Canaries, the Balearic Islands (except Minorca), a bit of North Africa, the Philippine Islands (discovered by Magellan and later occupied and named after Philip II), and the Americas—minus parts of the mainland and the greater part of the West India Islands, which by now had been appropriated by the English, Dutch and French.

THE GLORIES OF SPAIN

Spain's true glory survives in her art and literature, whose finest age was in the sixteenth and seventeenth centuries. Her artists include the famous names of El Greco (who came from Crete) and the great court portrait-painter Velasquez. The Spanish people have poetry and song in their blood, and their writers have produced a wealth of ballads, romances and stage plays. Foreigners can almost forgive Spain for the Inquisition as they smile over Cervantes' *Don Quixote*, that diverting parody (with its moral lesson for Spanish society) of outworn knight-errantry.

THE NETHERLANDS

The Netherlands, comprising modern Holland and Belgium, is a small tract of country with a big history. In the early sixteenth century it came into the full tide of European affairs. At that time the Habsburg Charles V ruled over the Holy Roman Empire, which included Germany and the Netherlands, besides Spain and its American conquests, and possessions in Italy.

Charles's troubles were almost as great as his empire. He was continually fighting France for dominance in Europe, and he found warfare a costly occupation. Now the solid and stolid burghers of the Netherland cities—Antwerp, Ghent, Bruges and others—were fat with the riches of trade and banking. One of Charles's troubles was to get them to aid him by loosening their purse-strings.

Even more troublesome was the spread of Protestantism. The teachings of Luther and Calvin found a ready soil in the Netherlands. Charles, the champion of the Roman Catholic Church, could not tolerate heresy. In 1522, he resorted to the terrors of the Inquisition to root out the poisonous growth. During the ensuing thirty years 30,000 men and women suffered a martyr's death at the stake or on the scaffold. But still the obstinate growth spread.

The persecution became even fiercer when, in 1555, Charles abdicated and his son, the intensely devout Philip II, ruled the Netherlands and Spain (1556). And now religion became merged with politics. Nobles and people alike, antagonised by the insolent Spanish troops and the savage assault on their creed, were driven to thoughts of independence. Philip had to defend his sovereignty and his Catholic faith. In 1567, he sent the Duke of Alva to crush the offenders, and six years of hideous slaughter and ferocious oppression followed. Alva himself boasted that he had put to death 18,000 men. But the country had found a resolute leader in William the Silent, Prince of Orange. In 1568 revolt broke out.

REBELLION AGAINST SPAIN

England's Elizabeth I, waging her own desperate contest against Philip, secretly abetted the rebellion. The southern provinces, less infected by Protestantism, joined in late and withdrew early. The seven Dutch provinces of the north, in which Calvinism was deeply rooted, formed the Union of Utrecht and, in 1581, boldly threw off their allegiance to the Spanish despot. Philip's next move was a drastic one. He offered a tempting reward for William's head. In 1584, the infamous blood-money was earned. William the Silent became silent for evermore. The very children in the streets cried for " the Father of his country ".

But the republic, for which he had suffered so much to create, continued to struggle. For five and twenty years it battled against the first military power in Europe. Elizabeth now openly aided her fellow-Protestants by land and sea. The defeat of the " Invincible Armada " in 1588 crippled Spain's naval power. Even Philip's huge resources were becoming exhausted. A series of brilliant Dutch victories, ashore and afloat (during which time Philip died), brought Spain at last to terms. In 1609, she virtually acknowledged the gallant little republic's independence. In 1648, the Peace of Westphalia confirmed it and the struggle which had lasted for eighty years was at an end.

RISE OF DUTCH POWER

During the century that succeeded the revolt of 1568 an astonishing display of persevering enterprise made the Dutch a leading commercial, colonial and naval power. They supplanted the Portuguese in the East Indies and Ceylon and drove out the English. They established stations in the Cape of Good Hope and West Africa. They explored the coasts of Australia and discovered Tasmania and New Zealand. They made conquests in the West Indies and South America and founded the settlements in North America which, when seized by the English, became the colonies of New York, New Jersey and Delaware. At sea they made themselves the masters of Spain, the equals of England. And, at the same time, they blossomed out in art and produced a line of superb painters which included Rembrandt, Vermeer, de Hooch and Hals. But in the eighteenth century, decline set in and Holland was finally forced to yield pride of place in worldly power to England.

Meantime, while the Dutch republic was bravely launched, the southern provinces had remained at their moorings. They differed considerably, in race and language, from Holland (or "The Netherlands", as it is officially called), being more akin to France, while Holland was nearer in character to north Germany. And they became strongly Catholic. For the present they were known as the "Spanish Netherlands". In time the southern provinces were to become Belgium. They, too, had their illustrious painters: the Van Eyck brothers, Rubens, Van Dyck and others of the "Flemish" school.

The histories of Holland and Belgium afterwards became increasingly interlocked with those of other countries.

The Flemish school of painting produced artists of exceptional merit, such as the brothers Van Eyck, Rogier van der Weyden and Hans Memling. Antonello da Messina took his knowledge of the use of oils and introduced the style to Italy.

IVAN THE TERRIBLE

The history of sixteenth- and seventeenth-century Russia is best glanced at quickly and then—except for a few saving features—forgotten. The country was still sunk in ignorant and brutal barbarism and semi-oriental tyranny. The civilised refinements of social and political life, as existing in western Europe, were practically unknown.

The outstanding figure of the period is the sinister Ivan IV, called "The Terrible", though he was not always seen in that character. His youth was wild and dissipated enough; but, a few years after his coronation in 1547—he was the first to be crowned Tsar—he mended his evil ways and introduced many reforms. But he could not keep it up. Ten years later the imperial penitent suffered a relapse. He imagined that every man's hand was against him and, half crazy with suspicion and fear, reacted savagely. Murders, executions and cold-blooded massacres reddened his hands. Then, in a final about-turn in 1584, he died as a monk.

Ivan was "terrible" to his "nobles" (they weren't a real aristocracy), who had ill-treated him in his youth and for whom he conceived a lasting hatred. But to the common people he was a friend, the "little father" of his people, the protector of the wretched serfs from the heartless tyranny of their great land-owning masters. Ivan tried to introduce skilled artificers from western Europe and anticipated some of the ideals of Peter the Great; but his well-meant efforts were thwarted. It was during his reign that the English explorers Willoughby and Chancellor, seeking a North-East Passage to the Spice Islands, opened up trade with Russia instead. Ivan fought many wars, successful and unsuccessful. Of the former were his campaigns against the Tatar khans who still occupied the south and east. Between 1552 and 1556, Ivan won Kazan and Astrakhan from them. In 1581, a Cossack chief began the occupation of Siberia. Within

seventy years pioneers had reached the Pacific and navigated the strait later named after Bering, its rediscoverer—a remarkable performance when you look at it and scale it out on the map.

A period of anarchy, social distress and foreign invasion followed soon after Ivan's death. The dynasty which had been founded in the ninth century by the Swedish Viking Rurik was extinguished and Poland made a bid for the throne. The Poles were, and still are, bitterly hated by the Russians. Their original offences were two-fold. First, they were Roman Catholics, while Russia was the home of the Eastern "Orthodox" Church with its different doctrines and practices. Secondly, they were united with the Lithuanians who, in the fourteenth century, had seized a large part of western Russia and subjugated its inhabitants. The Poles now dominated Lithuania, and most of the stolen territory was still in the aggressor's hands. Their attempt on the Russian throne was foiled by a great upsurge of patriotism and in 1613 a connection of the house of Rurik, Michael Romanoff, a lad of seventeen years, was elected as Tsar. That was the beginning of the dynasty that was to reign till the Bolsheviks massacred its last representatives in 1918.

Under the early Romanoffs, serfdom became more definitely established and peasants could be bought and sold like cattle. The Tsars recovered some of the lost western territory in the Ukraine. Intercourse with Europe increased and a crowd of foreigners who settled in Moscow began to exert an improving influence on the morals and manners and intellects of the uncouth court and society they found there. When Peter the Great was on the way to taking control, in 1689, Russia was still right at the bottom of the European class; but, given a progressive and enlightened teacher, it seemed that something might be made of her.

The persecutions carried out by Ivan IV earned him the name of the "Terrible".

In 1613, the patriarch of Moscow consecrated his nephew Michael as Emperor of all the Russias.

FRANCE AT THE ZENITH

French history in the sixteenth and seventeenth centuries is red with aggressive wars and religious persecutions. War was still a field of glory then, and roasting heretics was a plain Christian duty.

In the first part of the sixteenth century Francis I, King of France from 1515 to 1547, was worsted by the Habsburg Emperor Charles V in the contest for pre-eminence in Europe. Later, the balance of power between the two rival countries was somewhat evened up. Then, in 1558, Charles abdicated, having previously divided up his vast realms. His brother Ferdinand I received the Habsburgs' Austrian territories together with the throne of the "Holy Roman Empire", which practically amounted to Germany. His son Philip II got Spain and its possessions in the New World, together with the Netherlands and large domains in Italy and Sicily.

It was Spain's turn now to rise to greatness. France was suicidally tearing herself to pieces in religious wars. The fires of the Protestant Reformation which Luther had lighted in 1517 had showered sparks all over Europe. Germany was left divided between Roman Catholicism and Lutheran Protestantism. The French reformer Calvin, catching fire from one of the sparks, laid the foundations of the Presbyterian Church in Geneva, whence the flames spread to the Netherlands. In no country were religious passions more intense, or more closely associated with political questions, than in France. From 1562, over a period of forty years, the struggles with the Huguenots (as Calvin's followers were called in France) rent the country with ferocious civil wars, with massacres, murders and tumults.

At length the storm diminished. With the assassination of the last of the Valois kings, the Bourbon dynasty was begun, in 1589, by Henry IV—Henry of Navarre. The new sovereign was a genial soul, quick-witted, recklessly brave and possessed of an elastic conscience. A Huguenot himself, he performed the tight-rope feat of making friends with both religious parties. He achieved it by re-entering the Catholic Church and by conceding recognition to the Huguenots by signing in 1598 an edict at Nantes. The royal turn-coat, once in control of affairs, did much to repair his ravaged country and restore the shaken power of the monarchy. It was under his encouragement that the explorer Champlain laid the first firm foundations of the French colonial empire in Canada. An ill day dawned for France, when, in 1610, the wise and liberal Henry, thought by many to be one of France's greatest kings, was assassinated by a Catholic fanatic.

During the periods of religious strife, both past and to come, the Papacy was supported by one of the most notable religious orders that has ever been known. The Society of Jesus was conceived by a wounded Spanish soldier, Ignatius Loyola, and established in 1540. Its members, the Jesuits, consecrated themselves to a sort of crusade, under the captaincy of Jesus, for the promotion of the true Christian life. Unquestioning obedience to their superior officers was a distinctive feature of their strongly organised system. The Jesuits produced many renowned scholars and everywhere established schools where the pupils were given the best of educations and trained as rigid Catholics. The Order became the pre-eminent instrument of the Roman Church in its struggles to win back the straying Protestant flocks into the Catholic fold.

In the ensuing centuries the Jesuits spread their teachings from Europe to Africa, from America to the Far East. They roused the burning hatred of all Protestants, and even Catholic countries often grew to distrust them because of their political and commercial activities. Their enemies accused them—sometimes justly—of a complete disregard of

The assassination of Henry III in 1589 brought the King of Navarre to the throne as Henry IV of France.

Brilliant soldier and King of Sweden, Gustavus Adolphus, was killed at Lutzen in 1632.

Father Joseph, agent of Cardinal Richelieu, gained a breathing space in the Thirty Years' War by manœuvring the Diet of Regensburg (1630).

moral scruples, even to the point of instigating political assassination, to gain their ends. Such charges are now a thing of the past. To-day, the uplifting work of the Society is wholly concentrated on foreign missions, education and learning.

THE THIRTY YEARS' WAR

In 1618, one of the most shameless and ruinous of all European wars broke out in Germany. The Thirty Years' War was both a religious and a political struggle. It began formally with the refusal of the Protestant magnates of Bohemia to elect the Roman Catholic Emperor Ferdinand II of Austria to the vacant throne of Bohemia. They offered it instead to Frederick the Elector of the Palatinate. It soon degenerated into the usual scramble for political power and territory, in which the Empire, France, Spain and Sweden competed with each other. (England mostly—and wisely—kept out of the fray. During its later stages she was fully occupied with her own religious and political Civil Wars between Charles I and the Roundheads). Ferdinand, supported by his Habsburg cousin Philip II of Spain, started off with some notable successes. Thereupon, sympathy with the cruel sufferings inflicted on the vanquished Protestants and fears for the safety of his own country brought in the heroic Gustavus Adolphus, the king of Protestant Sweden. The ensuing military career of the liberator, with his new model army (which included a strong stiffening of Scots), his masterly tactics and leadership, had something of the brilliance and brevity of a shooting star. In 1632, after two years' campaigning, " the Lion of the North " fell in his last victory.

Eight years earlier one of France's most renowned statesmen, Cardinal Richelieu, had come into power under Henry of Navarre's son, Louis XIII. Richelieu was a man of sickly frame, iron will and cold heart. By his policy at home he strengthened the monarchy and made the royal will the law of the land. In foreign affairs he revived the old contest with the Habsburgs, in Germany and Spain, and laboured to make France great again. During the early years of the war his subtle diplomacy had been actively stirring up the Habsburgs' enemies. In 1635, with Gustavus Adolphus dead, he threw the French armies into the field.

Unhappy Germany! For thirteen years she was fated to be the main victim of the ravaging armies of all the contending powers. Not until 1648 was her agony ended, by the Peace of Westphalia. Richelieu had died in 1642, but his work had been carried on by an apt pupil, Cardinal Mazarin. It was to the latter's astute diplomacy, and the brilliant victories of the French generals, that France, after a separate treaty with Spain in 1659, emerged from the wars with her frontiers enlarged and strengthened and her power and influence gratifyingly exalted.

The Peace of Westphalia is a landmark in the history of Europe. There was to be no all-Catholic Germany: the Protestants of the north stood firm, as, substantially, they stand now. The emperor's authority was reduced to nullity: the conglomeration of separate " principalities ", some three hundred in number, of which the empire was composed were declared independent States. The real Habsburg Empire became an Austrian Empire, comprising the hereditary domain of Austria with various dependencies, including Bohemia, Silesia and such part of Hungary as wasn't in the hands of the Turks. By the treaty also Switzerland and Holland had their freedom from the Empire and Spain confirmed. Spain's great days were over and France's star had soared. Germany could no longer cause her anxiety. That exhausted country lay devastated, all prospect of nationhood lost to sight.

ABSOLUTE MONARCHY

In 1643, a child of five had mounted the French throne as Louis XIV. Widespread discontent with the autocratic government provoked civil war in the year of the Peace of Westphalia; but wily Mazarin steered the country back into calmer waters and buttressed up the monarchy again. The young king observed events with watchful eyes. When Mazarin died in 1661, Louis resolved that thenceforth he would be his own first minister and everybody's master. And he carried out his resolution. He made his personal authority supreme. Ministers and officials were responsible to him alone. The army and navy, taxation, commerce and industry —all were under his control. Parliamentary and popular rights were puffed away. If he did not actually coin the phrase

Threatened by the revolt of Parliament, Mazarin, the Queen Mother and Louis XIV were forced to flee from Paris.

Ambitious and autocratic, Louis XIV held court at Versailles.

" The State?—*I* am the State ", it perfectly expressed his views on the subject. And he claimed to rule by divine right, as " God's lieutenant ". Loving glory, he raised France to pre-eminence in Europe, in literature and culture and in the art of war. He was no genius, but he had great common-sense, a sound judgment and untiring industry. Finally, he was handsome, charming and elegant and possessed of a most royal dignity of deportment. The nation accepted him gladly and proudly as a sovereign who gave France security, order and glory.

The immense and splendid palace Louis built for himself at Versailles was an architect's delight and a courtier's paradise. The court which assembled in the vast halls and gardens became a luxurious centre of elegance, wit and beauty, governed by an exquisitely graceful and refined code of etiquette that set an example to Europe. There Louis bound the nobles by the silken chains of hoped-for gifts and perquisites. Insensibly they ceased to be powerful territorial lords and became mere satellites of the Sun-King, gaily-hued butterflies sipping the sweets of royal favour.

Such was Louis while treading the paths of peace. But the ambitious *Grand Monarque* soon found a use for his magnificent army and navy. His energetic minister Colbert had launched France on grandiose plans of commercial and colonial expansion which brought her into competition with Holland and England. "New France" in North America was extended from Canada to Louisiana. Possessions and trading stations were established in Madagascar and India.

But Louis' overruling aim was to extend France to its " natural boundaries " on the east at the expense of her neighbours. In 1667, he wantonly set in motion a series of aggressive wars that troubled Europe for thirty years and formed a preliminary to the crowning conflict of all. His armies marched into Flanders and Germany and landed in Ireland. His ships fought the Dutch and English fleets. Holland, Spain, Germany, Austria and England were all sucked into the vortex of universal combat. In 1685, Louis, a zealous Catholic, was led into committing one of his greatest errors. He revoked the Edict of Nantes which had given the Protestant Huguenots recognition, and hundreds of thousands of the persecuted sect fled the country. All Europe now regarded the vainglorious despot as a menace to its political and religious security. And amongst Louis' foes the most deadly and unappeasable was William of Orange, head of the Dutch State, who supplanted the Catholic James II on the throne of England in " the Glorious Revolution " of 1688.

In 1701, William formed the Grand Alliance of England, Holland and Austria; Marlborough's brilliant victories in the war of the Spanish Succession which followed, made Europe gasp; Louis's career of conquest was at last checked and France humbled.

France had indeed strengthened her eastern boundaries, in Spanish Flanders and Franche Comte and in Alsace. But for these gains, as for her arrogant master's whole system, she paid a ruinous price. The carnage of war, the flight of the Huguenots (who included many of France's most skilled and industrious citizens), and the maintenance of the gilded splendours of Versailles had all helped to drain the country's man-power and empty its purse. Far different now seemed Louis in the eyes of the nation. When the Sun King dipped to his setting in 1715 he left behind him the curses of a disaffected and exhausted people.

After a reign of 72 years, Louis XIV died in 1715.

THE UNTEACHABLE STUARTS

It seems strange that England, with its traditional (but hotly repudiated) claim to the overlordship of Scotland, should ever accept that country's rulers as its own. Yet that is what happened in 1603. On the death of Elizabeth I, James VI of Scotland, the son of Mary, Queen of Scots, was welcomed as James I of England. For James stood next in the line of descent from Henry VII, through the marriage of the latter's daughter Margaret to the Stuart King James IV. Scotland continued to be ruled as a separate kingdom, but the two Crowns were united.

The Stuarts were an unlucky family. Trouble dogged them like their own shadow. In England their kings, on the whole, were conscientious men, but they were blind to the changes of the times. On the fundamental issues of religion and parliament, king and people were ever locked in a mortal struggle.

James, with his grotesque figure, his self-importance and his bookish and lecturing habits, was hardly the man to fill Good Queen Bess's place in England's heart. The great queen had left the Anglican Church firmly established, but with a powerful Puritan opposition. The Puritans clamoured for the removal of all " popish " ritual and practices. Some hated church government by royally-appointed bishops, and favoured the Presbyterian system of freely-elected presbyters or elders. Others, the " Independents ", rejected the Anglican Church altogether and claimed complete independence for each congregation.

James was all for Church and bishops. He had had enough of Presbyterianism in his own country. Like Elizabeth, he regarded the Puritans' resistance as the sign of a dangerously independent attitude that might presently extend itself to politics. So he opposed the movement. Meantime we should credit him with the patronage of a noble scriptural and literary achievement: the new translation of the Bible, the Authorised Version, produced in 1611.

At the other end of the religious scale the Catholics came in for some severe treatment. They came near to repaying it in kind by the Guy Fawkes Gunpowder Plot of 1605, which we still celebrate with such explosive enthusiasm on 5th November.

James's overbearing attitude towards Parliament was the other great issue in the mortal struggle. The House of Commons, composed largely of country squires, merchants and lawyers, had long since become the centre of national affairs and had asserted itself even against Elizabeth in her last ten years. The Puritans were strongly represented there, so their religious resistance did, as James feared, extend itself to politics. The Commons had allowed themselves to be dominated by the popular and tactful Tudors, except for the last years of Elizabeth's reign, but this schoolmaster-king from over the Border got under their skin. His and their ideas of his rights—his " prerogative "—were poles apart. *He* believed in the theory that kings ruled by divine right and could make and unmake laws at their will. It was an old doctrine and there were many who believed in it. But it was so old, the Commons felt, that it had gone mouldy. *They* believed in Magna Carta and the people's ancient liberties—plus a few new ones.

Apart from this, it was generally agreed that the sovereign enjoyed the prerogative of dealing with certain special subjects, such as foreign affairs and other matters of State. The limits of these subjects were undefined, but James made them altogether too elastic and even lectured the Commons for debating such matters. Parliament should be seen and not heard, seems to have been his maxim. The Commons, however, thought otherwise and they bluntly asserted their privileges, including the rights of free speech, besides denouncing arbitrary taxation. The king's habitual laziness prevented an immediate clash, but the conflict of views remained as a storm cloud on the horizon.

Prompted by the revival of the anti-Catholic laws of James I, a plot was conceived to blow up the king and Parliament.

James, however, was wise, if unpopular, in establishing peace with the nation's old enemy, Spain. That country was beginning to show evidences of decline and had ceased to be the national bogey. James tried—unsuccessfully—to marry his son Charles to a Catholic Spanish princess. In the end he betrothed him to the French king's sister, Henrietta Maria, another Catholic. More to the taste of his people was the marriage of his daughter Elizabeth to Frederick, the Protestant Elector Palatine of the Rhine. It is from that ancient union that Britain's present line of sovereigns descends.

The Stuarts have the distinction of putting the first definite outlines of the British Empire on the map. Under their rule the idea of founding colonies in the New World came to the fore. In 1607, a settlement was planted in Virginia. In 1620, a body of Independent Puritans, the Pilgrim Fathers, fleeing from James's attentions, crossed the Atlantic in the little 180-ton *Mayflower* and sought freedom of conscience in New Plymouth. During the reigns of Charles I and II, colonies were founded as a refuge for various persecuted sects: Puritans in Massachusetts (which afterwards absorbed New Plymouth) and Connecticut; Catholics in Maryland; Quakers in Pennsylvania. Besides these, Rhode Island, New Hampshire and Carolina—later divided into North and South—came into existence; while New York, New Jersey and Delaware were—without the least excuse—seized from the Dutch. (The final colony, Georgia, was not founded till George II's time.) Other settlements were made in Newfoundland and the West Indian Islands and around Hudson Bay.

This strong westward tide of emigration was destined to prove of immeasurable significance in subsequent history. The new settlers found the Spaniards firmly rooted in the south. The ever-extending French settlements ranged from Newfoundland to Louisiana. But the future was to decide that, from the English colonies, the world power of the United States of America should arise and that the vast North American continent should be neither Spanish nor French but Anglo-Saxon.

THE PETITION OF RIGHT

Charles I, who succeeded James in 1625, was a virtuous, pious and cultured gentleman, but he had inherited his father's arrogant views on religion and Parliament and the royal prerogative. He soon had the Commons growling and snapping. He levied taxes and subsidies without parliamentary authority and imprisoned those who refused to pay. Whereupon the Commons, in the famous Petition of Right of 1628, formally denounced all such encroachments on the ancient rights of free Englishmen. Circumstances forced Charles to accept the Petition; but, as he was to prove repeatedly, his word could not be trusted.

Charles was devoted to the Anglican Church and frowned on Puritans. But he smiled on the " High Churchmen " who were introducing " popish " ceremonial and ornaments into the services and upholding the doctrine of the divine right of kings. In 1629, the Commons declared roundly that whosoever should propose changes in religion was a public enemy.

Parliament consistently withheld supplies of money as the one effective way of controlling the king's wilfulness. So, in 1629, Charles dismissed Parliament and tried ruling the country by himself. He continued to do this for eleven years, raising money by various questionable and unpopular means, including a " ship-money " tax to pay for new ships.

George Villiers, 1st Duke of Buckingham, supported Francis Bacon's impeachment.

He still regarded such measures as part of his royal prerogative.

Among the party that supported him were Sir Thomas Wentworth, afterwards Earl of Strafford, and William Laud, who became Archbishop of Canterbury. Wentworth was the king's strong man in civil and military affairs. He despised Parliament and Puritans equally. Laud, as leader of the High Church party, established the elaborate ritual that aroused the horror of all good Puritans. He was a sincere and well-intentioned man, and he corrected many church abuses. But he was intolerant and narrow-minded and he persecuted the Puritans mercilessly in the tyrannous Star Chamber and Court of High Commission. His severities drove many into the ranks of the Presbyterians and Independents. Thousands sought political and religious freedom in Massachusetts.

Charles and his over-zealous Archbishop presently decided to bring the Presbyterian Church, which dominated Scotland, more in line with the Anglican system. In 1637, the king imposed on the Scots the use of a Prayer Book after the pattern of the English liturgy. His action raised a howling whirlwind. A strong section of the people rose and, in 1638, swore a solemn Covenant to preserve their cherished Kirk at all costs. Charles gave up the idea.

The king's blind and obstinate pursuit of personal government created strong currents of dangerous resentment. In 1637, a rumble of the threatening storm was heard when John Hampden, a Buckinghamshire squire, refused on principle to pay ship-money.

THE LONG PARLIAMENT

At length Charles's empty pockets and an invasion by the Scots, who suspected his intentions, drove him to summon Parliament again. The assembly of 1640—the renowned Long Parliament—united the swirling currents of discontent into a tidal wave. Grimly the Commons settled down " to pull up all grievances by the roots."

There was to be no more personal rule: henceforth Parliament must be summoned every three years. Under the leadership of the parliamentarian Pym, the hated Star Chamber and Court of High Commission were abolished; ship-money and fines were declared illegal; Strafford and

Cromwell quickly became an influential member of Parliament and was consistently opposed to the king's autocratic rule.

Laud were imprisoned, and both were executed. But the Commons became divided among themselves, particularly over their Grand Remonstrance of 1641. The majority of the Puritans demanded sweeping reductions in the powers of the king and his allies the bishops. But a great many thought these went too far. The members were in fact lining up in opposite camps: King and Church against Parliament and Puritanism, Cavaliers against Roundheads.

In 1642, Charles cannily thought to take advantage of the cleavage. He suddenly descended on the Commons with an armed retinue to seize Pym, Hampden and three other prominent leaders. But the birds had flown. His high-handed breach of the privileges of the House brought the struggle to a crisis. Agreement was plainly impossible. The issue must be tried, it seemed, by " push of pike ".

In the First Civil War that began that year, two major factors ruined the king's cause: Oliver Cromwell with his Ironsides, and Scotland. Cromwell was a plain, country

At the trial of Charles I, sentence was passed that he be executed as a tyrant and public enemy.

squire and stern Puritan in whom a solemn sense of religious duty burned like a steady flame. His successes at Marston Moor in 1644 and Naseby in 1645 stamped him as the foremost cavalry leader of the day. As for the Scots, Pym bought their aid by promising extreme reforms in the Anglican Church, including the introduction of Presbyterianism.

With the end of the war, accordingly, the Presbyterian majority in Parliament started to enforce their system on the country. They never succeeded. The mass of the people were against it. So was the Army, with the powerful Cromwell as its champion. The soldiers were largely Independents who favoured toleration for all creeds except Catholicism.

Charles once more tried to profit from his enemies' disagreements. His dubious dealings, with Cromwell and the Scots, won back the latter to his side and plunged the country into the Second Civil War of 1648. But Cromwell crushed the Scottish army near Preston and the new outbreak was soon over.

Cromwell was now master of the situation. And his blood was up. The Army was weary of Charles' trickery and determined to bring him to account. It was enraged with Parliament for its recent negotiations with him. And the soldiers knew that the Presbyterian majority was hostile to them because of their armed power and their religious and political principles. Straightway they marched on London and violently purged the Commons of their opponents. The " Rump " of a few score men—mostly Independents—who were suffered to remain, then proceeded to the mockery of bringing Charles to trial. On the 30th January, 1649, to the horror of all Europe and most Englishmen, the condemned king, steadfast as ever to the principles of Church and Monarchy as he conceived them, was executed as a tyrant and public enemy.

Cromwell had replaced Charles's relatively mild tyranny with the dictatorship of the sword. The Rump now set up a Commonwealth and abolished the House of Lords. Meantime the dead king's elder son was proclaimed in Scotland as Charles II and Ireland broke into revolt. Cromwell crushed Ireland by a savage terrorism that ever after made his name a byword. The Scots were defeated at Dunbar in 1650, and afterwards brought under the English yoke. Prince Charles, with another Scottish army, was beaten at Worcester in 1651, and he escaped to France.

The victorious Cromwell now returned to the pressing problems of government and religion. He was not an autocrat by design. He firmly believed in Parliament. But, Parliament or no, he was determined to carry out his plans for the reformation of England and the creation of a godly State. First, there should be, within limits, toleration for all creeds except " popery ". Secondly, the reform in morals which the Puritans had already begun must be sternly enforced. The vices of drinking and swearing, the " popish " Christmas festivities and pagan May Day revels, the profaning of the Sabbath and such-like vanities and frivolities must be rooted out.

LORD PROTECTOR

But Cromwell knew that the bulk of the people—the greater part of them still Anglican churchmen at heart—were against him and his military rule. He dared not, therefore, summon a free parliament. Finding the miserable Rump Parliament unsatisfactory, he bundled the members out of doors in 1653. From then on until his death the Lord Protector, as he became, tried one government experi-

The Great Fire—the great conflagration which took place in London in 1666, lasted four days.

ment after another. But all failed because of the fundamental conflict of views between him and the country.

It was otherwise with foreign affairs. Cromwell's navy made its power felt from the North Sea to the Mediterranean and the West Indies. Commercial rivalry with Holland (which had just won its long struggle with Spain for independence) led to the First Dutch War of 1652-4, in which Blake brought the enemy to their knees. Trade also provoked a war with Spain. In 1655, Jamaica was taken. Soon England had recovered her Elizabethan supremacy at sea.

The Lord Protector's death in 1658 left a blank that no man could fill, though his eldest son Richard—" Tumbledown Dick " as folk called him—did his poor best. Quarrelling arose in the Army and its power broke. In 1660, what remained of the Long Parliament at last dissolved itself. General Monk, who commanded the English forces in Scotland, voiced the wishes of almost the entire nation when he negotiated for the restoration of the monarchy. Charles II entered London amid delirious rejoicings.

So the Stuarts were back again. But so was Parliament, both Lords and Commons. And the limits to the royal prerogative imposed on Charles I before the war were maintained. Henceforth Parliament must be the nation's supreme law-maker. There must be no more royal personal rule with its arbitrary taxes and illegal imprisonments.

THE CAVALIER PARLIAMENT

The year 1661 saw the assembling of the " Cavalier " Parliament. Charles had promised religious toleration, subject to Parliament's sanction. But the majority of the Cavalier Parliament, during this and the succeeding years, were eager only for a reckoning with their old Puritan oppressors and the restoration of the Anglican Church. The Act of Uniformity required all ministers to accept the Revised Book of Common Prayer. The great majority conformed. Those who refused were expelled from their livings. These stalwarts were the fathers of some of the modern Nonconformist sects. By the Corporation Act rigid Puritans were, in effect, excluded from local government. Charles tried to stop this trend by his First Declaration of Indulgence, but failed. The Conventicle Act forbade all religious meetings by Nonconformists. The Puritans rightly felt that they had been betrayed.

Now came a succession of misfortunes. The Second Dutch War of 1665-7, arising out of the old commercial rivalry, brought England little credit, though she retained the Dutch settlements in America which she had seized. In 1665, the Great Plague made London a city of the dead. And in the following year the afflicted capital was two-thirds destroyed by the Great Fire.

Charles's character now began to appear in murky colours. His tastes were all for ease and pleasure. His private life was shamelessly immoral. He was cynical and witty and very charming. But he was deep. Beneath his indolent exterior he nursed two aims: to rule unshackled by Parliament, and to secure toleration for the Catholic creed to which —so far as he had any religion at all—he himself was secretly attached. His chosen ally was Louis XIV, who also nourished two aims: a career of power and glory for France, and the crushing of Protestantism. The secret Treaty of Dover, of 1670, cynically disregarded all popular English feeling. The two royal conspirators were to divide Protestant Holland between them. Charles was to declare himself a Catholic at the opportune time. And Louis was to pay him a pension (to make him independent of parliamentary supplies) and, if necessary, send over troops to quell opposition.

In execution of this design Charles began the Third Dutch War in 1672. He likewise issued—solely by virtue of his royal prerogative—a Second Declaration of Indulgence suspending Parliament's penal laws against Catholics and (to cloak his primary aim) against Nonconformists too. But the Nonconformists refused to accept toleration at such a price. The fight between King and Parliament was on again. The Commons wrathfully demanded the withdrawal of the offending Indulgence. And Charles tactfully yielded. Thereupon Parliament clinched its triumph with the Test Act of 1673, which excluded from civil and military offices all who refused to receive communion in the Anglican church. Charles's brother James, Duke of York, a known Catholic, was among those thus disqualified. Next year, too, Parliament withdrew England from the Dutch war.

But the calculating king had not given up his secret aims. Presently his clever diplomacy carried him safely over another hurdle. In 1678, the arch-liar Titus Oates came forward with the scaremongering tale of a popish plot to murder Charles and crown his brother James. The country was panic-stricken at the prospect of a line of Catholics on the throne and Chief Justice Scroggs sentenced many innocent people to death on perjured " evidence ". The Earl of Shaftesbury, who led the opposition against the king's supporters in Parliament, introduced a plan to avert such a calamity by excluding James from the succession and substituting Charles's illegitimate son, the dashing and popular young Duke of Monmouth. Charles would never accept such an irregular course and the situation became highly explosive. In the end, however, he managed to outwit his opponents and went quietly on with his own schemes. But, in 1685, death brought to an end both him and his schemes.

It was during the wild excitement surrounding the Exclusion question that the two great opposing parties in Parliament first became organised under the nicknames of " Whigs " for those who supported the exclusion and " Tories " for those who opposed it.

James II, who now mounted the throne, quickly earned a bad mark with his subjects. It occurred in connection with the unsuccessful rebellion raised by the hare-brained Duke of Monmouth. Over a thousand of the rebel's ignorant following of yokels and miners were condemned, by James's atrocious Chief Justice Jeffreys in the " Bloody Assizes ", to death or slavery in the West Indian plantations.

Flushed by this success, James began on the headlong course he had already marked out for himself: to rule as a despot and to restore Catholicism. He prorogued Parliament for good. He chose Catholic ministers. He created a new Court of High Commission. He encouraged Roman rites. He officered the small standing army—which, to increase his power, he vastly enlarged—with Catholics. In 1687, imitating his brother Charles, he issued a Declaration of Indulgence to Catholics and Nonconformists; but, unlike his tactful brother, he obstinately upheld it.

These unteachable Stuarts!

In 1688, the determined king issued another Indulgence and ordered it to be read in the churches. William Sancroft, Archbishop of Canterbury, and six other conscientious bishops mildly petitioned to be excused. Whereupon James hauled them before the judges for sedition. When the judges acquitted them London blazed with triumphal bonfires.

The succession of Louis XIV's grandson, Philip, to the throne of Spain involved France and Europe in war.

The next shock came with the announcement that the queen had borne James an heir. The country had believed that such an event was unlikely and that James's successor would be his elder daughter Mary, who in 1677 had become the wife of the Protestant champion, William, Prince of Orange, the head of the Dutch republic. A Catholic succession once more loomed ahead. Half the country suspected a trick. The tale went round that somebody else's baby had been smuggled into the queen's bedchamber in a bed-warming-pan.

The heir, however, was genuine enough and the little innocent's coming speeded up a project already begun. A group, representing both Tory and Whig feeling, invited Prince William to come over and restore the liberties of England and the Protestant religion. Various common interests were now drawing the two countries together. Not the least of these was the need to combine against the towering ambitions of Louis XIV, which had made France a growing menace to Europe and England and their Protestant communities. William came. James marched to meet him. But his army melted away and all England rose against him. James skipped across the Channel. He was excluded after all. These unlucky Stuarts!

Parliament now set the seal on " the Glorious Revolution ". It crowned the nation's victory by establishing once and for all the constitutional rights and principles for which it had so long battled with the Stuarts. Among the measures taken during the new reign, Parliament declared it illegal to use the royal prerogative for suspending laws, or to levy loans and taxes or raise a standing army without parliamentary sanction. The Crown was settled on William III and Mary II (from 1689); afterwards, if they left no children, on Mary's sister Anne; and finally on the next Protestant heir, the Electress Sophia of Hanover—a child of James I's daughter Elizabeth—and her descendants. All Catholics were excluded. Liberty of worship was granted to most Nonconformists, though they were still barred from holding official positions. As for the doctrine of divine right, the new monarchs had to pitch it overboard. It could only apply to kings in the royal line of descent, and William and Mary ruled only under a parliamentary decree.

WILLIAM OF ORANGE

" Dutch William " is rather a tragic figure. He was a misfit in English politics and there was no love lost between him and his island subjects. His only concern with England was to draw her into the league he was trying to build up against the ravening aggression of Louis XIV. A heroic sense of duty to his fatherland ruled his life. He was a great diplomatist and an ardent soldier, though wanting in the supreme qualities of generalship. And he was a very sick man. His heart was cold, his manner surly and unsociable, and his wretched health often made him peevish.

But William's immediate task was to suppress resistance to his new throne. A rising in the Scottish Highlands took some time to settle. Meantime political and religious peace was secured by the establishment at last of the Presbyterian Kirk as the national Church of Scotland. In Ireland, which was mostly Catholic and violently anti-English, the much-excluded James II, aided by Louis, turned up in 1689. Next year, however, William trounced him in the battle of the Boyne and shooed him and his Frenchmen out of the islands. William secured peace with the Irish and their heroic leader Sarsfield on conditions which, under the compulsion of the

After the victory at Ramillies in 1706, the troops acclaim their great general, John Churchill, 1st Duke of Marlborough.

rabidly Protestant English Parliament, were soon flagrantly repudiated.

William was now free to turn to his arch-enemy. A ding-dong series of contests was waged in the Netherlands and elsewhere, on land and sea, till in 1697 both sides grew war-weary and peace was signed. The campaigns had brought little profit to the exhausted Louis.

The drums of war were not, however, to be silent for long. Charles II of Spain had died in 1700, bequeathing his vast empire—Spain, the Spanish Netherlands (reduced to the region of modern Belgium), extensive Italian possessions and immense territories in the New World—to Louis' grandson, Duke Philip of Anjou. The acceptance of the bequest would completely upset the balance of power in Europe and threaten another war. Actually, the danger had been foreseen and Louis had agreed to a treaty for the peaceful partition of the Spanish empire between his heir, the dauphin, and the Emperor Leopold of Austria's second son, the Archduke Charles. Now, however, Louis threw over the treaty and accepted the whole of the rich legacy for his grandson Philip. This, and his further actions, made war unavoidable.

In 1701, William crowned his life-work by the creation of the " Grand Alliance " of England, Holland and the Emperor Leopold to break Louis' overshadowing power. On James II's death, Louis recognised the latter's son as James III. That definitely put England's back up and made her entry into the war assured. But William was not to lead her. In 1702, he was killed by a fall from his horse.

Mary had died in 1694, and the sceptre passed to her sister Anne. The European stage was set for the titanic conflict of the War of the Spanish Succession. The man of the hour was John Churchill, the then Earl and future Duke of Marlborough. He stood high in the queen's favour because of her extravagant affection for his countess, Sarah.

Marlborough, as commander of the English and Dutch armies, immediately began operations in the Netherlands. His dazzling victories made all Europe gasp. In 1704, a combined army of the French and their Bavarian allies was threatening Vienna. Marlborough made an astounding surprise march of some 300 miles across Germany and completely broke the enemy forces in the battle of Blenheim.

Austria—and with it Germany—was saved. The long-standing belief in French invincibility was shattered. In 1706, at Ramillies, he sent another Franco-Bavarian host flying. In 1708, he scattered the French at Oudenarde and led the way to the mastery of the Netherlands. And in the following year he gave them another beating at Malplaquet. Such were the mighty hammer-strokes of the greatest general England had ever produced. Meanwhile, on other fronts, the French were driven out of Italy, though they were more successful in Spain. In 1704, England took Gibraltar and, in 1708, Minorca.

In 1710, however, troubles at home began to thicken round " Corporal John ", as his adoring soldiers called the great duke. Party politics were very bitter in those days and personal feeling ran high. Marlborough and the Whigs, who were then in power, wanted to fight the war to the end. The Tories, eager to displace them from office, were for peace. The country was weary of the conflict. The duke and his duchess had fallen out of favour with Anne. The upshot was that, in 1710, the Tories returned to power. They accused Marlborough of corruptly accepting gifts and bribes. The duke was able to answer the charges, but they gave a sufficient pretext for dismissing him from all his offices.

Peace was concluded by the treaties of Utrecht and Rastadt of 1713-14. Charles, now the Emperor Charles VI, received the Spanish Netherlands and most of the Italian possessions. Spain ceded Gibraltar and Minorca to England, while France abandoned her claims to Newfoundland, Nova Scotia and territories around Hudson Bay. England also received valuable trading rights, and the Protestant succession was recognised. Louis' grandson Philip kept Spain and its New World possessions, but the crowns of France and Spain were never to be united. England's main war aim was substantially realised. France was humbled and England, covered with glory, emerged as the leading power in Europe.

UNION OF THE CROWNS

Meantime a momentous event had occurred at home.

In 1707, England and Scotland became linked in the Kingdom of Great Britain under one king and with one combined Parliament, Scotland retaining her own laws and Presbyterian Kirk. The two ancient antagonists became partners.

The reign of " Good Queen Anne ", the last of the Stuarts, ended in 1714, and, in accordance with the Act of Succession, George, son of the recently deceased Electress Sophia of Hanover, was proclaimed king.

Looking back we can see what weighty achievements England made under the Stuarts: the settlement of the constitution on the lines that subsist to-day; toleration for Nonconformists; increased power and prestige in Europe; a growing empire. It was a period when England, France and Holland, like eager prospectors in a gold-rush, were staking out new and rival claims to commerce and empire in an expanding world. England took a full share of the rich spoils: the American colonies and settlements; Gibraltar and Minorca; the trading stations of the East India Company which foreshadowed the Indian empire; settlements in West Africa. There were notable advances in various sciences and Charles II gave a charter to the Royal Society in 1660, of which Sir Isaac Newton was at one time the president. And literature, too, had its glories. Milton composed his *Paradise Lost*, one of the grandest epic poems of all times, and Bunyan wrote *The Pilgrim's Progress*.

PRUSSIA AND FREDERICK THE GREAT

PRUSSIA EMERGES

Austria and Germany, France, England and Spain—these are the star performers who have figured in the foregoing scenes of modern European history. Now, in the first half of the eighteenth century, a new actor steps on the stage. Every country will cherish its own choice of hero, but all will emphatically agree that the newcomer is the villain of the piece. His name is Prussia and here are the opening lines of the part he is to play.

In 1648, the Peace of Westphalia, which brought the Thirty Years' War to an end, left the innumerable States which composed the Holy Roman, or German, Empire independent of the nominal authority of the Habsburg Austrian Emperor. They were free to go their own way, and none went so far as Brandenburg, the foundation-state of the Prussia that was to be.

EXTENDING PRUSSIA'S FRONTIERS

In the early fifteenth century, Brandenburg came into the possession of the Hohenzollerns. This obscure family had the knack of adding to its domains " steadily, steadily, bit by bit ". One of its more considerable early " bits " was East Prussia, a dukedom which the Brandenburg Hohenzollerns acquired in 1618. All Prussia, East and West, was originally a Slav country which later had been settled by German colonists and still later passed under the sovereignty of Poland. East Prussia, accordingly, was held by the Hohenzollerns as a duchy under Polish overlordship. West Prussia, which separated East Prussia from Brandenburg, remained under direct Polish rule.

ELECTOR OF BRANDENBURG

Of these and other beginnings Frederick William, the Great Elector of Brandenburg from 1640 to 1688, made much. He created a powerful army and a rigorous, efficient system of administration, ruling his subjects with the iron hand of an autocrat. Largely through his shrewd manoeuvres at the end of the Thirty Years' War, East Pomerania, on the Baltic Sea, together with some lesser " bits " were added to his domains. He likewise threw off the Polish overlordship of East Prussia. Altogether he may be said to have prepared the way for the rise of the autocratic and military state of Prussia whose career was to be of such calamitous import to Europe in the days to come.

ELEVATION TO MONARCHY

The most notable performance of the Great Elector's successor was to elevate his line to royal dignity. In 1701, he crowned himself King Frederick I of Prussia. Twelve years later the father of Frederick the Great stepped to the throne. King Frederick William I was a man of simple and honest character with a strong religious sense of duty to his kingdom. Yet the manner in which he performed that obligation revealed him as a boorish, miserly, and tyrannical drill-sergeant. His pride was centred in the immensely increased army which he built up and drilled and bullied into a perfect war-machine. For his Guards he collected—when needful, by kidnapping— tall and stalwart recruits from all over Europe and from them formed a regiment of giants. In his close-fisted thrift he cut down all extravagant spending, on clothes, servants and even funerals, so as to fill his coffers. In fact he made the state a military barracks supported on the twin pillars of the army and the treasure chest. So he developed the hateful military caste of the harsh and arrogant jack-booted Prussian gentry with their blind devotion to king and fatherland.

Frederick William's sorest trial was his undersized,

In the hope that his son, Frederick II (the Great), would be a hardy soldier, Frederick I had the boy educated in a rigorous, military manner.

Frederick II, humanist and scholar of considerable merit, had a great admiration for Voltaire, whom he invited to his villa, Sans-Souci.

son Frederick. To the old martinet's wrathful disgust, his heir was less interested in statecraft than in books and music—of all things! The young Frederick was strongly attracted by the polished literature and enlightened philosophy of the French, with their disturbing new claims for freedom of thought about religion and social rights and institutions. He himself wrote numerous works on history and politics, as well as on military subjects. After his succession to the throne in 1740, Frederick II's taste for culture never failed, but the competing responsibilities of kingship increasingly monopolised his interest and activities. He was a cool-headed and cynical character with few illusions about the goodness of human nature or the obligations of religion and morality in political concerns. Though he was the absolute master of the state, he regarded himself as its first servant, whose whole duty lay in advancing its power and welfare. Service and duty—these were the old Prussian ideals, the saving features of the unamiable Prussian character. The first years of Frederick's arduous and stormy reign were to reveal the character of the man to a startled Europe.

THE AUSTRIAN SUCCESSION

The Emperor Charles VI, who had recently died, had no son to succeed to his vast Habsburg dominions in Austria, Hungary, Bohemia and the Netherlands. Accordingly, to prevent the general scramble of a European war, he had persuaded the leading powers, including Britain, to concur in the descent of his domains to his young daughter, Maria Theresa. But on his death most of these promises proved worthless, for all too many of the powers harboured hopes of securing territorial gains by breaking them. In the ensuing war of the Austrian Succession the cool and calculating Frederick showed himself quick on the draw. Regardless of his plighted word, and deaf to the call of chivalry towards a young and inexperienced queen, he quietly set his machine-drilled armies a-marching and seized her province of Silesia. Whereupon France, her mouth watering for the Austrian Netherlands on her north-eastern borders, took the lead in a coalition against the distracted queen. In the end the

Frederick's taste for culture led to a dislike of the German language and a love for everything French. He wrote verse and prose in French.

The outstanding military skill of Frederick became evident during the Silesian war. The well-disciplined Prussian army became a perfect instrument of war in the hands of this man of ambition.

Hohenzollerns gained another " bit ", for the unscrupulous Frederick kept stolen Silesia. But, with Britain entering the lists to support Austria and check France, the war closed in 1748 with little further change.

Maria Theresa, however, was determined to recover her lost province. Her efforts to do so were accompanied by a remarkable change of partners in the European game of maintaining the balance of power. Austria had been trying for eight years to make an alliance with France, but without success. When Britain and Prussia signed a treaty of mutual defence with the object of protecting Hanover, France was left with no alternative but to come to terms with her age-old foe, Austria.

For a time, the German composer, Johann Sebastian Bach, was at the court of Frederick II. Frederick often played alongside the great composer.

THE SEVEN YEARS' WAR

So matters stood in 1756, the year of the outbreak of the

From 1756 to 1763, virtually the whole Continent was up in arms against Frederick. Although his army was sadly depleted by successive campaigns, Frederick's outstanding military skill enabled him to turn the Seven Years' War into a victory for Prussia.

Seven Years' War that was to involve all the European powers: Austria, France and Russia against England and Prussia (under Frederick the Great).

Our present concern is with Prussia's part in the conflict. And Prussia's concern was presently to escape annihilation by the ring of foes—France, Austria, Russia and Sweden—banded together to cripple her rising power. These were the years when Frederick, by his military genius and invincible resolution, earned from his people the title of " the Great ". In 1757, when it seemed that he must inevitably be crushed in the boa-constrictor coils his enemies were fastening on him, he struck the French and their allies a staggering blow in the battle of Rossbach and a month later routed the Austrians at Leuthen. For a time Britain aided him, too, with subsidies and troops, and by naval raids on France; but, in 1760, she withdrew her support. Frederick fought on doggedly, and his sadly-outnumbered forces won further astonishing successes. However, the overwhelming weight of his many antagonists nullified his victories. He suffered heavy defeats as well and Prussia was invaded and ravaged. The position of his decimated and war-battered troops, as they rallied round their indomitable captain, became desperate in the extreme.

PRUSSIA AS A POWER

But fortune favours the brave—even a brave thief—and in 1762 she gave another turn of her wheel. A new tsar, the half-witted Peter III, mounted the Russian throne. Peter idolised Frederick. He withdrew his armies from the field. And next year Maria Theresa gave up the exhausting fight. Prussia was saved at the eleventh hour. Frederick kept Silesia and kept it for good; but, for the rest, the years of incalculable bloodshed and suffering had been endured to little apparent purpose. They had, nonetheless, made one fact clear. Prussia, its military reputation assured, had become one of the great powers of Europe, the obvious rival to Austrian pretensions.

As for Frederick, the hero of his adoring people, he had saved his country from extinction and brought it glory and expansion, even if it was at terrible cost. He had begun his campaigns with a monstrous crime against the decencies of human conduct and definitely made Prussia the villain of the piece. Yet, if ever a fault can be atoned for by deathless constancy and resolution in the face of overwhelming odds, Frederick may hope for a charitable judgment of his offence. His less spectacular services to his country, in justice and administration, in finance and industry, were the expression of his abiding sense of duty to his people.

POLAND IS ANNEXED

Silesia did not satisfy Frederick's territorial appetite. There was that Polish province of West Prussia, tantalisingly separating East Prussia from the rest of his kingdom. If only that could be somehow gained . . .! Now Poland was an immense kingdom with a seething hotch-potch of races and creeds: Poles, Germans, Russians, Lithuanians and Jews; Catholics, Protestants, Orthodox Greek churchmen and again Jews. Possessing no aptitude for stable government, the country existed in a chronic condition of strife and turmoil. It was the obvious prey of its powerful and greedy neighbours, Russia, Prussia and Austria; and in 1772 they duly bore down on their victim, knife in hand, and hacked off a limb apiece from its living body. Prussia's share, of course, was the long-coveted West Prussia. Maria Theresa died in 1780 and Frederick the Great in 1786, but the vivisection of Poland went remorselessly on. In 1793, Russia and Prussia helped themselves to a second cut and two years later the whole trio of gluttons gobbled up what remained of the carcass. In what was one of the most shameless pieces of butchery in the bloodstained annals of Europe, Poland disappeared from the map.

Meantime events were occurring which drew the butchers' eyes westwards. In 1789, the French Revolution, which was to shake the thrones of Europe, had exploded with a roar.

RUSSIA OPENS A WINDOW

In the seventeenth century, Moscow was beginning to acquire a taste for culture from the foreign colony settled there. But Russia as a whole was still at the bottom of the European class in every aspect of civilised life, and was of little account in Continental politics. Her people were uneducated, her clergy slothful and backward. The refinements of social life hardly existed, for women were kept in strict seclusion. The manners of all classes were indescribably coarse and brutal. Drunkenness was a national vice, flogging a universal practice. Injustice, corruption and blatant bribery honeycombed the administration. Trade and commerce were hamstrung. Because of its long association with the Tatars and Constantinople, the imperial court was more Asiatic than European. And so things seemed likely to remain. Russia, clinging to her own barbaric ways and supersititions, was a stranger to civilised Western Europe.

Then came Peter the Great. In 1682, when he was a boy of ten, he could hardly be expected to take much interest in State affairs. But the delights of building and navigating ships and the fascination of the mechanics of war enthralled him. With other boys such enthusiasms might have led to nothing. But Peter was not as other boys: he was Tsar of Russia. The budding shipwright grew up to become the founder of the Russian navy. During these early years Peter gathered around him a band of close companions who, whilst indulging in hilarious schoolboy pranks and general high jinks, played with the utmost gravity at being grown-up soldiers and sailors.

In 1689, at the age of seventeen, Peter took to frequenting the foreign suburb of Moscow and began to absorb ideas. Soon he was taking his responsibilities more seriously. In 1695, he set out on a real war against the Turks on the Sea of Azov. Importing foreign artificers, and helping with his own imperial hands, he presently built a great fleet and won a brilliant victory. Peter was thrilled. Meantime, however,

he had gone off on a tour to Germany, Holland and England to see what he could learn about their ways. His busy mind was interested in everything and he had no royal scruples about working as a common dockyard labourer to gain practical experience. He became a Jack-of-all trades, from gunnery and shipbuilding to anatomy and engraving. He came back convinced that, if his country was ever to rise in the class, she must learn more from the West about the arts and sciences of civilised life, in war and peace. And, to open the lesson, he engaged a host of ships' captains, military instructors and other experts for service in Russia.

Some amusing scenes occurred after his return. As an indication of his westernising policy he forbade the almost religious fetish of wearing beards. To the horror of his court, he assembled his chief men before him and himself sheared off the offending facial growths.

After that he turned to a weightier matter. Russia's great need was an ice-free seaboard to enable her to develop industry and commerce and establish free communication with the great countries of Europe. Peter cast his eye longingly on the Baltic Sea: but those waters were controlled by Sweden. The Swedes, indeed, had been cutting quite a figure in Europe since the time of Gustavus Adolphus, and among their conquests were the Russian Baltic provinces. Peter, allying himself with Denmark and Poland, fought the Swedes from 1700 to 1721 and created a new standing army in the process. The end of the war left Livonia, Esthonia and other provinces in his hands. It also marked the finish of Sweden's little flutter as a major power. Meantime, in 1703, the victor had founded St. Petersburg, his "window to Europe", which soon afterwards became the capital city. His triumphs made an immense impression in Europe. Russia was no longer of little account.

During the years of fighting Peter completely reorganised the country's administrative system and expanded its indus-

From an early age, Peter the Great built his own boats.

Peter himself cut the long beards of the chief boyars.

After the death of Peter III in 1762, Catherine was crowned Empress of all the Russias.

tries and communications. Foreign institutions were copied. Officials were trained under his watchful eyes. He founded Russia's first museum and himself edited her first newspaper. He reformed the alphabet and the calendar. He reformed the Orthodox Church too—by cutting off its head: that is, by abolishing the Patriarch in favour of a Holy Synod or Council. Peter would have no " popes " in Russia to challenge his sovereign powers. His reforms had important effects on the class system. All the upper classes were combined in one comprehensive order of " gentry ", divided into various grades of nobility. Peter required them all to perform services, military or civil, to the State; but they weren't long in shuffling out of those obligations.

Notwithstanding all he achieved, Peter's greatness was not of the highest order. It was imperial power and prestige that he sought. He contributed little to the social, moral or cultural advancement of his subjects. His great gifts were the perception of his people's need to take lessons from the civilised West and the boundless energy by which he drove them into doing it. Russia was sunk in the sluggard's sleep: Peter was the strident alarm clock that woke her. Apart from this, he was a typically barbarous Russian, violent in manner and shocking in manners. He was a giant in strength and stature, standing 6 feet 6 inches high, and his passions and vices, his frolics and buffooneries, were on the same colossal scale.

Peter's forward impulse lived on after his death in 1725. His ideas found their most enthusiastic advocate in Catherine II (another so-called " Great "), who reigned from 1762 to 1796. Catherine's clever mind was aglow with the notion of making her rule outstanding in social refinement, literary culture and political power. She wrote, read and worked hard and corresponded with the foremost monarchs and men of letters of Europe. She planned to make a new and more humane code of laws and summoned a great elective assembly to discuss them. But, when the gentry found them too advanced for their liking, she weakly abandoned the project. That she left the miseries of the serfs unrelieved is evident from the repeated revolts that broke out and the savagery with which they were repressed. One useful reform, however, she did effect. For the first time in its history the country was given a system of district administration which served to coach the gentry in the work of local justice and self-

Catherine II of Russia was born Princess Sophia Augusta Frederica of Anhalt-Zerbst, in Germany.

government. But, when the French Revolution of 1789 began to rock the thrones of Europe, she definitely threw her progressive ideas overboard.

Catherine's skilful foreign policy gained Russia a notable increase in territory and prestige and brought her into many intimate contacts with the great Western powers. She cherished two aims. In the West she planned to recover from Poland the Russian-speaking Lithuanian provinces which had been wrested from Russia in the fourteenth century. In the South she dreamed of establishing her power on the Black Sea, controlling Constantinople and the straits leading to the open waters of the Mediterranean, and ejecting the Moslem Turks from Europe. The first aim, and more also, was achieved when Poland was heartlessly carved up and divided between Russia, Prussia and Austria. The southern dream was rather too much of a day-dream to be realised, but Catherine's wars with Turkey did win her the Crimea and a firm footing on the Black Sea, besides giving her the right to speak up for Christians under Turkish rule.

THE STORY OF SCOTLAND

There is no clear record of the first thousand years of Scottish history, but enough is known to enable us to trace in outline the growth of the ancient nation of Scots.

Three centuries before the birth of Christ the whole island of Britain was occupied by people who had come, originally, from the area of the Black Sea, and who spoke the Celtic language. At one time their civilisation had stretched from Ireland and Spain, eastwards to the Rhine, the Danube and the Alps; then the Romans, mainly by superior organisation, conquered them in continental Europe. In A.D. 43, the conquerors turned their attention to Britain.

All the Celtic tribes of Britain painted or tattooed themselves, and the proud Romans, amused by such barbarities, called them the *Picti*, or painted people. *Britanni* and *Britonnes* were Latin names for the Celts, which meant the People of the Designs.

ROMAN ADVANCE CHECKED

The highly trained, well equipped Roman Legions quickly overran the Celts of south-east England, exploiting the disunity among the tribes, who were always quarrelling among themselves. In Yorkshire, and the area of the Pennines, resistance was tougher, and the advance slowed down. Further north, beyond the rivers Forth and Clyde, the offensive was brought to a standstill, for there the Legions were faced by a solid confederacy of Celtic tribes, led by the Caledonians who occupied the land between the Forth and the Moray Firth.

The strongest fortifications in the Roman Empire were built in the land of the Caledonians, the men who never crouched in bondage. Their name still lives in place-names like Kirkcaldy, Dunkeld, and the sky-reaching peak of Schiehallion in Perthshire.

All the prowess of the Legions failed to subdue Scotland. The 9th Legion was annihilated there. The Roman historian Tacitus has recorded that the Roman Army, under the command of Julius Agricola, fought a pitched battle against a Celtic army of 30,000 men at Mons Graupius in September 84, and defeated them. The battle of Mons Graupius (probably Meikle Balloch Hill, near Keith, in Banffshire) was decisive. Despite the Roman claims of victory, Mons Graupius was their final effort at conquest. Thereafter they went over to the defensive.

They abandoned the fortress they had built at Inchtuthill, near Perth, and withdrew from their outposts. Then, about the year 122, the Emperor Hadrian built a massive wall from the Tyne to the Solway as a barrier against the unconquered Celts of the north. South of the wall, in the province called Britannia by the Romans, the Celts had been more or less subdued. They had given up their old habits and adopted Roman ways. The free Celts of Scotland, on the other hand, retained their traditions, including the tattooing, and were referred to as *Picti*, or Picts.

But the frontier was far from settled, so about A.D. 140 the Romans built another wall, from Forth to Clyde, as a forward defence line against the raiding Picts. This was the wall of Antonine. Still there were revolts and unrest, culminating in the great punitive expedition by the Emperor Septimus Severus in A.D. 209, which penetrated as far as the Moray Firth. After that the frontier area quietened down, the " frontier " being a broad, fluid zone based on Hadrian's Wall. To keep the peace, the Romans made treaties with certain tribes in the area between the walls, right up to the Forth-Clyde line. Some trading also took place, but the Pax Romana was an uneasy one.

CONVERSION TO CHRISTIANITY

Christianity was introduced. By the time the Roman Empire became officially Christian, in the 4th century, the Christian tribes living between the two walls tended to join forces with the Romanised Christians of the province of Britannia against the pagan Picts of the north. In 397, St. Ninian takes the stage, north of the Solway, as bishop at Whithorn. He was a local man, of the Novantae tribe, but trained at Rome. He did missionary work among the southern Picts, and extended his influence, through St. Patrick, to Ireland.

The Scots are first recorded in A.D. 360, as raiders of the Christian province of Britannia, like the pagan Picts and Saxons. (The Saxons, from about 450, occupied south-east England, while the Angles, their German kindred, spread from the Humber to the Forth).

The Scots were a Gaelic-speaking group from that part of Ulster known as Dalriada, but it is possible that they were, originally, Pictish colonists from Scotland and northern England. The Scots and Pictish languages had, however, grown apart. From Cornwall and Wales up to the Clyde the Celtic dialect was of Welsh type, and the Picts further north seem to have spoken a dialect nearer to Welsh than to Gaelic.

About the year 500, the Scots from Ulster were granted land in Argyll as vassals of the Picts. Then, in 563, St. Columba, who was an Ulster Gael, was given the Argyll island of Iona as a missionary base by Brude, High King of the Picts.

In the Celtic tongue, the land of the Picts was called *Alba*, as it still is in Gaelic. The Welsh call Scotland *Alban*, which probably means the Land of the Alps, or Bens. The Picts of Alba were organised in a number of sub-kingdoms under one High King, in much the same way as the Germanic tribes (Saxons, Bavarians and others) had their local princes who elected the Holy Roman Emperor of the German Folk.

The Scots sub-kings of Argyll, as vassals, fitted into the Pictish system. St. Columba converted the Pictish High King Brude to Christianity. The saint, and his Iona community, exerted such influence that the Anglic kingdom of Northumbria was also converted to Christianity. The spread of the Gaelic language in Scotland was also due to the influence of Columba and the Iona community.

The Angles of Northumbria, who had been troublesome to the Picts of Scotland for some time, became of little account after 685 when they were defeated in battle at Nechtansmere in Angus. But a new threat arose about the year 800, with Viking invasions from Norway and Denmark. The Vikings subdued much of England and Ireland, and took from Alba

About the end of the eighth century, the Vikings began to visit Scotland, but their first serious attacks began in the first half of the ninth century, culminating in an important alliance between Scots and Norsemen in 937.

the Shetland, Orkney and Western Isles, as well as areas of the north and west mainland.

THREAT FROM THE NORTHMEN

In the struggles against the Vikings, the Scots sub-kings of Argyll and the Iona community were in the front line of Celtic resistance. Kenneth Macalpin, a Scots sub-king, became High King of the Picts in 843. He was not the first Scots sub-king from Argyll to take this title, but after him the succession stayed in his family, and the High Kings of Alba became known as Scots, instead of Picts. Alba became Scotland, although, at first it was known as such only down to the Forth-Clyde line.

To the south and west of this line lay the Brittonic kingdom of Strathclyde and Cumbria, with its capital at Dunbarton. This kingdom extended from Clach nam Breatann (Britons' Stone) in Glen Falloch, north of Loch Lomond, to the Rere Cross on Stainmore in the North Riding of Yorkshire. As late as the year 1136, this southern limit was recognised by King Stephen of England as the frontier of Scotland.

The Scots kings controlled Strathclyde and Cumbria from 908, and formally annexed it in 1018. In 973, the Anglic province of Lothian, stretching from Tweed to Forth, was ceded to Kenneth II by King Edgar of England. The Germanic inhabitants of this province were not displaced, but Gaelic-speaking Scots moved in, and reached the Tweed, as place-names show. At the battle of Carham, in 1018, Malcolm II of Scotland defeated an English army under King Canute, and thus confirmed Scotland's frontier as the Tweed.

Although Scotland's frontier on the west was moved north to Solway and Esk in 1157 (formally ratified in 1237), the consolidation of the centuries-old Celtic kingdom into what we now know as Scotland took place in 1018. A few Norse groups still persisted in northern and western islands, and in outlying parts of the mainland like Kintyre and Galloway; but the kingdom of Scotland had taken shape. Its kings were enthroned at Scone, on the Tay, in the country of the Caledonians, the leaders of Pictish resistance against the Romans in A.D. 84.

The successive pressures of Romans, Angles, Danes and Vikings had moulded the people into a nation, and the sub-

kingdoms into one kingdom. The influence of Christianity, through such leaders as Ninian and Columba, kept it in touch with the general civilisation of Europe.

At this stage in their history the Celtic Scots were pastoralists; their husbandry was mainly cattle husbandry, but they did grow grain. The country was still largely afforested, but the fertile straths were cultivated. The people were convivial and musical, fond of heroic and satirical poetry, and epic tales. They had their own legal code. They were good at metalwork, enamel work, carpentry, and complicated stone-carving. The Norse and Anglic minorities intermarried with the Celtic majority, and this led to a mixture of cultures. Especially influential were royal personages and their marriages.

After the death of Malcolm II in 1034, the succession was in dispute. Under the old Celtic system of succession, the sub-king of Moray, named Macbeth, had a better claim than Malcolm II's grandson Duncan who was, in any case, an incompetent. By general consent, Macbeth became king in 1040.

Macbeth proved to be a good king. Shakespeare's play of the name is based on misinformation. The king had an international outlook. He visited Rome with Thorfinn, the Norse Earl of Orkney, and was the only Scottish king to do so. He employed a bodyguard of Norman cavalry, then the most modern troops in Europe, who sacrificed themselves for him resisting the invasion of Malcolm III, grandson of Duncan I. Malcolm was nicknamed Canmore, meaning Great Head.

As a refugee, the young Malcolm Canmore had lived in Northumbria with Earl Siward, his Danish uncle by marriage, and in the south of England at the court of Edward the Confessor. At Edward's court, Malcolm came under strong Norman influence; the king's mother was Emma of Normandy.

At this time the Normans were the leading European exponents of efficiency in government, civil and religious. Originally Vikings from Scandinavia, they had acquired a duchy in France, bringing their northern vigour to bear on the Greco-Roman civilisation of the Church. When Malcolm became king of Scots he brought in Norman efficiency experts to help his royal government. Besides being great systematisers in church and law, the Normans made good soldiers. They had better horses than the old-fashioned Celtic cavalry, and were tactically superior.

Malcolm III, about 1069, married the queen who was to become St. Margaret of Scotland. She was born in Hungary —a princess of the exiled Anglo-Saxon royal family—and had been brought up by her great-uncle, the Saint-King Stephen, who converted the Magyars to Christianity. From there she went to the Normanised court of Edward the Confessor, and after the Norman conquest of England in 1066 she came to Scotland.

Malcolm and Margaret, and their sons Edgar (1097-1107), Alexander I (1107-1124), and David I (1124-1153), modernised the kingdom, promoting new religious orders and establishing burghs. The king's burghs, modelled on the French, were fortified trading posts, which monopolised trade in their localities. By 1286, there were 35 royal burghs, and a further 13 belonging to bishops, abbots and nobles. The convention of royal burghs, which still meets, was a sort of economic parliament.

David I started a Scots coinage, but foreign money also circulated. More decisive for economic and cultural advance were the new religious foundations. The Celtic monastic movements of Ninian and Columba were by now spent forces, and the pious rulers replaced them with new vital movements which were based mainly on France.

RELIGION IN SCOTLAND

At Melrose, Newbattle, Dundrennan, and Kinloss, the Cistercians set the example of colonising wilderness, draining marshland for cropping, and breeding sheep for the wool trade with Flanders. Augustinian Canons at Scone, St. Andrews, Holyrood and Jedburgh stimulated a taste for more splendid ritual and comfortable living. The learned Benedictines had great houses, notably at Dunfermline where the royal family were buried. Other foundations were for Premonstratensians, Arrouasians, Cluniacs, Templars, and Hospitallers: all of them local branches of great international groupings.

In this religious revival dioceses were organised for bishops, some of them having magnificent cathedrals like St. Andrews, Glasgow, Aberdeen, Moray, Dunkeld, Dunblane, Brechin, Whithorn, Ross, Caithness and Argyll. Although it contained some clergy of French and English stock, the Church of Scotland was a fiercely patriotic body, and, in 1192, Pope Celestine III recognised it as " a separate daughter of the Apostolic See ", in no way subject to any archbishop in England.

NOBILITY

The sons of Malcolm Canmore, especially David I, modified the old Celtic feudal system of land-ownership and government in the direction of that evolved in France and Norman England. Titles to land were now recorded in written charters instead of being witnessed by large numbers of people at oral proceedings. The local sub-kings were renamed earls, and other Celtic offices and obligations were redesignated. Thus the Gaelic maor and toiseach gave place to a sheriff, operating from a castle commanded by a constable, and responsible for local defence, collection of royal revenue, registration of land-ownership, enforcement of payments due to the Church, and many other duties.

Some of the leading families of medieval Scotland were of Norman origin: the Bruces of Annandale; the FitzAllans, afterwards Stewarts, who held great lands in Renfrewshire; the Lindsays, from Lindsey in Lincolnshire; the Grahams from Grantham; the Ramsays from Ramsay in Huntingdonshire. The founders of these families in Scotland were friends of David I, who held the earldom of Huntingdon in right of his wife. But it is doubtful if all the Norman and other foreign officials introduced at this period received together as much as one tenth of the land of Scotland. Not one of them was made an earl.

The kingdom remained Celtic. The inauguration of the kings at Scone continued according to Celtic custom—a sennachie reciting the royal pedigree in Gaelic. The old Celtic Council of the Seven Earls persisted almost to 1300, though an assembly called by the French name *parliament* is attested a century earlier. Landowners had, of course, feudal rights and duties; but legalistic feudalism was much modified in practice by the traditional kinship groupings of the old Celtic clan system. Serfdom was on a small scale and local, and died out early as compared with the rest of Europe.

The marriage between Malcolm III, called Canmore, and Margaret, sister of Edgar Atheling, took place in 1069.

To enable them to cope better with aggressions by the Norman conquerors of England, the Scots kings moved their capital to Edinburgh, where the language of the Angles was in use. This spread through the burghs and the monasteries, and became the northern form known as Scots, or Broad Scots: the language in which Robert Burns and Sir Walter Scott were to write some of their finest work. The earliest major poem in Scots was written by Archdeacon John Barbour of Aberdeen about King Robert Bruce, who championed the nation's freedom against Edward I of England.

In 1286, King Alexander III was killed when his horse fell over a cliff in the dark. He was succeeded by his infant grand-daughter Margaret of Norway, who died in 1290. On her death, there were thirteen claimants to the throne. By ancient Celtic usage the best claim was that of old Robert Bruce of Annandale. His nearest rival was John Balliol. The Council of the Seven Earls decided for Bruce, but, when civil war was threatened, the Bishop of St. Andrews appealed for the arbitration of Edward I of England. Ignoring Celtic tradition, and basing his judgment on the European system of primogeniture, Edward decided for Balliol, who was installed as King of Scots in 1292.

Edward I soon began to assert claims of English overlordship, and tried to conscript Scots for a war with France in 1295. The Scots promptly renewed their Auld Alliance with France, and raided England. Edward came with an army, defeated Balliol in the spring of 1296, and marched as far as Elgin. He secured the homage of a number of Scots landowners. But, as soon as his back was turned, the struggle was resumed by Robert Wishart, the Bishop of Glasgow, and James Stewart, the hereditary steward of the kingdom.

One of Stewart's vassals was Sir Malcolm Wallace of Elderslie, whose second son, Sir William Wallace, proved a most inspiring leader. With young Sir Andrew Moray, who came with forces from the area of the Moray Firth, Wallace severely defeated an English army at Stirling Brig (1297). Then he suffered heavily in a holding action at Falkirk (July 1298) against Edward I in person.

After Falkirk, Wallace resigned his office of guardian, or regent, to two nobles: Robert Bruce, Earl of Carrick, in right of his mother, and John Comyn of Badenoch, a nephew of the exiled king John Balliol. Both had claims to the throne. For some years resistance was carried on by a varying syndicate of nobles and bishops, especially Wishart of Glasgow and Lamberton of St. Andrews; but in 1304 they compromised with Edward, waiting for him to die.

Although generally conciliatory at this stage, Edward was implacable towards Wallace, who was hanged, drawn and quartered in London on 23rd August, 1305.

But Wallace's cause was immediately revived by Bishops Wishart and Lamberton, and by the Stewarts and Bruces. Robert Bruce, seeking to win the support of John Comyn, his former colleague in the guardianship, met him in the cloister of the Franciscan convent at Dumfries on 10th February, 1306. Unfortunately they quarrelled, and Bruce stabbed Comyn. Friends of Bruce ran in and killed the wounded man. The resulting feud between Bruce and the Comyn party impaired the Scottish war effort, but Bruce had the people, the church and most of the nobles behind him, and learned how to make the best of his chances.

At Bannockburn, near Stirling, Bruce smashed a superior English army, led by Edward II, in June, 1314. He repeatedly raided northern England. He had his brother Edward Bruce made King of Ireland (1317-1318). In 1328, Edward III of England recognised the full separate sovereignty of Scotland by the Treaty of Northampton. Bruce died a year later. Scotland never had so good a king again.

The people of Scotland were prevented from reaping the full benefit of independence by a number of unfortunate factors, including fatal accidents to the better monarchs. Between 1377 and 1580, Scotland spent 52 years campaigning against a succession of aggressive English kings. For 89 years between 1406 and 1587 the country was run by cliques of courtiers because the monarchs were minors. Yet, despite all these drawbacks, the old-established nation made progress.

The native Scots Parliament was, for its period, an efficient body. Indeed, despite the radical weeding-out process in 1908, there remain in force to-day no fewer than 276 Acts of the Scots Parliament, passed between the years 1424 and 1707. Sir Archibald Alison, a trained lawyer and a historian of Europe, has written of the Scots Parliament: " The early precocity of Scotland in legislative wisdom, and the extraordinary provisions made by its native Parliament in remote periods, not only for the well-being of the people, but the coercion alike of regal tyranny and aristocratic oppression, and the instruction, relief and security of the poorer classes, is one of the most remarkable facts in the whole history of modern Europe ".

ALLIANCES WITH EUROPE

The Auld Alliance with France was a dominant cultural factor. Economically, too, Scotland had strong links with Flanders and the Baltic lands. Indicative of the international connections are the royal marriages of James II's reign. James II (1437-1460) married Mary of Guelders, a Flemish princess. His sister Margaret married the Dauphin of France, afterwards Louis XI; Isabella married the Duke of Britanny; Eleanor married Sigismund of Tirol, Duke of Austria; Mary married the Count of Grandpre in the Netherlands; Annabella married the heir of the Duke of Savoy. His son, James III (1460-1488), married Margaret of Denmark.

James IV (1488-1513) married Margaret Tudor, sister of Henry VIII of England, by which marriage the Stewarts inherited the English throne in 1603. James V (1513-1542),

Sir William Wallace was captured near Glasgow and taken to London where he was hanged, drawn and quartered.

Lord Darnley and fellow conspirators forced their way into the apartments of Mary, and murdered David Rizzio.

by his second marriage to Mary of Guise, was the father of the ill-fated Mary, Queen of Scots (1542-1567) whose first marriage was to Francis II of France. Her son, by her second husband, Lord Darnley, became James VI and I in 1603.

Scotland's international status, by the time of Wallace and Bruce, was already obvious from the reputation of such intellectuals as Duns Scotus and Michael Scott. Native universities were founded: St. Andrews in 1412, Glasgow in 1449, King's College, Aberdeen in 1494, Edinburgh in 1582, and Marischal College, Aberdeen in 1593. James IV had his sons tutored in Italy by Erasmus, the leading scholar of the age.

James V reorganised Scots law under a College of Justice, on an Italian model. James I (1406-1437) had been an accomplished poet in Scots, and a distinguished series of Scots makars flourished in the 15th and 16th centuries. Scots prose began to develop with the introduction of the printing press in 1508. The court Scots speech was employed by Parliament and the Law, as well as in commerce and familiar intercourse outside the Gaelic areas (which still covered about half Scotland).

Profound changes were caused by the local impact of the European religious revolution known as the Protestant Reformation. In this movement, two different tendencies converged: the earnest desire of idealists to reform the medieval Church according to their interpretation of the Word of God in the Bible (now made more generally available through the printing press), and the greed of landowners eager to seize the lands of the Church.

In Scotland about one third of the country's 30,000 square miles were owned by the clergy, who numbered about 3,000 in a population of about half a million. In neighbouring England, Henry VIII was seizing the monastery lands for himself, or for the upstart careerists backing his upstart Tudor dynasty. He encouraged his nephew James V to do the same in Scotland. But the Scots king remained loyal to the Roman Church and the French alliance.

War followed, and English armies devastated some of the chief Abbeys on the Scottish Borders, and elsewhere. Scotland was divided between Protestants backed by England, and Catholics backed by France, until the death of the queen-regent, Mary of Guise, in June 1560. Then the Protestants gained control, and in August, 1560, the Scots Parliament passed an Act repudiating the authority of the Pope, prohibiting the Mass, and condemning any doctrine or practice contrary to a Confession of Faith drawn up by a group of ministers led by John Knox.

Very soon, despite Knox's protests, two thirds of the Church lands were appropriated by nobles and lairds. The young Queen Mary Stuart, widow of Francis II of France, returned to Scotland in 1561. She was not yet 19. For six years she tried to cope with the new Protestant revolution. She married her Catholic cousin Henry Stewart, Lord Darnley, but quarrelled with him. On 9th February, 1567, he was strangled and his lodging blown up. The murderer was thought to have been the Earl of Bothwell, and this was the man Mary married three months later. Public opinion turned against her, and she abdicated on 24th July of that same year.

In 1568, after escaping from prison, she was defeated at the battle of Langside, and fled to seek asylum in England with her Protestant cousin Elizabeth Tudor. Elizabeth confined her in various English castles, and finally had her executed in 1587, on the ground that her prisoner was a troublesome focus of Catholic plots abetted by Spain.

Mary's son, James VI, had been brought up a Protestant. During the king's minority Andrew Melville had the Kirk established on a Presbyterian basis by the General Assembly at Dundee in 1581. Its theology was borrowed mainly from the French lawyer, John Calvin, who worked from a base in Geneva. England now became the chief political ally of the new Scottish Establishment, and English gained currency through the availability of the Bible in that language, which Scots could understand although they did not speak it. But the old cultural connections with France, now half Protestant, continued for another century.

Under the Presbyterian system the Church of Scotland was governed, at parish level, by a Kirk Session consisting of the minister and elders; by Presbyteries which ruled groups of parishes; by Synods which regulated groups of Presbyteries; and by a General Assembly. This form of Church government seemed too democratic and republican to James VI, and he took steps to establish Episcopacy, that is government by bishops and archbishops. After his accession to the English throne in 1603, the king's greater patronage enabled him to get the necessary Acts through the Scots Parliament.

The reign of Charles I saw the outbreak of the First Civil War (1642).

His son Charles I, who succeeded him in 1625, was a sincere Episcopalian, but less tactful than his father. He at once made enemies of the nobles and lairds by revoking all grants of church lands made by the Crown in the previous two generations. At his Scottish coronation in 1633 he tried to bribe the landowners with peerages, in the hope that they would give over land to his bishops. They accepted his peerages, but ganged up against him in the so-called National Covenant of 1638, which was a restatement of a Covenant against Popery signed in 1581.

At this time thousands of Scots soldiers of fortune were fighting in the Thirty Years' War of religion in Europe, and many of them signed up with the Covenanters. In 1638, the General Assembly re-established Presbyterianism. Charles tried to coerce the Scots, who occupied Newcastle-upon-Tyne, and cut off London's coal supply. This encouraged the English Parliament to resist the king's arbitrary rule. Charles came to Scotland and agreed to the Scots' terms, which were the establishment of Presbyterianism, and selection of the Scots Privy Council and State Officials in consultation with the Scots Parliament. This is the germ of that constitutional monarchy which is now practised in Great Britain under the Cabinet system.

Returning to England, Charles I started to fight Parliament there in 1642. At first he won battles. The English Parliament therefore negotiated with the Scots Parliament for armed support, and signed a Treaty in 1643 called The Solemn League and Covenant, in which they undertook to establish Presbyterianism in England and Ireland.

The Scots army, under Oliver Cromwell, helped to win the decisive battle of Marston Moor. Despite the brilliant campaigning of the Marquis of Montrose, with his Highland clansmen and Irish mercenaries, the cause of Charles was lost, and he surrendered to the Scots army in Nottinghamshire. On his refusal to accept the Covenants of 1638 and 1643, they handed him over to the English Parliament, on condition that no harm should befall him. Cromwell, however, had the king beheaded on 30th January, 1649.

Within a week the Scots Parliament proclaimed Charles II as king. They sent envoys to the Netherlands, inviting the king to sign the two Covenants. Charles II delayed, while Montrose, on his instructions, began a new campaign in Scotland. This was a failure, and Montrose was hanged as a traitor to the 1638 Covenant. Charles then signed the Covenants and sailed to Scotland. He was crowned at Scone on 1st January, 1651.

Charles's invading army was smashed by Cromwell at Worcester in September of that year. From then until his death in 1658, Cromwell ruled the whole island, and Ireland, dictatorially. In his Commonwealth Parliament, Scotland had 30 members out of a total of 460, and some of these were English officers of Cromwell's own storm troops.

The Parliamentary union was repealed on the restoration of Charles II in 1660. Charles also repudiated the two Covenants and restored Episcopacy. The Episcopalians started fining people for not attending their services. Covenanters held armed mass meetings, called conventicles, on the moors. Feelings were bitter when James VII and II, a devout Catholic, succeeded in 1685. Hundreds of Covenanters were sent to America as slaves. Repression was sometimes severe, and excesses were committed by both sides.

At the end of 1688, some English magnates invited Protestant William of Orange to be king. By then, James's government in Scotland had few friends, and he fled to France. John Graeme of Claverhouse struck for the king, but was killed in the hour of his overwhelming victory at Killiecrankie on 27th July, 1689, and the rising was over. The Scots Parliament restored Presbyterianism, which remains the religious Establishment of Scotland under the Union of Parliaments, made in 1707.

The motives which brought about the Parliamentary Union of 1707 were mixed: partly religious and political, partly commercial.

Queen Anne (1702-1714) was the last Protestant sovereign of the Stuart line. The problem of the royal succession became acute when she died leaving no healthy heir. Her half-brother James, the son of James VII and II, was a Catholic, and backed by French imperialism which was, at that time, a terrorist system under Louis XIV. Majority opinion in Scotland and England favoured succession by the Protestant Elector of Hanover, the future George I, whose mother, the Electress Sophia, was the daughter of James VI and I.

Commercially, Scotland had suffered from the religious wars, and a series of bad harvests. Her trade in France and Flanders had been almost lost because of Louis XIV's wars. The trading venture on the Isthmus of Panama, sponsored by the Scots Parliament, had been sabotaged by William of Orange and his rich London backers, and adversely affected by disease and accident. The morale of the Scots capitalist class was low, and many minds began to warm to the idea of sharing in England's growing overseas monopolies and plantations.

THE UNION OF THE CROWNS

After prolonged debates the Scots Parliament accepted the Articles of Union in 1706, although they would have preferred a federal union under which a Scots Parliament would have been retained for certain spheres of government.

The Scots Law and Law Courts, the Scottish Presbyterian Church, the rights of the Royal Burghs, and certain private rights, were preserved under the Treaty. The United Kingdom came formally into being on 1st May, 1707. Since then, the Scottish nation has evolved without the complete self-government it had possessed for two thousand years, but individual Scots have continued to make distinguished contributions in countless fields all over the world.

The eighteenth century opens a distinctive chapter, almost a new book, in Britain's story. In the previous century, Englishmen had fought and suffered for two inspiring causes: the Protestant creed against the Catholic, and Parliament against royal despotism. Both these tremendous questions had now been substantially settled. The fires of religious and political passion had burned low. Men turned to less lofty and more practical affairs: the pursuit of worldly gain and the party strife of Whig and Tory at home; commerce and empire abroad.

The change in the character of the times is illustrated by a typical figure, Sir Robert Walpole. This coarse-mannered, good-humoured, unsentimental country squire headed the government for twenty-one years from 1721. His long and mainly peaceful " rule ", coupled with his financial genius, gave the country a healthful, if humdrum, breathing space between wars. But his cynical outlook and his corrupt parliamentary methods lowered the moral standards of public life.

With the change in the country's mood, men became more tolerant in religion. But they also grew lukewarm. The Church had lost its former vigour and left the mass of the people without spiritual uplift. However, from 1739 onwards, a powerful corrective appeared. John Wesley and his colleagues organised the Methodist movement. The passionate zeal and earnestness of Wesley's life-long crusade made the teachings of the Christian faith once more a living inspiration in daily life.

WHIG AND TORY

In the cockpit of politics and creed, Whigs and Tories fought each other with beak and spur. Tories and Whigs alike, of course, supported constitutional government by king and Parliament. But, in any contest for power between the two institutions, the Tories would generally side with the Crown, while the Whigs would defend the rights of Parliament. In religion, the Tories stood stoutly for the Anglican Church; the Whigs stood as staunchly for fair play for Nonconformists; and both held Roman Catholicism in horror. The land-owning country squires and the country parsons were mostly true-blue Tories. The wealthy merchants, the town tradesmen, and the general body of the Nonconformists supported the Whigs. The lords and the Anglican bishops were divided between the two camps.

Parliament itself stood for government by the property-owning classes. The mass of the people had no vote. The great aristocratic families formed the bulk of the governing class. They dominated the House of Lords and powerfully influenced the Commons. And, until late in the eighteenth century, everybody accepted this as right and proper. The elegant and cultured members of upper-class society were a superior breed of men. The lower orders " knew their place ".

The House of Commons—the focus of public affairs—was composed of upper- and middle-class members. The elections to it were very unequally representative and often scandalously corrupt. Many constituencies, containing only a handful of voters, returned as many members as the whole of Yorkshire or Devonshire. Peers and other local magnates controlled numerous " pocket " and " rotten " boroughs. Once elected, many members sold their support to the Crown, or the party in power, for pensions or offices of profit. Yet the Commons, despite their faults, could on occasions display a robustly independent and truly national spirit.

A FOREIGN KING

George I, Elector of Hanover, who begins our period, had at least one distinguishing feature. His accession in 1714 introduced the Hanoverian line from which our present sovereign descends. Otherwise he was a dull dog, a gross, plodding, awkward German with unprepossessing looks and very little in the way of personality. He couldn't speak English. He didn't understand or want to understand English politics. His one wish was to spend as much of the year as possible in his beloved Hanover.

George's deficiencies had some important consequences. In earlier times the government had been directed by the king with the advice of his Privy Council. Later, a smaller council, the germ of our modern Cabinet, was selected from it. The members were chosen, or dismissed, by the king, whose servants they were; and they might be men drawn from different political parties. But these conditions had been for some time changing. The smaller council was becoming more like the Cabinet of to-day, in which the members are the servants of Parliament, chosen by the leader of the party in power (the prime minister) from among his own followers. It was far from having reached this stage under George I, but that homesick monarch's frequent absences in Hanover, and his ignorance of English, accelerated the movement. He was only too pleased to resign the tedious burden of government work to his ministers while he

George I, Elector of Hanover, spoke no English, and left all administrative duties in Britain to his ministers.

himself played truant. A further consequence was that the more prominent of those ministers gradually began to usurp the place of the sovereign in the foreground of national affairs.

THE JACOBITES

The Whigs now came into power and they remained there for nearly half a century. The Tories were cold-shouldered because a great many of them still clung to the ancient doctrine of the divine right of hereditary royal succession and hankered, though indecisively, after the " legitimate " Stuart king, the Old Pretender, James II's son. The Whigs, on the other hand, stood for the supremacy of Parliament, which, by " the Glorious Revolution " of 1688, had gained control over the monarchy. The menace of the " Jacobites " —so called from *Jacobus*, the Latin form of James—became a reality in 1715. A rising broke out in the Highlands of Scotland and the north of England, but it quickly collapsed.

One of the few excitements of George I's dull reign, the South Sea Bubble, was fully in keeping with the commercial outlook of the times. In 1719, the South Sea Company, a prosperous trading venture, offered to take over the National Debt in return for certain commercial privileges. A wild rush to buy the company's shares followed. The market price of the £100 shares leaped to over £1,000. Then doubts began to arise concerning the company's true prospects. There was a rush to sell. The shares slumped; the bubble burst. A furious agitation against the company and the government arose. There had been bribery in high places. Before the commotion died down the government had fallen almost into the same condition as the bubble.

In 1727, George I died and his son succeeded him. George II was a fussy little man, but shrewd and straightforward, and brave of heart. In 1739, the first real break in the long peace of Walpole's rule occurred. Spain had granted Britain limited trading facilities in the West Indies. The British traders presently began to forget all about the limits and Spain got very angry. She caught one of the offenders, a Captain Jenkins, and, according to his story, sliced off one of his ears. The mutilated Captain appeared before the House of Commons with the ear—or at all events *an* ear—in a bottle. It was like waving a red flag before a bull. The Commons lost their judgment in their indignation and Walpole was driven to declare war. The conflict was not over-successful and it helped to bring about Walpole's fall.

More than that, it was the prelude to a succession of wars of immeasurably greater import which arose out of national rivalry and self-preservation.

AUSTRIAN SUCCESSION

Spain was allied to France and soon Britain was at grips with both over the question of the succession of the Emperor Charles VI's daughter Maria Theresa to the vast Habsburg possessions in Austria, Hungary, Bohemia and the Netherlands. It is interesting to record that in the war of the Austrian Succession when Britain entered the arena on Maria's side, the fiery little King George fought like a lion in the battle of Dettingen. When the War ended, in 1748, Maria Theresa secured most of her rights, but had lost Silesia to Prussia.

Meantime, in Britain, another Jacobite rising had threatened the Hanoverian throne. Its hero was Charles Edward, Scotland's " Bonnie Prince Charlie ", the glamorous Young Pretender and son of the Old Pretender. Charles sailed over from France and landed in the West Highlands in August, 1745. He was a leader such as Scotland loved, brave, hardy and gallant and noble of character. Many Highlanders flocked to his standard with burning enthusiasm. In September, his forces were in Edinburgh. At Prestonpans he scattered an English army like chaff. Then began his sensational dash over the Border. Carlisle and Manchester were taken. In December, he stood in Derby. London had a bad attack of the jitters. But the bold invader had reached his farthest south. The English Jacobites failed to rise. Aid from France was barred by the British Navy. Sadly against his inclinations, Charles turned back.

He struck the English another blow at Falkirk, but it was his last considerable success. An army under George II's son, William, Duke of Cumberland, followed him into the hills, where his Highlanders insisted on retreating. And on Culloden Moor his forces were irreparably broken. For five months the prince was hunted from place to place, while

The Battle of Culloden in 1746, was the final death-knell to Jacobite hopes for a Stuart on the throne of Scotland.

the noble-hearted Flora Macdonald and other faithful adherents aided and shielded him. The British government had put a price of £30,000 on his head; but there were no Judases in the Highlands. At length, with all hope gone, the prince escaped back to France. The Stuart cause was laid in the dust for ever and Jacobitism in politics afterwards died a natural death.

The embers of the rising were stamped out with brutal ferocity. " Butcher " Cumberland made Culloden a massacre. The fugitives were hounded down. Scores of Jacobites were hanged or beheaded or exiled. Harsh measures were taken to prevent further outbreaks and to establish more settled conditions in the country.

The prevailing Highland clan system, romantic and picturesque though it might be, was a barbarous survival from the Middle Ages. Each clan formed one great family. Its members were bound to their hereditary chief by the closest ties of loyalty and devotion. He commanded his followers in war or foray. As judge and administrator of the law he had power over life and limb. The authority of the distant king of England was set at naught. Such primitive conditions were obviously out of place in a civilised realm, and they were now rigorously brought to an end. The warriors were disarmed; their native dress was prohibited— though later it was revived. The roots of the clan system were destroyed: the chiefs became commonplace landlords on the English pattern, and their judicial powers were abolished.

THE HIGHLAND CLEARANCES

The century from about 1745 onwards witnessed a remarkable transformation in all Scotland. We shall read presently of the fundamental changes wrought in England by new methods of agriculture and by the Industrial Revolution and its Machine Age. The same movements, bringing the same unparalleled but unequally shared prosperity, operated in Scotland. At the same time, with the spread of education and culture, aided by the new roads and railways, the gentle arts of civilisation came to embrace the whole country. Edinburgh, indeed, earned the proud title of " the Athens of the North ".

The wild Highland region, however, though it became more quiet and orderly, enjoyed only a Cinderella-like share in these benefits. It was no place for mechanised industries. The soil was poor and could not support the existing population. Many of the landlords, finding it more profitable to turn the glens into sheep-runs, callously evicted the tenants from their wretched little hillside crofts. It is calculated that, even before the War of American Independence of 1775, some 30,000 distressed Highlanders quitted their homeland and emigrated to the New World.

Yet, all in all, the period marks the fusion of Highlands and Lowlands in the making of modern Scotland. And the national talents and abilities of Scotland, as displayed in war and politics, in colonisation and industry, in the fields of thought and learning, have ever since added an asset of incalculable worth to the partnership business of Great Britain and its overseas empire.

To return to European affairs: the peace of 1748 was scarcely even a truce for Britain and France. In the competition for world trade and dominion they were natural rivals. (Holland, another strong candidate in the seventeenth century, was now left behind). During the war the two countries had been energetically jumping each other's claims in

Dissension among the Marathas forced the British, under the governorship of Lord Wellesley, to establish themselves as the paramount power in western India.

America and India. Now they continued their operations with undiminished gusto.

The British colonies in North America (with Georgia now added) stretched in a continuous line along the Atlantic coast. Behind them lay French Louisiana and Canada. The French had conceived a grandiose design. They would connect their two great possessions with a chain of forts and pin the British down to the coastland strip. And this they proceeded to do.

In India the principal British settlements were Bombay, Calcutta, and Madras. The French East India Company had its headquarters at Pondicherry in the Carnatic. The vast native Mogul empire was falling to pieces and its provincial nawabs and rajahs were setting up as independent rulers. The struggle between the French and British rivals took two forms: direct fighting, and manœuvres for winning over the local rulers. Robert Clive now appeared on the scene. At the age of nineteen he had arrived in India as a clerk to the East India Company. Presently he abandoned his uninteresting desk for the livelier field of action. In 1751-2 his astonishing dash and courage won and held Arcot, the capital of the Carnatic, against odds of twenty to one and restored the pro-British nawab to power.

THE YEAR OF VICTORIES

In 1756, the Seven Years' War broke out in Europe, and drew these widely spaced colonial hostilities into a single combination. Maria Theresa hungered for the recovery of Silesia and negotiated an alliance with France. Britain, already fighting the French, sided this time with Prussia. Spain came in later. As usual, Britain started badly. But then the island race produced a superb war-leader—as it does from time to time. William Pitt took charge of affairs. He was a strategist on the grand scale. His eye took in the four corners of the world of combat. His energy was terrific, his self-confidence boundless, his enthusiasm and burning oratory irresistible. He gave new vigour to the operations in Europe; but his eyes were fixed on the lands beyond the oceans. 1759 was " the year of victories ".

Guadeloupe, the richest sugar island in the West Indies, was taken. The battle of Minden brought imperishable

All French hopes of retaining a colony in Canada were squashed when Quebec, the key to Canada, fell to the dying hero, Wolfe.

glory to Britain's red-coats. The French navy was crippled in the battles of Lagos and Quiberon Bay. Quebec, the key to Canada, fell to the dauntless determination of the dying hero, General Wolfe. Then, in 1760, Montreal went the way of Quebec.

Meantime, in 1757, Clive in India had scored the sensational victory of Plassey. By 1760, he had, in effect, established British supremacy in Bengal, while other captains were happily prising out the French from the regions farther down the coast. Next year Pondicherry, the last French stronghold, surrendered.

To-day, we rightly take a more sober view of the " glories " of war. But no Briton can resist a surge of patriotic pride as he reads of the terms of the Treaty of Paris concluded in 1763, notwithstanding that Britain relinquished Guadeloupe and many of the other valuable prizes she had taken. France ceded to Britain, Canada, a portion of Louisiana lying east of the Mississippi, several West Indian islands and the West African settlement of Senegal, while Spain handed over Florida. France received back her trading settlements in India, but her political power was broken. French Louisiana west of the Mississippi was transferred to Spain. The treaty sounded the death knell of the French dreams of empire in North America and India and established the bases of Britain's imperial power.

There are, alas, some depressing footnotes to the story. One is that Maria Theresa never recovered Silesia. Another concerns Robert Clive.

CLIVE IN DISGRACE

From 1765 to 1767, Clive, as Governor for the East India Company, performed services of the highest order in reforming the greedy and oppressive administration of the Company's get-rich-quick officials. On his return to England his enemies accused him of accepting gifts of money from the Indian princes. The charge was true. But it was the commonly accepted practice of the Service, and Clive had availed himself of it to a far less extent than he might have done. In 1774, sick and distressed, he died by his own hand.

The third footnote we shall come to all too soon.

On George II's death, in 1760, his grandson had come to the throne. George III was a conscientious, courageous and well-meaning young man, but extremely narrow and obstinate in his views. Unlike the earlier Georges, he had been brought up as an Englishman, and he positively gloried in the name of Britain. He had made up his obstinate mind that he would play a more active part in the government than his predecessors had done. " George, be a king ", his mother had urged. And George resolved that he would. So he appointed his own ministers when he could and, largely by the familiar method of bribery, organised a party in the House of Commons on whose support he could depend. Among these " King's friends ", as they were named, the Tories were predominant, for the Tory party had by this time become reconciled to the Hanoverian succession.

TAXATION OF THE COLONIES

We now come to the most depressing of all the footnotes to the story of the Seven Years' War. The immense conflict had left Britain loaded with debt, much of which had been incurred in securing the American colonies from French designs. It was now necessary to garrison America for defence against the Red Indians and possible insurrections of the French settlers remaining in Canada. The mother-country thought her offspring should bear a small part of her financial burdens. Accordingly, in 1765 and 1767, several duties were imposed on them: a stamp duty on legal documents, and taxes on tea and a few other imports into the colonies. These levies aroused hot resentment and active opposition, being condemned as infringements of the colonists' rights of self-government. The settlers stood out mainly for the time-honoured English principle of " no taxation without representation ". They declared, moreover, that they were no longer children subject to their mother's arbitrary authority. And finally, with the overthrow of French power, they felt themselves strong enough to stand on their own feet.

To quiet the storm, all the duties except the levy on tea were repealed: but the actual right of taxing the colonies was specifically maintained. So far the British government had acted reasonably and even generously, if at times with little tact. But in 1770, King George got matters into his own determined hands. Pitt, who had been made Earl of Chatham, had finally retired from office and the king's tame minister, Lord North, was head of the government. George had always wanted to make a firm stand against his presumptuous subjects in America and now he was able to do so.

DECLARATION OF INDEPENDENCE

In 1773, an Act of Parliament virtually gave the East India Company the monopoly of supplying tea to the colonies and put the American merchants out of business. Immediately the flames of enraged protest broke out anew. But narrow-minded and obstinate George did not heed them. His disobedient subjects, with their mistaken ideas of their rights, must be chastised. He would " be a king " indeed. His principles of colonial government were in fact rather out-of-date. To persist in them, in the face of the intense bitterness of feeling aroused, was crass stupidity. None the less, we must do him justice. His attitude was shared by many and he received much support in Parliament and the country. Accordingly, strong measures were taken to reduce the king's naughty children to submission. In 1775, the quarrel ended in war. On the 4th July, 1776, the colonies which had revolted issued their Declaration of Independence. The history of the United States of America had begun.

During the next four years, France and Spain, still smarting from the humiliations of the Seven Years' War, flung themselves eagerly into the fight against their old enemy, and Holland joined them. The sorry tale closed in 1783, when Britain was driven to acknowledge defeat and let her children go. There were further losses too: Minorca and Florida to Spain; Senegal and other possessions to France. And for much of this we have to thank the well-intentioned folly of George III. (*See* " The New World and the U.S.A.").

While Britain was thus losing one empire she was on the way to building up another. In India, Acts of Parliament passed in 1773 and 1784 made the East India Company's rule subject to Crown control. The succession of able governors-general sent out, beginning with Warren Hastings, extended the sphere of British influence, British justice, and settled government, step by step. By 1815, it embraced three-quarters of the sub-continent. Beyond the Indian Ocean

On 5th September, 1774, the Continental Congress met to air the grievances of the people against the British Parliament's violation of their colonial rights and liberties.

Charting the eastern shores of the Australian continent, Cook was nearly wrecked on the Great Barrier Reef. By throwing heavy equipment overboard, he managed to sail his ship to Batavia for repairs.

other fields of opportunity were being developed. The talented and industrious navigator, Captain Cook, had explored the east coast of Australia in 1770. Eighteen years later the penal settlement of Botany Bay was founded and, after this somewhat dubious beginning, the early years of the nineteenth century saw the first opening up of New South Wales. (*See* " The Southern Continent ").

THE FRENCH REVOLUTION

In 1789, the peace of Europe was shattered by the convulsions of the French Revolution.

Europe was shaken as by an earthquake, and Britain was inevitably drawn into the tremendous conflict that followed.

The Earl of Chatham had died in 1778, and, five years later, his gifted son had become Prime Minister at the age of twenty-four. William Pitt the Younger, who died in office at the age of 47, lacked many of his famous father's great qualities, but his unshakable resolution and self-confidence were to prove Britain's main driving force in the perilous years ahead.

The story is told in the following articles on " The French Revolution " and " Napoleon Bonaparte ". There you may read of the glorious naval victories of Jervis and Duncan and Nelson and of Wellington's final triumph over Napoleon at Waterloo in 1815. You will also learn how the Bourbon kings were restored and Belgium and Holland united, and how Britain's empire was expanded by the retention of many new conquests, including Malta and Mauritius from the French, British Guiana, the Cape of Good Hope and Ceylon from the Dutch.

Before the flames of war died down they had scattered some sparks abroad to add to Britain's difficulties. In 1798, Ireland had broken out in rebellion. The rising was quickly stifled, but it had an important sequel. By the Act of Union of 1800, Ireland was united with Great Britain, the Dublin parliament closed its doors, and henceforth Irish members sat in Parliament at Westminster. Farther afield, a quarrel with Britain's former colonies over her claim to prevent neutral ships from trading with France or her allies had led, in 1812, to a war which left some bitter feelings in its wake.

Great Britain was the first nation in Europe where skilled men banded together to form friendly trade societies.

The Duke of Wellington (1769-1852), soldier and politician, eventually became Prime Minister in 1828.

INDUSTRIAL REVOLUTION

The second half of the eighteenth century saw the beginnings of another kind of revolution, one which completely transformed the daily life of the people and changed Britain from a mainly agricultural to a mainly industrial country. The Industrial Revolution, as it is called, was the most significant movement that had occurred in our social history.

During the eighteenth century, agriculture itself was revolutionised. New methods of cultivation and the growing of root and other crops vastly increased the yield of husbandry. Scientific breeding and improved feeding doubled the weight of cattle and sheep. Millions of acres of open land were enclosed. But now the machine age had come to give a startling impetus to industry. Mechanical inventions in the textile industry had begun in the previous reign. They now followed each other in a steady succession. The Scotsman James Watt brought out his improved steam-engine, which began the age of steam-power for machinery, and George Stephenson built his first locomotive. Discoveries were made for smelting iron with coal and coke instead of with charcoal. New canals and better roads facilitated inland transport. It was Britain who led the world in the Industrial Revolution, and her trade and wealth rose by leaps and bounds. So did her population.

But there was another side to the picture. The increasing prosperity was not equally shared. The altered agricultural conditions dislodged large numbers of small farmers and peasants from their holdings. The new machines transferred the village industries of spinning and weaving to the urban factories. So there set in a steady drift from the country to the new and rapidly growing towns. And the towns were hideous, insanitary slums, dark blotches on the face of " England's green and pleasant land ". Labour was cheap and wages low. Factory hours, and working and living conditions, were becoming positively and revoltingly inhuman.

The outcome was a deep and sullen discontent that fostered the class war between Capital and Labour which remains with us to-day. Riots and other disturbances became frequent. Parliament, ignorant of the true condition of affairs, was unsympathetic. Accordingly, a long-standing demand for its " radical ", or root, reform was pressed forward. The House of Commons, it was asserted, should be made more fully representative of the people. But the government feared that the agitators were infected with the spirit of the French Revolution—of which, indeed, signs were not wanting—and repressed their activities. The Combination Acts of 1799 and 1800 made trade unions illegal. The era of reform had not yet come—but it was on the way.

ARTISTIC FLOWERING

Now for a brief mention of the prolific literature of the period. Pope's witty, polished and artificial style of verse is typical of the " classical " era. The works of such poets as Wordsworth, Coleridge, Byron, Shelley, and Keats mark a reaction against it and a return to Nature. Scotland's great contributions, in poetry and prose, were the writings of its national bard, Burns, and " the wizard of the North ", Sir Walter Scott, while Ireland produced Oliver Goldsmith. And we have to thank Defoe for *Robinson Crusoe*, Swift for *Gulliver's Travels* and Gray for his *Elegy in a Country Churchyard*.

In other artistic fields, such as painting, playwriting, architecture, furniture, china and pottery, Britain was pre-eminent: Handel (a German who became a naturalised Englishman) in music; Hogarth, Reynolds, Gainsborough, Romney, Constable and Turner in painting; Sheridan and Goldsmith in playwriting; Vanbrugh, the Adam brothers and Nash in architecture; Chippendale, Sheraton and Hepplewhite in furniture; and Wedgwood and many others in china and pottery.

The year of Waterloo saw Britain clothed with power and glory, though temporarily exhausted by an overdose of war. Her far-flung empire and world-wide commerce were secured by her invincible navy. Her immense achievements in the war had made her name honoured throughout Europe. She had given to the common cause two supremely great commanders—Nelson at sea, Wellington on land. Her free institutions were the envy and the inspiration of all oppressed peoples. True, she was suffering from grave social and economic weaknesses; but these she might be expected to overcome in her own way. Meantime, the British Lion's roar reverberated unchallenged around the world.

George III never tasted the sweets of victory. The unhappy man became insane and, from 1811, his son acted as regent.

AUSTRIA AND MARIA THERESA

British history books have been inclined (with our approval) to give scant attention to the more easterly parts of Europe as being mostly beyond Britain's horizon. Many of the events which occurred there, however, did and still do intimately concern her. The development of aeroplane, radio and other modern communications, moreover, has brought those distant regions well within our compass. One can no longer neglect their close acquaintance. And to understand their present position, it is necessary to know something of their past.

Our immediate story centres round Austria. Her previous history may be briefly summarised as follows: before his final abdication in 1558, the Habsburg emperor Charles V shared out his far-reaching possessions, giving to his brother Ferdinand (who was already King of Bohemia and Hungary) the Habsburg Austrian inheritance and the sovereignty of the make-believe Holy Roman (or German) Empire. The Thirty Years' War, which ended in 1648, left that sovereignty even more unreal than before, by making the numerous component States of the empire practically independent. The wars against Louis XIV of France, which closed in 1713-14, presented the Austrian emperor with the Spanish Netherlands (roughly equal to modern Belgium), together with most of Spain's Italian possessions. In the War of the Austrian Succession, fought from 1740 to 1748, and the Seven Years' War that opened in 1756, Maria Theresa, the young heiress of the Austrian dominions, lost Silesia to the Prussian robber-king Frederick the Great, who thenceforth stood as a serious rival to Austrian power. Finally, the iniquitous partitions of Poland between Russia, Prussia and Austria added large portions of that dismembered kingdom to Austria in 1772 and 1795.

During this lengthy period Austria was almost barren of distinguished rulers, but it did produce one notably influential and attractive figure in Maria Theresa. At her accession in 1740 she was twenty-seven years old, and her youth and beauty, her noble character, her gracious charm and queenly bearing won the hearts of her subjects. In all the wars and diplomatic manœuvres of her 40-years' reign she took a leading part. When Frederick the Great filched Silesia, her moving appeal to the chivalry of the fiery Hungarian nobles rallied them to her support in passionate devotion. But Frederick's guns spoke more loudly than hers and all her efforts to recover the lost province were in vain. In the first partition of Poland her noble heart recoiled from the base design, and only considerations of state constrained her to acquiesce in it. Meantime she worked devotedly and wisely to bring peace, prosperity and unity to the varied races under her rule.

New social and political ideas were rife in her time. Enlightened rulers, such as Frederick of Prussia and Catherine II of Russia, showed praiseworthy zeal in trying to improve the conditions of their subjects by fostering trade and industry, lightening the peasants' burdens, increasing those of the over-privileged nobles and clergy, and practising toleration in religion. Maria Theresa trod this path of reform. But, like the other well-meaning sovereigns, she had no intention of abating any of her autocratic powers. She granted favours rather than conceded rights. After her death in 1780, her son Joseph II, who reigned till 1790, enthusiastically followed in his mother's footsteps. But the headlong pace of his reforms aroused determined and widespread opposition, especially from the privileged classes, and the greater part of the emperor's beneficent work was undone.

TURKISH THREAT

Perhaps the most valuable of the forgotten services that Austria rendered to Europe is that she kept the conquering Turks at bay.

The Moslem hordes, after storming the ancient Eastern capital, spread jubilantly over the Balkans and, in 1526, stood before the gates of Vienna. Thus they threatened the whole house of Western Christendom. They had captured the porch and forced their way into the hall. Whether they would be able to flood over the main interior apartments depended primarily on Austria, who stood as a lion in the path of their advance. Her roarings were not always convincingly leonine, but she clawed the enemy valiantly in an almost non-stop fight, generation after generation. In the first half of the seventeenth century the early fire and energy of the invaders showed signs of waning, but presently they flared up again in another grand assault. It was then that Austria really roared. By one victory after another, following on brilliant successes gained over the enemy by Poland, her armies rolled the Turks back across Hungary. In 1699, the beaten foe was forced to relinquish the whole of that kingdom to the empire and other districts to the gallant Poles. The liberation of the Christians in the Balkans—Greeks, Bulgars, Serbs and others—remained for the distant future to achieve. But the menace to Central and Western Europe was dispelled.

For most of her long reign, Maria Theresa held the reins of government in her own hands. Of strong character and dedicated nature, she was prepared to help her people, provided her authority was not lessened.

THE FRENCH REVOLUTION

The French Revolution of 1789 was gunpowder. When it was touched off the blast rocked Europe. The like of it had never been known before. To understand how the devastating upheaval occurred, we must go back in history a little.

The eighteenth century has been called the Age of Enlightenment in Europe because men's eyes were then everywhere opened to changed views of the principles of society and government. At the beginning of the century most of the Continent was ruled by autocratic sovereigns. The nobility were a privileged class. The Church was influential, wealthy and quite opposed to progressive ideas. And, like the nobility, it was largely exempt from taxation. The common people were still oppressed by many feudal burdens which had survived from the Middle Ages. Over large areas the peasants remained serfs. The criminal laws were ferociously cruel and free speech was gagged

These indefensible conditions were accepted in France, as elsewhere, because they had always existed. The Church taught that man, through Adam's sin, was naturally evil and quite incapable of devising a better social system. The time came, however, when intelligent men began to question this ancient doctrine. They could no longer believe that man was essentially base and his condition beyond repair. On the contrary he was fundamentally virtuous and capable of infinite improvement. He possessed the divine gift of *reason*. Given the opportunity, he could sweep away all the errors and injustices of the old, outworn, man-made system and rebuild society on the rational foundations of justice, liberty and equality. This promising change of outlook was immensely stimulated by the work of English philosophers and natural scientists. John Locke had produced his illuminating theories of the processes and capabilities of the human understanding and the true principles of social, political and religious life. Isaac Newton, with his discoveries of the law of gravitation and the composition of light, had brilliantly advanced man's knowledge of the natural laws which govern his earthly habitation and shape his course.

That the audacious poaching on their traditional preserves was strenuously resisted by the privileged classes was only to be expected. The Church was especially alarmed because the new ideas encouraged heretical ideas about the divine government of the universe. Many of the reformers were " deists ": they believed in the existence of a supreme deity, but not necessarily in the revealed God of Christianity.

New social and political ideas were rife in Austria, Prussia and Russia. It was France that had spread them there, after taking fire from the example of Britain and her American colonies. But, while the so-called "enlightened" sovereigns shied at the thought of their people having actual *rights*, France, as we shall see, carried the doctrine to fulfilment.

THE SPREAD OF NEW IDEAS

In 1726 a deistic French writer, named Voltaire, a man of keen wit and brilliant intelligence, visited England. To his eager mind it seemed the Island of the Blessed. Under the Hanoverian kings the royal power was curbed by an elected parliament. There was no arbitrary taxation, and nobles and clerics alike had to pay. Within certain limits, every man was at liberty to speak and write and worship as he pleased. The people were free, prosperous and happy. After his return home in 1729, Voltaire, during the rest of his long life, continually employed his energies, like a French St. George, in slaying the dragon of tyranny and privilege. Freedom for all in thought, word and deed, was his demand as the essential first step in the march of reform. He was especially bitter against the higher clergy. With scathing tongue and biting wit, he contemptuously denounced them as worldly-minded and intolerant enemies of progress.

The Cathedral of Notre Dame (from a 17th-century print).

The coronation of Louis XVI and Marie Antoinette, daughter of Maria Theresa, took place in the ancient cathedral at Rheims in the year 1774.

The marriage between Marie Antoinette and Louis, dauphin of France and future Louis XVI, took place in 1770.

His teachings spread apace. The new ideas were eagerly debated, and a flood of books and pamphlets sowed them broadcast. Then a new voice arose. Rousseau, in his *Social Contract* of 1762, proclaimed that the principle of good government was based on the will of the people with every citizen sacrificing his personal interests to the welfare of the community. His doctrines rang through France.

Matters had been going from bad to worse from the time of Louis XIV, who died in 1715. Afterwards, in the time of Louis XV, the War of the Austrian Succession and the Seven Years' War had further drained France's man-power and finances, and had destroyed her hopes of colonial empire in Canada and India. Louis XVI, who succeeded his grandfather in 1774, was excellent at repairing locks but, though full of good intentions, too weak and changeable in his efforts to repair the shaken kingdom. His queen, the fascinating Marie Antoinette, daughter of the Austrian Maria Theresa, was gay, frivolous and pleasure-loving. Her womanish whimsies and baleful influence on public affairs made her unpopular at Court and detested by the nation.

In 1778, France, eager to revenge her territorial losses to Britain in the Seven Years' War, sided with the American colonies in their War of Independence. Revenge is sweet, but it cost France a lot of money, and the colonists' triumph was a dangerous stimulus to the spirit of liberty at home.

THE SPREAD OF DISCONTENT

On the eve of the Revolution, then, France presented the picture of a landscape black with stormy discontent. The autocratic Louis XVI could tax, or imprison, or silence his subjects at will. The favoured and proudly exclusive nobility idled away their days in the gaieties of the luxurious and extravagant Court at Versailles. Both they and the higher clergy had forfeited the peoples' respect. The humble and hardworking parish priests were grossly underpaid. The industrious middle-classes chafed against unequal taxation and privilege. The toiling peasants, though often hungry, were not on the whole as badly off as those of some other countries; but they were taxed almost to the limit and were further exasperated by out-dated feudal obligations. The administration was hopelessly corrupt and inefficient and

confused in its policy. No national parliament existed to ventilate the country's grievances. The nearest approach to one was the assembly of the clergy, nobles and middle-class burgesses in the States-General, and it had not been summoned since 1614!

The spark that at last fired the gunpowder was the government's bankruptcy. Money *must* be raised by some means. But how? " Not from us! " protested the nobles and clergy. And " Not from us! " echoed the middle-classes. From the peasants then? Impossible. Many of the poor growling wretches were already being filched of three-quarters of their earnings by the State and their local lords. In desperation Louis was driven to take council with the nation. He summoned the old States-General.

When the deputies met at Versailles on 5th May, 1789, the atmosphere was charged with excitement and hope. We may say that the Revolution had begun. From the outset a deadlock occurred between the three orders of the church, the nobility and " the third estate ". The latter comprised the rest of the nation; but it was represented chiefly by the " bourgeoisie "—the well-to-do higher members of the middle-class. The privileged orders refused to co-operate with the commoners. Whereupon the latter broke away and declared themselves a National Assembly, swearing that they would never separate till they had given France a new constitution. The lesser nobility and the country clergy supported them and it was not long before the king, yielding to the force of public opinion, ordered the others to join the Assembly. It was a signal triumph for the commoners.

Meanwhile tempers were rising in Paris, and Louis was persuaded by Marie Antoinette and a group of die-hard courtiers to summon a body of troops to stand by. Immediately the cry went up that the Assembly was in peril. The people flew to arms. On 14th July, an infuriated and lawless mob, equipped with pikes and cannon, stormed the Bastille, the grim old prison which in their eyes was a visible symbol of royal tyranny. The spectacular triumph was itself a symbol of the crash of the old order. And it gave the Paris mob—a half-starved rabble of criminals, scoundrels and other desperadoes—its first taste of blood.

The exultant citizens set up a commune or municipal

Mirabeau tried by oratory and political manœuvre to form a government based on British parliamentary procedure. That this plan failed was due largely to the intervention of Marie Antoinette.

On 14th July, 1789, the populace took the Bastille by storm.

government, and recruited a National Guard. The humiliated Louis was compelled to sanction these measures and to wear in his royal hat the abominated tricolour cockade, the red, white and blue revolutionary badge. In the prevailing tumults, which were aggravated by bread-riots, Paris gave the lead to the provincial towns. The peasants rose and burned their hated lords' castles. Many of the nobles skipped abroad and sought foreign aid to crush the insolent upstarts who were wantonly wrecking the venerable institutions of their country.

In October, the shifty conduct of Louis and some of his die-hard court advisers provoked a fresh outburst in Paris. A mob of hungry people, followed by the National Guard, forced the king and queen to remove from Versailles to the Tuileries palace in Paris. It was like imprisoning them in a gilded cage. The National Assembly followed and resumed their sittings in a nearby building. Paris now controlled the king as well as the administration and the army. But how long would it be before the brutal Paris underworld controlled them all? Already they suspected the bourgeoisie in the Assembly of looking only to their own interests.

The cross-currents in the revolutionary tide-race now

became clear. It was not an oppressed peasantry that had released the flood-waters. That was the achievement of the bourgeoisie and lesser nobles, who, as intelligent men, were weary of the abuses of the old order. Later, when the obsolete machine of royal despotism and class privilege had been scrapped, the contest changed its character. It became one between the moderate bourgeoisie, who were content with the constitutional reforms achieved, and the inflamed masses, who clamoured for ever more radical measures.

It was in these distracted conditions that the Assembly set itself to the exhilarating work of making the nation's dream come true by rebuilding society anew. One of its earliest acts was perhaps its most notable. The Declaration of the Rights of Man boldly asserted the claim of all citizens to liberty, equality, justice and a voice in legislation and taxation. The principles of this historic manifesto were to be the rallying cry of reform, for generations to come, in France and in all other oppressed countries.

By September, 1791, the monumental task of framing the new constitution was completed. The evils of centuries were boldly swept away and free France was gloriously set on a new course. A limited monarchy was created, together with a Legislative Assembly, or parliament, to be elected by all save the poorer classes. The privileges of the nobility were abolished. The vast estates of the Church were confiscated. The bishops and parish priests became salaried civil servants elected by the people without troubling to consult the Pope. And Louis, with a wry face, had to swallow it all.

Magnificent as was the overall achievement of the Assembly, some of its measures had raised up bitter enmities. The civil constitution of the clergy shocked devout Catholics and definitely alienated the king. Most of the bishops and half the parish priests resigned their livings in protest and became steadfast opponents of the Revolution as an enemy to religion. The poorer town and country workers were angered at their exclusion from parliamentary elections and the neglect of their economic grievances. Storm-clouds were gathering on the horizon.

One of the blackest of them loomed up just across the Rhine, where the emigrant nobles had organised a small army. Louis and his queen were secretly intriguing with

From 1614 until 1789, the States-General was not summoned. On 5th May, 1789, it met for the last time, becoming known thereafter as the National Constituent Assembly.

Danton, powerful orator and revolutionary leader, was a member of the Tribunal, but was more moderate than Robespierre.

Incited by agitators, the populace of Paris invade the Palace of Versailles, compelling the king to move to Paris.

Prussia and the Austrian emperor, Marie Antoinette's brother. The people pricked up their ears in alarm. They scented collusion between the nobles abroad and those at home. The Revolution was threatened from within and without. Then, in June 1791, the double-dealing Louis, carefully disguised, made a dash for the border. But his carriage was stopped at Varennes, and back to their gilded cage the fugitive and his queen were hurried. A republican party now raised its head and denounced Louis as a traitor. The passions of the populace were rising. Their distrust of the moderate bourgeoisie deepened into a settled hate.

Events followed thick and fast like snowflakes in a blizzard. The Legislative Assembly which had taken over from the old Assembly in October, 1791, contained many deputies hostile to the king. Of these the Jacobins were the most forthright. They belonged to a powerful political club, one of many which had sprung up to press forward the aims of their members. The Jacobins began as clean-handed moderates. They ended as red-handed extremists.

The Assembly faced a critical situation. Austria and Prussia had threatened to intervene and restore Louis' authority. It was not surprising. When your next door neighbour goes crazy and sets his house afire and—worse still—when he encourages your servants to do the same with yours, you need to do something about it. France, of course, flamed with indignation. In April, 1792, she declared war; but, by August, Prussian and Austrian troops were on French soil. A crisis had arisen. And in that crisis the king failed his country and revealed his complicity with the enemy.

A huge shadow had already fallen on the scene, the shadow of the Jacobin, Danton. The great, coarse-faced, popular leader, with his voice of thunder and his violent counsels, dominated Paris. With panic and wild rumours of treachery filling the air, the Tuileries palace was stormed. The king became a close prisoner. The tumultuous citizens set up a new, strongly Jacobin commune of hot-heads. The revolutionary tide-race brought a lot of human scum to the surface. In September, hundreds of suspected aristocrats and priests, who had been hunted out and thrown into prison, were ferociously massacred. Only by terror could the secret enemies of the Revolution be quelled. On 22nd September, a National Convention formally abolished the monarchy and proclaimed France a republic.

Meanwhile the patriot-soldiers, bawling out the rousing strains of their new war song, the *Marseillaise*, were marching confidently to the front. They were desperately raw and

The king is made to appear before the people, his head covered by the traditional red beret of the revolutionaries.

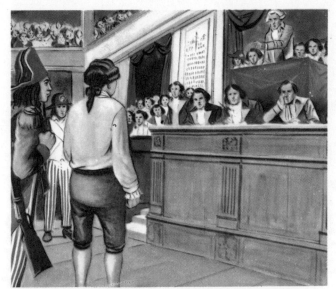

The trial of the king, Louis XVI, by the Convention was a complete mockery.

ragged, but they were ardent, and they actually forced the allied army back. Then they marched gaily onward. They invaded Germany and Savoy, defeated Austria and occupied the Austrian Netherlands, or Belgium. Liberty, equality and fraternity were proudly proclaimed to all oppressed peoples. Yet the pity of it is that the patriots were already betraying those principles. The intoxication of victory had bred in their hearts the old despots' lust of conquest and territorial gain.

Now came the final reckoning with the king. There could be but one meet penalty for traitors. The British had exacted it from Charles I in January, 1649. The French inflicted it on Louis XVI in January, 1793. Like Charles he died bravely. His whole life had been a tragedy. Fate had given him a giant's part to play; and he was only a pigmy. A thrill of horror ran through Europe and soon an avenging coalition, including Britain, Holland, Austria, Prussia, Spain and Sardinia, was formed against the regicide country. Britain was bound to be drawn into the conflict by the French occupation of Belgium. It was a long-standing principle with her that no great rival power must be allowed to dominate the Low Countries, and thereby hold a pistol to her head.

The tide of success turned against the French. In March they were driven out of Belgium. Their General Dumouriez deserted to the enemy. The road to Paris lay open. Royalist and priestly insurrections broke out.

Now indeed France stood at bay. And nobly she faced her foes. In that hour of direst peril one supreme resolution animated her: to fight to the death for her newly-won liberties. Pending the preparation of a new republican constitution, a Committee of Public Safety, with almost absolute powers, was created by the Convention. The Jacobins controlled it. The hot-headed Paris commune and the riotous Paris mob were its allies. France became a nation in arms. And the burning ardour of her fighting men, the bristling bayonets and thundering artillery, won their reward. By the close of the year 1793, the foreign " tyrants " were everywhere hurled back. The insurrections at home were ruthlessly stamped out. Next year the Austrians were driven from Belgium in what was to prove their final evacuation of the country, and the French marched in and occupied Holland.

While the soldiers were thus rolling back the foe in the

field, the government were hounding down the " traitors " within the gates. The man of the hour was a lean, ghastly-hued, self-righteous lawyer, the elegant Robespierre. The gleaming vision of an ideal republic, inspired by the teachings of Rousseau, possessed his mind. He pursued it in all honesty and sincerity, with single-minded and merciless intensity. All who opposed its progress were traitors to a sacred cause. Under him, during the ten months from September, 1793, the Reign of Terror, already begun, reached the apex of its systematic ferocity. Thousands of suspected men and women were pitilessly butchered. The guillotine was seldom idle. It claimed Queen Marie Antoinette. It claimed Danton when the fanatical Robespierre found him too squeamish for his designs.

At last the country sickened of the red tyranny. In July, 1794, Robespierre was overthrown and the guillotine took him too. The Paris commune was abolished, the Jacobin Club closed. The Terror was over. In 1795, the administration was entrusted by the Convention to a new body of five members, "the Directory". It ruled France for four years and proved itself hopelessly corrupt and inefficient. The aggressive wars in which it engaged led to the formation of another coalition of European powers. In these campaigns a certain young general named Napoleon Bonaparte covered himself with glory and won the enthusiastic admiration of a nation that longed for a strong master-hand to bring it peace and orderly rule. Napoleon was more than ready to supply the need. In November, 1799, by a military conspiracy, he turned out the unpopular government; whereupon he was made First Consul of the State with practically supreme power. So, with a final explosion, the Revolution rumbled to its end in a new dictatorship.

Yet its principal achievements were secure. The spirit of individual freedom, of political liberty and equal justice, lived on and presently gained new triumphs. The unfair feudal privileges of the clergy and nobility had been buried too deeply ever to be resurrected. Religious toleration was won. And this was not all. France, the first great Continental power to establish democratic rule, stood as a lighthouse whose rays illuminated Europe. The principles of social and political reform, the Rights of Man, proclaimed in the throes of her great Revolution, took root among her neighbours and, in the fullness of time, everywhere bore fruit.

During the period of the Terror, carts loaded with condemned political prisoners passed through the streets of Paris.

NAPOLEON BONAPARTE

It was only by chance that France's greatest military genius was a Frenchman at all. Corsica, where he was born in 1769, had only been acquired by France from Genoa the year before. Actually Napoleon was the second son of a poor Corsican lawyer of noble and, probably, Italian descent. From the age of ten, however, when he began his military studies in France, he received a French education at Brienne and later at Paris.

HIS AMBITIONS

The Revolution broke out in 1789, and four years later the young Napoleon had become an artillery officer of considerable reputation. At that time the naval base of Toulon, assisted by a British squadron, had gone over to the royalists. Napoleon's quick eye discerned the key to its recovery. The British withdrew; the insurgents surrendered. In 1795, however, Napoleon's fortunes were at a low ebb. He was just a thin, little, sallow-faced officer, only about 5 feet 2 inches in height, with awkward manners and untidy dress. Yet his striking features and penetrating eyes gave some hint of powerful qualities within.

When a chance of advancement came he seized it boldly. By prompt action he saved the government from a royalist insurrection. His foot was now planted on the ladder of success. He entered society, where he fell in love with, and married, the beautiful widow Josephine Beauharnais.

In 1796, the coalition of European powers which had been formed against revolutionary France had come to grief. The Directory of five members who ruled France decided to make a wide-ranging attack on Austria and entrusted the command of the operations in northern Italy, where Austria was the dominant power, to Napoleon. The ball was now at his feet, and brilliantly he played it. The King of Sardinia went down before him. Austria followed, and in October,

Nelson, brave man and brilliant tactician, was mortally wounded at the Battle of Trafalgar.

1797, he shot the ball clean into the goal. By the Treaty of Campo Formio Austria ceded Belgium and the German districts on the French side of the Rhine and left France practically in control of northern Italy.

Britain, France's most determined foe, guided by her staunch-hearted premier William Pitt, now faced France alone. And not France only: Holland and Spain had ranged themselves against Britain. In 1797, she struck some telling blows at sea. Jervis scattered the Spaniards at Cape St. Vincent, and off Camperdown Duncan captured half the Dutch fleet. Earlier, too, Britain had taken Ceylon and the Cape of Good Hope from the Dutch and a few other trifles from Spain and France.

EGYPTIAN CAMPAIGN

How to strike back in the face of Britain's naval superiority?—that was the question that agitated Napoleon. He thought to find the answer in Egypt. By a blow there he would assail his stubborn enemy's power in the Mediterranean and India. In 1798, eluding Nelson's frigates, he landed an army near Alexandria. But Britain's one-eyed and one-armed admiral scented out his fleet lying at anchor in Aboukir Bay. And by brilliantly daring tactics and devastating gunfire he annihilated it. The " Corsican ogre " was bottled up. He hadn't found the answer to his question after all.

FIRST CONSUL

Meantime, events at home were shaping favourably to his secret political ambitions. In 1799, leaving his army behind him (the British practically destroyed it later), he slipped back to France. There he overthrew the unpopular government and made himself First Consul of the State.

Within four years the obscure Corsican had climbed to the top of the ladder. Yet it was only a beginning. His whole career was to blaze him forth as a superman. His supreme

The Institute of Egyptology is a relic of Napoleon's Egyptian campaign of 1798. The " Rosetta Stone " was one of the great discoveries.

military talents apart, he was endowed with astonishing industry and physical stamina. He could work or ride for hours on end. Food and sleep seemed unnecessary to him. His ambitions, like his vanity and selfishness, were boundless. No moral scruples restrained him. No man must stand in his way.

In 1798, a new coalition, this time bringing in Russia and Turkey, had been formed. The Allies started by carrying all before them; but the crushing defeats of the ill-fated Austrians, in 1800, by Napoleon at Marengo and General Moreau at Hohenlinden, counterbalanced their successes. The coalition collapsed and the territorial situation remained much as before—except that Britain had captured Malta. The French held Belgium and the Rhine and controlled most of northern Italy, with the " free " republics they had created there, as well as Switzerland and Holland. In 1802, Britain, with Pitt temporarily out of office, patched up a peace treaty. But it couldn't last and next year the guns were banging again. In 1804, Pitt returned to the helm; and Napoleon attained the glory of being crowned Emperor of the French.

TRAFALGAR

The contest had now ceased to be one with revolutionary France. It had become a struggle with Napoleon, as he sought, like another Charlemagne, to subject all western and central Europe to his power. " Boney " never forgot that his most deadly foe was Britain and he early planned to invade the island. But his design was foiled by the watchful British Navy and shattered in 1805 by Nelson's famous victory of Trafalgar—won, alas! at the cost of the hero's life.

Meantime another coalition—of Britain, Russia and Austria against France and her lackey Spain—was trying its luck. It hadn't any. Between 1805 and 1807 " the little corporal ", as his idolising soldiers called their invincible general, knocked out Austria at Ulm and Austerlitz, Prussia (who had by now entered the field) at Jena, and Russia at Friedland. Then he extinguished the shadowy authority of the Austrian emperor in Germany by abolishing the now defunct Holy Roman Empire. And he hemmed in Austria and Prussia by creating various new States which would be under his influence: the German Confederation of the Rhine, the Duchy of Warsaw and the Kingdom of Westphalia. Between whiles he sent an army to expel the King of Naples and take over his realm of southern Italy.

CONTINENTAL BLOCKADE

But he still had to settle scores with Britain. And he couldn't get at her. The two antagonists, indeed, were fighting each other with one hand tied behind their backs: for France lacked an adequate navy and Britain lacked an adequate army. Napoleon, however, had another arrow in his quiver. Britain, he said, was " a nation of shopkeepers ". Pitt, her great leader, was dead. Touch her merchants' pockets and they would soon clamour for peace. So, in 1806, he declared a complete continental blockade, forbidding all commerce with the stubborn islanders. The shaft proved to be a boomerang. It caused serious loss and discontent in Britain; but France, her allies and dependants suffered as well —though it was a grand time for smugglers. And it led Napoleon to undertake one new conquest after another, in order to enforce the co-operation of all the European states, till the time came when he over-reached himself.

But that time was not yet in sight. After Friedland, Napoleon had a friendly little chat with Tsar Alexander I on a raft moored in a river near Tilsit. The Russian monarch was captivated by Napoleon's magnetic charm and the treaty of 1807 was the result. Alexander agreed to support the blockade, and the precious pair planned to commandeer the fleets of Denmark and other neutral countries. That would have tied Britain's other hand by imperilling her naval supremacy. But George III's resolute Foreign Secretary, Canning, forestalled the plotters. He dispatched a fleet to Copenhagen and seized practically the entire Danish navy.

PORTUGAL OVERRUN

However, things were still going well on land for Napoleon. His armies overran Portugal; and in 1808, by force and the meanest trickery, he took possession of the Spanish throne. When Austria, in 1809, once more ventured to raise her head he promptly laid it low again at Wagram. Meanwhile he annexed the Papal States in central Italy. Then, in 1810, he added a new splendour to his line. Divorcing Josephine, who had failed to bring him an heir, he wedded the illustrious

Shortly after the indecisive battle of Borodino, Napoleon retreated from Moscow.

Although Napoleon stayed only about ten months on the island of Elba, he helped to plan a road system.

After his escape from Elba, Napoleon made a last desperate attempt to lead the French to victory. The Hundred Days' campaign resulted in a decisive defeat at Waterloo. France did not want their former hero and Napoleon was forced to surrender to the British.

Archduchess Marie Louise, the Austrian emperor's daughter.

He now stood at the summit of his fortunes. Western and central Europe lay at his feet and Russia was his ally. He had shuffled the thrones of Europe like a pack of cards, making his brothers Joseph, Louis and Jerome Kings of Spain, Holland and Westphalia, his brother-in-law General Murat King of Naples, his friend the King of Saxony Grand Duke of Warsaw.

While he thus stands on his dizzy pinnacle of power let us observe him from another viewpoint. Napoleon was a far-seeing statesman and administrator as well as a soldier. He restored order and financial stability in France and reconstituted the laws in clear and practical codes. He created a new nobility. He made peace with the Church after the repression it had suffered during the Revolution. He reorganised education, constructed splendid roads and made Paris a city of beauty.

Napoleon's immense empire was like a cage of lions cowed by their master's whip. But if his hand should ever falter . . .

Three enemies in particular he must beware of: untamable Britain; Russia; and the rising national spirit of the peoples he had trodden down and humiliated. This last was a new historic feature which, later, was to spread with tremendous effects. Hitherto kings and princes had annexed and disposed of countries like personal possessions. But now, with the example of France and its Revolution before them, the subject peoples were growing more conscious of their distinctive unity in blood and language and national traditions. They believed that all foreign conquests were evil. They felt that they were entitled to live under their own native rulers in accordance with their own ancient institutions.

RETREAT FROM MOSCOW

The first signs of faltering in the lion-tamer's hand was seen in Spain. The proud Spaniards were fiercely patriotic. They rose against the French invaders as one man: not so much in organised armies as in irregular bands of " guerrillas ". Their unquenchable spirit at last gave Britain an opportunity of striking effectively at Napoleon on land. In the Peninsular War of 1808-1814, Sir Arthur Wellesley (soon to be famous as the Duke of Wellington) drove the French armies out of Portugal and Spain. Meantime the changeable Tsar Alexander had changed again, partly because the continental blockade was injuring his country's commerce. The dear friends of Tilsit parted company. Napoleon invaded Russia. And in those vast snow-clad wastes, he at last over-reached himself. Of some 600,000 men who marched into Russia in June, 1812, less than 100,000 came out six months later.

BATTLE OF THE NATIONS

This colossal disaster, following on the example of successful Spanish resistance, inspired a passionate national awakening in Germany. In 1813, at Leipzig, in the four-day " Battle of the Nations "—Russia, Prussia, Austria and Sweden against France—Napoleon suffered total defeat. Next year the allies entered Paris. Napoleon abdicated and was sent to Elba.

The Congress of Vienna sat down to reshuffle the fallen emperor's carefully arranged pack of cards. Three famous statesmen represented Britain, Austria and France: the wise Castlereagh, the despotic Metternich and the astute Talleyrand. France was reduced to its former boundaries. The Bourbon kings were restored there (but an earlier Charter of Liberties confirmed the main principles of the Revolution) and also in Spain and Naples. Belgium and Holland were united under the Dutch king, Germany became a loose confederation of thirty-nine States, including Prussia, under Austrian leadership. Prussia received part of Saxony and districts along the Rhine. In Italy, Austrian influence prevailed, though almost all the former States were revived. Russia grabbed most of Poland. It all showed a disappointing disregard for the new spirit of nationalism.

FINAL EXILE

Suddenly, in 1815, while the Congress was still sitting, came a thunderclap. The Corsican ogre had escaped. He was in France, with a wildly enthusiastic army at his back. But his final ruin came with the epoch-making triumph of the Duke of Wellington, clinched by the Prussian Blucher, at Waterloo. After that it was St. Helena for " the disturber of the world's peace ". And it was on that remote, rocky Atlantic island that, on 5th May, 1821, he passed away.

BRITAIN AFTER WATERLOO 1815·1914

The nineteenth century is so densely packed with stirring events and great movements that they seem to roll out by mass production.

The victory of Waterloo in 1815, which ended the Napoleonic wars, left Britain the dominant world-power. She ruled a far-flung empire. She was supreme on every ocean. She led all nations in the Industrial Revolution, which had begun in the previous century and given her the trade markets of the world. Her heroic contributions to the defeat of the French tyrant had crowned her with universal respect and honour.

Yet with all this she was suffering from a grave internal sickness that affected all sections of the community. Her immense war effort had left her, for the time being, as exhausted as a boxer after a gruelling twenty-round contest. The Industrial Revolution, which had transformed her from a mainly agricultural to a mainly industrial country, had degraded the social and economic conditions of the workers while filling the purses of their employers. The war, and the trade slump that succeeded it, had temporarily dislocated industry and hit the manufacturers. And there were other evils. Under the savage criminal laws an offender could be hanged for stealing five shillings or a sheep. Indeed there were more than two hundred crimes punishable by death.

These social injustices provoked frequent outbreaks of violent discontent. The landed aristocracy governed the country. The mass of the people had no vote and so were unable to ventilate their grievances in Parliament. The government feared that the widespread agitation for reform was a dangerous insurrectionary movement and they set themselves resolutely to crush it. Yet it was evident to enlightened and sympathetic observers that searching reforms were long overdue. The growing " Radical " party sought them in changes in the constitution of Parliament, changes which would make that assembly more truly representative of the nation. " Reform Parliament ", was their cry, " and Parliament will reform the laws ".

In 1820, while the country was distracted by these commotions, poor, mad, old George III passed away and the Regent, his son George IV, came to the throne. The so-called " first gentleman in Europe " was a man of some wit and taste, but for the rest he was a selfish character, a ruinous spendthrift, and a dissolute dandy and rake.

In 1822, a freshly constituted Tory government adopted a new attitude towards the question of reform. They believed that a sympathetic parliament was fully able to correct the popular grievances without reforming its own constitution. In 1823, Robert (afterwards Sir Robert) Peel, the Home Secretary, reduced the number of capital crimes by a hundred. (It was the same Sir *Robert Peel* who created the " Peelers ", or " Bobbies ", by establishing the London Police Force in 1829.) In 1824-5, the government somewhat relaxed the provisions of the Combination Acts, which had previously made trade unions illegal; though it was not till some fifty years later that the movement gained its charter of freedom. Steps were also taken to promote freer foreign trade and to reduce the cost of living.

Another reform, of a different character, effected under a later Tory government, marked a sensible advance in the enlightened principle of religious toleration. The remaining penal laws imposed on Nonconformists and (with a few exceptions) on Catholics during the old struggle with the Anglican Church, were formally abolished in 1828-9.

But the government's attempts at social improvements were mere tinkerings with an engine that required a thorough overhaul. It was Parliament itself that needed repair and, in 1830, when dandy George's worthless life closed, parliamentary reform was the burning question of the day.

Boxing as a sport was revived in the early eighteenth century in England.

The practice of employing children in mills and factories was abolished in the nineteenth-century.

McAdam's system of road-making improved the appalling condition of the eighteenth-century roads of Britain.

In 1823, Britain sent troops to Portugal's aid when her independence was threatened by Spain.

Before this unlamented event occurred the brilliant Foreign Secretary, Canning, who had headed the government in its reforming zeal, had been pursuing a similarly " liberal " policy in foreign affairs. After the fall of Napoleon, some of the restored continental rulers had applied themselves to stifling the principles of free constitutional government and national independence, which had everywhere been stimulated by the French Revolution of 1789. Canning boldly championed movements for reform in Spain and Portugal, and for outright independence in Spain's American colonies where the decline of Spain's influence combined with the successful revolt of Britain's North American colonies was causing unrest, and in Greece. Masterful Britain had her finger in every pie.

BALKAN RISING

The Turks had controlled the Balkans for centuries. When the Greeks rose against those brutal tyrants, Canning led Britain to draw the sword in their support. The British Lion's active intervention, however, was mainly prompted by the fear that, if the watchful Russian Bear were left to deal with the situation alone, it would plant its great paws permanently upon the eastern Mediterranean and menace British interests there and on the overland routes to India.

The wrongs of the Greeks had aroused the warmest sympathy in British hearts. Numbers of volunteers had gone forth to strike a blow at the abominated Turk. Among the leaders was the noble-hearted poet Lord Byron, who laid down his life for the cause. At last, when the Greek fortunes were desperate, Britain, Russia and France sent out a fleet and, at the battle of Navarino, fought in 1827, won an annihilating victory. Two years later, plucky little Greece regained its freedom.

In 1830, with the accession of George IV's brother, the simple, warm-hearted and breezy sailor-king William IV, another little country struck a blow for freedom. The Belgians rose against their masters, the Dutch House of Orange. Canning was dead, but Britain had found another forceful and liberal-minded Foreign Secretary. Lord Palmerston was a statesman who was always ready to lecture poor, ignorant foreign diplomats on the superior British principles of free constitutional government and to speak up for British interests abroad. It was with his enthusiastic

support that Belgium eventually succeeded in gaining her independence.

Revolutionary ideas were evidently very much in the air. Britain's social and political reformers had caught a touch of the infection and temperatures were rising. The demands now put forward were a clear challenge to the long-standing privileges of the land-owning governing class. They were two-fold. One was for a fairer rearrangement of the antiquated parliamentary constituencies—the county areas and the boroughs (towns). These constituencies mostly elected two members apiece, quite regardless of how many voters each contained. Indeed, all the evils and injustices still remained uncorrected and even intensified. Populous new factory towns such as Birmingham and Manchester returned no separate representatives. But the " pocket boroughs " and " rotten boroughs ", some of them with only one or two voters, still elected their pair of members. And the old bribery and control of elections by the wealthy went on merrily.

The other demand was for an extension of the franchise, or

In 1827, Britain, Russia and France defeated the Turks at the Battle of Navarino.

111

In 1830, William Huskisson, M.P. for Liverpool, was killed at the opening of the Liverpool-Manchester railway.

right to vote. At that time, in the English country areas, the privilege was restricted to landowners. Tenant-farmers and farm labourers had no say. In the boroughs the various qualifications were quite senseless; but in most places the voters were relatively few. In Scotland and Ireland things were just as bad, if not worse.

The Whig and Tory parties in Parliament were naturally reluctant to surrender the powers enjoyed by the governing class which they represented. But they both agreed that something must be done. The Tories were, by temperament, opposed to sweeping changes. The Whigs were more just and open-minded. Only the small group of Radicals (which formed the extreme Whig wing) stood, as a body, whole-heartedly for reform in principle as a step towards democratic or, popular, government.

In 1831, a battle royal began. The Whig government under Earl Grey introduced its boldly-conceived Reform Bill. The measure proposed to rearrange the parliamentary constituencies and sweep away many of their evils and injustices, and (as later amended) to extend the franchise to the middle classes—the farmers in the country and the shop-keepers in the towns who owned or rented property of a certain minimum value.

To the die-hard Tories the Bill came like a blow between the eyes. *They* would have called it the *De*form Bill. The measure was blocked by violent opposition. But a fresh general election returned Grey to Parliament with a handsome majority, for the country had set its heart on the Bill. Grey now got a second Bill through the House of Commons, but the Lords threw it out. And now the fat was in the fire. The country was seething. Grey piloted a third Bill through the Commons. The Tory Lords cut its heart out. After that the issue was stark and clear. Peers or people—which was it to be? Revolution, remember, was in the air.

GREAT REFORM BILL

The fateful issue was never tried that way. The king agreed, if necessary, to exercise his power of creating new Whig peers to cancel out the Tory majority in the Lords. Under that threat the peers doffed their coronets, as it were, and surrendered. On 7th June, 1832, the storm-tossed Reform Bill at last reached port with the royal assent.

Thus the people made the first great breach in the ancient stronghold of the governing aristocracy. True, it was only the middle classes who entered the citadel, but it was a very considerable beginning, and, in 1867, an even wider breach was opened in the defences. The Reform Act of that year gave the vote to householders and lodgers in the towns and certain householders in the counties, that is, to almost all the working class except agricultural labourers. And in 1884, these labourers too were given the vote. It is impossible to overstate the far-reaching consequences of this bloodless revolution. Britain became a democracy. Politically Jack was now as good as his master. Power had passed into the hands of the people—meaning the males. It only remained for that power to be organised to give it full expression, and a decisive advance towards that end was made with the formation of the Independent Labour Party in 1893.

In the year after the passing of the Act of 1832, the Whig government demonstrated that a reformed Parliament would in fact reform the laws. They attacked the shocking scandal of child labour. Amongst other inhumanities, little children of seven were kept toiling in the textile factories for twelve or more hours a day. The Factory Act of 1833 (one of a long series to come) prohibited the employment of children under nine and limited the hours of those under thirteen to forty-eight per week. Then, as a doubtful treat, the latter group were given schooling for two hours a day. The government also made a money grant for educational purposes. These were the first effective steps taken by the State towards the free, compulsory, universal education that children " enjoy " to-day. In the same year, thanks mainly to William Wilberforce and his fellow-workers, the monstrous institution of slavery was abolished throughout the British Dominions.

VICTORIA'S REIGN

King William died in 1837, and Queen Victoria began her memorable reign. The new queen was the daughter of William's brother Edward, Duke of Kent. She was an inexperienced young girl of eighteen, endowed with character, grace and dignity, and filled with a deep sense of her royal responsibilities. In all the varied events of her reign she exerted her influence in tireless devotion to the duties of her exalted office. Her accession ended the connection of the Hanoverian line with their continental kingdom, for the

Queen Victoria was welcomed to Paris by Napoleon III.

After the Mutiny of 1857, the governing of India was taken over from the East India Company by the Crown.

succession to Hanover was barred to females. In 1840, the queen was happily wedded to Albert of Saxe-Coburg-Gotha, the future Prince Consort.

The 1830's and 1840's were the boom time of the Railway Age in which Britain took the lead. The Stockton and Darlington line, opened in 1825, and the Liverpool and Manchester line which followed in 1830, had begun the new era of transport by steam-powered locomotives. By 1848, there were some 5,000 miles of railways in the United Kingdom, giving an immense impulse to every branch of industry and untold convenience to the general public.

SIR ROBERT PEEL

The Tory party had been badly shaken by their defeat on the Reform Bill of 1832. They were, however, rallied by Sir Robert Peel, and the new party that gathered round him declared themselves sympathetic to all necessary popular reforms. Peel was Prime Minister in a Tory government from 1841 to 1846. During that time he improved the hours and conditions of labour in the mines. He took another long step towards Free Trade by removing or reducing a host of duties. He reimposed the Income Tax that has vexed the taxpayer ever since. And then he took a further plunge into Free Trade. As a protection to agricultural interests the then existing Corn Law duties restricted the import of foreign grain. The cry now was that these " starvation laws " made bread dear for the hungry poor. In 1846 Peel abolished the iniquitous duties—and thereby abolished himself from office. He died four years later. He knew that he was attacking the interests of his land-owning Tory supporters, but he was a statesman who had the honesty and courage to put the public welfare before that of party. The workers remembered him with heartfelt gratitude. His action split the Tories into two opposing camps—Free Traders and Protectionists. It was not long, however, before Britain went over almost entirely to Free Trade. For a great while after this, party politics became rather confused. Indeed the very names of the parties underwent a change: " Conservative " for " Tory ", " Liberal " for " Whig ".

Meantime the irrepressible Lord Palmerston was finding plenty of foreign pies for Great Britain to put her finger in. The first important one was Russia's. Britain looked with unfriendly eyes on that aggressive and despotic power not only as a threat to her political interests, but as an enemy to human freedom. In 1841, Palmerston scotched Russia's designs for controlling the Dardanelles and Constantinople. A year earlier he had gone somewhat farther afield. He started a little war with China. It resulted in opening up the country to European trade and giving Britain Hong Kong. Nearer home, Palmerston gave encouragement and, where he could, actual aid to a crop of revolutions which, in 1848, had sprung up in Austria, Germany, Italy and France in support of progressive government and national freedom. The causes of these uprisings dated back to the French Revolution. Unfortunately, however, the new growths mostly withered away.

In 1853, Palmerston helped to bring about a real showdown with Russia. The Turkish empire was breaking up and the Russian Bear was hungering after some of the pieces as greedily as the wild bear hungers after honey. All attempts at restraining the brute miscarried and so the Crimean War of 1854-6 was waged against her by Britain and France— another interested party. The bitter combats of the Alma, Balaclava, Inkerman, and Sebastopol, the heart-stirring, suicidal charge of the Light Brigade " into the jaws of death ", and the sublime mission of Florence Nightingale to the neglected sick and wounded, are events in the struggle that will always fire the blood of British people. The peace terms duly chained up the Bear, but only for a time. It was in 1856 that the queen instituted the coveted Victoria Cross decoration " For Valour ".

THE MUTINY

Only a year after this, Palmerston (who had become Prime Minister) was faced with a more perilous trial of strength in India. In 1857, British authority was paramount throughout India proper and in Assam and Lower Burma on the east, and Sind and the Punjab on the north-west frontier. (The conquest of Burma was completed in 1886.) Suddenly the Mutiny exploded like a thunderclap. The causes of the uprising were numerous: a considerable decline in discipline among native troops; discontent and suspicion over British measures affecting native customs, caste and religion; and many others. The accumulated grievances were touched off by a mere mischance. Cartridges issued to the Sepoy soldiers, the tops of which had to be bitten off before use, were rumoured to be smeared with the fat of animals sacred

From 1874 until 1880, Benjamin Disraeli pursued a foreign policy which strengthened Britain's Imperial power.

to Hindus or untouchable by Moslems. Inflamed by this "outrage", the revolt spread with lightning speed over the northern and central provinces. The fighting took on the fury and ferocity of a struggle of wild beasts. Yet within a few months the back of the mutiny—it was never a national rising—was broken. By the following year, 1858, British authority, which had seemed imperilled, was restored.

The rule of the East India Company was thereupon taken over wholly by the Crown. And in 1877, Queen Victoria was proclaimed Empress of India.

The years following the Mutiny saw some noteworthy happenings in Europe. By 1860, most of the disjointed states of Italy had won their freedom from foreign rule and in 1861 they became united in a single kingdom. The remainder followed within nine years. Palmerston, needless to say, gave the movement his blessing. Prussia, too, came to the fore, till, under the steady guidance of the "Iron Chancellor" Bismarck, it had lowered the crest of Austria, and brought together a powerful confederation of North German States. But Bismarck was not yet satisfied. In 1870-1 the ravening Prussian Eagle dug its talons deep into France. Alsace-Lorraine was torn from her side. France once more became a republic. And, with its growing militarism and imagined racial superiority, the German Empire—a combination of the northern confederation and the southern states—was born, to cast its baleful shadow over Europe till it deepened into the black night of two World Wars.

GLADSTONE AND DISRAELI

At home, the death of Palmerston in 1865 left the political arena clear for the combats of two famous antagonists—Gladstone and Disraeli.

Benjamin Disraeli, the Conservative leader, was the baptised son of a Spanish Jew. He was clever, quick-witted, and ambitious. His great aims in life were to help the workers, to popularise the monarchy, to foster the unity, might and glory of the British Empire, and to exert Britain's influence boldly abroad. Gladstone, who became the Liberal leader, was a man of strong moral and religious principles. He had a terrifically powerful personality and a torrential gift of

speech that made him the greatest parliamentarian of the age. He disliked Disraeli's "Imperialism"—his inflated and aggressive notions of empire—and he strongly opposed over-much meddling in the affairs of other nations. He was a master of finance and a sincere social and political reformer.

It was Disraeli who carried through the Reform Act of 1867. That measure had extended the franchise to the town workers and others. And the workers were mostly uneducated. "We must educate our new masters", a politician of the time had remarked. And after the Liberals, under Gladstone, came into office they took that mission in hand. The Education Act of 1870 opened the path of schooling to every child by setting up local School Boards and providing for the building of more schools. It was not, however, till twenty-one years later that education became everywhere both compulsory and free. What those facilities meant to the future of the people hardly needs emphasising. It was like opening the eyes of the blind.

In 1874, Disraeli secured another term of office. He introduced several useful reforms concerning public health, housing, trade unions and other matters. Then he turned to deal with a tangled situation abroad. In 1877-8 the Russians, free now of their flimsy chain, defeated Turkey and liberated the greater part of the Balkans from the Moslem tyranny. "Imperialist" Disraeli (now Earl of Beaconsfield) thought the peace terms gave Russia far too much control in the Near East and backed up his protests with a display of troops and warships. Thanks to the astuteness of Disraeli and Lord Salisbury, the Foreign Secretary, Russia was forced to accept drastic modifications at the Congress of Berlin, and Turkey placed the island of Cyprus in British hands.

Another tangle was Egypt and the recently-opened Suez Canal, which provided a new sea-route to India. France and Britain held a considerable financial interest in the canal and the country. When the Khedive, the ruler (nominally under the Sultan of Turkey), became insolvent, Disraeli, in 1879, arranged for Britain and France to take over administrative and financial control of the country. Next year Gladstone returned to office and in 1881 Disraeli died. The Egyptian army rose against the foreign intruders. The French withdrew from the scene, and the peace-loving

On 6th May, 1882, Lord Frederick Cavendish, First Secretary for Ireland, was murdered in Phoenix Park, Dublin.

Gladstone was compelled to send ships and men to suppress the rising and protect the Canal. Then came a fanatical religious outbreak in the Sudan. Gladstone refused to take it in hand, but sent out General Gordon to withdraw the scattered native garrisons serving under British officers. Gordon, unfortunately, got cut off in Khartoum, and, in 1885, the dilatoriness of Gladstone's cabinet in sending troops to his relief resulted in his death. The people never forgave Gladstone for that. Britain remained in occupation of Egypt, and in 1896-8 Sir Herbert Kitchener brilliantly reconquered the Sudan.

Gladstone's long career, however, was destined to receive its finishing stroke from another quarter. The age-old irrepressible Irish demand for self-government, or " Home Rule ", had broken out in violent excesses. Gladstone felt that it would be wise and just to concede it. But all he succeeded in doing was to split the Liberal party on the issue. Many of his followers went over to the Conservatives, who looked on Home Rule as a very dangerous venture. That was in 1885-6 and for most of the remaining years of Victoria's reign the Conservatives, with their new " Liberal Unionist " allies, were in power. The Radical, or extreme Liberal Unionist, Joseph Chamberlain, who became Colonial Secretary in 1895, carried on Disraeli's Imperialist policy with glowing ardour, so that it continued to be a distinctive slogan of the Conservative-Unionist party. Gladstone retired in 1894 after a public career of more than sixty years. Four years later he died.

In the last quarter of the century imperialism was at its zenith. It had not always been so. About the mid-century many statesmen considered the colonies rather an encumbrance. It was largely resulting from this attitude that a number of the separate provinces of Canada and Australia, and also New Zealand (annexed in 1840), were made self-governing. Then, from 1867 onwards, the Canadian provinces, except Newfoundland, were federated as a single Dominion and, in 1901, the Commonwealth of Australia came into being. In Africa, self-government was granted to Cape Colony in 1872, and to Natal in 1893. All this was a very different policy from that which had lost Britain the American colonies in the previous century.

Colonial progress in Africa was complicated by the pre-

Following the murder of Europeans in Alexandria, the British fleet bombarded the city to suppress the rising and protect the Suez Canal.

As a reaction against British occupation a revolt broke out in the Sudan (1883).

sence of the Boers and the native tribes. British soldiers and statesmen had long been busily painting the map red in their conflicts and manœuvres with Kaffirs, Zulus, Boers, and others. In the final quarter of the century half a dozen European powers were engaged in grabbing as much territory as they could lay hands on. Britain naturally was not behindhand.

BOER WAR

But, in 1899, the most vexatious of Britain's colonial wars had broken out there. Sixty years earlier some thousands of Boers (descendants of the original Dutch settlers) had trekked northwards to escape from British rule. A series of unfriendly contacts ensued as the British, in the painting-red process, followed them up. Eventually the Boers were established in the Transvaal and Orange Free State as two independent republics, subject to certain British treaty rights. When gold was discovered in the Transvaal, outsiders—mostly British—poured into the country. Although these " uitlanders " paid enormous taxes, Kruger, the Boer President of the Transvaal, treated them very oppressively. In particular he refused to grant them the franchise which would have given them a vote—perhaps a predominant one—in the government of the country. He was, of course, fully entitled to do this, but his attitude was bound to infuriate the " uitlanders " and antagonise the British government. Kruger, however, was intensely patriotic and his ideal had always been " South Africa for the Boers ". Quite understandably, he hated the imperialist British and dreamed of driving them out of the land, maybe with foreign aid. The hare-brained Jameson Raid over the Transvaal Border and its swift suppression further inflamed his enmity and stimulated his hopes. Negotiations for a peaceful settlement broke down. Each side felt that it was suffering intolerable grievances and it seemed impossible to reconcile them. Kruger would not make satisfactory concessions on the franchise question. He had been heavily arming his country and in September, 1899, Chamberlain arranged for more troops to be sent out. Kruger replied with an ultimatum and in October war followed, the Orange Free State lining up with the Transvaal.

The Boers proved unexpectedly tough and elusive fighters. In 1900, however, Lord Roberts and Lord Kitchener (the Sir Herbert of the Sudan War) at last got the upper hand and the two republics were annexed. It was not, however, till 1902 that the beaten Boers laid down their arms. Only four years later they were granted self-government, and in 1909 Cape Colony, Natal, the Transvaal and the Orange Free State were combined in the Union of South Africa.

In 1901, the Victorian era had ended with the death of the queen after the longest reign in British history. Her passing plunged the empire into mourning. Her wise and sympathetic attitude had won the people's love and reverence. It had made the monarchy the symbol of empire, the link that united the far-flung units of that immense community of peoples in a common bond of loyalty.

VICTORIAN ACHIEVEMENTS

The years from 1815 to 1901 were a period of notable achievement in every phase of Britain's national life. No large-scale wars checked her progress. Her political system was transformed from an oligarchy to a democracy. The working classes, newly educated and organised, marched forward to power. The gloomy squalor of their lives was lightened. Britain, " the workshop of the world " and leader in the Industrial Revolution, multiplied its commerce and shipping, its manufactures and national wealth, although there was a serious set-back from the '70's onwards in the collapse of her agriculture under the pressure of foreign competition. Immense progress was achieved in the sciences of biology, geology, chemistry and physics. Advances of incalculable value were made in medicine, the most rewarding of which was Lister's discovery of the saving power of anti-septics in surgical operations. Besides the coming of the railways the period saw the first motor cars (speed limit four miles per hour to begin with), the introduction of gas and electric lighting, the development of the electric telegraph and telephone. These are only a few of a host of material benefits which included also cameras and bicycles. There were gains of a higher character: the growth of a more humane attitude towards the underdogs of society, and a deep concern with religion.

The long Roll of Honour in literature is starred with

In 1885, the German engineer, Gottlieb Daimler, perfected the 4-stroke motor which he fitted to a three-wheeled carriage.

brilliant names: the poets Tennyson, Wordsworth, Browning, Matthew Arnold, and Swinburne; the novelists Hardy, Dickens, Thackeray, " George Eliot " and the Brontes, besides those spell-binders, in both prose and verse, Kipling and Robert Louis Stevenson; the historians Macaulay, Carlyle, and John Richard Green; and countless writers on various aspects of thought and learning.

As for wordly dominion, Britain was the leading maritime world power. Her empire included Gibraltar, Malta and Cyprus in Europe; Canada, Australia and New Zealand; India, Burma, Ceylon, Hong Kong and the Malay States; broad domains in Africa; innumerable scattered islands in the East and West Indies and elsewhere in the Atlantic, Pacific, and Indian Oceans; mainland settlements in Central and South America; and stations in China.

Yet, before the end of the century, clouds were gathering on the horizon. Britain could not expect to retain indefinitely her lead in world trade, and it was being steadily reduced by her foreign competitors—especially Germany and the United States. And Germany, the strongest military power in Europe, was making a sudden and challenging increase in her navy.

Edward VII, who succeeded his mother in 1901, was a king of great personal charm, good nature and social tact.

In 1902, a Unionist government passed an Education Act which abolished the School Boards and provided for additional technical and secondary instruction. In the same year Chamberlain presided over a sort of empire family gathering or conference of colonies, which had been granted self-government—Canada, Australia, New Zealand, Newfoundland, Cape Colony and Natal. Resolutions were passed favouring Imperial Preference—the fostering of empire trade by taxing foreign goods more highly than empire goods. In 1903, Chamberlain boldly launched a crusade renouncing Free Trade and adopting Imperial Preference as a step towards closer empire union. The Unionist party, however, was in two minds on the subject and in the general election of 1906 they were thrown out of power.

LABOUR PARTY

The new Liberal government displayed many advanced

In 1899, the Boer War began after a breakdown in talks between Boer and British representatives.

At the end of the eighteenth century, enclosure of the fields was begun, restricting hunting to more modest areas.

Radical ideas of social reform. But the outstanding feature of the parliament was the first appearance of a strong Labour party. The working class had arrived to stay. They brought with them some disturbing notions. The most widespread was the doctrine of socialism, which had been developing since the previous century. Socialism means, among other things, a war on capitalism and excessive private profits, with State ownership, for the benefit of the community rather than the benefit of an individual.

PEOPLE'S BUDGET

Many social evils were now tackled and a start was made in providing school meals for the children of the poor and paying old-age pensions. Then came a battle royal. In 1909, David Lloyd George, a fiery Welsh Radical, introduced his "People's Budget". It was avowedly intended, by increased taxation, to take from the rich to help the poor. The Lords threw out the measure, though they were not supposed to meddle with "money bills". But, when another general election in 1910 again returned the Liberals to

The long reign of Victoria saw tremendous progress made in the fields of politics, industry and science.

office, the Lords had to swallow the unpleasant medicine.

Meantime, the Government had set themselves to abolish the power of the peers (the majority of them Conservatives) to override the House of Commons. The bill introduced by Premier Asquith provoked a lively commotion. But the Lords were worsted in the end. After 1911 they could only hold up bills for a period of two years. And they could not even do that with financial bills.

Edward VII's reign, which ended in 1910, had seen some notable mechanical developments. In 1901 the first transatlantic wireless message was transmitted from Cornwall to Newfoundland. In 1909, the Frenchman Bleriot achieved the epoch-making first aeroplane flight across the English Channel.

NATIONAL HEALTH INSURANCE

In 1911, after George V's accession, a measure of the highest social value was carried through Parliament by Lloyd George. The National Health Insurance Act provided for pay and free medical attendance for manual workers and many other employees, together with unemployment pay for workers in certain selected trades. (In 1920, the benefit was extended to most of the other industries.)

About this time Ireland was getting fighting mad again over Home Rule. In 1912, the Liberals introduced a new bill to grant it. Ulster, the north-eastern province, the greater part of which was predominantly pro-British and intensely Protestant, declared that it would fight rather than submit to an Irish parliament dominated by Catholics. Only the coming of a greater clash of arms in 1914 caused the problem to be shelved.

The aggressive attitude of Germany and the mutual distrust of the Great Powers had long been shaping events towards a world catastrophe. The nations had already lined up. By 1882, Germany, Austria and Italy had sealed the Triple Alliance. France replied with a Russian alliance in 1893. In 1904, Britain concluded the *Entente Cordiale*, or cordial understanding, with France. In 1907, she extended it to Russia. So, in 1914, the Triple Alliance and the Triple Entente stood face to face, like two angry neighbours gnashing their teeth at each other over the garden wall. The stage was set for the First World War.

BENJAMIN DISRAELI

Britain's Great Jewish Premier

Benjamin Disraeli—" Dizzy " to his friends and supporters —is the most colourful and intriguing figure in nineteenth-century British politics. His solid achievements and bizarre personality seem quite at odds with each other. With his deathly pale face, coal-black glossy hair and dark, blazing eyes, his dandified dress and beringed fingers, he appears like some exotic plant that has found its way into the trim English political garden. His contemporaries were divided in their opinions as to whether he was a charlatan or a man of sincere principles; few are quite sure about it to-day.

Disraeli's father was a Spanish Jew who renounced the practice of his faith when Benjamin was in his thirteenth year —he was born on 21st December, 1804—and permitted all his children to be baptised as Christians. Benjamin, none-the-less, remained proud of his race and its great spiritual and cultural history. When he left school at fifteen he was already aglow with a sense of his inward powers and athirst for fame. Continuing his studies at home, he revelled in the classical Greek, Latin and English authors and spent twelve hours a day conning his books. The music of fine language completely enthralled him and he threw himself ardently into cultivating his own powers of speech and writing. Presently he decided that the one satisfying field for his consuming ambitions was politics.

EARLY POLITICAL AMBITIONS

It was long, however, before he became free to open the gate into that preserve. He tried his hand in the law— unwillingly. He tried financial speculations—disastrously. Extensive travels on the Continent and in the Near East gratified his longing to see more of the world and its peoples. Before he was twenty-one he had written a remarkable novel

Benjamin Disraeli, Earl of Beaconsfield (1804-81), great premier of Queen Victoria's era.

which made him the talk of the town. It was the first of a life-long series which were unique in using works of fiction to set forth his political views. There followed a gay spell of fashionable social life. He met the leading figures of society, literature and politics. Finally, he stood for Parliament, having declared quite gravely that he intended one day to be prime minister. It was not until 1837, the year of Queen Victoria's accession, that Disraeli, then thirty-two, first entered the House of Commons as a member of the Tory party. He had already become a man of reputation and originality of ideas, but people still regarded him with suspicion and doubt.

Britain at this time was ripe for change, both social and political and Whigs and Tories alike were being forced by a growing popular agitation to adopt a policy of reform. The Whigs, however, had taken the lead in the movement. It was they who had pushed through the Reform Bill of 1832 which extended the franchise to the middle classes. The Tories, as upholders of the privileged aristocracy and country gentry, were naturally more cautious in advancing the popular cause, and as a result they had fallen out of favour with the electors. Disraeli's brand of Toryism gave them a new idea to think over. He had developed the theory that the founda-tions of British life were the Crown, the Church of England and the landed aristocracy. He believed that the masses were deeply loyal to these institutions and Tory at heart. He had always concerned himself about the hardships of the people and his aim now was to persuade his party to adopt their cause as its own. This "Tory democracy" plan would, of course, challenge the Whigs' pre-eminence in the reform movement. To the politicians of the time, however, the idea must have seemed like trying to mix oil and water.

But how was a young Member of Parliament, however highly charged he might be with energy and self-confidence, to effect such a change? Disraeli lacked all the advantages of birth and social influence. If he was to rise it must be by his own genius. His very personality was against him. His race, his florid oratory, his showy mannerisms and fantastic dress branded him as an outsider. They were, indeed, the expression of his romantic and orientally imaginative character; but they were un-English. His quick wit and cleverness and undis-guised ambition made him distrusted. All his life he had to contend with this feeling. Yet in time his commanding talents won for him a devoted and enthusiastic following. In the parliamentary debates the members found that he knew what he was talking about. As for the talking itself, his picturesque oratory and his rapier-like wit and biting sarcasms swept them off their feet. And with his keen intelligence he could read other men's minds at a glance and learn how to influence their actions.

QUEEN VICTORIA

The supreme instance of his personal magnetism appears in his relations with Queen Victoria after he had become a minister of the Crown. At first the queen strongly disapproved

In 1846, Disraeli led Tory opposition to Peel's repeal of the Corn Laws. Although the repeal went through, Disraeli had split the Tory Party and shortly afterwards the Government was out of office.

of him. Disraeli courted, flattered and amused her whilst tactfully and humbly deferring to her royal wishes. The queen was completely won over by his charm and the two became fast friends.

The spell-binder came into the full blaze of the parliamentary limelight during the agitation over the repeal of the Corn Law duties by the Tory premier Sir Robert Peel in 1846. In his devastating attack on the great leader, Disraeli's withering powers of scorn and irony won him a tumultous oratorical triumph. The duties were indeed repealed; but Disraeli had fatally shaken Peel's prestige. The Tory party split in two; the government fell; and Disraeli had established his reputation. Gradually he became the acknowledged leader of the Conservative party in the House of Commons. (From Peel's time onwards, the Whigs and Tories slowly regrouped themselves and became known as " Liberals " and " Conservatives ".) Under the influence of this new dignity Disraeli wisely abandoned his flashy manners and preposterous dress. In 1852, when Peel was dead, a Tory government, led by the Earl of Derby, gave him his first seat in the Cabinet—though it lasted for only a brief period—as Chancellor of the Exchequer.

DISRAELI AND GLADSTONE

The quick changes of fortune that followed brought Disraeli at length into the long duel with Gladstone that forms one of the most famous contests in British parliamentary history. The two combatants were natural enemies. Gladstone was a man of deep moral and religious principles and human sympathies. He had entered public life out of a sense of almost sacred duty. His supporters revered him as an inspired prophet. His opponents denounced him as a self-righteous hypocrite. No one but Disraeli could vie with him in oratory or parliamentary adroitness. He looked on Disraeli as insincere and cynical, a man possessed of a devil. Disraeli thought him slightly unbalanced. Gladstone guided his political course by lofty principles sincerely held. Disraeli, less morally earnest, cared more for practical measures than theories. Gladstone stood for political and administrative reform, such as an extended franchise and government economy, but he opposed too much State interference in social affairs. Disraeli wanted to shine as a practical Tory

democratic social reformer. The ups and downs in the campaigns of the two giants—the one so grave and passionate (and prosy), the other so brilliant and impassive (and flippant)—kept the country in a ferment of delicious excitement. There were no film stars or football favourites then to focus popular interest.

STRUGGLE FOR REFORM

The first great pitched battle was fought over the Reform Bill of 1867, by which, under the pressure of a riotous popular demand, it was intended to extend the vote to the town workers. Disraeli and most of the party leaders accepted the proposal in principle but differed on how far it should go. Few cared for a real democracy, but all were eager to claim the credit for introducing the reform in the expectation of capturing the votes of the new electors. Accordingly, the Bill which Disraeli, then Chancellor of the Exchequer in another Tory government, brought forward in 1867, provided for extending the franchise but limiting its range, by various safeguards against " going too far ". Gladstone and other reformers brought up their heavy artillery and delivered a crashing attack on the measure. The government was called upon to remove the safeguards. It was a blatant competition for party advantage in courting popular favour. The opposition parties were strong. The government was threatened with defeat and the consequential discredit of resisting the wider extension of the franchise. Disraeli, however, rose to the occasion. By prodigious efforts of eloquence and astute party tactics he silenced the enemy batteries. Turning completely about face, he agreed to the removal of the safeguards. The Bill was passed; the Tories could claim credit for it; and, in a phrase of the day, " the Whigs were dished ". Furthermore, the adroit Disraeli could now feel that he had won over his party to the cause of the people. Which was just as well for the party. The day of aristocratic privilege was passing; the future lay with democracy.

A year later Disraeli at last attained his early ambition. In his own expressive but somewhat undignified phrase, he " climbed to the top of the greasy pole " and became Prime Minister. But he soon slithered down again. The electors showed their appreciation of the Reform Act by returning a Liberal government in which Gladstone, also for the first time, became premier. Six years of fruitful legislation followed, the rival leaders busily sniping at each other all the time. Then, in 1874, the swing of the political pendulum installed Disraeli once more in office. He was nearly seventy now and a sick man. Yet the ensuing years were an outstanding period in his career. Still strong on his Tory democracy policy, he carried out a useful programme of social measures concerning public health, housing, slum clearance and trade unions. And his bold and romantic temperament launched out on new courses overseas. He had often displayed his pride in Britain's greatness. From about this time his ideas expanded. He was fired with the purpose of reinforcing the unity, power and glory of the British Empire. It was a policy of " Imperialism ", and it was to become one of the distinctive doctrines of the Conservative party for nearly half a century. To the peace-loving Gladstone, however, it seemed dangerously aggressive towards other countries and wholly unprincipled. Disraeli was treating the interests of Britain as paramount; Gladstone proclaimed the broader principles of international right and justice.

PURCHASE OF SUEZ CANAL

The first notable display of the new spirit took the form of a dramatic financial deal. The Suez Canal, which had been opened in 1869, was Britain's trade-route and life-line to India. More than half the shares in the Company that controlled it belonged to a French Company; the remainder were held by the Khedive of Egypt. About 15th November, 1875, Disraeli learned that the Khedive, whose purse was empty, was about to sell his shares to a French syndicate. Disraeli promptly decided that Britain's interests could never permit the deal. The Khedive's price for his shares was £4,000,000 and he wanted the money by 30th November. Disraeli lost no time. By the 25th he had overreached the French financiers by contracting to buy the shares for the British government. But how was he to find the money in time? The consent of Parliament was necessary, but the Houses were not then in session. Disraeli decided to take a risk. He borrowed the funds, at twenty-four hours' notice, from the Jewish international bankers, the Rothschilds.

Gladstone, mortified by his rival's success, talked of having him impeached, but nothing came of it. Disraeli's vision and promptitude had secured for Britain, not merely a highly profitable investment, but a share in the control of the Canal that was to be a weighty factor in future political developments.

EARL OF BEACONSFIELD

Next year, when ill-health made his duties in the House of Commons beyond his strength, the queen created Disraeli Earl of Beaconsfield. Thenceforth he carried on the premiership in the quieter waters of the House of Lords. In the same year his imperialism and his devotion to the queen blended in a proposal to exalt Her Majesty with the new title of " Empress of India ", which was duly proclaimed in 1877. Disraeli foresaw that the title would be regarded by the princes and peoples of India as a recognition of their country's distinctive position and that it would strengthen the ties of loyalty that bound them to the British Throne.

The years 1876-8 brought on a major engagement between the two rival captains. It occurred over "the Eastern Question". Briefly, the Moslem Turkish Empire had long been breaking up, Russia had long coveted Constantinople, and Britain, because of her interests in the Near East and India, had long determined that she shouldn't have it. To that end it had been her settled—and successful—policy to keep Turkey on its feet notwithstanding its shaky, corrupt and debased condition. In 1875-6, risings among the Christian subjects of the Turks in the Balkans had been savagely repressed by their masters and thousands of Christians in Bulgaria massacred by the Bashi-Bazouk Turkish irregulars.

A wave of horror swept over Britain as tidings of the Turkish atrocities of pillage and torture and murder came in. Gladstone, in a blaze of righteous wrath, fomented the storm of indignation with the demand that the miscreant Turks should clear out "bag and baggage" from the scene of their crimes. In 1877-8 Russia, posing as the Christians' champion, took the field, defeated the Turks and compelled them to sign the treaty of San Stephano which, among other provisions, set up Bulgaria as a great inde-

Because of the culpable delay of the Government, a British relief force was too late to save the beleaguered General Gordon's army at Khartoum.

In 1879, the British army had to contend with war with the Zulus, and only when their king was taken prisoner were the Zulus finally defeated.

pendent State under Russia's control. With Russian soldiers almost at its gates, Constantinople was again threatened.

TREATY OF SAN STEPHANO

Britain's anger over the Turkish atrocities was by now swallowed up in her traditional fear of Russia's fell designs. London was swept by a war fever and the streets rang with a rousing popular song:

We don't want to fight;
But by Jingo, if we do,
We've got the men, we've got the ships,
We've got the money too.
We've fought the Bear before,
And while Britons shall be true,
The Russians shall not have Constantinople.

That just about summed up Dizzy's feelings. It was, as usual, " Britain first! " with him. He had previously sent the fleet into the Dardanelles. He now brought Indian troops to Malta and called up the reserves. Russia took the hint. A conference of the great powers assembled in Berlin. Disraeli and Lord Salisbury, the foreign secretary, took a firm stand. The Treaty of San Stephano was drastically modified. Turkey was bolstered up again, Russia's designs were checked and Britain acquired from Turkey a protectorate over Cyprus as a base for keeping an eye on future events.

PEACE WITH HONOUR

When Disraeli returned home in 1878, sick in body but bringing " peace with honour ", he had won a bloodless victory for Britain. His triumph had raised him to the peak of his career and his countrymen acclaimed him with wild enthusiasm. All of which was gall and wormwood to Gladstone, who felt that Disraeli's conduct was a piece of selfish British Imperialism practised at the expense of the Balkan Christian peoples. And it must be said that Salisbury himself confessed later that Britain " had backed the wrong horse ", and subsequent events have gone far to confirm his opinion.

Gladstone believed that Imperialism encouraged wars, and about this time it did in fact provoke two, though in each case against Disraeli's wishes. Both were signalised by initial

disasters before the final triumph was won. The first outbreak occurred in South Africa, where, after the Transvaal had been annexed without fighting in 1877, the neighbouring Zulus were crushed two years later. The other conflict broke out in Afghanistan in 1878-80, over the strengthening of the Indian north-west frontier against the bogey of Russia's intrigues.

VICTORY FOR GLADSTONE

In 1879, Gladstone opened a new whirlwind campaign on the home front with a furious cannonade against Imperialism. The wars in South Africa and Afghanistan, with their early disasters, had greatly disturbed the country. The Turkish atrocities still lingered reproachfully in the public memory. These circumstances served as Gladstone's ammunition. He had reached the age of seventy, but the undiminished force of his burning eloquence swung his audiences over to his side. A severe trade and agricultural depression added to the electors' growing discontent with the government. In the General Election of 1880, Disraeli was turned out in favour of a Liberal administration with Gladstone at its head. And in the ensuing year the battle of the giants ended with Disraeli's death.

A MAN OF GENIUS

It is difficult to read the riddle of the Earl of Beaconsfield's character. Undoubtedly his guiding star was personal ambition. But that does not necessarily mean that he was cynically insincere in the major principles he adopted and constantly followed. He started his career as a political adventurer and, like other politicians, sometimes trimmed his sails to the changing winds of circumstance. Yet it is quite probable that he believed his doctrines to be good, not only for himself and his party, but for his country too. Historians differ in their opinions on the subject. What stands beyond question is that he was a man of genius and exuberantly powerful personality and that he was filled with a great love of Britain, in whose history he played a distinguished and not unfruitful part. To which we may add that he remade and revitalised the Conservative party, and created a new and inspiring conception of the grandeur of the British Empire and its majestic standing in the world at large.

FRANCE AFTER NAPOLEON

The downfall of Napoleon left France in complete turmoil. More than twenty years of revolution and war had sapped her man-power and emptied her purse. It was in the fervent hope of a return to peace and order that, in 1814, she accepted the restoration of the Bourbon monarchy in the person of Louis XVIII (Louis XVII, the son of the guillotined Louis XVI, has got lost to history: he probably died in prison in 1795, some say of poison). The new king—a clever, witty and corpulent old gentleman—had to face the task of steering the nation from the old order to the new. He did so by granting a Charter that preserved the main principles of the Rights of Man won by the Revolution of 1789. The political "franchise" however—the right to vote in parliamentary elections—was soon restricted to the richer members of the middle-class.

Louis, like all his successors, had to wade through a whirlpool of political agitation. France was distracted by conflicting parties, ranging from extreme royalists (eager to return to the bad old days of absolute monarchy) and Bonapartists (who longed to revive the Empire), to republicans and "liberals". Liberalism was a theme that, as the century wore on, was to effect a transformation in European political and social life. "Liberal" means "free", and the middle-class disciples of the movement were everywhere strenuously working for the same rights and reforms as France had gained. In France itself the Liberals felt that Louis' Charter did not go far enough towards popular government.

Louis skilfully steered a middle course through all these swirling currents; but, after his death in 1824, his autocratic successor Charles X was less wise. He practically destroyed the constitution—and himself with it. In July, 1830, Paris—always excitable and ready for violent measures—rose in revolt and Charles abdicated.

This popular explosion did not stand alone. There was a growing spirit of nationalism in Europe which impelled subject peoples to denounce their foreign tyrants and seek independence under their own rulers and institutions. The two upsurging movements of nationalism and liberalism, the one seeking national freedom, the other individual freedom, naturally became closely associated. Several upheavals had already occurred. Spain's Southern American colonies had broken free and Greece had risen against the brutal Turks. In 1827, at the battle of Navarino, the combined fleets of France, Britain and Russia annihilated the Egyptian and Turkish navies. As a result of this, Greek independence was assured. Following the Paris revolt in July, 1830, Catholic Belgium arose against her harsh Protestant Dutch masters and gained her independence. Other countries were less fortunate. In Germany, Spain, Sardinia, Italy and Poland the popular movements were almost everywhere repressed by the despotic rulers.

After Charles X's fall, the French crown was conferred on a member of the younger Bourbon line, Louis Philippe, the so-called "citizen king", who had long been making professions of his great affection for democracy. At first popular in Paris, under his Charter, constitutional government was preserved, but there was precious little advance in democratic principles, a circumstance which was to prove unfortunate for the king.

The nineteenth century, which was so prolific in popular stirrings, witnessed the growth of socialism. The movement gained force and urgency from the miseries of the poor resulting from the Industrial Revolution that was spreading from Britain to the Continent. The essential first step in establishing it was to secure an extension of the franchise to all, so that the workers might voice their grievances in parliament. Louis Philippe's government obstinately refused to concede this and other popular demands to his subjects;

Faced with almost impossible tasks, the Congress of Vienna met to decide the disposition of Napoleon's empire. All Europe sent important statesmen to attend the Congress and the well-organised social life of the Congress was a byword.

and in 1848 Paris protested in its usual explosive manner by staging another revolt. Last minute promises of reform were of no avail. Louis Philippe abdicated and hastily got himself smuggled across to Britain, and the insurgents deciding that they had had enough of the Bourbons, proclaimed a republic.

YEAR OF REVOLUTIONS

The year 1848, due mostly to the encouragement of the French revolt, produced a positive rash of outbreaks on the face of Europe—in Austria, Italy and Germany. But the strong medicines of the despots soon purged it away. The day of freedom had still not yet arrived. Even in France the insurgents, in the end, gained little except universal suffrage. A National Assembly did in fact confirm the republic, but the Socialists, who had been foremost in the street fighting during the revolt, were sternly crushed as dangerous fanatics. As for the new republic, that soon met its fate at the hands of a remarkable individual who now comes striding to the front—Louis Napoleon, a nephew of Napoleon Bonaparte.

The great emperor had by this time acquired something of a halo. The sufferings which his ambitious career had inflicted on his people were forgotten. He was the national hero who had covered France with glory and whose conquests had been made with the sole purpose of bringing the blessings of universal peace and liberal government to Europe. Louis Napoleon now stood forth as the heir to his glory and his liberalism and as the friend of working and middle classes alike. His own career already resembled that of the hero of an adventure story. He had fought for the nationalist cause in Italy. He had made two unsuccessful snatches at the French Crown. He had suffered banishment to America, exile in England and imprisonment in a French fortress from which he escaped five years later. And through it all he had steadfastly nourished the conviction that he would one day revive the Napoleonic line.

In 1848, he was elected president of the Republic. And four years later, by a shameful combination of force and flattery, deception and faithlessness, yet with the overwhelming approval of the people, he wrung the neck of the infant republic and made himself Emperor Napoleon III. (The great emperor's son had been Napoleon II, King of Rome, but he never actually ruled.) The adventurer's dream was at last realised. Once in power he began by ruling as an autocrat. Yet he sympathised with nationalist aspirations abroad, and in France, circumstances led him to concede liberal reforms.

As a usurper Napoleon III always had at the back of his mind, in company with higher motives, the thought that there was nothing like the glory of successful war for rallying the people round the throne. In 1854-6 he joined with Britain in the Crimean War against Russia. In 1859, he fought for the cause of Italian unity by allying himself with Victor Emmanuel II, King of Sardinia, against Austria. But midway in the operations, he was overcome by the horrors of the battlefield, the magnitude of the task he had undertaken and anxieties at home. So he made his peace with Austria and left his ally (from whom he acquired Savoy and Nice) to seek his own salvation.

The emperor's concluding military adventure was an encounter with a machine, a machine of high power and deadly efficiency—the Prussian army. The menacing growth of Prussia at this time towered over Austria and dominated

The landing in Algeria marked a renewal of French colonial expansion.

With the consent of the great majority of the electors, Louis Napoleon became Napoleon III, Emperor of France.

the North German States. That the two jealous neighbours would some day be at each other's throats seemed inevitable, yet the conflict that presently arose was wholly unnecessary. Its immediate cause was the offer of the vacant throne of Spain to Leopold of Hohenzollern, a distant relative of the Prussian King William I. The French fears of encirclement could have been dispelled peaceably. But the scheming Bismarck and the Prussian war party were spoiling for a fight, and their opposite numbers in France were frantically eager to oblige. So, in July, 1870, France threw down the gauntlet.

It was as if she were possessed of a devil, like that of the Gadarene swine, which drove her to destruction. Self-assured but lamentably unprepared, she hurled herself against the deadly, efficient Prussian war machine. Disaster followed on disaster. A French army 170,000 strong was shut up in Metz. Within seven weeks of the opening of the war another army of 100,000, including Napoleon himself, was encircled at Sedan and, on September 2nd, forced to lay down its arms. France, aghast, deposed the inglorious Bonaparte emperor

For nearly thirty years, Prince Otto von Bismarck was the power behind the throne of Germany.

On 17th November, 1869, the Suez Canal was officially opened to traffic. The first ship through was the French imperial yacht Aigle, *with the Empress Eugénie on board.*

and, setting up a new republic, gallantly continued the losing fight. Paris was besieged and bombarded. The ardent republican, Gambetta, made a spectacular escape from the city in a balloon to organise a volunteer army. But it was all of no avail. The Metz army surrendered. On 28 January, 1871, after a siege of 131 days, starving Paris capitulated and an armistice was signed. Meantime the exultant victors, arrogantly installed in the palace of Versailles, proudly proclaimed the new German Empire.

LOSS OF ALSACE

The harsh peace terms reduced France to the depths of shame and humiliation. Alsace and part of Lorraine were wrested from her. Alsace, it is true, was mainly German in population, but it had lived as a part of France for two centuries. An enormous indemnity was exacted, the German troops remaining in occupation till it was paid. France never forgot her abasement. In the years to come France nursed a burning thirst for revenge and the recovery of

On 2nd September, 1870, after the Battle of Sedan, Napoleon III, with 80,000 men, surrendered.

the lost provinces, till the First World War came to slake it.

Sad at heart, the Third Republic turned to setting its shaken house in order. After a period of fierce political strife and civil commotion the National Assembly, in 1875, decided, by a single vote, that France should remain a republic. A new constitution was created by a series of laws which set up a parliament of two houses: a Chamber of Deputies, elected by universal manhood suffrage, and a Senate, under a president elected by the two houses. The new constitution endured, in substance, until 1940. Before the end of the century several liberal laws were passed; free compulsory education was established; and the Socialists grew into an organised political party.

INDUSTRIAL GROWTH

During the nineteenth century France shared, of course, in the universal advances in science and industry: railways, the electric telegraph and telephone, steamships and the like. The progress of the Industrial Revolution was less disturbing there than in Britain. While France has her heavy and light industries (iron, steel, coal, motor-cars, luxury goods and so on), agriculture is the predominant occupation. The greater part of the land is tilled by thrifty and industrious peasant-proprietors who are deeply attached to their holdings. Of the specialised crops, the grape-vine, cultivated for the wine industry, is the most noted. The republic also built up a vast colonial empire, though much of it was sandy waste. Including her ancient possessions, it embraced great areas on the continent of Africa and in Indo-China; five towns in India; Guiana: and various American and Pacific islands. Two famous canals are associated with the great French engineer Ferdinand de Lesseps: that of Suez, opened in 1869; and that of Panama, begun in 1881 but afterwards taken over by the United States.

In foreign affairs, Europe was hurtling towards the catastrophe of the First World War of 1914. The great powers were lining up, the Triple Alliance of Germany, Austria and Italy facing the Triple Entente of Britain, France and Russia, and the strains and stresses that precipitated the final clash were building up. The spark that was to set the blaze alight was touched off on June 28th, 1914.

GARIBALDI
And the making of Italy

Giuseppe Garibaldi's life-story forms the liveliest chapter in the history of his time and country. It shows how a man with the heart of a roving adventurer helped to achieve a seemingly impossible feat of patriotism.

When he was born—in 1807 in Nice—no other country of Europe had fallen from such a height to such a depth of political fortune as Italy. Once, she had been the heart and centre of the great Roman Empire and the cradle of learning and culture. Later, the old Imperial City of Rome had become the high seat of the popes whose spiritual authority extended over the Catholic Church of the West. But, since the fall of the empire in the fifth century, Italy had been the dismembered prey of a succession of foreign invaders—barbarian, French, German, Spanish, Austrian and others. In Garibaldi's youth it was the long-standing Austrian tyranny that dominated and oppressed her people.

Under such circumstances what hope—what thought indeed—could ever arise of making Italy a free and united nation? Yet in 1848, in common with so many other European countries, revolution broke out in Italy. The French Revolution of 1789 and Napoleon Bonaparte's tyrannous conquest of Europe set in train a universal demand for the rights of man, for liberal reforms and for national freedom. It was then that the first cries for liberation and unity—feeble as yet as the bleating of a lamb—were heard in modern Italy.

ITALY UNDER AUSTRIAN DESPOTISM

But the cries were ruthlessly silenced, the weak and scattered risings suppressed. The representatives of the kings and emperors who assembled at the Congress of Vienna in 1814-15, after Napoleon's downfall, wanted no more popular upheavals. Italy was partitioned into eight kingdoms and duchies, much on the former lines and mostly under rulers with Austrian connections. So the Austrian tyranny was firmly re-established. Lombardy already formed part of the sprawling empire; now Venetia was added to it. All the other States could look to Austrian armies to support their despotic rule.

Yet the struggle still went on, and in 1831 it was galvanised anew by a young Genoese idealist, Giuseppe Mazzini, who founded the association of " Young Italy ". Mazzini fervently proclaimed the fight for freedom and unity as a religious duty. And it must be won, not by looking to foreign aid, but by massed popular risings against the arch-enemy Austria. " Do it yourself! " was his slogan. His numberless conspiracies—he was an indefatigable plotter—had little practical success; but his untiring efforts and passionate faith lastingly strengthened and ennobled the rising spirit of Italian nationhood.

IN EXILE

It was one of his plots that, in 1834, brought the twenty-seven-year-old Garibaldi into the field of action. The new recruit was a sailor and the son of a sailor, a strong-willed and self-reliant young merchant-captain whose voyages had taken him up and down the Mediterranean and beyond. Garibaldi's part in the new scheme was to join a ship in the King of Sardinia's navy and win over the crew. (The so-called " Kingdom of Sardinia "—one of the eight Italian States—embraced, in addition to the Mediterranean island, the mainland provinces of Piedmont, Savoy and the Genoa district. As Piedmont was its real centre, the kingdom is commonly called by that name). But, as usual, something went wrong with Mazzini's designs. Mazzini had to fly.

After Mazzini's release from prison, he was forced to go into exile. He went to Marseilles where he organised La Giovine Italia, *or* Young Italy *movement with whose help he hoped to liberate Italy from foreign and domestic tyranny.*

Garibaldi, sentenced to death, skipped away to South America.

The hot-bed of revolution was to prove the cradle of his fame, the arena where he revealed and developed his remarkable qualities as a leader of fighting men. With the tough, red-shirted legion of Italian exiles which he enlisted, this steady-eyed, utterly fearless and self-confident adventurer set the world agog. His rousing exploits and dare-devil escapades bordered on the unbelievable. Impelled by a passion for freedom—anywhere and everywhere—he fought in two revolutions. At different times he figured as privateer, naval commander and general. His skill and audacity won a chain of victories in the field. He became a master of guerrilla warfare.

REVOLUTION IN ITALY

Fourteen years later Italy, ringing with his fame, beckoned him home. For it was 1848, the " Year of Revolutions ". Europe was astir again. Italy was in a ferment. Sicily (which, with southern Italy, formed the kingdom known as " the Two Sicilies ") revolted. Parliamentary constitutions were won in four States: the Two Sicilies; Piedmont; Tuscany; and the Papal States, which were ruled by the Pope as a sovereign prince. Milan threw out its Austrian garrison. Venice declared itself an independent republic. And a new, royal leader had arisen in Italy. Many patriots had built their hopes on Charles Albert, the descendant of the House of Savoy who ruled Piedmont. He had disappointed them in the past, but now he had come forward with his army to strike a blow against Austria. It seemed that the war of liberation had really begun. The bleating of the lamb had sharpened to the tiger's snarl. Italy's hopes soared.

They soared only to fall the farther. Around Custozza, in July, 1848, Charles Albert's army suffered heavy defeats. Austria's grip on the north was everywhere restored, save in Venice.

The focus of interest shifted to the Papal States. The progressive Pope Pius IX had warmly favoured liberal reforms. Now, however, taking fright at the revolutionary excesses of the highly excitable Roman mob, he changed his views and decamped. He found refuge in the kingdom of the Two Sicilies, where the Spanish Bourbon King Ferdinand II was steadily engaged in stamping out the rebellion in Sicily.

Garibaldi, with a few score of his Red Shirts, had landed in Italy in the previous June. After some sharp encounters with the Austrians in the north, he eventually turned his steps towards Rome, gathering a nondescript force on the way. In February, 1849, Rome proclaimed itself a republic, and soon Mazzini arrived from his London exile to direct its fortunes. Meantime, the fugitive Pope had appealed to the Catholic powers of Europe to restore him, and France responded with a powerful army. King Ferdinand, too, sent troops to his aid. Garibaldi, with his scratch legions, bravely fought them both, but the odds against him were overwhelming. In July, the republican leaders were constrained to surrender and Pope Pius returned to his realm.

VENICE SURRENDERS

Garibaldi, however, scorned to lay down his arms. Away in the north, Venice, hard pressed, was still stubbornly battling with the Austrian White-Coats. Garibaldi, with some 4,000 volunteers, set out to their aid. Italy will never forget that famous march. With the soldiers of France, Ferdinand and Austria striving to encompass him, the wily leader, by masterly tactics and invincible endurance, escaped their clutches. Not for nothing had he learnt his lessons as a " guerrilla " fighter on the wide pampas of South America. But he never reached Venice. That heroic city, besieged and blockaded by land and sea, reduced to starvation, and smitten with cholera and typhus, at last lowered its flag.

Italy now lay once more beneath the grinding heel of the despots. Garibaldi withdrew from the scene and eventually sailed for New York. There for a long time he worked as a candle-maker, then captained a trading-ship to China, and back via Australia. In 1854, he went to England, where he received a rapturous welcome. During these and the ensuing years a new dawn was breaking for Italy. The European situation was changing. The wrongs of the Italians became a subject of general concern. The British government's openly expressed sympathy served as an active help in their

A landowner in the Piedmont district, Cavour worked for the political, industrial and agricultural development of his country, eventually becoming Prime Minister of Piedmont in 1852. He then worked for the unification of Italy, supporting with some reserve, Garibaldi's enterprise. Cavour lived to see Victor Emmanuel of Piedmont proclaimed king of Italy.

In an endeavour to expel the Austrians from Italy, King Victor Emmanuel II had an interview with Garibaldi, the patriot, and appointed him commander of the Alpine Corps.

Garibaldi and his "Thousand" landed at Marsala on 11th May, 1860. On the 15th of May, he had defeated the Neapolitan troops at Calatafimi, and on 20th May, Palermo was taken.

struggle. Austria's power was declining; that of Piedmont was rising. Victor Emmanuel II, an ardent patriot and a more resolute king than Charles Albert, now ruled the State, guided by his capable minister Count Cavour, who had sworn to make Italy united or die.

Piedmont still enjoyed the benefits of the free parliamentary constitution granted in 1848. Cavour was a staunch supporter of liberal principles of government and a consummate diplomatist. Under his directing hand the country steadily advanced in military power and economic prosperity. Gradually the patriots realised that their brightest prospects of unity and freedom lay in the liberal rule of the House of Savoy. Garibaldi was among them. The republican and revolutionary Mazzini held aloof. He distrusted all monarchies and wished Italy to work out her own salvation. Cavour believed that the cause could never be won by popular revolutions alone, but that foreign aid was essential. Working tirelessly and patiently, he urged his king forward, boldly defied Austria and won France as an ally.

FINAL VICTORY

In 1858-9, the French Emperor Napoleon III secretly agreed with Cavour to support Piedmont if Austria attacked her. Cavour's clever manœuvres assured that war did in fact break out; and Austria got such a drubbing that she might have been driven out of Italy if Napoleon had not withdrawn his troops, thus leaving his ally in the lurch. However, Victor Emmanuel did very well in the end. He won Lombardy by the sword; and, in 1860, the duchies of Tuscany, Parma and Modena and the northern Papal State of Romagna came over to him.

Garibaldi had returned to Italy in 1854, and later taken a hand in hammering the Austrians. In 1860, an adventure after his own wild heart opened up. The turbulent Sicilians had invited him to lead a revolt against their new, semi-idiotic King Francis II. It was for this desperate exploit that the great guerrilla captain enrolled that motley and ill-armed band of Red Shirts who are known to fame as "The Thousand". Landing in Sicily, they advanced on Palermo. The city was defended by a garrison of some 20,000 royal troops; but the Red Shirts fought their way in and, by amazing boldness

and good luck, forced its surrender. Garibaldi, strongly reinforced, then crossed over to the mainland, drove the royal forces before him, put the king to flight and entered Naples in triumph. He had liberated the whole of southern Italy and Sicily. It was his greatest hour. Cavour now intervened with a bold stroke. Following his advice, King Victor Emmanuel marched down through the Papal States to join hands with Garibaldi and mopped up the Marches and Umbria during his progress. In 1861, he was proclaimed as the first King of Italy. Soon afterwards the new kingdom suffered a grievous loss in the death of Cavour. The great statesman had worn himself out with his onerous duties.

Venetia and the Papal State of Rome still remained outside the fold. But in 1866, with her eye on Venetia, Italy joined Prussia—another rising State—in a war against Austria. The Italians got rather a bad mauling, but Austria got a worse one from Prussia, and as a result Venetia was successfully shepherded into the fold.

FRENCH TROOPS LEAVE ROME

France was the main obstacle in Rome. Her troops were still stationed there to defend the Pope's sovereignty. In 1870, however, Prussia again came to the fore and toppled Napoleon III from his throne within seven months. Necessity compelled the French to withdraw from Rome. And, as they walked out, the Italians walked in. The Pope, of course, retained his spiritual authority. But he lost his ancient territorial realms. Italy's *Risorgimento*, or resurrection, as her people proudly call the liberation movement, was at length completed.

The irrepressible Garibaldi performed many more notable feats before his death in 1882, but they are of relatively minor importance. He would have been a glamorous and exhilarating figure under any circumstances: the times gave his talents free rein. His irregular strong-arm methods, serene self-assurance and independent spirit constantly made him a sore trial to Cavour and other leaders. He was the rough fighting man, with no head at all for the wiles of diplomacy. But he takes his stand with Mazzini, Cavour and Victor Emmanuel as one of those who achieved the " seemingly impossible feat " of freeing and uniting Italy.

1848: THE YEAR OF REVOLUTIONS

The European events of 1848 give one a Guy Fawkes Day feeling: the fireworks were going off everywhere. The causes go back to the French Revolution of 1789. That explosion started a chain-reaction which went fizzing across Europe and beyond. As the revolutionary armies marched into the neighbouring countries they proclaimed the Rights of Man and the doctrines of liberty, equality and fraternity. In so doing they gave rise to the later middle-class "liberal" crusade, for political and social reform. Furthermore, when Napoleon crushed Europe beneath his heel, a new passion for national independence developed among all subject peoples. And, alongside these upsurges of feeling, socialism had intensified its struggle to right the wrongs of the labouring classes. So the three movements of liberalism, nationalism and socialism, which were to transform completely the people's lives during the nineteenth century, marched boldly forward.

LIBERAL YEARNINGS

It helps us to realise the crying need for reform which existed in every country in Europe if we try to picture the oppressive conditions of the times. Austria affords a glaring instance of them. The emperor could make laws and levy taxes at will. The Press was muzzled, free speech curbed and new ideas banned. Police spies were everywhere. Many of the peasants were still serfs, oppressed by privileged nobles and bigoted priests and victimised by harsh criminal laws unfairly administered. The only effective remedy was a parliamentary constitution, with a wide franchise, or suffrage, that would give the people a vote and voice in their own government.

After the downfall of Napoleon in 1814, the autocrats of Austria, Prussia and Russia had rigidly set themselves against all progressive ideas. They wanted no more revolutions, French or otherwise. Europe needed peace. So they banded themselves together, as a sort of police force, to keep things as they were. Britain, guided by her forceful Foreign Secretaries Castlereagh, Canning and Palmerston, associated herself with them in the keeping of the peace, but no further. She would not lend herself to attempts to stop the clock of progress. The police force, accordingly, was not always effective. Though many of the agitations which arose, up to 1830, were crushed, France threw out her autocratic King Charles X and Greece, Belgium and the Spanish American colonies secured their independence.

FRANCE SETS THE PACE

When the struggle was renewed in 1848, most of Europe was affected but it was chiefly in France, Austria, Italy and Germany that the fireworks started a real blaze. The French set the example by the wild uprising of Socialists and others. France became a republic, with Louis Napoleon as president, and secured universal manhood suffrage. Austria, under its Foreign Minister Metternich, was the most purblind and obstinate opponent of reform. She was also the very centre of nationalist grievances. The Habsburg Ferdinand I ruled despotically over a quarrelsome menagerie of peoples of different race, language and traditions: Germans, Czechs, Poles, Magyars, Roumanians, Croats, Serbs, Italians and others. It was Metternich who ruled the country, however, and his rigid, illiberal policy was the main cause of the rebellion of 1848. The excited students of Vienna started a lively revolt that set Metternich flying for his life (in a laundry cart) and brought the frightened emperor to terms. The Italian States arose against their hated Austrian and Spanish Bourbon masters. Germany had long been hungering for the union of its various States in a single empire. Street fighting in Berlin

Inspired by the Revolution in France and Belgium in 1830, the population of Warsaw rose up against the Russians.

The first revolution in the Year of Revolutions broke out in Sicily ; the population demanded independence.

In Vienna, the one-day revolt of 13th March, 1848, by a group of students, gave the people of the city their freedom and forced Metternich to resign.

When William II ascended the throne of Germany, he allowed Otto von Bismarck to hold the reins of government. Bismarck was later dismissed, William assuming command.

and other cities now won the promise of a constitution.

Yet, with some few exceptions, such as universal suffrage in France and the new (but very undemocratic) constitution in Germany, these revolts all came to nothing. The autocratic monarchs, letting loose their armies, won the day. None-the-less the clock of progress had by no means stopped. If we follow the general history of the countries involved we shall hear it ticking on.

In Italy it is at its loudest. For centuries the divided country had been the spoil and battle-ground of alien powers. But, in 1859, fortune gave her a leader in the gallant and progressive Victor Emmanuel II, whose kingdom of Sardinia included also Piedmont and Genoa. Under him, with the able assistance of his Prime Minister, Count Cavour, she resumed the passionate struggle against her foreign tyrants. By 1861, most of the disjointed States had won freedom and unity. Nine years later the remainder followed. It was in these campaigns that the noble and valiant Garibaldi and his thousand Red Shirts earned imperishable glory. Victor Emmanuel became the first king of the united country and a parliamentary constitution was granted. Long before the outbreak of the First World War Italy had developed into a major industrial, naval and military power.

BISMARCK

Germany's future, from 1862 to 1890, was largely marked out by the wily diplomacy and inflexible purpose of Prussia's "Iron Chancellor", Bismarck. By 1866, Prussia had seized Schleswig-Holstein from Denmark, thrashed Austria and established the Confederation of the North German States. In the Franco-Prussian War of 1870-1, which brought about the downfall of Napoleon III, she dealt her neighbour a sledge-hammer blow and annexed Alsace-Lorraine. The German Empire of the northern and southern States was proclaimed. Under its constitution universal male suffrage was introduced; but there was no real democracy and the emperor, or Kaiser, exercised the widest autocratic powers. Expanding industry fostered the growth of socialism. Bismarck strove to suppress it; but, in the interests of the monarchy, he favoured some State socialism, such as sickness-

and old-age-insurance, to content the restless working classes.

To strengthen the country's international position Bismarck, in 1879 and 1882, formed the Triple Alliance with Austria and Italy which lasted till 1914. Meantime extensive colonies were founded in Africa and the Pacific. In 1888, the sabre-rattling and vainglorious Kaiser William II stalked to the throne. Germany was already infected by an arrogant spirit of militarism and fancied racial superiority, and the intemperate outbursts of "the All-Highest" kept Europe in a constant state of tension. The empire, with its expanding population and wealth, competed with the world in industry and commerce and challenged it in naval and military power. It all led to the tragedy of 1914 and the outbreak of the First World War.

REFORMS IN AUSTRIA

Austria's crest had been irrecoverably lowered in her 1866 scrap with the Prussian Eagle. The Emperor Francis Joseph whose reign extended from 1848 right down to 1916, turned his attention to the internal discontents of his ramshackle empire. Initially a despotic ruler with no sympathy for liberalism or nationalism, his attitude, after the war, relaxed a little. In 1867, the two parts of the realm, the Austrian provinces and Hungary—thenceforth known as Austria-Hungary—were granted self-government in home affairs, each with its own parliament. In Austria, all men of twenty-four years were given the vote in 1906; but the franchise in Hungary was always very restricted. The empire now looked to the south-east, the Balkans, for its future. But this was a troubled field, in which the Russian Bear was already prowling and growling. It was also an area where nationalism won some notable triumphs: Serbia, Roumania, Montenegro and Bulgaria threw off the cruel Turkish yoke. It was a Serbian spark that set Europe afire in 1914.

By then most of Europe—to sum up our original theme of reform and nationalism—had won some measure at least of parliamentary constitutional government. Even in Russia reform had advanced a step. Germany and Italy had each achieved unification and nationhood. Belgium and the Balkan States, too, had gained their freedom. The age of the abolute monarchs in Europe was over.

BISMARCK
The Man of "Blood and Iron"

Among the historic characters who have shaped the Europe of to-day, Bismarck towers up like a grim mountain peak. During the twenty-eight years of his power, his strong hand and calculating mind created the German Empire whose grandiose and swollen ambitions, after his departure, precipitated the catastrophe of the World War of 1914. The huge shadow of that ruthless and dynamic figure still lies across our path.

Otto von Bismarck was born in Brandenburg of an old Junker family on 1st April, 1815, the year of Waterloo. The Junkers were an aristocratic and rigidly conservative class of proud and privileged landowners, army officers and civil service officials who exercised a dominant influence in the Prussian State. From them sprang the harsh and arrogant jack-boot Prussian gentry.

Bismarck's early years were spent in a Prussia that had endured many troubles and changes since the death of the great Frederick. Feeble rulers had weakened it internally. Napoleon had broken its military backbone. Then came a revival of spirit under the impulse of the new national, political and social movements that were agitating Europe in general.

"Germany" was still only a conglomeration of great and petty States, of which Prussia was one. The liberating doctrines of the French Revolution and the sufferings of the subsequent wars had deeply affected German thought and feeling. They had aroused a hunger for national unity and for liberal institutions which would give the people greater individual freedom, and for parliamentary government instead of autocratic rulers. In Prussia, during the period of revival, many advances were won by that kingdom. Feudal injustices were swept away and the peasants redeemed from serfdom. The administration was reformed. A new and

more democratic conscript army made Prussia a nation in arms. A patriotic spirit of self-sacrificing and all-embracing duty and service to the Fatherland was fostered.

The Congress of Vienna, which sat in 1814-15 to settle the affairs of Europe after Napoleon's downfall, had scant sympathy with these ardent aspirations. Germany was grouped into a loose confederation of thirty-nine independent States under the headship of Austria, and an assembly, the Federal Diet, was set up to conduct its affairs. Of the northern States, Prussia was the most powerful. Her possessions reached from the Rhineland on the west of the Rhine to Silesia and East Prussia, though there was a big break—formed chiefly by Hanover—in the middle. Prussia was obviously a dangerous rival to Austria for the leadership of the Confederation.

The outlook for national unity and reform now became distinctly gloomy. The rulers of the various confederate States, with few exceptions, were intensely jealous of their sovereign independence and opposed to liberal progress. In Prussia the reform movement was eventually stayed and largely defeated by the conservative Junkers. The Federal Diet was not a people's parliament but an assembly of the rulers' envoys. But often, when the direct road to your objective is blocked, a way round to it appears by chance, and something of the kind happened in the approach to the unity of Germany.

From 1818 onwards a *Zollverein*, or customs union, was formed by Prussia and an increasing number of states, but not including Austria. This commercial organisation, with its customs-parliament, gave a considerable fillip to trade; but it did a great deal more. As a practical working measure, it further encouraged and familiarised the idea of a political union, this time with Prussia holding the sheltering umbrella and Austria left out in the rain.

The year 1848 was "The Year of Revolutions" for nationalism and reform all over Europe. Germany broke out into fierce riots and furious street-fighting. The uprisings, however, were relentlessly suppressed and the unprogressive constitution granted to Prussia in 1850 was like giving the agitators a stone when they had asked for bread. The rebellion had achieved nothing.

So far we have said little about Count von Bismarck, because there was little to say. In his university days he had shown himself a hard drinker and a great practical joker and fought at least twenty-five students' duels. His relish for food, drink and tobacco became, in fact, gigantic. He once avowed that no man should die till he had smoked a hundred thousand cigars and drunk five thousand bottles of champagne. Time made him a man of tremendous strength and stature. He had a compelling gift of speech and a bluff and boisterous geniality that proved irresistible. (But he was cold and hard within.)

In the Year of Revolutions, Bismarck attracted considerable notice by coming out as a strong supporter of the Prussian monarchy and traditions and a determined enemy of liberal-

The inhabitants of Berlin rose in revolt on 18th March, 1848.

At Sadowa, a small village near the Elbe, the Prussians defeated the Austrians on 3rd July, 1866.

ism. But it was not until 1851-9, when, as Prussian envoy, he attended the Federal Diet at Frankfurt, that he made a significant display of his powerful qualities. It was then that he became convinced that a war to the death with Austria was an essential step towards the supremacy of Prussia. Later, he figured in the diplomatic service at St. Petersburg and Paris. His travels in Britain and France and his diplomatic offices gave him a supremely valuable insight into international politics. In 1862, when he was forty-seven, his great moment arrived.

In the previous year, William I had ascended the Prussian throne. William was a well-intentioned, soldierly autocrat who believed firmly in the divine right of kings but was not wholly opposed to reforms. He regarded the unification of Germany, minus Austria, under Prussian leadership as his country's sacred mission; yet he was neither so bold nor so unscrupulous as Bismarck in pursuing that aim. In 1862, a political storm blew up over a plan for reforming and increasing the army. The House of Representatives, which had been created under the constitution of 1850, contained a strong party of liberal and more advanced democratic reformers, and the plan was rejected. A straight fight thereupon opened between the progressive parties and the king. William, at his wits' end, called in Bismarck and appointed him minister-president (prime minister) to deal with the crisis. Bismarck dealt with it in characteristic fashion. " Blood and iron " were to be his methods, not parliamentary rule. In flat defiance of the Liberals, he weeded out his opponents, gagged the Press, raised taxes illegally and spent the proceeds on the army reforms.

But this success was a mere skirmish compared with the contest he was to wage on a wider field next year. The King of Denmark was also Duke of Schleswig and Holstein. The population of those provinces, however, was largely German, and Holstein was one of the member-States of the German Confederation. In 1863, when King Frederick of Denmark died without children, a dispute arose about the succession to the duchies. The Danes wanted to incorporate them completely with Denmark. The German Confederation wanted them both for themselves. Bismarck eventually made up his mind that they should be added to Prussia, though Prussia hadn't a shadow of right to them. But he must proceed warily. Almost everyone in Germany was against him, in-

cluding the Federal Diet, his own king and the Prussian parliament. And there was the awkward fact that the Danish succession to the duchies had been guaranteed under treaty by Russia, Britain, France and other countries, including Prussia itself.

Next year, then, to cloak his designs, Bismarck persuaded Austria to co-operate with Prussia in occupying the duchies and forcing Denmark at the sword's point to cede them to the two allies jointly. This done, he set about ridding himself of his now unwanted partner and securing the stolen prizes for Prussia alone. But would any of the foreign powers intervene to check his little game? Not Russia, he thought: he had already cultivated the Tsar's friendship. Not Britain, he felt sure: to his mind her foreign policy was feeble. There remained France: Bismarck quieted her by spoon-feeding the Emperor Napoleon III with vague hints of territorial compensations—all of which in fact came to nothing. Thus secured, Bismarck went ahead on a course that made a conflict with Austria all but unavoidable. In 1866, Prussian troops marched into Holstein and the occupying Austrian forces withdrew. "When rogues fall out honest men come to their own"—sometimes. The German Diet sided with Austria. Whereupon Prussia declared war on both the Confederation and Austria.

The Prussian army had been organised and drilled and equipped till it had become a fighting machine of deadly might and efficiency. Six weeks proved long enough for it to overthrow the Confederation forces and lay Austria low in the decisive defeat of Sadowa. Prussia stood forth as master in Germany. The long-standing pre-eminence of Austria was forever destroyed. The disputed duchies were annexed. The " break " in the Prussian domains was closed by the acquisition of Hanover and the neighbouring States. In 1867, the North German States were combined into a close federation under the predominance of Prussia and with Bismarck as Chancellor. The southern States were left alone for the time being, for Bismarck realised that they were not yet ripe for inclusion with the Prussianised north.

This glorification of Prussia had been achieved by Bismarck's boundless audacity, astuteness and resolution. Calmly and unfalteringly, he had enforced his will, regardless of opposition or of right or wrong.

These, however, were only the first fruits of his activities.

131

With the defeat of the French in 1870, the German Empire, as visualised by Bismarck, was born.

He now turned to ripen and complete the harvest. He would bring in the southern States. Once again he must walk delicately. The apprehensions of France at Prussia's rising power would have to be reckoned with, and Bismarck probably came to believe that the issue would eventually be decided by a clash of arms. In the end he made a conflict certain by a piece of diplomatic trickery that goaded Napoleon III into the formal declaration of war. Thus France was made to appear, in the eyes of the world, as the aggressor. Germany was merely defending itself against a jealous rival. And the southern States, sufficiently ripened now by the sun of German patriotism, rallied to Prussia's side to fight in the common cause.

The story of the final crisis and of France's humiliating defeat in the war of 1870-1 is a tragic one. With the end of the fighting the harvest was all gathered in. France lost Alsace and part of Lorraine and had to pay a large indemnity. North and South were brought together, under Prussian domination, in the new German Empire. And Europe was faced with the startling spectacle of a Germany that had become, in the space of only nine years, the strongest and most efficient power in Europe.

During the remainder of his career Prince von Bismarck, as he now became, overshadowed Europe with his vigorous personality. The diplomats of every country recognised and feared his intellectual superiority and masterly statesmanship. His position, as minister-president of Prussia and Imperial Chancellor, coupled with the confidence and trust of the Kaiser (Emperor) William I in his popular servant, placed the direction of Germany's public affairs almost wholly in his hands. Under the constitution of the empire the ruling power was vested in the King of Prussia as Kaiser and his Chancellor, together with an Imperial Council, in which Prussia held a leading position. There was also an assembly, the Reichstag, which, being elected by universal manhood suffrage, was representative of the people; but, as far as its effective powers were concerned, it was much like a chained dog.

There was no more need of " blood " in the Chancellor's policy, but there was a plentiful use of " iron ". Bismarck was a ruthless upholder of the brutal old Prussian traditions of State policy. His foremost aim was the greatness of Prussia and the empire it had created. He had already shown that to secure that end, all means, fair or foul, were considered justified. Moral obligations—truth, honour, good faith, justice—were cynically disregarded. Might was right. The Iron Chancellor would tolerate neither rivals nor opposition. His enemies he hounded to ruin. Those who had served him, but could serve no longer, he cast aside like worn-out gloves.

None-the-less he did not always have things his own way. In particular, the continual conflict he waged with the Liberals and Socialists was by no means always successful for him. Strangely enough, his adroit tactics gave birth to the first comprehensive system in Europe for insuring the workers against sickness, accident and old age. Bismarck was not playing Father Christmas: he was trying to make socialism appear unnecessary by granting these concessions voluntarily.

In his foreign policy the Chancellor strove to keep Germany out of further wars and to preserve the peace of Europe. The empire was satisfied with its gains; its present need was to consolidate and organise itself. Bismarck wanted to be good friends with Britain and Russia. Yet, in the long run, the alliance he made with Austria and Italy led to distrust and to the counterbalancing "entente" between Britain, France and Russia which completed the line-up of the First World War.

The years brought a menacing change in the attitude and outlook of the German nation. A new generation grew up that was *not* " satisfied ". Under Bismarck's rule, Germany had been Prussianised, not only in its administration, but in the arrogant Junker militaristic traditions and methods. Intoxicated with their past triumphs, the Germans yielded themselves to the heady doctrine of their superiority in race and culture, in science and efficiency and in war. As the empire's population, trade and commerce increased, an inevitable demand arose for further expansion and dominion as a world-power in competition with other States.

The ageing Chancellor tried to curb the excesses of the excited young hounds who were yelping around him. But he could not divert the approaching course of the empire's destiny. In 1888, William I, his master and friend, died and another kaiser " who knew not Joseph " presently came to the throne. Conflicts of temper and policy quickly developed. William II kept Europe in continual alarm by his displays of the mailed fist of German might and his challenge to Britain's naval supremacy. Moreover, he meant to be his own master and, therefore, his own Chancellor. In 1890, to the consternation of the empire, he dropped the pilot who had guided Germany for twenty-eight years and embarked on the uncharted course that culminated in the calamity of 1914.

For that calamity Bismarck cannot be held directly responsible. His part was this: he unified the German people in a powerful empire; and he infused into that empire the pernicious Prussian doctrines of statecraft by which he had created and sustained it. How he would have acted had he lived in 1914—he died in 1898—no man, of course, can tell. His career shows that, when it seemed good policy, he could exercise a wise restraint. But what his rash successors did with the deadly weapon he had placed in their hands the world knows to its cost.

The German Empire has crashed; but its creator, notwithstanding all his faults—particularly his repression of his countrymen's healthy democratic growth—is still honoured by most Germans as a great national hero.

SPAIN LOSES SOUTH AMERICA

Spain cut a sorry figure in Europe after the War of the Spanish Succession which ended in 1713. After Britain's North American colonies revolted in 1775 she tried to pay off old scores by operating with the French and Dutch pack that were yelping around Britannia's skirts at the same time. But it was in the Napoleonic wars that Spain once more performed a star part. True, she was on the losing side at Trafalgar: but it was no disgrace to be beaten by Nelson. Where she earned lasting fame was in defying Napoleon, after he had driven out the Spanish Bourbon king Charles IV and the Crown Prince Ferdinand in 1808 and set up his own brother Joseph in their stead. The unquenchable national spirit of her people gave the Duke of Wellington his opportunity in the Peninsular War; between them they opened the first cracks in the Corsican ogre's European empire. After Napoleon's fall in 1814, Ferdinand returned to rule over what was still a far-flung empire, extending from the Balearic and Canary Islands and North Africa to the Philippines and the Americas.

But in the Americas, Spain's hold had long been slipping. The colonies were governed by viceroys sent out from home. They, and their officials, controlled the settlers, body and soul, by their complex and oppressive administration. All commerce with foreign countries was forbidden. The royal officials formed a privileged class and their meddlesome powers aroused constant discontent among the Creoles (those born of Spanish parents in America) and other sections of the population, which included the native Indians, negroes imported from Africa and those of mixed white, Indian and negro blood. The settlers began to demand a fuller share in their own government and, when this was not forthcoming, ideas of separation from the mother country naturally arose. One of the strongest ties that had bound the peoples to Spain was that of religion. The Jesuits, who laboured devotedly in converting the Indians and advancing the development of the country, were zealous supporters of the monarchy, and the influence they exercised over their flocks was profound. In 1767, however, having fallen out of favour with the reforming King Charles III, the Jesuits were driven out of the American colonies. Their departure seriously weakened many of the peoples' attachments to the Crown.

The successful rebellion of Britain's North American colonies in 1775 set many of the southerners thinking. Then came the French Revolution of 1789, proclaiming to the world the principles of liberty, equality and fraternity, followed by the movements for liberal reforms and national independence which agitated Europe in the 1820s. The disturbing new doctrines quickly found their echo in southern America. And in between, when Napoleon dethroned Charles IV, it must have seemed to many of the colonists that self-government had become an even stronger right. Thus the movement towards independence accelerated until, beginning in 1809, the colonies, like a mettlesome bunch of corralled broncos, one by one kicked their way through the fence and galloped away to freedom.

The outstanding hero of the liberation was the soldier-statesman Simon Bolivar, the son of a Spanish nobleman. Bolivar was born in Venezuela and he had sworn to set that colony free. Besides being a great commander, he was a man of liberal ideas and swift and resolute action. In 1810, he instituted the first locally-formed government in Venezuela. In his campaigns against the royal troops the Liberator, as his grateful followers called him, fought more than 200 battles. He won countless victories, but he suffered defeat, disgrace and exile as well. Yet his spirit never faltered. In 1819, he performed one of his most famous military feats. To aid a revolt in Colombia he set out from Venezuela with a " foreign legion ", of which British and Irish adventurers formed the

Itúrbide, a Spanish army commander, went over to the side of the revolutionaries against Ferdinand VII of Spain. He had himself proclaimed Itúrbide Augustin I of Mexico, but after a short, extravagant reign he was forced by Congress to abdicate.

backbone. Suffering intense hardships, his army tracked its way over the freezing Andes in to the scorching plains beyond. There the ragged and weary troops soundly defeated a royalist army and broke the power of Spain in Colombia.

When Bolivar died, in 1830, he had not only performed his vow to free Venezuela; his ardent leadership had led to the liberation of Colombia, Ecuador, Panama, Peru and Bolivia (named after him) as well. By that time, actually, all of Spanish South America, the Isthmus and Mexico had freed itself of the Spanish yoke.

BRITISH SUPPORT

Meantime, these independence moves had been causing growing concern to the autocratic sovereigns of Austria, Russia and Prussia. They feared their effect on the restive elements in their own realms. So, together with France, they proposed to help helpless Spain regain her territories. But here Britain spoke up—and, incidentally, hit back at Spain for her support of Britain's own revolted colonies. Her Foreign Secretary Canning favoured liberal reforms and flatly declared that Britain would oppose intervention. In 1823, President Monroe proclaimed the famous doctrine that has ever since been a cardinal principle of the United States' foreign policy. In effect it said to Europe " Hands off America! " Next year Britain formally recognised the republics of Mexico and Colombia, as a start. And that was that.

The colonists' break with Spain has not been everywhere and wholly a gain for them. The mother country had at least given them the order and security of centralised rule. Freedom has been followed by much material prosperity; but it has also brought to many of the republics unstable governments, characterised by frequent internal revolutions and wars, with unequal political rights and much social backwardness.

Meantime little Portugal's vast Brazilian colony was following the same path as its neighbours. In 1822, King John VI's son, Pedro, who governed the colony as regent, declared for independence with himself as emperor. Then in 1889, after a revolution, a republic was proclaimed.

Simon Bolivar, liberator and statesman, secured independence from Spain for Venezuela, Colombia, Ecuador, Panama, Peru and Bolivia.

North American assistance and the British fleet came to the aid of the insurrectionists in Argentina, Uruguay and Chile.

The Spanish reaction to the movements for independence in South America, resulted in the rebels being shot without pity.

The loss of southern America was not even the beginning of the end of the Spanish empire: Florida and Louisiana had already passed to the United States. Presently came the turn of Cuba. The condition of revolutionary chaos that ruled in the island occasioned the intervention of the same powerful neighbour. As a result of the ensuing Spanish-American War, of 1898, Cuba became an independent republic and the Philippine Islands were ceded to the States. Next year Spain sold the last of her Pacific islands—the Carolines and others—to Germany. Thus ended the magnificent overseas empire that had once made Spain so immensely rich and powerful. All that remained to her were the Canary and Balearic Islands and her holdings in North Africa.

Spain has made little advance in modern democratic government. The liberal reform movement of the 1820's gained no effective hold on her people. When the First World War began, her Bourbon king, Alfonso XIII, ruled over a nation that enjoyed little of truly representative parliamentary government.

THE SICK BEAR

From the time—1703—when Peter the Great founded St. Petersburg and so opened a window on Europe, Russia drew increasingly closer to the West. In the Napoleonic Wars she played an important part by providing the conqueror of Europe with his first real setback. After the emperor's fall, she joined Prussia and Austria in opposing all European movements for social and political reform. Her own domestic history during the nineteenth century centres round the same obstructive policy.

ALL-POWERFUL TSARS

The tsars were complete autocrats. They could make wars and laws, and tax or imprison their subjects as they pleased. Their army of officials and secret police were the oppressive, and often corrupt, agents of the tsar's grinding tyranny, and frequently far worse than their imperial masters. The peasant masses were ignorant, superstitious and down-trodden serfs, bound to the soil and to the exacting service of the land-holding gentry.

The new ideas of reform which flooded in from the West were enthusiastically adopted by teachers, writers and other men of enlightened mind. The tsars, however, believed that the old medieval Russian ways were the best. They regarded the clamour for representative parliaments, popular education, freedom of speech and the Press and such-like nonsense as a danger to the State, and waged merciless war against them. The leaders of the reform movement were flogged, hanged, imprisoned, or exiled to the horror of the Siberian mines. But persecution could not stamp out the

flames. The fight went on. Violence begat violence. The more desperate agitators, the "Terrorists", systematically marked down the most conspicuous of the offending officials, and even the tsar himself, for assassination. And, while the intellectuals were raising their voices, the wretched peasants were roaring out for the breaking of their chains. Those were terrible and threatening times. It was as if the tsars were sitting on a volcano. If one day it should erupt—like France in the Revolution of 1789 . . . Some concessions were in fact exacted from the government. Decrees of Alexander II in 1861 and Nicholas II in 1906 emancipated the serfs. And in the latter year the first duma, or representative parliament, was elected. But the successive dumas were rigidly controlled and liberal progress stifled; these concessions existed only on paper.

TRANS-SIBERIAN RAILWAY

During these times more substantial things than ideas entered the country. The Industrial Revolution and the Machine Age found their way there and the textile, metal and other industries notably expanded. Railway building began in the 1830s, and between 1891 and 1905 the great Trans-Siberian line, from Moscow to Vladivostok on the Pacific, a distance of nearly 6,000 miles, was constructed. The growth of factories and of town life inevitably fostered the rise of socialism, and the clamours of the industrial workers joined in the chorus for reform.

Meantime the empire was making a vast expansion abroad. From early times the rulers of Russia had coveted Constanti-

Wanting equal civil rights and a say in the government of the country, a peaceful demonstration of thousands of workers, led by the priest Georgy Gapon, on 22nd January, 1905, marched to the Winter Palace of the tsar. Unfortunately the tsar was not at the palace and the troops, taking fright at the size of the demonstration, fired on the crowd killing about 1,000 people.

In a desperate attempt to save the monarchy in Russia, Nicholas II abdicated in favour of the Grand Duke Michael. The failure of the abdication was to be anticipated and, in any case, the Grand Duke Michael refused the crown. The royal family were imprisoned and finally shot. The popular uprisings which started in Russia with apparently economic beginnings very soon assumed a political aspect.

nople and control of the Bosphorus and Dardanelles straits, which would give them a warm-water port and access to the Mediterranean. They were, indeed, interested in the whole Balkan peninsula. In the early nineteenth century that region still formed part of the Turkish empire. Many of the oppressed subject peoples were of the same Slav blood and Orthodox Christian faith as the Russians. The tsars, who were the heads of the Orthodox Church, considered themselves their natural protectors and made the most of the fact to further their imperial ambitions.

CLASH WITH BRITAIN

Throughout the nineteenth century the Turkish empire was breaking up, and Russia coveted some of the pieces. Her designs, however, were steadfastly opposed by the other interested powers, especially Britain and Austria-Hungary. Britain saw in them a menace to her interests in the eastern Mediterranean and the overland route to India. Austria-Hungary had its own ambitions in the Balkans. Accordingly it became the settled policy of these powers to keep Turkey on her feet as a bulwark against Russian encroachments.

Some of the encounters that arose, include the liberation of Greece in 1829, the Crimean War of 1854-6, and the Russo-Turkish War of 1877-8 which freed Serbia, Roumania and Montenegro. Bulgaria became completely independent in 1908, and later the new States did some extensive poaching on such territories as had been left to their old Moslem oppressors. None-the-less (and whatever Russia may think about it) though the Turkish republic which has superseded the former empire retains only a foothold in Europe to-day, its flag still flies over Constantinople. It was the continuing rivalry of Russia and Austria-Hungary in this uneasy region which kindled the spark that blew up Europe in 1914.

JAPAN AT BAY

Russia had better luck in Asia and along her southern boundaries. Half the great land mass came into her grasp, extending as it did from Siberia in the north to the borders of Persia, Afghanistan and China in the south. But, when she

About the year 1900, the revolutionary movements in Russia began to develop into something more definite. One of the boldest and most resolute leaders was Nikolai Lenin, returned from exile in Siberia, who united the efforts of those anxious to overthrow the imperial régime.

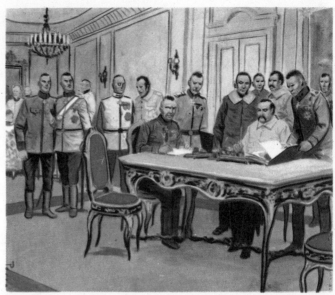

The Treaty of Brest-Litovsk between Russia and Germany was signed on 3rd March, 1918, and Russia withdrew from the First World War.

started encroaching on Manchuria and sneaking down into Korea, she encountered a road-block. For opposite Korea lies Japan. And Japan regarded the peninsula as her own particular preserve. The outcome was the war of 1904-5. Japan had recently made herself a strong naval and military power. The result of the war astonished the world. The Russian fleets were annihilated, and the Russian armies driven back. Japan acquired Port Arthur and later Korea was annexed.

The news of these disasters reached home at a time when the liberal and socialist agitations had produced a universal ferment of rebellious discontent. Bad harvests brought famine to millions of peasants. The humiliating defeats in the Korean war were charged to the scandalous mismanagement and corruption of the government. The national indignation flared out in widespread strikes, peasant risings and other disorders. Nicholas II was forced to summon the duma; but its activities were hamstrung as before.

When the First World War opened, Russia lined up in the Triple Entente which had been formed with France in 1893 and with Britain in 1907. But the country was utterly disorganised by its violent internal discords and its incapable, dishonest government. The shamefully ill-equipped Russian troops were mowed down by the Germans like grass before the scythe.

THE BOLSHEVIKS

In 1917, the volcano erupted. The monarchy perished. The extreme Bolshevik ("majority") revolutionary party, in a rising organised by their ruthless leader Lenin, and his associate Trotsky, seized power and set up a dictatorship of the workers. This epoch-making convulsion known as the October Revolution was the initiation of a fully Communist State controlled for the benefit of the working classes. In 1918, Russia signed the treaty of Brest-Litovsk with Germany and withdrew from the war. A few months later, Nicholas II, the last of the Romanoffs, and his family were massacred.

In the long and agonising period of intellectual awakening Russia brought forth a noble and vivid literature. The works of Turgenev, Tolstoy, Dostoyevsky and Chekhov are read the world over.

THE NEW WORLD AND THE U.S.A.

America was discovered by chance—as if you were looking for a sixpence and found a sovereign. The Portuguese, ambitious to convert the heathen and tap the dazzling treasures of the East, pioneered the Cape route to India. Perseveringly they felt their way round the Cape of Good Hope to India, to the Spice Islands (particularly the Moluccas), the prime object of their quest, to China and Japan. In 1492, Spain entered the race.

The geographical knowledge of those times had some remarkable gaps. The 1492 map of the globe made by the German mariner Behaim shows western Europe and eastern Asia with little but a width—greatly underestimated—of ocean in between. The existence of such trifles as the American continent and the Pacific Ocean was entirely unsuspected. The Viking discoveries of 500 years earlier were unknown or forgotten in Europe generally. Columbus, like other leading geographers, believed that the earth was a sphere and not flat. Accordingly, if you sailed west long enough, you must eventually reach the east. That was the theory he burned to test. His ultimate aims were the same as the Portuguese, but the pursuit was intensified by his ardent and mystical temperament. He believed himself to be divinely destined to perform some great work. A lot of people thought both him and his theories just plain crazy.

Crazy or not, he at last gained support for his daring venture from Queen Isabella of Castile. In 1492, with three small ships and crews who were already half-unmanned by fear, he sailed out to brave the terrors of " the Sea of Darkness ". Five weeks after leaving the Canaries his quaking and rebellious crews were relieved by the sight of land ahead. They had made the Bahamas. Columbus thought he had reached the fringes of Asia and the Indies—hence the misleading name of the West Indies to-day. Afterwards he hopefully made three more voyages, searching for a strait leading to the Spice Islands, and in 1498 he sighted the mainland of South America.

DISCOVERY OF NEW WORLD

It was some time before the truth was known, though more voyages of exploration continually increased Europe's meagre knowledge of the newly-discovered lands. In 1497-8 England took a turn. Another Genoese navigator, John Cabot, sailing under the patronage of Henry VII, discovered what was probably Newfoundland and explored the North American coast from Labrador southwards. In 1500, the Portuguese Cabral sighted Brazil and claimed it for his king. Next year Amerigo Vespucci, a Florentine, explored the northern and eastern coasts of South America and later somehow gave his Christian name to the new continent. In 1513, the Spanish adventurer Balboa, climbing a mountain in Darien (Panama), looked out in astonishment on the Pacific. And in 1520, Magellan penetrated the straits that now bear his name and sailed for ninety-eight long days across the vast empty wastes of the Pacific. So Europe gradually learned its geography lesson: a new continent and a new ocean lay between the Atlantic and the East Indies.

Spain and Portugal between them claimed all the new discoveries, and to avoid disputes a remarkable arrangement was effected. The Pope laid down a dividing line which, with subsequent changes, gave Brazil to Portugal and the rest of the Americas to Spain. Whereupon Spain resolutely set itself to exclude all other countries from trade or colonisation in her allotted domain. England and France, however, were to have something to say to that.

As the Spaniards spread from the West Indian islands to the mainland they found ample compensation for having missed the Spice Islands. They had discovered El Dorado, the land of gold, instead. The evidence of its abundance made gold their prime object. In 1519, Cortez, one of their

On reaching the island which he named San Salvador, Columbus and his men give thanks to God for their safe delivery.

Conquistadors, or Conquerors, with six hundred adventurous soldiers behind him, marched into Mexico and found such marvels as took the invaders' breath away. They had come upon a highly organised civilisation, that of the Aztecs, which itself had succeeded that of the Mayas. In the densely populated lake-island capital (now Mexico City) they gazed on magnificent stone palaces and temples and paved streets, and on every hand their eyes were dazzled by a splendour of gold and silver and precious stones beyond all they had ever dreamed of. The Aztecs had a system of writing and a calendar. But their religion to European eyes was barbarous: human beings by the thousand were sacrificed to their gods. Cortez made short work of it all. Within two years he had captured King Montezuma and destroyed his capital. The Aztec empire, with its gold and silver mines, passed into the hands of Spain.

The next glittering prize was Peru. Pizarro, a cruel and treacherous Conquistador, set off in search of it. And he, too, found an elaborately organised civilisation in being. Its buildings were massive masterpieces of masonry. Its roads — one of them 3,000 miles long — were of astonishingly skilled construction. In 1533, Pizarro, having started with 183 men, entered Cuzco, the capital city. Two years later the Inca empire followed the same road as the Aztec and a new stream of silver and gold and gems flowed into Spanish coffers.

By the second half of the sixteenth century the main lines of the Spanish conquest, from Mexico to Chile and Argentina, had been marked out. The Portuguese, too, were gradually exploring and settling Brazil. America had entered on a new phase of its history, the era of European domination. The native " Indians " (another " howler " of naming), as a whole, had little reason to love their new masters. They were reduced to virtual slavery, though the Franciscan, Jesuit and other Roman Catholic priests laboured heroically for their spiritual and bodily welfare. With negro slaves from West Africa added to the racial hotchpotch we get the makings of much of the mixed population of to-day. Spanish and Portuguese rule lasted down to the nineteenth century, when the various colonies freed themselves.

Notwithstanding Spain's claim to sovereignty, the history of North America was destined to be written mostly by the

The despotic rule of Montezuma, the last Aztec emperor of Mexico, was due to end with the arrival of the Spaniards.

English and French, with a brief paragraph by the Dutch.

France was early on the scene. From 1534 onwards, Cartier discovered and explored the St. Lawrence. England didn't really wake up till Elizabeth I's reign. Those were the great days when England's rumbustious mariners roved the seas, seeking adventure and discovery, treasure and spices, trade and colonies. To such men the Americas beckoned irresistibly, and the nation's bitter hatred of her old enemy Spain added zest to their response. Drake, sailing in 1577, circumnavigated the globe and wrought havoc on Spain's Pacific ports. Frobisher and Davis, between 1576 and 1587, went groping after a north-west passage to the Indies. Gilbert, in 1583, claimed Newfoundland for England. Raleigh tried—unsuccessfully—to plant a colony in "Virginia" in 1585 and 1587.

In the seventeenth century the idea of colonisation came to the fore. England, France and Holland were cut-throat rivals for commerce and empire in an expanding world. Spain's preposterous claims to sovereignty in North America were blandly ignored. English colonies were planted, the

The first permanent colony in New England was formed by the passengers aboard the little ship, Mayflower.

first permanent settlement being in Virginia in 1607. Later those settled by the Dutch were seized (and their capital, New Amsterdam, was renamed New York). Finally the thirteenth colony, Georgia, was founded in 1732. Other settlements were made in and around the West Indies, Newfoundland and Hudson Bay. In 1655, Cromwell's conquest added Jamaica to the bag.

THE RACE FOR COLONIES

So much for England. But France was continuing her activities too, her head filled with dazzling designs of the great colonial empire which she planned to create in North America. In 1608, Champlain had established the first permanent white settlement at Quebec. Other stations sprang up in Newfoundland and Nova Scotia and round Hudson Bay; but by the terms of the treaties of Utrecht and Rastadt, France lost these in 1713-14, after the War of the Spanish Succession. Meantime French trappers and missionaries were ranging and settling in the St. Lawrence Valley. In 1682, La Salle, sailing down the Mississippi, reached its mouth in the Gulf of Mexico. The whole region was claimed for France and named Louisiana and a colony was established on the lower reaches of the river. This was steadily linked up with Canada by a chain of forts and trading posts. For the French had conceived a masterly design. They would make the whole interior country their own and pin down the English on the Atlantic coast. But the Seven Years' War of 1756-63 wrecked that plan. With the fall of Quebec and Montreal the empire that France had laboured over for a century and more was shattered for ever. France was left—as were the Dutch—with only her West Indian islands and a holding in Guiana on the South American mainland. (Later, Britain, too, got a slice of Guiana.)

When England established her colonies in the New World it was as if she had cast a stone into the water whose ripples encompassed the globe. For from those settlements sprang the United States, the future world-power. It was English blood that first flowed into the veins of Uncle Sam. The march of events was to declare that North America should be neither Spanish nor French but Anglo-Saxon. The language and literature of England, her legal system and

The first shot fired at the Battle of Lexington was to re-echo throughout the country. The people rebelled against the government imposed upon them and demanded the right to govern themselves.

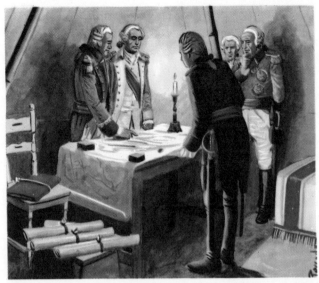

Although General Washington was not a brilliant tactician, by sheer force of character he inspired confidence and a strong national spirit in the country, which was to make him the guiding spirit of the American revolution.

parliamentary government and free institutions were to prevail in that wider field. England was the Mother of North America.

But there was soon to be a bitter family quarrel. The unhappy dispute centred mainly on the claim of Britain to tax her children without their consent. And it led to the War of American Independence.

The first shots were fired at Lexington and Concord, Massachusetts, in 1775. In the same year the American Congress, acting for the thirteen colonies, took defensive measures and appointed George Washington, a rich Virginian tobacco planter, commander-in-chief of the " rebel " forces. Washington had already won distinction in the French wars and shown himself to be a fearless soldier and a man of untiring energy and cool judgment. A rather significant encounter had taken place at Bunker Hill, near Boston. The British General Howe, with reinforcements from home, had fought an engagement which, though successful, had shown that the despised American volunteers could stand up to the disciplined regulars. In 1776, Washington succeeded in forcing Howe out of Boston. On 4th July, Congress drew up its famous Declaration of Independence, asserting the right of all men to life and liberty under their own chosen form of government. Later in the same eventful year Howe drove Washington from Long Island and occupied New York.

Two notable events starred 1777. Howe crushingly defeated Washington at Brandywine Creek and captured Philadelphia. But at Saratoga the British suffered a disaster that was to have momentous consequences. General Burgoyne foolishly got himself and his entire army of 3,500 men surrounded and was forced to surrender.

The general result of the fighting up to the winter of 1777-8 was deeply discouraging to the Americans. Washington, with his small, defeated army, spent the season at Valley Forge, Pennsylvania. His men were half-naked, half-frozen and starving. Sickness and desertions almost halved their numbers. Only the unconquerable spirit of their beloved general kept the remainder together. Only the amazing slackness of General Howe saved them from total annihilation.

But in 1778 the tide began to turn. The news of Saratoga had electrified France. Thirsting to avenge her recent loss of empire, she sprang to the colonists' aid. Next year Spain joined her, and in 1780 Holland followed. The effects were crippling. Britain's sea communications were disrupted and she had to defend herself against the fleets of her enemies in the West Indies, the Mediterranean and India. At the same time the American cause was strengthened by a tonic draught of French supplies and trained soldiers. Meantime, Clinton, who had superseded Howe, extended the war into the southern colonies. For three more years the stubborn fight continued, in this and other areas. Then, in 1781, at Yorktown, Virginia, came the last decisive grapple. The British General Cornwallis and 7,000 men, besieged and blockaded by American and French land and sea forces, were compelled by Washington's brilliant strategy to lay down their arms.

Britain had been defeated by her own muddles and miscalculations, by the decisive efforts of France and her European allies, and by the grit and resolution of Washington. The great captain's noble strength of character had won the deep devotion of his countrymen and inspired them with his own undauntable will to win.

In 1619, a Dutch ship from the coast of Guinea sold the first negro slaves to the tobacco planters of Virginia.

AMERICAN CONSTITUTION

In 1783, the peace treaty was signed and Britain recognised the independence of the United States. The western boundary was fixed at the Mississippi; Florida was restored to Spain. In 1787, a Convention drew up the Constitution of the new Federation which, with various amendments, remains in operation to-day. Under its provisions each State has its own legislature, with power over local laws and taxation. National affairs are dealt with by Congress. This central parliament consists of the Senate, of which two members are elected by each State, and the House of Representatives, whose members are elected by the different States on a population basis. The head of the Federation is the President, elected for a term of four years. The President wields very extensive powers. He is commander-in-chief of the army, navy and air force. He appoints the great government officials. He can, within certain limits, veto laws passed by Congress and, if his position is strong, he can largely control government policy. In 1789, Washington was unanimously elected as the first President. His subsequent services in welding the separate States, with their mutual jealousies and conflicting interests, into a united nation were a fitting sequel to his achievements during the fighting.

The ensuing years saw the great advance westward. Lusty pioneer hunters and traders blazed the trail. The settlers followed with axe and plough and rifle. The Indians were pushed ever farther back. The tide surged on, beyond the Appalachian Mountains, across the Mississippi into the Wild West, the Great Plains, the Rockies, and so to the Pacific shore. In 1803, a colossal piece of bargaining was concluded. Three years before, Spain had ceded Louisiana to France. Now Napoleon sold it for hard cash to the United States, whose territory was thereby doubled. In 1819, Spain ceded Florida. By 1848, wars with Mexico had roped in Texas, California, Nevada, Utah, Arizona and New Mexico and the occupation of the Pacific coast was completed. Finally, in 1867, Uncle Sam again opened his purse and bought Alaska from Russia. Thus many new States were formed, and later admitted to the Union, till they reached their present number of fifty. Roads, railways, canals and steamers revolutionised

With the capitulation of General Cornwallis on 19th October, 1781, the British cause collapsed.

The Federals suffered heavy defeat at the Battle of the Potomac when the Confederates fought bravely in defence of Richmond.

transport and communications. Towns and cities sprang up. Industries flourished and European emigrants flocked to the new land of freedom and opportunity.

Meantime other events were occurring. In 1812-14, the Americans were fighting their British cousins again over their right to trade with France and her allies. In 1823, President Monroe gave Europe the "Hands off America!" warning and in 1861, the fearful convulsion of the American Civil War began. It had many causes. In the industrial North, the home of the shrewd dollar-making Yankee business magnates, life was based on individual freedom and enterprise. In the South, the immense cotton plantations of the rich and easy-going gentry depended wholly on negro slave labour. The North abominated slavery and demanded its abolition. There were clashes of interests, too, on economic matters. North and South were in truth at one in despising each other's whole way of life. And, finally, the southern States strongly resented any outside interference in their affairs. In 1860, South Carolina seceded from the Union to be followed by ten other southern States. Here was a question even more fundamental than that of slavery. Could any State be allowed to divide the nation's strength?

All these issues were tried out, from 1861 to 1865, in the exhausting blood-letting of one of the most terrible civil wars in history. Four million men fought in that devastating struggle; 600,000 lost their lives. The South found its supreme general in the gallant soldier and brilliant strategist Robert E. Lee. Ulysses Grant, by his grim and relentless determination, led the armies of the North through seas of blood to their final triumph.

But the hero of the conflict was President Abraham Lincoln, who had been "raised" in the direst poverty in a log cabin. Though opposed to slavery as an inhuman aristocratic system, the preservation of the Union was to him the prime need. For, he declared, "a house divided against itself cannot stand". And he meant it to stand, so that it might carry on its destined work of creating a free democracy—"government of the people, by the people, for the people". To that cause he devoted all his wisdom and patience, his great heart and his passionate oratory. To that cause he kept the nation true through long years of stress and trial till the preservation of the Union and the abolition of slavery were alike assured. Alas! within a week of victory the nation's saviour was assassinated.

Towards the end of the century the nation began to assert itself more vigorously as a world power. In 1898 it fought a high-speed war with Spain, which led to the cession of the Philippines and other Pacific islands (granted independence in 1946) and the freeing of Cuba. The same year saw the annexation of the Pacific Hawaiian Islands. In 1914, the Panama Canal was opened. The States' territories and possessions now included various Pacific and West Indian Islands and the Canal zone. In modern times the part played by America during and after the two World Wars has been decisive.

The Americans have served mankind in other fields as well. Alexander Graham Bell (actually a Scotsman by birth) invented the telephone in 1876. Thomas Edison invented the electric light bulb and the phonograph, or gramophone, about the same time. The Wright brothers, in 1903, produced the first power-driven heavier-than-air flying machine. The United States, collaborating with British and Canadian scientists, produced the first atomic and hydrogen bombs and stands to-day as the only serious rival to Russia in the development of space flight. In literature the American contribution has been as notable and original as it is copious. Of the works beloved by junior as well as adult readers, none of us is ever likely to forget Longfellow's *Hiawatha*, Harriet Beecher Stowe's *Uncle Tom's Cabin* and Mark Twain's *Tom Sawyer* and *Huckleberry Finn*.

MODERN AMERICA

The over-all story is that of staggering expansion. The population of the Federal Republic has soared to 180 millions. The output of its coal, iron, steel, petroleum and other industries is colossal. Its cotton and tobacco plantations, its cattle ranches and cornlands, are immense. Its manufactured and agricultural products reach all the markets of the world. It has well over 200,000 miles of railroad. It is the leading military, naval and air power. It is the champion of democracy and free parliamentary government. And it is the one power strong enough to tilt a lance with Soviet Russia, and the stifling Communism it seeks to impose on the world.

THE FIRST WORLD WAR

In 1914 Europe was heading for the abyss of war. The great powers were suspicious and fearful of each other's designs. Among them Germany had become the bully of Europe. Her aggressive brandishings of the mailed fist had provoked one international crisis after another. The Prussian military caste and the blustering Kaiser William II were arrogantly bent on punching their way to the fore. They had deluded themselves with the notion that the German "herrenvolk" were a superior breed of men and that the other peoples of Europe were in decay.

GRIEVANCES

Germany complained of many wrongs. In 1879 and 1882 she had sealed a Triple Alliance with Austria and Italy. Yet she declared that the answering Triple Entente concluded by France, Russia and Britain between 1893 and 1907, encircled and threatened to destroy her. Furthermore, British imperialism had appropriated the richest of the world's colonial prizes and left her late-arriving competitor without "a place in the sun".

While Germany was chafing under these grievances, France was still smarting from her crushing defeat in 1870-1, as well as from later humiliations, and hungering after the recovery of Alsace-Lorraine. Austria-Hungary and Russia were rivals for a controlling influence in the Balkans. In 1908, the former had annexed Bosnia and Herzegovina. Those provinces were peopled by Yugo-Slavs (South Slavs) who, like their kindred in Serbia and Austria-Hungary, were passionately yearning for unification in a comprehensive and independent Serbian State. Serbia, therefore, under Russian patronage, was Austria's bitter enemy. The tsar would have stood up to his rival there and then had he dared; but Germany stood menacingly behind her Austrian ally. Germany was already at odds with Russia in the Near East, where the former, ever seeking expansion of her political and commercial power, had gained a dominant influence over Turkey. As for Britain, while Germany's designs in the Near East challenged her interests there, Germany's ambitious naval plans threatened her very existence as an island power.

ARMS BUILD-UP

In the friction and tension of these conflicting interests a dangerous race in armaments had set in. Britain and Germany were frantically building warships against each other. Germany, already the mightiest military power in Europe, made a further immense increase in her army. What precisely Germany's ambitions were in 1914, and whether or not she was spoiling for a fight, are even now disputed questions.

The spark that actually touched off the great explosion was a relatively trivial affair. The heir to the Austrian throne was assassinated in the Bosnian capital by a Serbian subject of the empire. Austria, with some show of reason, blamed Serbia for the crime and deliberately rushed to war against her. Russia, as Serbia's patron, prepared to come to her aid. Germany, supporting Austria, declared war on Russia and her ally France. Britain entered the lists on 4th August, after Germany had invaded Belgium: for that brutal act was a cynical infringement of the little kingdom's guaranteed neutrality and a direct threat to Britain's maritime security.

So the Triple Alliance and the Triple Entente drifted into war. And it was to be a war on a new and mighty scale, with the combatant nations throwing all their resources into a

The assassination of the Austrian Archduke Francis Ferdinand on 28th June, 1914, was the spark which exploded into the First World War.

Having rapidly overrun a large part of Belgium, the German army was halted at the ring-fortress of Liége, which held out heroically against the enemy for more than ten days.

For four years, but in particular for four months of 1916, Germans and French attacked and counter-attacked at Verdun without any final result. It was essential that, during the 1916 offensive, the German army should be tied down in that area while the British army organised itself for a large-scale attack on the Somme.

struggle to the death: men by the million; the new aeroplanes and airships; improved submarines; heavier artillery and more machine-guns; poison gas; and the tank.

THE MIRACLE OF THE WAR

Germany had to cope with a war on two fronts. She counted on a swift victory and acted on a preconceived plan. This was to strike through Belgium, sweep round towards Paris, squeeze the French armies together and destroy them and so bring France to her knees before the slow-moving Russian legions were ready to engage. The plan might have succeeded had it been followed out closely. The Belgian frontier fortresses tumbled down. The French in the north and the British Expeditionary Force under Sir John French on their left flank, were in grave danger of being enveloped. The dogged British stands at Mons and Le Cateau enabled them to extricate themselves; but by the end of August the enemy stood within striking distance of Paris. Then the exultant Germans, overrating their successes, made a false move and Joffre, the French commander, saw that they paid for it. On 5th September, he turned and counter-attacked and drove the startled enemy back from the River Marne and across the Aisne. This was the famous " miracle of the Marne " that saved Paris and perhaps France.

YPRES

In Belgium, the fall of Antwerp on the 9th October was followed by a German drive for the Channel ports, the possession of which would have cut Britain's communications. But the British blocked the way at Ypres and, in a series of battles that raged with unsurpassable fury from 19th October to 22nd November, they fought the enemy to a standstill. The German hopes of a swift victory were shattered. Thenceforth the struggle became static along a 350-mile line of trenches stretching from the North Sea to Switzerland. The Allies had suffered over a million casualties.

In the East the Russians were taking a mixed diet of defeat and victory. In East Prussia they were knocked spinning in the battle of Tannenberg. In the south they routed the Austrians in Galicia.

GALLIPOLI

In 1915, the deadlock on the Western Front led the Allies to look eastwards. Turkey had joined the enemy powers in the previous October; whereupon Britain had annexed the island of Cyprus and declared Egypt a British protectorate. Russia was being hard pressed. Accordingly, a plan was formed for forcing the Dardanelles and taking Constantinople. This would give a knock-out blow to Turkey in Europe and enable aid to be sent to Russia. When a naval bombardment failed to silence the forts, troops were landed on the Gallipoli peninsula. It was an operation of immense difficulty and only the dare-all spirit and superb dash of the attackers, especially the "Anzacs" from Australia and New Zealand, made it possible. Even so their valour was of no avail. There was bad staff work and bad luck and around the end of the year the hopeless project was abandoned.

Meantime Turkey was receiving attention in Asia. Indian divisions advanced up the River Tigris in Mesopotamia (Iraq) and in September captured Kut. There, however, General Townshend was later besieged by a superior Turkish force. All attempts to relieve him were repulsed and in April 1916, after a fighting siege of nearly five months the garrison was forced to surrender.

ITALY CHANGES SIDES

The combats on the Western Front during 1915 produced little change. Sir John French was then superseded by Sir Douglas Haig as commander of the British forces. At home, Asquith's unsatisfactory ministry was replaced by a coalition government of all parties. Italy, renouncing the Triple Alliance, joined the Allies and kept the Austrian armies occupied. On the eastern front the Russians were driven back and badly shaken. Serbia was crushed and Bulgaria joined the Austro-Germans in the crushing.

VERDUN

In 1916, Britain realised that she must throw her full weight into the scale to help make good the Allies' appalling casualties; she adopted conscription. This year Falkenhayn, the German commander, worked on the idea of bleeding France

The Battle of Jutland, which was fought on 31st May, 1916, between the battle fleets of the German navy and the British navy, was the only important naval encounter of the First World War. Although the British suffered greater losses in ships and men, the German battle fleet was forced to retire because of the successful blockading of their ports by the British navy. Britain's command of the sea was intact and the Germans had to fall back on submarine warfare.

Despite the deliberate sinking of the Lusitania *and constant provocation on the seas, President Wilson of the United States stuck to his policy of neutrality. When, however, a plot was uncovered in which Mexico was to provoke war with the United States, President Wilson finally declared war against Germany.*

to death by continuous attack on a vital point. From February to September he battered away at the great fortress system of Verdun. France bled indeed, but not to death. Haig, at the cost of 750,000 casualties, relieved the pressure on the fortress by a sustained offensive in the Somme valley and Verdun remained untaken. Russian successes led Roumania to join hands with the Allies in the wild war-dance; three months later she lay prostrate beneath the enemy's jack-boot. In Britain, the end of a year of exhaustion and failure brought a new vigour to the conduct of the war when the human dynamo, Lloyd George, became Prime Minister.

SUBMARINE WARFARE

The British Navy was bearing the brunt of the operations at sea and strangling Germany with its ever-tightening blockade. Only once—in the Battle of Jutland on 31st May, 1916—did the main fleets engage. The immediate result was disappointing and inconclusive. But the German Navy, having prudently retired to harbour, never afterwards ventured far out except to surrender at the end of the war. Instead, contrary to international law, the enemy, from January 1917, concentrated on unrestricted submarine warfare. Shipping of every nationality, armed or unarmed, proceeding to or from British ports was attacked without warning. Germany was feeling the pinch of Britain's hunger-blockade. The war in France was in a condition of stalemate. An all-out submarine campaign, it was confidently expected, would reduce Germany's arch-enemy to starvation and submission in six months. The expectation came perilously near to being realised, and only the Allies' tireless exertions and clever devices enabled them to swat the mosquito-like swarms of U-boats that assailed them. Innocent-looking " Q "-ships that lured the enemy to destruction, camouflaged hulls to reduce visibility, depth charges, mines, guarded convoys and new shipbuilding—all these were among the measures that slowly gained the mastery over the deadly pests. What the piratical submarine campaign did help to do, however, was to persuade at last the United States to enter the war in April, 1917.

GAIN AND LOSS

Unfortunately this heartening event was accompanied by another disheartening event. In March, revolution broke out in Russia. The imperial government was overthrown; the army fell to pieces; and in December the country's new masters signed an armistice with Germany. Russia was " out ".

There was no lack of fighting in the West during 1917. The Allies had mustered nearly four million men, a third of them British, with more coming. The Aisne, Vimy Ridge, Messines, Passchendaele and Cambrai (where the British tanks first definitely showed their possibilities) are names associated with local or incomplete successes and failures, with dauntless valour and limitless endurance, but also, alas! with hideous and colossal slaughter. To add to the tale of disappointment, the Italians suffered a heavy defeat at Caporetto.

THE NEAR EAST

The most cheerful campaigning news came from two minor fronts. In Palestine a British force under the brilliant cavalry commander Sir Edmund Allenby thoroughly trounced the Turks at Beersheba and went on to capture Jerusalem. Next year the army gave the enemy another good licking and reached Aleppo, right up in northern Syria. In these masterly campaigns Allenby received valuable aid from that romantic and almost legendary hero "Lawrence of Arabia" and the wild Arab tribesmen who fought under his magnetic leadership. In Mesopotamia, the shame of Kut was wiped out in 1917 by the recapture of the town and the taking of Baghdad, followed in 1918 by the conquest of the whole country.

THE SOMME AND VICTORY

The year 1918 brought the long and bitter contest to a crisis. Ludendorff, who had taken over the German command in the West, massed all his forces for a determined snatch at victory before the American armies were ready. The submarine campaign had failed. The British blockade was succeeding. From March to July, Ludendorff delivered a series of terrific attacks that were savagely driven home. The Allied armies reeled before the staggering blows. The British front was pierced. The onrushing Germans once more reached the Marne. But it was their final effort and the Allies recovered in time. Foch, now supreme commander in France, was able to strike back. And American aid was coming in fast to make ultimate victory sure. Then, on 8th August, in the Somme area, Haig, with 450 tanks rumbling ahead of his troops, launched an offensive that broke the German front and scored a spectacular triumph. The victory was followed up by repeated attacks that stabbed all up and down the enemy line. The Germans were forced back in a general retreat. Haig's mighty blows smashed through their final defences. Germany's military power cracked. All her partners were throwing up the sponge. Mutiny broke out

in the fleet. Revolution flared up at home. The Kaiser left Germany for Holland. On 11th November, Germany surrendered and signed armistice terms dictated by the victors. The Allies, with the British Commonwealth and Empire forming the hard core of their forces, had won what was perhaps the most titanic war in history.

PEACE TERMS

In 1919, the victorious Allies assembled in Paris to settle the peace terms. The Conference was dominated by three powerful personalities: President Wilson of the U.S.A., an idealist with visions of a new and exalted world order—for which the world was not yet ready; "Tiger" Clemenceau, whose consuming aim was to rend and bind France's prostrate foe; and the British Premier Lloyd George, who, while bent on making Germany pay, tried to put the brake on the two extremists.

The new British invention, the tank, was first used on a big scale in the battle of Cambrai in 1917. The successful tank attack was not followed up.

Lenin and Trotsky were the chief architects of the revolution of 1917. Overthrowing the provisional revolutionary government, the Bolsheviks, or extreme party, came to power. Of the two men, Trotsky was the more moderate.

On 11th November, 1918, Germany was compelled to sign an armistice at Compiégne. The German delegates accepted all the terms laid down, including the immediate withdrawal of their troops from all occupied territories.

145

Shortly after the surrender of Germany and Austria, military and civilian delegates of various nations assembled at Paris in 1919, to discuss the terms of the peace.

The peace treaties (beginning with that of Versailles, 1919) and other measures redrew the map of Europe and grappled with world-wide problems. Germany was disarmed and forbidden to rearm. She was presented with a colossal, and quite unpayable, war bill. A great part of the Rhineland—the German province bordering Belgium and Luxembourg—was to be "demilitarised", its fortifications dismantled. The region was also to be occupied by Allied troops for a period of fifteen years. France realised her old dream of recovering Alsace-Lorraine. The German colonies, which had already been captured, were divided among the Allies. Britain and the Dominions received German South-West and German East Africa (the latter was afterwards named Tanganyika) together with other colonies in Africa and in the Pacific. They were to be governed by the new possessors as trustees or guardians under the newly-created League of Nations. Britain also received Palestine and Mesopotamia

When peace came it was welcomed by the defeated as well as the victorious. Large and emotional demonstrations expressed a universal sense of relief. Here a tumultuous and joyful crowd in the streets of London celebrates the conclusion of the peace agreement.

on the same terms, but later these areas were formed into independent States. Northern Schleswig was returned to Denmark.

In settling the racial tangle of Central Europe, the Allies gave the fullest possible recognition to the rights of the subject peoples which had been so blatantly ignored by the Congress of Vienna in 1814-15. The ramshackle Austro-Hungarian Empire had already broken up and the Habsburg dynasty fallen. From its parts were formed the republics of Austria (woefully diminished), Czecho-slovakia and Hungary. Long-suffering Poland reappeared as another republic. The Yugo-Slavs largely attained their ambition in the formation of the kingdom of Yugoslavia—the former Serbia much enlarged. The Baltic provinces, which had been surrendered by Russia to Germany in 1918, became free republics. The flight of the Kaiser had brought the Hohenzollern dynasty to its end, and Germany started life afresh as another addition to the list of new republics.

Remembering the suffering and havoc of the war years (the British Empire alone mourned nearly a million dead), the victors laboured to prevent further armed conflicts by means of a great League of Nations. By a Solemn Covenant, signed eventually by member States all over the world, the nations agreed to submit future disputes to arbitration and to combine against any aggressor. Unhappily the effective-ness of the noble aim was imperilled from the first. The United States, fearing to entangle itself in further European quarrels, repudiated its idealistic President's labours and refused to join the League.

The war gave a "new look" to Europe. Four ancient and powerful empires—Germany, Austria-Hungary, Russia and Turkey—closed down and an assembly of new and untried republics opened up. The last of the old despots had their crowns knocked off. The kings who retained theirs ruled as constitutional monarchs. The day of universal democracy seemed to have dawned. But it was a red dawn, a herald perhaps of stormy weather. Many of the infant republics were unstable, mere lambs in their powers of self-defence, but wild-cats in their mutual rivalries.

The Allies, due to circumstances, had made a daring experiment. How successfully it would work out remained to be seen.

146

BETWEEN THE WARS

When the First World War armistice with Germany was concluded in 1918, Europe presented a spectacle of unparalleled ruin and disorder. Twenty-five million people, it has been estimated, had perished of wounds, starvation and disease. Hunger stalked the earth. Everywhere the countryside had been ravaged, homes wrecked, factories destroyed. International credit, on which commerce depends, was shattered. Trade crashed. Unemployment rose to staggering proportions. Labour unrest threatened social order.

Britain's share of these sufferings was far less grievous than that of the devastated Continent. The upheaval brought many changes into her political and social life. Her women's splendid war services were recognised in 1918: the vote was granted to those of thirty years or more who possessed a prescribed property qualification. Adult suffrage for all males (irrespective of the previous property and lodger's qualifications) was also given. Ten years later women were put on the same footing. Thus the ideal of equal adult suffrage was at length attained.

SOCIALISM

The war had greatly advanced the Socialist movement, and in 1924 the first Labour government came into office. In 1931, a National government, formed from all parties, abandoned Free Trade and adopted the policy of Protection and Imperial Preference.

Meanwhile important developments in overseas affairs occurred. In 1922, Britain withdrew the protectorate she had established over Egypt and declared the country to be an independent State. British troops, however, remained in occupation for defence purposes.

In 1920-22, agreement was reached over the vexed Irish question. The "distressful country" was divided into two regions: six counties of Ulster ("Northern Ireland"), and the rest of the island ("the Irish Free State"). Each was given its own parliament; but, while Northern Ireland remained a part of the United Kingdom, the Free State became a self-governing Dominion, like Canada. From 1932 onwards, however, the Irish republican party broke one link after another in the slender chain that bound the Free State to Britain. In 1937, the break became all but complete when "Eire"—in English "Ireland"—declared itself an independent State.

During the war the self-governing Dominions had nobly rallied round the mother country. At the same time the already growing feeling of their own distinct nationhood had strengthened. The Imperial Conference of 1926 and the Statute of Westminster of 1931 declared Great Britain and the Dominions to be equal, self-governing communities, united by a common allegiance to the Crown and freely associated as members of the British Commonwealth of Nations. The Dominions then concerned were Canada, Australia, New Zealand, Newfoundland (which, however, threw in its lot with Canada in 1949), the Irish Free State and South Africa. India had not yet attained "Dominion" rank: but despite internal differences, it was training hard for self-government and, by the India Act of 1935,

greater authority was given to the provincial assemblies

In the early 1920s, the voice of radio, or wireless broadcasting, began to be heard in almost every household. In the late 1930s television programmes followed.

In 1936, the good and well-loved King George V passed away. He was succeeded by his son Edward VIII, who, because of his intention of marrying a divorcée, abdicated before he was crowned. Thereupon the sceptre passed to his brother George, Duke of York. While these changes were taking shape other countries were seeking their ideals of government by violent means. In Russia, the Bolsheviks fastened their grip on the country's European and Asiatic territories. These they grouped together as the Union of Soviet Socialist Republics—"Soviet" being the name given to the early revolutionary workers' and soldiers' councils. And on these they rigorously imposed their system of Communist government.

Communism is a form of Socialism, though in some respects it is fundamentally opposed to it. The Bolsheviks derived their main doctrines from the brilliant, fanatical, and rather disagreeable German-Jew Karl Marx, who wrote some famous works on the subject from 1848 onwards. His ideas were eagerly taken up by advanced thinkers all over Europe, but it was left to Russia to try them out on a large scale.

Under the ruthless Lenin and, after his death in 1924, the grim and cunning cobbler's son Stalin, Communism meant the dictatorship of the Bolshevik party, with State control of land, industry, labour and pretty well everything else for the benefit of the workers. All other political parties were suppressed, and all the powers of government were concentrated in the hands of the Bolshevik leaders and their associates. Here lies one of the basic differences between

Before the First World War, the right to vote in local and parliamentary elections was denied to women. Women's right to vote was courageously fought for by Mrs. Pankhurst.

present-day Communism as prevailing in Russia and the Socialism found in the western countries. Under the latter system, though the aims are comparable, they are sought through the will of all classes and parties, freely expressed in elected representative parliaments.

Communists, to a more extreme degree than Socialists, are determined enemies of the " capitalist " system of the West, under which—so they assert—the employers dishonestly grind their profits out of the toil of the workers. Russian Communism is hostile to religion, though it grudgingly tolerates it. Communism is, indeed, almost a religion in itself to its fanatical disciples, and it is their avowed intention to impose it on all the capitalist countries.

The Bolshevik Revolution of 1917 is the most momentous political and social event of modern times. Practical experience has modified some of its extreme dogmas; and its triumph has been achieved at the cost of countless lives, appalling suffering and inhuman tyranny. But the Bolsheviks have shown the world what a Communist State can achieve. Their rule is fully as despotic as that of the tsars. But they have completely reorganised and immensely developed agriculture and industry. They have spread education among the people. They have improved living conditions generally and given the despised peasants a new outlook on life, a new position in their fatherland.

Once the new Russian government was firmly established the other great powers had to recognise it. France, indeed, in 1935, concluded a pact of mutual assistance with " the Reds ". She also made military alliances with Czechoslovakia and Poland. For France, dangerously weakened by internal discords, was jumpy. She dreaded a war of revenge by a restored Germany.

FASCISM

The post-war sufferings and disappointments of Italy made that country a fertile soil for revolutionary ideas. The discontented workers hailed the Bolshevik Revolution with envious enthusiasm. Civil war was brewing. But a powerful figure appeared who gave a new turn to events. Benito Mussolini, the son of a blacksmith, was a man of violent and boastful character, fiery patriotism and flaming ambition. Supported by the bludgeons of his blackshirted Fascist gangs

(named after *fasces*, or rods, which in ancient Roman times had been carried before the chief magistrates), he seized power in 1922 and set himself up as dictator. Mussolini did not abolish capitalism, though he strictly controlled it. And he allowed the monarchy to remain, though with little power. But he destroyed parliamentary government, democratic and liberal institutions and free thought and expression. The individual citizen was left with no rights: the State was all and his duty was but to obey. All opposition was crushed with calculated brutality. Mussolini believed in might, not right; in war, not peace.

With the reins of power firmly in his hands, the dictator gave the disorganised country fresh heart and won its rapturous devotion. He brought efficiency to the slack administration. He reformed agriculture and industry under State control. He carried out immense and beneficial public works. All in all, he aroused Italy to a new fervour of proud nationalism. He even entertained fantastic ideas about reviving the glory of the ancient Roman Empire. In 1935-6, cynically disregarding the solemn covenant of the League of Nations, he invaded and annexed Abyssinia. The member-states of the League were too much concerned with their own particular interests and rivalries to act together and bridle the aggressor. Their feeble attempts showed that the League—which, unhappily, the Americans had from the first refused to join— had no teeth, and the result was only to embitter Italy against Britain and France and throw her into the arms of Germany.

THE RISE OF HITLER

And what of Germany? The ruinous post-war economic depressions hit her all the harder because of the staggering burden of reparations, or compensation for war damage, heaped on her shoulders by the victorious Allies. She was let off eventually; but, in the universal trade slump then prevailing, the miseries of want and mass-unemployment remained. Added to these hardships were the bitter humiliation of defeat, the widespread belief that her armies had not really broken in the war and the feeling that the Allies had tricked her into submitting to the harsh terms of the peace treaty. The resulting sense of national grievance, and the growing infection of the country by Russian Communism, prepared the way for the sensational uprising of the ex-house-

In 1923, Adolf Hitler held a rally of the National Socialist Movement in Munich. His attempt to proclaim a national revolution failed, and he was sentenced to five years' imprisonment.

The Falangists in Spain drew support from Italy, France and Germany. Franco's first attack, launched on 8th March, 1937, failed after a desperate four-day battle.

At Guernica, the Basque town, left-wing forces barricaded themselves in during April, 1937. Before surrendering to the Falangists, they set fire to the town and destroyed it.

painter and corporal, Adolf Hitler, and his Nazi party.

Mussolini's success in Italy gave Hitler the cue for action. He was a man inflamed with German racial pride and patriotism. His heart was filled with violent hatreds—of the Allies, of Communists, of Jews, of the parliamentary government of the German Republic set up after the war. The restoration and boundless expansion of Germany and its " superior " people in an all-powerful military and autocratic State was his consuming passion. By 1933, with the aid of his stormtroops, he had carried all before him and made himself dictator. As in Italy, so in Germany: under the merciless Nazi tyranny all opposing political parties were silenced, all democratic rights suppressed. The Jews—the victims of Hitler's fiercest hatred—were persecuted atrociously. Hitler was an evil genius. His daring aims and fanatical personality intoxicated the nation with bright visions of a fatherland restored to power and prosperity under his leadership.

Hitler, shrewdly judging that the war-weary western powers would not use force to restrain him, proceeded to flout the Versailles treaty by rearming Germany. In March, 1936, he defied the treaty again by marching his troops into the Rhineland.

SPANISH WAR

Now comes a lurid side-show. The scene is Spain. Its internal history had for long been a tale of conflict between the supporters of the oppressive monarchy and Roman Catholic Church, the military adventurers who repeatedly aimed at political power, and the Socialists, Communists and revolutionary extremists who demanded a free republic with a democratic constitution. In 1931, the last-named had their way. The Bourbon king departed and a republic was proclaimed. The new government became increasingly pro-Communist and anti-clerical and the struggle of opposing forces and ideas continued.

In 1936, it boiled over in a civil war of unspeakable ferocity. All Europe was stirred by what seemed a vital contest between the forces of Communism and religion, democratic freedom and Fascism. Volunteers rushed into the fray like ardent crusaders to fight, on one side or another, for the cause they held sacred. To Hitler and Mussolini the free-

for-all fight afforded a useful opportunity to try out their new weapons and tactics of war in aid of General Franco and his Fascist, anti-Communist aims. So for three years the wretched country was bled and bombed and ravaged till Franco finally triumphed. His mildly Fascist dictatorship still holds Spain down; but it is qualified by the promise of an ultimate return to monarchy and constitutional rule.

Meantime, nearer home, Hitler continued on his breakneck course. In March, 1938, he seized Austria. Next he cast a hungry eye on the Bohemian frontier districts of Czechoslovakia, which were largely German in population. But Czechoslovakia was allied, not only, as we have seen with France, but also with Russia, and Britain, too, might be aroused if he attacked it. Unfortunately, the republic's backers were totally unprepared for war. Neville Chamberlain, the head of the National (practically Conservative) government in Britain, was pursuing a policy of " appeasing " Hitler by a sympathetic discussion of Germany's grievances. In September, at Munich, he practically handed the coveted districts to Hitler on a plate. The gratified dictator thereupon declared that his territorial appetite was satisfied. Henceforth all was to be peace and concord. Europe breathed again. Six months later the arch-hypocrite swallowed the remainder of the Czechoslovakian republic. Chamberlain woke up and rearmament was pressed forward.

For some years past the warmongering Hitler and Mussolini had been acting together like a pair of crooks planning a burglary. Japan—another power that, by its war on China, had foresworn its obligations under the League of Nations—had joined them, and the villainous trio eventually leagued themselves together in an unholy military alliance.

After Czechoslovakia came Poland. Hitler demanded the return of Danzig, which had been made a free city by the Versailles Treaty. Poland refused and France and Britain promised to support her. The dreaded war was drawing near now and both sides angled for the friendship of Russia, whom Britain and France had antagonised by the surrender at Munich. It was Germany who secured a treaty with Russia, ensuring her neutrality in the event of war. On 1st September, 1939, Hitler invaded Poland. Two days later Britain and France declared war.

THE SECOND WORLD WAR

In 1939 Europe was flung into the furnace of the Second World War, and from the opening of the second conflict it became all too clear that it would far surpass the first in its destructive powers. The new or improved weapons which had come into use were incomparably more deadly. They had effected a revolution in the horrid science of war. Armies were mechanised. Tanks, used in hundreds, gave them their " punch ". Aeroplanes dominated land, sea and sky. Radio transformed communications and radar contributed its uncanny aid in tracking aircraft and shipping.

As in 1914, the British overseas Dominions rallied to the mother country. But the Irish Free State (now a sovereign independent State) chose to remain neutral.

On 1st September, 1939, Hitler had invaded Poland. That was the decisive outrage which led Britain and France, two days later, to declare war.

THE PAUSE AND ATTACK

Unhappy Poland was throttled in a month and then carved up between Germany and Russia. In the West things were singularly quiet till April, 1940. Then suddenly the Germans pounced, by land, sea and air, on Denmark and Norway, largely to gain a base for attacks on British shipping. Gallant British and French attempts to oust the invaders failed. On 10th May, the Germans burst into Holland and Belgium. In Britain, acute dissatisfaction over the failure in Norway and the critical situation in Belgium and northern France overthrew Chamberlain's government. Mr. Winston Churchill was then elected leader of a Coalition Government and thenceforth his inspiring personality and his powerful and many-sided genius was to be the supreme directing force of all his country's energies.

DUNKIRK

The Germans now launched a masterly non-stop surprise attack in the Ardennes with their Panzer (" mail ") divisions of armoured troops. Employing a new technique of massed tanks and low-flying dive-bombers against an enemy woefully inferior in mechanisation and aircraft, their columns smashed clean through the Allied line. By 20th May they had driven right across northern France to Abbeville and reached the English Channel. The Anglo-French-Belgian forces cut off in the north were hemmed in. The Belgians, exhausted, gave up the fight. Their Allies were relentlessly squeezed into a narrow bridgehead around the French seaport of Dunkirk. Annihilation threatened them and only a miracle could avert it. The amazing thing is that the miracle happened. Ships of the British Navy and merchant fleet, seconded by a host of yachts, tugs, barges and other odd craft, many of them manned by their volunteer owners, performed the impossible. Between the end of May and early June, no less than 338,000 of the hemmed-in British and French troops were snatched from the German jaws that were closing on them and brought safely across to England.

THE DEFEAT OF FRANCE

But France was beaten. Her more southern armies were still in the field; but the country was infected with political unrest and the troops had little heart for continuing the struggle. On 22nd June, the aged Marshal Petain's government signed an armistice which surrendered all northern and western France to Hitler's control. Meantime the " valiant " dictator of Italy, Mussolini (who had previously allied his country with Germany after falling out with the League of Nations over the seizure of Abyssinia), decided that the time was ripe for declaring war on France and Britain.

BRITAIN STANDS ALONE

Britain, sadly battered but defiant, stood alone amid the

The first act of provocation by German troops was the over-throwing of frontier posts on the Polish border.

Dive-bombing by the high-speed German Stukas pulverised the Polish defences.

On 21st June, 1940, near Compiégne, armistice terms were handed to Marshal Petain. Germany claimed the right to occupy the eastern and northern zones of France.

With the fall of Bardia on 5th January, 1941, the British offensive rolled on to Tobruk, which fell on 24th January. The Italian forces then retreated farther to the Sirte area.

wreckage of the Allied cause, and the triumphant Hitler now bent all his efforts to the task of smiting her down. Invasion preparations began; but first, German mastery of the air must be assured. In early July, a contest of deadly intensity was waged between the R.A.F. and the German Luftwaffe of four times its strength. On London the bombs rained down death and devastation regularly night and day for three weeks and more. But her tight-lipped citizens showed an awestruck world that " she could take it ". The ruinous raids were extended to the big industrial areas and ports and continued throughout the winter and spring of 1940-1. But by October, 1940, Hitler had been forced to admit defeat in the air and to postpone his unsolicited visit to Britain indefinitely. For the rest of the war, with intervals, air raids (including the later flying bombs and rockets) became an accepted feature of everyday existence.

The land war that had been lost in the West could only be re-won, if at all, by a stupendous effort. That effort was not made till 6th June, 1944 (known to the Allies as " D-Day "). We can, therefore, turn to the other theatres of war and follow the operations there up to that date.

WAR IN AFRICA

One of the liveliest of these theatres was North Africa. There, the fortunes of the desert war ebbed and flowed like the tide. The enemy's purpose was to destroy Britain's power in the Mediterranean, Egypt and the Red Sea and thereby sever her communications with the East. Already their submarines and aircraft had made the Mediterranean a perilous place for Allied shipping. Now, the completion of the work was left to the braggart Mussolini. Italy's land, sea and air power, being free from other commitments, was overwhelmingly superior to that which Britain could muster on the spot. The Italian General Graziani, therefore, was in high hopes, when in September, 1940, he invaded Egypt from the neighbouring Italian colony of Libya. In December, General Wavell's Army of the Nile went out to meet him. By February, 1941, his tanks and infantry had done some remarkable work. They had driven the Italians out of Egypt, reached Benghazi (500 miles from the starting point), annihi-

lated a great enemy army and taken 130,000 prisoners, 400 tanks and 1,290 guns. The British losses were under 2,000 men. So much for Graziani's hopes.

GREECE, SOMALILAND AND ABYSSINIA

Unfortunately these dazzling successes were now to be interrupted. Greece was being attacked by Germany, and General Wavell's force was heavily drawn upon to aid her. The aid, especially in aircraft, proved insufficient. Greece fell and the British troops were transferred to Crete. But there too, when the Germans followed with airborne troops in May, their complete mastery in the air won the day. So Germany established her footing in the eastern Mediterranean.

Incidentally, in 1941, some slight consolation for these failures was forthcoming from East Africa. British Somaliland, which had been taken by the Italians in the previous year, was regained. Italian Somaliland and Eritrea were captured. And stolen Abyssinia was recovered for its rightful ruler.

ROMMEL AND EL ALAMEIN

Back in Libya, in March-April, the first ebb tide in the fortunes of war had set in. Germans, under the daring Rommel, had taken over and the British, drained in numbers and weakened in tanks, lost almost all their recent gains. The valuable seaport of Tobruk, now besieged, still remained to them, but General Wavell's main force was hustled back into Egypt. In the ensuing period (during which General Auchinleck replaced Wavell) the tide ebbed and flowed in the most bewildering manner. At length, in May-June, 1942, Rommel's superior tanks and guns had their way. Tobruk fell. The British were forced back, in a dour fighting retreat, deep into Egypt. At El Alamein they stood only sixty miles from Alexandria, the key to communications with the East. But there they turned at bay.

General Alexander now assumed control in Egypt. Under him, General Montgomery, a careful organiser and gifted strategist, was given command of the reinforced army soon to become famous as the " Eighth Army ". On 23rd October, the decisive eleven-day battle of El Alamein began. It ended

On 8th November, 1942, strong American forces landed at Casablanca, Morocco. These land, sea and air forces began a pincer movement on Tunis in conjunction with the British Eighth Army driving up from Libya.

in the complete rout of the German and Italian armies. The tide had turned again in Britain's favour and this time finally. Montgomery now trundled the beaten foe before him westwards for a matter of 1,400 miles till he reached Tripoli in January, 1943. So much for the daring Rommel.

MOROCCO, ALGERIA AND TUNISIA

In December, 1941, the United States had entered the war in circumstances to be related presently. In November, 1942, Anglo-American armies, under the American General Eisenhower, had effected landings in the French colonies of Morocco and Algeria, which were still under the control of Pétain's defeatist government. Later, they were joined by an army of French and colonial troops, ready to strike a blow for fallen France. The Allies' purpose was to co-operate

with the Eighth Army in expelling the enemy from North Africa. This would open up the Mediterranean for Allied shipping and for further promising ventures. In April, 1943, the armies of Generals Eisenhower and Montgomery joined hands. The Germans were feverishly pouring fresh troops into neighbouring Tunisia; but in May, General Alexander, acting as Deputy Commander of the Allied forces, gave them the knock-out blow. A quarter of a million prisoners went into the bag and North Africa was cleared.

THE ITALIAN CAMPAIGN

The first of the further promising ventures was General Alexander's conquest of Sicily in July-August. The next comprised landings on and around the " toe " of Italy in September. Already, however, Mussolini had been thrown out by his own people and a new Italian government secretly agreed to unconditional surrender. But the Germans took over the defence of the country, and the Anglo-American and other troops (the Eighth Army among them) had to fight for every foot of ground bit by bit, up the leg of Italy. On 4th June, 1944, two days before D-Day, they got about as far as the knee. The Americans jubilantly entered the capital city of Rome and the enemy was in full retreat to new positions farther north.

THE INVASION OF RUSSIA

The next theatre of war to be visited is an unexpected one. Hitler's treaty of friendship with Russia in August, 1939, had been a mere stop-gap. He had never felt sure of his new and powerful friend's sincerity and a time came when, apart from other considerations, he needed to secure command of Russia's vast resources in food, oil and other supplies. So, in June, 1941, he suddenly turned about and launched his armies against her. Britain no longer stood alone. She had gained an ally. True, her new partnership was an uneasy one. Russia was a revolutionary, Communist and aggressive State and there could never be any real trust or cordiality between the two countries. But all differences were for the

Russian forces made a determined stand following the rapid advance of the Germans. Taking advantage of bitter winter conditions, they attempted to wear down the Axis armies. As no headway was being made, the opening of a " Second Front " was proposed to the Allies.

In an attempt to secure the oilfields of the Caucasus, the German army launched an offensive in August, 1942. During this campaign, they were halted at Stalingrad. After a tactical surrender by General Paulus, the Wehrmacht made a skilful withdrawal from the Russian front.

moment submerged in the immediate need to smash the common enemy. Britain regularly sent large consignments of war material to Archangel, though she could ill spare them, and the convoys suffered heavy losses from German submarines.

Hitler's legions, operating over a front that reached from the Baltic to the Black Sea, drove rapidly and confidently forward. By December, 1941, they stood within forty miles of Moscow. In the south they reached the River Volga in August, 1942. But there, at Stalingrad, a titanic three-month contest ended in complete disaster. It was war on a gigantic scale, with millions of troops and thousands of tanks and guns engaged on fronts hundreds of miles long. The weight of the inexhaustible Russian masses—" the Russian steam-roller "—told in the end. The invading hosts were ground down, or pushed back, with staggering losses. When D-Day dawned, the Russians had almost entirely liberated their homeland and were still pressing westwards on the heels of the exhausted foe.

PEARL HARBOR

The Far East front opened even more sensationally than the Russian. Japan, like Italy, had sided with Germany because of the opposition of the League of Nations to a war of aggression, in this case against China. Possessing the third largest fleet in the world, her ambition was to be top dog in the East. On 7th December, 1941, when the United States was still at peace, she made a diabolically treacherous raid by carrier-borne aircraft on Pearl Harbor, in the Hawaiian Islands, and put the unsuspecting American Pacific Fleet out of action. It was a major catastrophe; but it brought the United States into the war. For several months afterwards the faithless Japanese were indeed top dog in the Pacific. Britain could do little against them. Her resources were already stretched to breaking point in other quarters and she was lamentably weak in the Far East.

WAR IN THE FAR EAST

The top dog was quick to take advantage of the situation and bite and bite again. The greater portion of the East Indies, the Philippines and New Guinea, was snapped up. On 15th February, 1942, British arms suffered a humiliating disaster: the key naval base of Singapore, attacked from landward, was stormed. In March, Rangoon, the capital of Burma, fell and the whole country was yielded up when the British and Indian army withdrew behind the Chindwin River into Assam. India itself stood in danger.

By May, however, Uncle Sam was recovering his breath after the foul blow below the belt at Pearl Harbor. During the ensuing two years a series of combats (in many of which Australian units distinguished themselves) raged with sustained and devastating fury. The naval air battles of the Coral Sea and Midway Island, and the sea-land-air contests for the Solomon Islands (notably Guadalcanal), New Guinea, the Gilberts and the Marshalls, are among the star American victories in that vast ocean war. By D-Day the United States was edging towards Japanese home waters.

The world position of the Allies had tremendously improved since 1941-2. Everywhere their cause was on the up-grade. Thus it was that, in 1944, a reinforced and re-equipped army, trained in jungle fighting and covered, transported and supplied by a powerful air force, was able to stage a come-back in Burma. (American and American-trained Chinese forces co-operated in the ensuing campaigns.)

A notable victory in the battle of Arakan, on the south of the fighting line, put the army in good heart. But then the ferocious and fanatical Japanese launched a heavy attack in the centre and actually won a foothold in India. The critical battle was still undecided on D-Day.

THE WAR AT SEA

The last front to be surveyed is the sea front. The whole Allied position depended on command of the ocean routes for the transport of troops, food, munitions and other supplies. The responsibility, for this and for all the other multifarious operations at sea, was almost entirely Britain's till the United States came in. Apart from the Pacific area, no really considerable actions were fought, though there were many notable smaller engagements. Aircraft, carrier-borne or shore-based, became a dominating factor in all naval operations. The most dramatic episode was the chase of the *Bismarck*, Germany's powerful new 45,000-ton battleship, in May, 1941. Starting out from Norway on a shipping raid on 22nd May, she was sighted off Iceland, engaged by battleships and aircraft, lost, picked up again, crippled by aircraft and destroyers and finally sunk by gunfire 300 miles off Brest on 27th May.

The supreme enemy effort, as in the First World War, was concentrated on the submarine campaign, supplemented by commerce-raiding ships and mines. This time, however, aircraft and new types of magnetic and acoustic mines were extensively used in co-operation. So great was the havoc wrought among warships and supply vessels, that there were black periods when it looked as if the U-boats were going to win the war for Germany. The Allies grappled with the deadly menace by every available means: the marvellous "Asdic" submarine-detecting system, new ship-construction, guarded convoys, carrier-borne and long-range aircraft, mines, radar and other offensive and defensive measures. The sinkings gradually diminished; but it was not till the fourth year of the war that the U-boats were definitely mastered.

In attempts to stave off defeat in 1944, German scientists were able to perfect two reprisal weapons : the V1 (inset), known as the " Doodle-bug ", and the V2. These flying bombs caused great material damage and considerable loss of life in the south of England, but did not alter the final result of the war.

On 6th June, 1944, the Allies opened the Second Front with the landing of troops in Normandy. At first all men and materials were put ashore on landing craft, but on D-Day plus 10, artificial harbours were brought into use.

In the Far East, the American armies were driving the Japanese back to defeat. To hasten the end of the war in that sector, atomic bombs were dropped on Hiroshima and Nagasaki in August, 1945.

D-DAY, 6th JUNE, 1944

And now we come to Britain on D-Day, 6th June, 1944. The Allies had gone forward on every active front, but the fact remained that Germany, the main enemy, was still intact. Not an inch of her soil was trodden by an invader. The Allied leaders, President Roosevelt of the United States, Mr. Churchill and the Russian Premier Stalin, had long been nursing plans for remedying this state of affairs by simultaneous attacks from east and west. Now, Britain and the United States stood ready to carry out their part of the design in the greatest amphibious military undertaking in history. It had taken years of detailed study and preparation. It involved the assembly of hundreds of thousands of men, thousands of aircraft, vehicles and ships. In addition there was a complex array of new and ingenious military devices and engines of war, including " swimming " tanks, submarine cross-Channel petrol-supply pipes, floating piers and artificial harbours.

General Eisenhower was appointed Supreme Commander, but the opening moves, before he crossed over to France, were in charge of General (later Field-Marshal) Montgomery. The Allied plan of campaign was to seize and secure bridgeheads along the fifty-mile stretch of sandy beaches between Cherbourg and Le Havre in Normandy and then to break out in a general onslaught on the German armies. It was to be the supreme crisis of the war. If the assault failed the failure might well be beyond remedy.

THE LANDINGS AND VICTORY

But it did not fail. Foul weather, powerful beach defences, the fiercest enemy resistance—all were overcome. The Allies were already lords of the air and the sea, and Germany and the invasion area had been thoroughly softened by intense bombing. Nothing could resist the dash and courage of the British, Canadian and American assault forces. The bridgeheads were won, extended and linked together. In late July the break-out began and grew and grew into a grim pursuit across northern France and Belgium of a desperate and failing foe. General Eisenhower had taken over operational

control on 1st September. Enemy resistance now stiffened, and the autumn and winter were periods of hard and steady slogging. But the end of March, 1945, saw the Germans driven over the Rhine with the Allies forcing the crossing after them. Then followed the drive into the heart of Germany. Before April was out the enemy lines buckled and broke beneath the Allies' relentless hammer-blows. Prisoners surrendered by the thousand. Connection was made with the Russians advancing from the east. Hitler committed suicide. In Italy, General Alexander had reached the top of the " leg " and Mussolini had been shot by Italian patriots; while on the 2nd May the German armies in Italy laid down their arms.

Five days later Germany surrendered unconditionally.

VICTORY IN THE FAR EAST

Only Japan was left to be reckoned with and the reckoning —which was aided by a new British Pacific fleet—was short and sharp. Already the Americans were back in the Philippines and other strategic islands, and Burma had been recovered. By the end of July, Japan's remaining naval power was utterly destroyed. In August, military history was made with the dropping on her towns of the first atomic bombs. On the 14th August, she gave up the struggle. The Second World War was over.

PEACE AT LAST

Britain, supported by the Commonwealth and Empire, could review her part in the conflict with justifiable satisfaction. She had given her all and bled herself white. And she had added another name to the roll of the world's great men. Winston Churchill had proved himself the grandest war leader of all times. His rock-firm faith and unflinching courage, his rousing ardour and limitless energy, had inspired Britain to defy the German tyrant when his power seemed unassailable. So Britain had once more saved Europe by holding, alone and unaided, the last bastion of freedom till the time arrived when Russia and the United States marched forward with their saving power.

THE POST-WAR WORLD

The Second World War left Europe bankrupt and ravaged. Industry and commerce were in chaos. Millions of people were hungry and homeless. Had it not been for the generous economic aid of the United States it is hard to see how the stricken nations could ever have struggled to their feet again.

UNITED NATIONS ORGANISATION

In 1945, fifty countries, including this time the U.S.A. and Russia, signed the Charter of the United Nations Organisation (U.N.O.) that was to supplant the old League of Nations. It was a further brave endeavour to prevent future wars, besides undertaking various social and economic services on an international scale.

The victorious Allies remained in occupation of the enemy countries: Russia in the eastern parts of Europe; the U.S.A., Britain and France in the western, and the U.S.A. in Japan. The central and south-eastern European States which Germany had overrun were restored, with some boundary alterations. More royal crowns toppled down, Italy, Yugoslavia, Bulgaria and Roumania all becoming republics. Unhappily, few of these countries enjoyed real independence. They lay under the huge shadow of Communist Russia. And that shadow threatened to creep over all Europe. The U.S.S.R. had emerged from the war as the strongest power in Europe. Only the U.S.A. could challenge it in population, material resources and organisation. The production of atom and hydrogen bombs and rockets—carrying nuclear warheads—of inter-continental range has immeasurably increased the tension.

The western Allies, including the United States, were anxious to set up a repentant Germany, as a counterpoise to Russia. This, of course, did not suit Russian designs.

Accordingly, in 1949, Western Germany alone was formed into a Federal Republic. In 1955, it became an independent sovereign State. It continued to be closely associated with the western powers and rapidly advanced in industrial prosperity. As a counterblast, Russia set up Eastern Germany as a " Democratic " Republic, which it kept closely under its control.

N.A.T.O.

A further security measure against the great Bear was taken in 1949. U.N.O. was supplemented by the North Atlantic Treaty Organisation, a defensive pact between the U.S.A., Canada, Britain, France, Italy and other Western powers. Western Germany was admitted to it in 1955. Russia was, and still is, very sore about it.

The shattering convulsions of the war had left the whole world in a condition of acute social and political unrest. Socialism spread with irresistible force, while in France and Italy Communism firmly established its disturbing influence. In France, conditions became so chaotic and alarming that at last the people turned in despair to the soldier-statesman General de Gaulle for salvation. In 1958, they gave de Gaulle almost dictatorial powers to set the country on its feet again and to prepare a constitution for a new republic—the Fifth.

In Britain, in the general election of 1945, the Socialists swept the country. There was an urgent feeling that society must be created anew on truly democratic lines. The State must ensure a higher standard of living for ordinary people. All the political parties were pledged to social reform. But, while the Socialists sought it through State ownership and control in industry and the public services, the Conservatives believed in private ownership, free competition and individual

From 25th April to 26th June, 1945, representatives of 50 countries met to form an organisation to include all nations. The aims of the United Nations Organisation, to maintain peace and settle all international conflicts, have not always been realised.

Under Stalin's dictatorship, Communism engulfed the satellite countries. Russia was the centre of political power, authority and thought, and at all political meetings the emblem of Communism appeared with huge portraits of Stalin. After his death the " Iron Curtain " lifted a fraction.

Korea had been divided into two, the north becoming a People's Republic under Communist control. In 1950, the North invaded the South, resulting in United Nations intervention. For three years, all the major powers were directly or indirectly involved in the Korean war.

In the waging of the Cold War between the Eastern and Western blocs, great sums had to be devoted to defence expenditure. Increasingly large amounts were spent on rockets, launchers and propellants, thus leading directly to programmes of space exploration.

enterprise. The Liberal party had so declined that it hardly counted.

So the Socialist government built up its brave new world of the "Welfare State". It nationalised the Bank of England, the coal mines, railway and road transport, cables and wireless, gas and electricity. By the National Insurance, Assistance and Health Service Acts of 1946 and 1948, the State provided a generous scale of sickness, unemployment, old-age and other benefits and a free health service for all. The period during which the Socialists' old enemy, the House of Lords, could hold up legislation was further reduced, from two years to one.

The year 1952 was saddened by the death of George VI, the best of kings, and gladdened by the accession of his daughter, Queen Elizabeth. In 1947, Her Majesty had married Lieutenant Philip Mountbatten, a great-great-grandchild of Queen Victoria, and now known to all as "Prince Philip".

GROWTH OF NATIONALISM

Among the restless agitations intensified by the war none was more insistent than that of nationalism, with its demand for independence, among the peoples of Africa and Asia. Britain, for her part, had already granted freedom to a number of her Dominions in different continents. —Canada, Australia, New Zealand, the Irish Free State and South Africa. She now had to deal with a chorus of clamorous demands for the same right from the Asian, African and other countries still under her rule. It had always been her policy to train her colonial subjects in self-government and fit them for independence. Post-war conditions led her to increase the pace. As a result, India and Pakistan—the States into which the Indian Empire split—Ceylon, Ghana, Malaya, Sierra Leone, Nigeria, Cyprus, Tanganyika, Jamaica, Trinidad and Tobago and Uganda have attained independence, while at the same time becoming members of the British Commonwealth of Nations. Burma, Eire, Somaliland and South Africa have broken away from the British connection altogether.

France and other countries have similarly acknowledged that some of their colonies have reached the school-leaving age.

The Near East, where Arabs and Jews were at daggers drawn, was a hot-bed of nationalism; and in Egypt, Britain badly burnt her fingers. In 1956, she withdrew her remaining troops from the Canal zone. Colonel Nasser, the fiery and ambitious President of the Egyptian Republic and champion of Arab nationalism, thereupon seized the Canal, which of course is a vital international waterway. Britain (led by Sir Anthony Eden, the Premier of the Conservative government then in power) joined a vigorous Franco-Israeli attack. They invaded Egypt. But this act of high-handed "Imperialism" was out of date. World opinion condemned it utterly. U.N.O. intervened and the invasion was called off, leaving Colonel Nasser in possession of the booty.

The coming of the longed-for era of settled peace and international concord is still delayed by the aggressive Communist policy of Russia. Repeated endeavours to come to an agreement for banning atomic warfare and generally reducing armaments have so far been frustrated by mutual distrust. And away in the Far East another thunder-cloud is looming. Modern China, that country, with its 650 million people, has embraced Communism and associated itself with Russia. Peace and concord—the winning of these blessings still remains the prime problem which mankind has to solve. Let that be achieved and we shall enter fully upon an era of dazzling possibilities for mankind.

Never before has life offered such a wealth of thrilling opportunities to man's undying spirit of adventure and enterprise and progress. The openings are everywhere: by land, sea, and air, in science and industry, in literature and the arts, in public service. Already we are in the Space Age. Russian and American "cosmonauts" have orbited the earth. Russian and American rockets have dented the moon. Then in July 1969, to the wonder and admiration of the entire world, American astronauts actually set foot on the moon.

INDIA'S AGE-OLD STORY

The Indian sub-continent is built on an imposingly large scale. Its extreme measurements are nearly 2,000 miles in length and breadth. Its peoples number some 500 millions and speak over 150 different languages. It is a hotchpotch of religious creeds: Hindu, Moslem, Sikh, Jain, Christian (claiming about ten million followers) and others. India is a land that makes geography interesting, for geography has largely shaped its history. The Himalayas, the highest mountain range in the world, wall it off from Central Asia, save for the high passes, especially the famous Khyber and the Bolan, of the north-west. Through those natural gateways a succession of invaders has poured down on to the rich alluvial plains of the north.

The plains are watered by three great river systems: the Indus, the sacred Ganges and the Brahmaputra, all measuring between 1500 and nearly 2000 miles, with their tributaries. The vast, sweltering, level expanse, over 200 miles wide, has ever been the main setting of India's story. Two-thirds of her population are massed there to-day. Southern India—the Deccan—has played a far less formative part.

Nearly three-quarters of the people depend for their livelihood on the soil, millions of them tirelessly cultivating their little patches of wheat and millet, rice and other produce in thousands of self-contained villages. But India is a sun-baked land and success or failure depends on the seasonal monsoon rainfall. The vagaries of these life-giving rains have repeatedly brought widespread drought, flood, famine, pestilence and death from starvation.

India can boast one of the world's most ancient civilisations, one indeed which may be related to that of Sumeria which began about 3000 B.C. At the same time, a people of advanced culture were settled in the Indus valley. They had cities containing brick houses, stately palaces, temples and public baths. Fate swallowed them up, though how we cannot say. A new people—called the Dasyus—appear out of the nowhere of history; but we know little about them either, save that they had dark skins and flat noses. Then, from perhaps about 2500 B.C., tribes of the lighter-skinned Aryans or Indo-Europeans came streaming through the passes and began definitely to mould India's history. These tribes have a particular interest for us. Their Sanskrit language reveals similarities to those of the European peoples, including English, which strongly suggest that somewhere in the distant past they sprang from a common source. Sanskrit became the parent of Hindi (which is now the official language of the present Indian Dominion) and other Indian tongues. The Aryans' tribal hymns, the Vedas, are one of the oldest collections of the world's literature.

The Aryans slew, enslaved, expelled or mingled with the flat-noses. Gradually, in the passing of the centuries, they enlarged their conquests and settled down to till the land. Family groups formed innumerable separate villages, each under a headman or leader. Potters, weavers, carpenters and smiths practised their hereditary crafts. The nobles wore armour, fought from horse-drawn chariots and hunted with dogs. Chariot-racing, wrestling, dancing, music—and gambling—formed the favourite amusements. In time, splendid cities arose where wealth and luxury, art and literature, science and learning abounded. Trade and commerce expanded. It was through the contacts and gradual commingling of the two races that the religious and social system of the Hindus, who to-day form two-thirds of India's peoples, was broadly shaped.

HINDUISM

The system of Hinduism thus developed is a good deal more

Benares, holiest city of Hinduism, lies on the banks of the sacred river Ganges. Millions come each year as pilgrims for ritual washing in the waters. From the temples, flights of steps lead down to the river's edge.

Many divisions of caste split up the Indian people. On the left are a low caste couple, with a man and woman of high caste on the right. The children belong to an intermediate caste.

The advance of Alexander the Great into the Indian subcontinent ended at the river Ganges.

than a religion. It is also a code of everyday conduct. And it is a very mixed affair. On the one hand it exhibits the crudest superstitions. Stones and trees are worshipped. There is a bewildering multitude of gods, of which the foremost are the supreme Brahma the Creator, Vishnu the Preserver and Siva the Destroyer. On the other hand the system is enlightened by the lofty principles of India's great philosophers. The doctrine of rebirth is an outstanding feature of Hinduism. Man dies only to be born again. And the character of each rebirth, whether for better or worse, depends on how he behaved himself in his previous life. A wrongdoer may be reborn as an insect, a worm, even a vile pig. In time —but commonly almost an eternity of time—he may attain the state of *nirvana*, or eternal bliss.

Hindu society is dominated by the caste system, which itself claims a religious origin. Every individual is born into a particular group which encloses him like the walls of a fortress. Within those walls the rules of his daily life are unalterably fixed. He may not marry into another caste. His food and drink, his company at table and, usually, his occupation are strictly determined. Originally four principal groups were recognised: the Brahmins or priests; the warriors; the farmers, traders and craftsmen; and the menial or servile group. From the latter probably descend the present-day 40-50 millions of the despised "untouchables", contact with whom is rank pollution. Well over 3000 castes exist to-day. They are mostly based on a man's calling or occupation, but they are also associated with distinctions of race, tribe or religion. Westerners find it hard to understand the all-powerful hold that this deep-rooted and exclusive system exerts. It splits the Hindu people into irreconcilable fragments and hinders all national unity and progress. Modern conditions are tending to relax caste distinctions; but progress is slow and difficult.

BUDDHISM

The most famous of India's philosophers, Gautama Buddha, who lived from about 560 to 480 B.C., was much concerned with the problem of rebirth, or reincarnation. Like many other sages, he found life a dubious blessing on the whole, its pains and sorrows far outweighing its fleeting joys. To discover an escape from the nightmare round of rebirth became his earnest study. And presently he believed he had

succeeded. Man must renounce all his natural desires— for the passing pleasures of existence, even for existence itself as a separate individual. Instead, he must devote himself to helping others along life's troubled way. Thus freed and purified he would, as we might say, short-circuit reincarnation and attain *nirvana*. Visionary and mystical doctrines make a very strong appeal to the Asiatic temperament and Buddhism spread far and wide over the East. In India, however, it had lost its popular hold by the eleventh century.

During the period of Aryan-Hindu supremacy, many other invaders paid a call on the country, including Alexander the Great in 327 B.C. These incursions brought India into contact with Greek and Roman civilisation and added a few more ingredients to the existing mixture of race and creed. But the basic pattern of Hindu life suffered remarkably little change.

In the rise and fall of rival kingdoms that occurred during these times, one name at least has won imperishable renown: Asoka, who ruled from about 274 to 232 B.C., and by conquest extended his empire over most of India. But the horrors of war soon sickened him. He became an earnest Buddhist and devoted himself to the moral and material welfare of his subjects and the spread of the charitable doctrines of his adopted creed. His work died with him; but in the East he is still revered for his rare and noble conception of the true duties of a king.

MOHAMMEDANISM

Now comes the violent jolt. In the seventh century came the startling rise of Mohammed of Arabia and the later spread of the conquering Moslem arms and religion. In the seventh and eighth centuries the wave of advance overflowed into north-west India. From the late tenth century onwards it was carried forward by Turkish and other peoples who had adopted the Moslem creed. The era that followed was filled with fierce and stubborn fighting as the invaders gradually advanced eastwards over the plains. The various Hindu States into which India had split went down one by one.

In 326, Alexander the Great crossed the Indus near Attock and gained a great victory. Although the Greeks only remained in India for two years, their culture had an influence on Indian history out of all proportion to the length of their stay.

The final phase set in with the arrival, in 1525, of the Moguls. By the seventeenth century, that famous dynasty held sway over almost all India. The Hindus became a subject people, their race despised, their religion contemptuously tolerated by their arrogant Moslem masters.

FOUNDER OF THE MOGUL EMPIRE

One of the few Mogul emperors who tried to reconcile the two races was Akbar the Great, who ruled in the time of England's Elizabeth I, from 1556 to 1605. He is a most attractive character, quick-minded, kindly and affable, just and merciful. He was strong and brave and, it is said, could pacify the worst tempered " rogue " elephant. He couldn't read or write, but he had a devouring curiosity for knowledge of every sort. His military conquests made him the real founder of the Mogul empire. His settled ambition was to unite all India and its peoples in one great and prosperous whole. To that end he sought to close the breach between his Moslem and Hindu subjects. He treated them as equals and even devised a new religion blending features of their, and other, creeds, though few people adopted it.

Unfortunately, his successors didn't inherit his wisdom and the Hindus sank again under oppression and persecution. Within a century of Akbar's death, the great Mogul empire was breaking up into a number of separate States, some Hindu, others Moslem. Soon the emperors' power was reduced to a shadow.

The Moslem tyranny made India a country of two sharply divided and antagonistic peoples; and, despite the later changes in their relationship, the gulf between them still remains unbridged. Yet the Moslems have made valuable contributions to every branch of Indian life—religion, language and literature, painting and architecture, industry and craftsmanship, social customs. Delhi, for long the Moslem capital, and other magnificent cities became luxurious centres of refined culture. Their splendid palaces and pavilions, their mosques and minarets, with their dazzling ornamentation of gold and precious stones, seem like something out of fairyland. The gleaming white marble mausoleum, or tomb, of the Taj Mahal at Agra is a sight that none who has seen it will ever forget.

We come now to a complete change in the character of our story. In the great European age of exploration, the Portuguese, seeking the treasures of the East, had reached India (Calicut) in 1498. Albuquerque, who was sent out as viceroy of the East in 1509, built up a maritime empire which included trading posts in India (Goa and others), the Spice Islands, Africa, the Persian Gulf and Ceylon. Less than a century later the English and Dutch were disputing the market. In those days, when the glory of the Mogul dynasty was at its height, the Indian trade was a prize of fabulous worth. Its principal commodities were superfine muslins, cottons and silks, rice and sugar, precious spices, costly gold- and silver-ware and jewellery.

COMING OF THE EUROPEANS

The English East India Company was formed in 1600, the Dutch in 1602. Both Companies established trading stations, or " factories ", on the Indian coasts, the English starting with Surat in 1612. Soon the Portuguese were driven from the eastern part of the field, except that they retained Goa, Damao and Diu in India. In 1639, the English Company founded Madras and later set up stations in Bengal, including Calcutta in 1690. In 1668, the Company acquired the island of Bombay from Charles II, who had received it as part of the dowry of his Portuguese bride, Catherine of Braganza. At the end of the seventeenth century, the Dutch were on the way out from India to concentrate on the East Indies, from which they had driven the Portuguese and the English. The final struggle was to be waged between Britain and France, as part of the world-wide contest for trade and empire. The French East India Company had its headquarters at Pondicherry, founded in 1683.

By the mid-eighteenth century the native nawabs and rajahs had made themselves practically independent of the dissolving Mogul empire and had taken to fighting each other. India fell into a condition of complete anarchy. It was an obvious field for the French and British to exploit, although one must remember that the Companies had been started as trading associations without any thought of gaining political power. Money-making was their business, not empire-making. However, the arrival of Joseph Dupleix, the French governor of Pondicherry, quite altered the situation. Dupleix saw possibilities. By using his superior French troops in the

The search for a sea-route to the Indies, in which so many brave men had given their lives, is almost over : Vasco da Gama's fleet is about to enter the Bay of Calicut.

Asoka, an emperor of North India from 274 to 232 B.C., embraced Buddhism and attempted to spread it throughout his lands. He had a column erected, named after him Asoka's column, whose capital was decorated with four lions above a base over a lotus. On the base is the wheel of life, a Buddhist emblem, which is featured on the Indian flag.

native quarrels and setting up puppet princes of his own choice, he might build up a powerful French political empire. He made a promising start. In 1749 and 1751 he got his own candidates installed as Nawab of the Carnatic and Nizam of Hyderabad.

The British realised that they would have to fight the French, join in the political game, and restore order to the distracted country. Otherwise they might as well pack up and go home. Empire-building was being forced upon them. Fortunately they had the right men for the work. One of them was Robert Clive. Clive's astonishing feat of taking Arcot, the capital of the Carnatic, in 1751, and defending it for fifty days against odds of twenty to one, made a profound impression on the Indian mind. British prestige soared. Next year, a French army was forced to surrender before Trichinopoly and the British candidate was hoisted to the Carnatic throne. Dupleix, his ambitions foiled, was called home.

BLACK HOLE OF CALCUTTA

The year 1756 marked the opening of the Seven Years' War, in which Britain and France finally fought out their struggle for world-championship. It was a memorable year in the Indian field of combat. The wild and dissolute young Nawab of Bengal, Surajah Dowlah, seized Calcutta, and the inhuman atrocity of the "Black Hole" followed. 146 British prisoners were packed into a small, ill-ventilated military gaol in the height of the tropical season and only 23 ghastly

spectres emerged alive. Next year, the avenging Clive bore down on the offender. Calcutta was retaken; and then, with an army of 3,200 British and sepoys (native troops), Surajah Dowlah's host of 50,000 men was utterly routed at Plassey. Down in the south, in 1760, Dupleix's successor was decisively beaten by Sir Eyre Coote at Wandiwash and next year Pondicherry fell. By 1760, Clive had made the British the effective masters of Bengal and laid the foundations of Britain's Indian empire. The treaty of 1763 which ended the Seven Years' War left the French power in India broken beyond repair. Clive performed further invaluable services from 1765 to 1767 and succeeded to a great extent in checking the scandalous abuses of the Company's administration. In 1772 he was charged with accepting bribes from the Indian princes and two years later he died tragically by his own hand. The young hero may have been a hopeless scapegrace at school, but he proved himself a military genius and a notable statesman.

The Company was now well launched on its political career; but the British government decided that it was not equal to the added responsibilities. Measures were taken for bringing the administration under Crown control, and British rule expanded down to 1815 under a succession of excellent governor-generals. The most fruitful events of this period occurred between 1798 and 1805, when the Marquis of Wellesley was governor-general. Tippoo, the villainous Sultan of Mysore, had become an enthusiastic ally of Napoleon. And Napoleon was in Egypt harbouring designs to overthrow British power in India. But Wellesley struck first. In 1799, his younger brother, Sir Arthur Wellesley (later destined to meet Napoleon at Waterloo) gave Tippoo a sound beating and stormed his capital, Seringapatam, the sultan himself dying in its defence. The governor-general's forward policy immensely extended Britain's rule.

By 1857, British and native troops had fought a succession of wars, against Gurkhas, and Mahrattas, Burmese and Afghans, Baluchis and Sikhs. Though the native princes of Rajputana and numerous other States, embracing some two-fifths of the country, were allowed to retain their thrones as subsidiary allies, British authority was paramount throughout India proper and in Assam and Lower Burma, Sind and the Punjab (the conquest of Burma was completed in 1886). Meantime, the English language was adopted in State-aided schools and such of the native scholars as attended them were afforded a Western education. The mid-century saw the spread of railways, the electric telegraph and other Western inventions.

INDIAN MUTINY

And then, in 1857, came the Mutiny. The outbreak began at Meerut. The sepoys murdered their officers and then seized Delhi, where the Europeans and Christians were massacred. The revolt spread through the whole Bengal army. Dreadful deeds were done at Cawnpore: women and children were brutally butchered. At Lucknow the British were besieged by a great host. But soon the military recovered from the first shock. Delhi was retaken after a terrific assault. Lucknow was relieved. Next year the Mutiny was a spent force. It had failed largely because most of the Indian princes remained loyal and few of the civilians supported it. But the fearful atrocities committed left bitter feelings behind. In August 1858, the British government passed an India Act transferring the administration from the East India Company to the British Crown and giving the Governor-General the title of Viceroy.

The famed Ajanta Caves are in Hyderabad State. These Buddhist temples, cut into the rock, were constructed between 200 B.C. and A.D. 600.

In 1877, Queen Victoria was proclaimed Empress of India.

COMING OF INDEPENDENCE

Our story now takes its final turn. Western education and ideas had spread in India. After the Mutiny a growing demand arose among the educated middle classes for a fuller share in the country's administration. In the 20th century many went further, notably Mahatma Gandhi, a revered social and political reformer. These agitated for complete independence. It had long been Britain's policy to train her colonial subjects for the responsibilities of self-government. Yet many British statesmen and officials in London cold-shouldered the movement in India. They were not altogether opposed to it but their attitude was one of exasperating distrust and self-conscious superiority. After the First World War the Indians felt strongly that their loyal services deserved some reward in the direction of self-rule. The government was still slow to respond; but the fuller Indianisation of the Civil Service (the body of officials who administered the country) was seriously begun in the 1920's.

The situation was difficult. India had had no experience in self-rule or parliamentary institutions. The masses were illiterate. The native princes were jealous of their rights. The caste system split society into fragments. The feud between Hindu and Moslem divided the nation.

Clearly progress must be sought by slow and cautious stages. Two of these stages were reached in 1919 and 1935. A certain share of responsible self-government was granted to the " British " provinces (as distinct from the native States) through popularly elected local councils and parliaments. Furthermore, an All-India Federation including the native States was planned. But these measures did not meet the insistent claims of the rising spirit of Indian nationalism and neither the Hindus nor the Moslems were satisfied. The ensuing struggle became one between these two religious parties. The Moslems feared that the Hindus, with their vastly superior numbers, would in time dominate the government; and they demanded to be formed into a separate State. Feelings ran high. During and after the Second World War —in which India again made notable sacrifices—riots and massacres became frequent.

In 1947, the British government announced its intention of withdrawing from the scene and leaving India to settle its problems by itself. This bold step forced the conflicting parties to realise that they must come to an agreement promptly if civil war was to be avoided. As a result two independent States were created: Moslem " Pakistan " (lying in two widely separated districts), and Hindu " India ". Both States later became republics, but they retained their connection with Britain as free Dominions within the British Commonwealth of Nations.

It had been realised by all that the tension of religious feeling was so acute that disturbances would almost certainly follow partition and the withdrawal of Britain's strong arm. What in fact did occur, most especially in the Punjab, was an appalling calamity. The Punjab, with its mixture of religions, was now divided between the two Dominions. Immediately after partition popular upheavals of uncontrollable fury arose. Eleven million refugees—Hindus, Moslems and Sikhs—migrated from one side of the new border to the other. Frenzied massacres, burnings and plunderings, famine and pestilence and universal chaos attended their panic-stricken flight and, before the wave of madness ebbed, perhaps 500,000 souls perished.

The Partition plan left the native States to decide their own future and all have since allied themselves with one or other of the Dominions. The position of Kashmir, where Moslems predominate, is nonetheless still undecided. After its maharajah joined India, his Moslem subjects rebelled and there was fighting between India and Pakistan. In 1949, a truce was arranged, with a cease-fire line that left the country divided between the combatants. This condition of stalemate still continues and further embitters the strained relations existing between the two Dominions.

The British Empire in India came to an end in 1947, but some irritating thorns still festered in the country's flesh. While the French had relinquished their remaining colonial possessions, the Portuguese still stood fast in Goa, Damao and Diu. Indian nationalism was bent on their recovery, but Portugal held on. Whereupon, in 1961, Indian troops proceeded to extract the offending thorns by a piece of drastic surgery. So Portugal lost the territories it had held for 450 years.

The new Dominions face some gigantic problems. They have to educate the ignorant, tradition-bound and poverty-stricken masses. They must increase food-production to feed a rapidly rising population which they must simultaneously curb. They must expand their industries—cotton, jute, hides and skins, tea and sugar, rubber, coal, iron and steel and manufactures—to pay for the improved social services of the new and modernised India they are striving to build, and to provide employment for the new generation of scientists and skilled technicians. They have to fuse or reconcile old ideas and institutions with new ones, the traditional Hindu and Moslem ways of life and thought with those imported for the West. Especially do they need to relax the caste system which is hamstringing social and political unity. Britain has bequeathed them, among other legacies, the principles of free parliamentary democracy. Communism is only a small voice in the land at present, though it may well speak louder in the times to come. The soul of the present-day Republic of India was the leader who embodied its finest liberal ideas, the late Prime Minister, Pandit Nehru. Only time can show what course the country will take in the future.

CANADA, THE FIRST DOMINION

Canada comprises all Northern America north of the United States, except Alaska, which became the 49th State in 1959. It is larger than the U.S.A. and practically as big as Europe. The most stirring events of its history occurred in its youth. What race was to rule that vast piece of the earth's surface, with its mighty rivers and lakes, its massive mountains and boundless prairies? Was it to be French or English?—that was the great question. The answer looked uncommonly like being "French".

DISCOVERY OF CANADA

The region had been first put on the map about the year 1000, when the Northman Leif Ericsson explored the coast. But it was not till the great burst of exploration following the voyages of Columbus that it was firmly drawn there. There were yawning gaps in the geographical knowledge of those times, when the existence of the American continent and the Pacific Ocean was quite unsuspected. Columbus, in 1492, thought he had reached the fringe of Asia and the Indies and that the coveted Spice Islands were nearby. Cabot had comparable delusions when, in 1497, he discovered what was probably Newfoundland. In the teeming cod fisheries of those fog-laden waters French and English sailors were thenceforth to compete regularly and fiercely.

In due time Europe learned its geography lesson. Magellan discovered his strait to the Pacific through the tip of South America and the search began for an alternative north-west passage. It was on that quest that the Frenchman Jacques Cartier set out in 1534. Of course he didn't succeed; but, during his three voyages up to 1541, he found the Gulf of St. Lawrence and explored—as far as Quebec and Montreal —the broad river highway of the same name, that leads from the Atlantic to the Great Lakes. Some "Indians" told him the country was called Canada. That was really the native word for a village; but the name has stuck.

It was not till some sixty years later that the French began real colonisation. In 1604, Samuel de Champlain started a settlement in Nova Scotia. In 1608, he founded and named Quebec and afterwards discovered the lake called after him. "New France", or French Canada, was coming into being. Companies were formed for trading and colonising. Missionaries penetrated the primeval forests, zealously labouring to convert the natives.

In 1663, the country passed under direct royal government. Further explorations had been made beyond the Great Lakes and on to the rolling prairies. La Salle sailed down the Mississippi and, in 1682, reached its mouth in the Gulf of Mexico. The whole vast valley was claimed for France and named Louisiana after Louis XIV. The main river system and the Great Lakes were on the way to passing under French control. In 1742, French explorers penetrated so far into the west that they may have sighted the towering mountain barrier of the Rockies.

Meantime the English were not altogether idle. Frobisher and Davis pursued the search for the north-west passage. Gilbert claimed Newfoundland for his queen, Elizabeth. In 1607, Virginia, the first of the thirteen Atlantic colonies, was established.

In 1609, Henry Hudson, an Englishman sailing under the Dutch flag, navigated the river which bears his name. Next year, in England's service, he entered the strait and explored the bay (that huge bite out of the land measuring 600 by 1000 miles) named after him. The stalwart navigator deserved a better fate than the one he suffered. His crew mutinied and set him adrift, with eight others, in a small boat. Save in old tales of Indian folklore, that was the last ever heard of them.

A Viking fleet must have been an awe-inspiring sight. The skill and courage of these seamen took them from Norway, across the mighty Atlantic Ocean, to Greenland, and Vinland (Rhode Island or Nova Scotia) in North America.

John and Sebastian Cabot, sailing from Bristol with 18 men, made their landfall in Newfoundland in the year 1497, claiming the land for Henry VII.

The coastline of Labrador stretches for about 1,000 miles along the Atlantic, from the Strait of Belle Island to Hudson Strait. It is indented with many bays and fjords.

Following on the lost mariner's discoveries, an intense competition in the valuable fur trade set in between English and French traders. In 1670, Charles II granted a Charter to Prince Rupert and a band of aristocratic associates establishing the Hudson's Bay Company. It gave the Company the lordship and the trading monopoly of a vaguely defined but enormously wide-ranging area stretching out all around the Bay. The barter trade with the Indians in furs and skins flourished. But great losses were inflicted by the French and their Indian allies in murderous assaults on the Company's forts and garrisons.

ANGLO-FRENCH RIVALRY

Such clashes were all of a piece with the general situation from early times. Whenever and wherever French and English traders and settlers met they fought as bitter rivals. Each side—the French more effectively—enlisted the savages as allies, and the fighting reached a pitch of hideous and pitiless ferocity as the Indian braves made gruesome play with tomahawk and scalping knife. In the later conflicts North America was merely a fringe of the world-wide battlefield, centred in Europe, on which the two powers fought out their long struggle for power and dominion and commerce. Louis XIV's soaring ambitions were checked by the terms of the Treaties of Utrecht and Rastadt, however, and after the War of the Spanish Succession (1702-13), France was compelled to abandon her claims in Newfoundland, Nova Scotia and around Hudson Bay.

But, though the French had to pack their bags in those outer areas, they remained very much at home in the regions of the St. Lawrence gulf and river, the Great Lakes and Louisiana. And they steadily proceeded with the grand design of linking up Canada and Louisiana with a chain of forts and trading posts in order to hem in the English colonists on the Atlantic coast and make the whole of the interior their own. It was a masterly plan. But it was over-bold. There were only about 70,000 Frenchmen in the country against perhaps two million English, though the former were far better organised for united action.

During and after the War of the Austrian Succession (1740-8), British colonists, co-operating with troops from home, vigorously prosecuted the national feud in North America. But the time was now approaching when the answer to our opening question was finally spoken. In the Seven Years' War (1756-63), Britain and France fought out to the finish their global struggle for empire. In the American arena, Canada became a major battlefield. In 1758, the powerful French fortress of Louisburg on Cape Breton Island, commanding the entrance to the Gulf of St. Lawrence, fell before a combined naval and military attack. The following year was notable for one of the most glorious triumphs of British arms.

James Wolfe, a major-general at thirty-two, had been sent out to attack the key fortress of Quebec. The young commander's sickly constitution, pale features and gawky figure scarcely seemed the stuff that heroes are made of. But within his valiant heart an unconquerable spirit and almost sacred sense of duty glowed. He faced a formidable problem. The citadel stood in a position of immense natural strength on the cliffs towering above the St. Lawrence river. The able French commander, Montcalm, was satisfied that it was impregnable. Wolfe tried hard to draw him from his fastness for a fight in the open; but Montcalm sat tight. Time was pressing, for the hard Canadian winter, when the St. Lawrence freezes up, was approaching. Wolfe determined on a fantastically daring plan for gaining a footing on the high plateau to the west of the city, the Heights of Abraham, and to bring the enemy to battle. The cliffs seemed hopelessly inaccessible, and several attempts to scale them failed. But an obscure foot-path zig-zagging up its bush-clad face had been discovered. The word was given. Silently, in the grey light of dawn, a picked landing party scrambled up the cliff. They gained the summit. The main army under Wolfe swarmed up after them. The French were taken completely by surprise. Shattered by the deadly British volleys, they fled in disorder. Quebec was won. But it was won at a grievous price. The gallant Wolfe, shot in wrist, groin and lungs, paid for it with his life, as Montcalm paid for its defence with his.

Next year the surrender of Montreal completed the conquest of Canada, and in 1763 the Treaty of Paris confirmed the doom of the whole French empire in North America. Canada was to be British.

But with this question answered another quickly arose, as we shall see presently. The province of "Canada" included in the French surrender formed only a small part of the Dominion of to-day. It comprised the more or less settled areas along both sides of the St. Lawrence and around the Great Lakes. The vast regions to the north and west, including the Hudson Bay Company's territory, were largely an unexplored wilderness.

"Canada" was occupied almost exclusively by French settlers. These, it is interesting to note, had already come to regard themselves as distinctively Canadian rather than French. They were in fact French Canadians. They presented a knotty problem in statecraft to their new rulers, a problem as tricky as breaking in a horse. The British had to rule, and if possible to reconcile, a hostile people who were as highly civilised as themselves and completely alien in their way of life. The French were Roman Catholics. They were quite unfamiliar with British parliamentary institution; they themselves lived under a modified feudal system. To this system, and to their religion, language and laws, they were stubbornly devoted.

The British government fortunately had the wisdom to realise that the horse they had to "gentle" was a mettlesome creature. The Quebec Act passed by George III's parliament in 1774 has ever been regarded by the French Canadians as their Charter of Liberties. Taken with the treaty of 1763, it left them in full possession of their Church and language, while their civil law was permitted to stand alongside the British criminal law.

We are now coming to our second question. In the war of 1775-83, the thirteen American colonies broke away from Britain. The American "rebels" tried, as it were, to lasso the French Canadians and draw them over to their side as rebels too. What was the response? Would Canada also sever her connection with the British Crown? Not so. The American lasso missed its aim. The Quebec Act had done its pacifying work. The just and sympathetic attitude of the popular British Governor, Sir Guy Carleton, did the rest. When, later, the Americans invaded the country, the French remained loyal and the invaders were thrown out. The event was all but

The administration of Lord Durham, governor of Canada, stirred up the wrath of suspicious French colonists, but created the conditions for dominion status. Ontario and Quebec were rejoined and given greater independence.

decisive for Canada's destiny. And it was confirmed when Britain and the United States fought each other in the war of 1812-14. Three times the Americans invaded the country and three times the Canadians—French and British standing shoulder to shoulder—sent them skipping. Canada was not to be absorbed into the United States. It was to remain a jewel in the British Crown.

The American War of Independence had important consequences for her northern neighbour. Large numbers of the Americans had remained passionately loyal to Britain. When the war ended and the break became complete the United Empire Loyalists, as they were called, were regarded as traitors and shamefully persecuted. Homeless and penniless, multitudes of them fled, or were driven, from the country.

Some 40,000 of the unhappy victims found refuge in Canada, where they joined the French and British settlers of Nova Scotia, founded New Brunswick and opened up virgin ground in Ontario. They brought with them a deep-rooted affection for Britain and British institutions and with it a bitter hatred of the Americans and the United States which has not completely evaporated in the far more friendly relations of the two countries to-day. At the same time the loyalists presented the mother country with a new conundrum. They had made Canada a country of two totally opposite peoples, one for the most part English-speaking and strongly Protestant, the other French and ardently Catholic. How to persuade the two bodies thus joined together—like the Siamese Twins—to live in harmony was to be one of Canada's persistent problems.

The British Prime Minister, William Pitt, decided that they shouldn't remain joined. So, in 1791, Canada was divided into two parts separated by the Ottawa river: on the west, *Upper Canada* (Ontario), which was predominantly Anglo-Saxon; on the east, *Lower Canada* (Quebec), which was mostly French. (Nova Scotia and New Brunswick were not affected.) Each province was governed by a Lieutenant-Governor and Council in association with an elected assembly, or parliament; the ruling power, however, remained with the British Crown. The modest share in popular government thus granted, while preserving the old French laws and institutions in Lower Canada, was something quite new to the French. It gave them an apprenticeship in British parliamentary methods. And to both British and French it marked the first steps on the road to full self-government.

Unfortunately the plan didn't work. A clamour arose for less official control and more democratic ways. In 1837, rebellions broke out in both provinces. The government quickly crushed them, but for a long time afterwards they left the French with very sore feelings against their British "oppressors".

REUNION

However, the British government sent out a Whig statesman of democratic views, Lord Durham, to investigate the colony's troubles. Lord Durham advised that the severed Siamese Twins should be reunited. But far more noteworthy was his recommendation that they should be given self-government in their own affairs. That proposal introduced a memorable new principle which, in an ever-expanding form, was to govern Britain's attitude towards her colonies in general— Canada, Australia, New Zealand and many others. The historic importance of the principle lies in this: it solved the puzzle of how to satisfy the colonies' rising spirit of independent nationalism and yet retain them in the Empire and the later Commonwealth.

In 1841, then, Ontario and Quebec were joined together under a single government and parliament; and nine years later, during the governorship of the understanding and popular Lord Elgin, self-government followed. But matters did not rest there for long. The two races remained hopelessly at loggerheads. The United States was suspected of designs on its northern neighbour's possessions. Canada was eager to expand and develop. Everything suggested a wider union of the scattered provinces.

So, in 1867, a start was made. Ontario, Quebec, Nova Scotia and New Brunswick became federated as the Dominion of Canada. Each province preserved its separate parliament, but a strong central government ruled from Ottawa, the new capital. The Dominion's first premier, the Scotsman Sir John A. Macdonald, is gratefully remembered by Canadians for the leading part he took in the movement and in his "national policy" of building up a prosperous and self-supporting country within the British Empire. In 1869, Hudson's Bay Company's territories were purchased by the Dominion, the Company surviving merely as a trading concern.

EXPLORATION

While Canada was thus growing up politically it was stretching its limbs in other ventures. In 1789, another Scotsman, Alexander Mackenzie, travelled in his birch-bark canoe down the river in the North-West Territories now called after him. In that frozen country of Indians and Eskimos and polar bears he gazed out on the Arctic Ocean. Four years later he crossed the Rockies and beheld another ocean—the Pacific. From the 1820s onward, exploration and settlement accompanied the intensified fur-trading operations of the Hudson's Bay Company over a vast range of territory extending from Ontario to the Pacific. In 1858, the new colony of British Columbia was established. With immigrants pouring in, the Middle West was rapidly settled. Land-hungry pioneers spread from Manitoba over the boundless forest and prairie lands of Saskatchewan and Alberta, the future "bread basket" of Canada and one of the world's great wheat-fields.

The westward advance was furthered by the construction

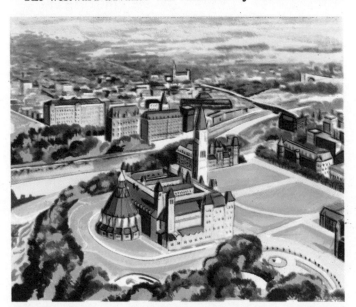

Between 1800 and 1858, Ottawa grew from a handful of houses into a city, endowed with parks, monuments and civic buildings.

The indigenous population of Canada was a mixture of Eskimo and Indian.

of the trans-continental Canadian Pacific Railway, completed in 1885. So new provinces were formed and admitted to the Dominion. In 1896, a more exciting event brought a frantic rush of prospectors to the Yukon: gold had been struck in the Klondike district. Meantime industrial manufactures were growing.

Since the death of Sir John Macdonald in 1891, his nation-building policy has been steadily pursued, notably by the two premiers Sir Wilfrid Laurier—a French Canadian, who held the office for fifteen years, and, W. L. Mackenzie King, who died in 1950 and who though not consecutively held the same high office for twenty-one years.

During the World Wars, the self-governing Dominions rallied round the mother country and after the first conflict, Canada, amongst others, became one of the freely associated members of the British Commonwealth. During the second war, Canadian scientists made important contributions to the development of the first atomic bomb.

CANADA'S POTENTIAL

Canada is still a comparatively young and growing country. Already she has become one of the world's great industrial and commercial powers. But she has still greater expectations from her almost unlimited natural resources. She is rich in furs, timber, wheat and fruit. Her mineral wealth includes iron, nickel, gold, silver, copper, asbestos and aluminium as well as the priceless uranium which is essential for the production of nuclear energy—and the atom bomb. Canned meat, flour, textiles, paper, and the wood pulp which forms its principal ingredient, are among her major industries. Her population of 20 millions (which includes Scandinavians, Germans and other Europeans, together with Indians and Eskimos) is all too small for the country's needs. Over 30 per cent. of the people are French speaking; in the province of Quebec 85 per cent. That province, indeed, presents a puzzling spectacle. It is a *French*-speaking community in a *Canadian* nation which itself belongs to the *British* Commonwealth.

Canadians are almost aggressively proud of their distinct and vigorous nationality. French and English Canada do not always see eye to eye, but they are at one in regarding themselves as first and foremost Canadians.

"THE AFRICAN LION"

The story of Livingstone

David Livingstone was a lucky man in at least one respect. He discovered his true calling early in life. From his pious Scottish parents he acquired a vigorous mind and body; they were too poor to give him much else of consequence. David's father was a tea salesman, living, at the time of his son's birth on 19th March, 1813, at Blantyre, near Glasgow.

David attended the village school till he was ten and afterwards worked in a cotton factory—from 6 a.m. to 8 p.m. daily. That still left him ten hours a day to spend and he found ample use for that golden spell in trout-fishing (and salmon-poaching), scrambles after geological specimens, hunts for medicinal herbs, and above all reading. Soon his taste for learning led him to an evening school, where for two hours daily he wrestled with Latin—then the basis of education. Returning home, he continued his scholarly labours till midnight or later.

Travel books were a continual delight to the boy who was himself to become quite a considerable traveller; but as he grew older he turned more to scientific works. Somewhere about his twentieth year this serious-minded and self-reliant youth experienced a strange spiritual revelation. His deep religious feelings urged him to dedicate his life to some practical work in the service of his fellow-men. He resolved to be a medical missionary.

Step by step he proceeded to qualify himself for that office. His character—firm, lofty of purpose, kindly and sympathetic—was already suited to it. He attended Glasgow University to study medicine, Greek and theology, paying for the winter sessions he spent there by returning to work at the cotton factory during the summer. He sat for, and passed, the examinations of the London Missionary Society. Two years in the London hospitals were followed by a medical degree and ordainment as a minister of the Scottish Independent Church. In December, 1840, he sailed for Africa and in March of the following year, his age being then twenty-eight, he landed at Cape Town.

At that time the map of Africa south of the equator was agreeably easy to draw. It was little more than an outline, with a blank—unexplored, darkest Africa—in the interior. The Portuguese were established in Angola on the west coast and Mozambique on the east. The British had taken, and extended, the Dutch colony at the Cape. The Arabs held a string of ports along the Indian Ocean from Cape Delgado northwards. At this time the abominable slave trade, though banned by Britain and the other European powers, still persisted, especially with the Arabs through their great market at Zanzibar.

In May, 1841, Livingstone set out from Port Elizabeth for the 530-mile journey by ox-wagon to Kuruman in the Bechuana country, the London Missionary Society's remotest outpost from the Cape. He was eager to penetrate the wild country to the north where no missionary had ever yet set foot. For more than two years, operating from Kuruman, he laboured in that field. In one period of six months he covered a thousand miles. Sometimes he deliberately cut himself off from his European companions so that he might live among the natives and learn their languages and customs. Their religion was a revoltingly barbaric hotchpotch of magic and witchcraft. Some of the tribes had never before seen a white man. Others had encountered Portuguese traders and acquired guns from them to supplement their native spears.

Livingstone went fearlessly into their squalid villages and sat around their camp fires. Teaching and doctoring, he adopted them as his children and cast his spell upon them. For him the colour bar did not exist. He seemed to understand by instinct the working of their primitive minds. When, as often happened, he encountered unfriendly tribes, he adopted a quietly resolute but tolerant attitude. One day he came upon the treacherous Bakaa tribe. These savages had recently murdered a European trader and his escort and regarded Livingstone as a possible avenger. The chief and his attendants eyed him suspiciously, while the other armed tribesmen took cover. When the Doctor trustfully ate the food brought to him they crept out again. Whereupon the strange white man calmly lay down for a sleep. When Livingstone left them the hatchet had been buried unused.

In August, 1843, Livingstone and his colleague Edwards carried Christianity 220 miles north of Kuruman and erected a mission house at Mabotsa. About this time the Doctor had an experience which few have undergone and survived. The district was infested with lions. Going out with a native hunting party, Livingstone fired both barrels of his muzzle-loader at one of the brutes. The lion sprang at him, buried his teeth in his shoulder and shook him as a terrier does a rat. Then a native caused a timely diversion. The lion turned on his new assailant but eventually dropped dead from the delayed action of Livingstone's bullets. The Doctor

David Livingstone explored regions never before seen by white men.

bore the marks, and suffered the effects of that encounter for life. He enjoyed a happier experience in January, 1845, when he married Mary, a daughter of the Scottish Dr. Moffat, one of the founders of the Kuruman mission station. He had gained a companion who was to accompany him bravely on many of his expeditions into the wilds.

In June, 1849, Livingstone attempted an undertaking approaching the impossible. In his ambition to found a mission station still farther north, he resolved to cross the almost waterless Kalahari Desert. He set out with about twenty natives and two white companions: William Oswell, a noted scholar and big-game hunter, and Mungo Murray, another sportsman. During the 600-mile trek the party nearly died of thirst. But they won through at last; and were the first Europeans to sight Lake Ngami.

Plagued by mosquitoes and tsetse-flies, Livingstone and Oswell pushed on to Linyanti, where, in August, 1851, they discovered the upper reaches of the Zambezi river—and also stark evidences of the slave-trade. The wretchedly poor tribes were reduced to raiding each other and bartering their captives to half-caste Portuguese traders in exchange for food, clothing and guns. The revelation gave a new character to Livingstone's mission. He had long formed the opinion that something more than the present system of missionary work was needed to spread the faith over the vast regions of Central Africa and bring the natives to a real understanding of the Christian way of life. Their own savage and degraded standards must be raised. He saw more clearly now that the rudimentary native industries must be fostered and trade routes to the coast opened up. Commerce with the outside world would improve the tribesmen's living conditions and make them independent of the slave-dealers. At the same time it would bring the uplifting ideas of Christian civilisation in its wake. On this long-distance project Livingstone now concentrated his energies. He determined to blaze a trail to the coast.

Accordingly, having sent his wife and children to Britain, Livingstone, in November, 1853, began his great trek westwards. Starting from Linyanti with twenty-seven picked natives, he travelled northwards and westwards by canoe along the rivers and then on foot. In the Chiboque country, Njambi, the chief of the fierce slave-raiding tribesmen, barred his path. The savages surrounded Livingstone's camp,

Stanley finds Livingstone near Lake Tanganyika.

At a point where the river Zambezi forms the boundary between Northern and Southern Rhodesia, are the mighty Victoria Falls, first discovered by Livingstone.

brandishing their swords and levelling their guns. The Doctor sat calmly on his camp stool, his gun across his knees, and called their bluff. Njambi climbed down. The party proceeded on its way.

During that perilous and exhausting 1,600-mile journey, starvation, malaria and dysentery reduced Livingstone to a skeleton. At length, however, in May, 1854, the travellers reached the Atlantic coast at Loanda in Portuguese Angola. But the almost superhuman feat of courage and endurance failed in its main object. In existing conditions the country was impossible as a trade route. It took Livingstone a year —during which he went down with his twenty-seventh attack of fever—to get back to Linyanti. And in November, 1855, he was on his travels again, with an escort of 200 natives, to try the east with its great Zambezi waterway. On the way he beheld the magnificent spectacle of the mile-wide Falls, with their 420-ft. drop, which the Africans called Mosioatunya, " Smoke-that-thunders ", and which the Scotsman named after Queen Victoria. The journey then continued, overland or by river, till, after some 1,300 miles, it ended at Quelimane, Mozambique, in May, 1856.

Livingstone had now been in Africa for fifteen years. During that time he had covered well over 4,000 miles of tropical jungle and forest, desert waste and swamp, and crossed the entire continent. He had penetrated the haunts of wild beasts: lion, elephant, rhinoceros, hippopotamus, buffalo, boar and crocodile. He had exposed himself to the attacks of mosquito and tsetse-fly. And he had compiled a mass of scientific information about the country, its races, animals, plants and minerals. Only his magnificent constitution, calm determination and missionary zeal could have carried him through—unless we may add the call of the unknown which, one may guess, ever sounded in his ears. Now he felt that he needed a holiday at home.

When he landed in Britain in December, 1856, he was surprised to find himself famous. Honours were showered upon him. Society lionised him. But " the African lion ", as his friend Oswell called him, had as little liking for being treated as a lion as he had for being maltreated by one. Soon after he had written his *Missionary Travels* he was off to Africa again. And this time he left in style. The British

Henry Stanley, having made several visits to Africa, traced the course of the Congo down to the sea.

government, which had become interested in developing East Africa, appointed the popular hero Her Majesty's Consul there and commander of an expedition for exploring the country and promoting commerce, civilisation and the extinction of the slave-trade. Livingstone was furnished with a paddle-steamer for river work and a staff which included a navigating officer from the Royal Navy, a botanist and physician and a geologist. Leaving Liverpool in March, 1858, with Mrs. Livingstone and her youngest son on board, the expedition arrived two months later off the Zambezi delta.

Explorations by land and water were made far up the Zambezi, Shire and Rovuma rivers and, in September, 1859, Livingstone discovered Lake Nyasa. The results, though important, were hardly up to expectations. The Doctor's hopes of the Zambezi as a commercial highway were dashed by the discovery of the Kebrabasa rapids. On the other hand, his survey of the Lake Nyasa district heralded the British Protectorate of Nyasaland.

But there was no falling off in the dangers and hardships endured. Livingstone ran into a little war between the Portuguese and a notorious slave-raider and saved the Portuguese governor's life by dragging him from the battlefield while the bullets were whizzing around him. At the Kebrabasa rapids Livingstone's canoe was sucked into a whirlpool and its occupant narrowly escaped disaster.

The party's progress took them along the main path of the Arab and Portuguese slave-trade, and the gruesome signs of the diabolical traffic multiplied around them. They found whole villages burnt and depopulated, entire districts smitten with starvation, disease and death, as a result of the atrocious inhumanity of the raiding bands. Four out of every five of the yoked and manacled captives collapsed, or were callously butchered, on the long trek to the slave markets.

There were other trials and tragedies. Fever levied a heavy toll, and amongst those who died was Mrs. Livingstone. Unhappy discords marred Livingstone's relations with his colleagues. As a self-reliant and masterful individualist, he was a failure in team-work with Europeans and many found him difficult to get on with.

On his second return home in July, 1864, one thought was in the forefront of Livingstone's mind. He would awaken the conscience of his countrymen to the unspeakable iniquities of the commerce in human flesh and blood. That his crusade was, in the long run, mainly responsible for suppressing the odious traffic may be counted among his noblest achievements.

A year later, when he was fifty-two, Africa called to him again. The Royal Geographical Society invited him to tackle the problems of defining the watershed, in the region between Lakes Nyasa and Tanganyika, that divided the great rivers of the continent and of fixing the true sources of the White Nile. (Actually, the latter question had already been settled, but no one at that time could be positive about it.) Livingstone agreed to go, though as ever his avowed primary concern was his work among the natives. Sailing in August, 1865, he arrived off the Rovuma river in high spirits in the following March.

The high spirits were soon lowered. For three years he explored the region of the lakes till, in March, 1869, he reached Ujiji on Lake Tanganyika. During his painful progress all but five of his attendants deserted him. He suffered hunger and sickness, the loss of his medicine chest—almost a sentence of death in itself—and the attacks of savage tribes. Often his need for safety and sustenance drove him to travel with the very Arab slavers whose nefarious trade it was his purpose to destroy.

HIS DISAPPEARANCE

At this stage a curtain of silence falls on the scene and Livingstone becomes lost to the world. " Is he dead or alive ? " is the question all were asking. On 10th November, 1871, a newspaper reporter, H. M. Stanley, sent out by an American journal, found the answer. There can be few who have not read of the dramatic meeting between seeker and sought at Ujiji. Stanley walked forward and politely doffed his hat. " Dr. Livingstone, I presume ? " he said.

Throughout the two years and more of silence Livingstone, assailed by ever-recurring weakness and often carrying his life in his hands, had steadfastly pursued his geographical mission. Now, fortified by Stanley's supplies, he obstinately refused to return home till he had finished his task. He never did finish it. The time came when even his powerful frame wore out. On 1st May, 1873, certain of his faithful black attendants found him kneeling at his bedside in an attitude of prayer. Livingstone was dead. A feat of rare devotion has made the names of his servants, Susi and Chuma, memorable. The heart and other organs of their " great master " were removed and buried beneath a big tree. Then Susi and Chuma, with a supporting party, bore the crudely embalmed body over swamp and desert, through forests and across rivers, in a heroic eight-months, trek to the coast. The dead chief must be buried in his own country.

On 18th April, 1874, the great-hearted missionary's remains received the final honour of interment in Westminster Abbey.

Livingstone was the greatest of all pioneer-missionaries. His thirty years of travel and travail covered one-third of the immense African continent and opened a way for Christianity and civilisation in Central Africa south of the equator. When he died the map was far less easy to draw: he had added so much detail to it. Under the inspiration of his splendid example, Stanley and a host of missionaries and other explorers carried on his work.

THE CARVING-UP OF AFRICA

Apart from the European settlers, the Mediterranean regions west of Egypt are peopled largely by Moslem Berbers and Arabs. Egypt's population includes Arabs, Moslem and Coptic Christian peasants, mixed negro-Arab Nubians, and European and other foreigners. From the south of the Sahara to the Gulf of Guinea are the negroes, many of them fine, strong, athletic people with lustrous black skins. The 4 ft.-6 in.-high, pot-bellied pygmies of the equatorial jungle are friendly, chocolate-coloured folk. Ranging over much of the country, south of the equator are the lighter (sometimes much lighter)-coloured Bantu, whose numerous tribes include the Xosas and Zulus. The yellow-brown Bushmen of the Kalahari Desert are very shy and backward. The Hottentots of the south-west are closely related to them, but more progressive.

EARLY CULTURE

The continent has never been wholly dark. Indeed its northern parts have displayed some of the brightest lamps of ancient history. The first of these were Egypt, and Phoenician Carthage. Then came the Greeks with their splendid city of Cyrene, followed by Alexander the Great with his even more splendid city of Alexandria, which was a celebrated centre of literature and learning in all its aspects. Under the Romans the whole coastal region became provinces of the empire, and their cities basked in the light of Latin culture. Later in the queue of arrivals came the Arabs. From about the middle of the seventh century A.D., they carried their arms, their creed, their language and brilliant culture from the Red Sea to the Atlantic. The Romans had done some exploration southwards, but they found the Sahara Desert rather discouraging. The Arabs, mounted on the camel, did better. They laid down caravan routes, opened up commerce with the interior, established trading settlements far down the eastern coast and drew maps of the country. They have left an abiding mark on northern Africa and its Berber inhabitants. From the eleventh century onwards, various European peoples, bent on trade or conquest, put in an appearance. And in the first part of the sixteenth century the Turks occupied Egypt and spread their rule westwards over their regencies of Tripoli, Tunisia and Algeria.

Long before this, however, the great European movement of maritime exploration had begun. From the fourteenth century onwards, the Portuguese, in their quest for African possessions and the rich trade of the East, inched their way round the huge pear-shaped continent and, by the mid-sixteenth century, reached India and beyond. A flourishing traffic in gold, ivory and slaves developed on the north-west African Guinea coast. The discovery of America by Columbus had greatly increased the demand for slaves and luckless West African negroes were shipped to the West Indian plantations to satisfy it. The slave-trade and the quest for gold presently brought English, Spanish, French and other adventurers to the region. Numerous forts and trading posts were set up. The British colony of Gambia began to take shape. Farther south the Portuguese, about 1483, had dis-

covered the mouth of the 3,000-mile-long Congo River. During the sixteenth and seventeenth centuries they seized the trading towns which the Moslems had established along the eastern coast (though they lost many of them again later) and advanced far up the 2,000-mile course of the Zambezi.

Meantime interesting events were taking place up in the north-east. Abyssinia (officially called Ethiopia) was the domain of a Christian king known vaguely to Europe as Prester John. The name was the subject of an old legend. The original sovereign of the fable was believed to have ruled over a vast empire in the Far East. He modestly claimed to be the greatest monarch under heaven. And he kept an eye on his subject princes by means of a magic mirror which reflected everything they were doing. By the fourteenth century the legend had transferred the august potentate's realm to Abyssinia, which had been a Christian land since the fourth century. The Portuguese were at pains to track down the country and, as a result, its geography became quite well-known to them.

The lure of the East Indian markets led Dutch, English and French traders to establish ports of call on the long haul round Africa. The Dutch installed themselves at the Cape in 1652, the English in far-away St. Helena and the French in Madagascar and the neighbouring islands. Before these rivals Portuguese power waned.

These and other varied ventures paved the way for territorial claims, but they left most of the vast African interior a blank on the map. But a change was on the way. By the late eighteenth century Europe had become seriously troubled about the iniquities of the slave-trade. In 1807 Britain, for her part, declared it illegal, and within thirty years the other European powers also abolished it. None-the-less the odious traffic long persisted, particularly under the Arabs through their great market at Zanzibar. Britain had now become

James Bruce, Scottish explorer, and his bearers meet warriors of a hostile tribe during the exploration of Ethiopia. Bruce traced the Blue Nile to its meeting point with the White Nile.

intent on real African trade and colonisation, especially in the north-west. A settlement which had already been formed at Sierra Leone, on the Guinea Coast, for freed slaves, developed into the colony of that name. (The Americans followed suit with the negro colony of Liberia.) The Gold Coast was taken over to check the slave-trade. Meantime, during the Napoleonic wars, Britain had taken possession of the Dutch settlement of Cape Colony, and in 1814, it was formally ceded to her.

MAPPING OF AFRICA

While these events were occurring, a new phase of European infiltration had set in. Systematic exploration had begun. Much of the work of African discovery was necessarily directed towards tracing the course of the four great rivers leading into the interior—the Nile, the Niger, the Congo and the Zambezi. Between 1770 and 1772, the Scotsman James Bruce travelled through Abyssinia and determined the course of the main Nile tributary, the Blue Nile. In 1796-7 Mungo Park, another Scotsman, followed the Niger for 300 miles. In 1805, after he had covered 2,000 miles, the natives attacked his party and Park was drowned. Not until 1830 was the final stretch of the river traced. Meanwhile, from 1823 onwards, extensive explorations were made between Lake Chad and Timbuktu.

In 1858, J. H. Speke and Richard Burton reached Lake Tanganyika, and four years later Speke solved the age-old riddle of the source of the White Nile by locating it in Lake Victoria.

By the mid-nineteenth century, Christian missionary work among the natives, coupled with compassionate efforts to combat the horrors of the slave-trade, had been taken up by bands of devoted labourers. Discovery, trading and territorial acquisitions were "fringe" benefits in their endeavours to spread the Gospel tidings.

Dr. Livingstone—yet another Scot—is the most illustrious of these dedicated missionary explorers. During his first visit, from 1841 to 1856, he crossed the great Kalahari Desert, traversed the continent from west to east and followed the Zambezi to its mouth. His arduous labours filled in much of the map of Central Africa. On his second trip, from 1858 to 1864, he explored the lower Zambezi and discovered Lake Nyasa. From 1866, he perseveringly investigated the region of Lakes Nyasa and Tanganyika. For over two years the world had no news of him.

Meantime an American newspaper sent out its correspondent H. M. Stanley, to look for the missing explorer. Stanley succeeded in 1871, but nothing could induce Livingstone to return home. At last his powerful frame succumbed to disease. On 1st May, 1873, his native servants found their master kneeling at his bedside—dead. The cruelties of the Arab and Portuguese slave-drivers had always stung Livingstone's heart to pity and indignation. His passionate protests were largely responsible for bringing the abominable traffic to an end.

Among the great doctor's successors Stanley, the once ill-used workhouse- and ship's cabin-boy, stands pre-eminent. In a series of expeditions up to 1889, he explored the equatorial forests of Central Africa, followed the Congo to its mouth, and with amazing energy opened up that region as no man had ever done before. He also discovered Lake Edward and Mount Ruwenzori.

By this time the process of carving up the continent had received a sudden acceleration. "The great scramble" for

" The Great Trek " was stimulated by rapid British expansion in Cape Colony. The Boers, with their team of oxen, crossed the Orange and Vaal rivers to open up new homes for themselves in the north.

territory had begun. There were various reasons for it. Britain had gone all "Imperialistic" and colonial expansion ministered to national pride. Her merchants and manufacturers, moreover, were seeking new markets and more raw materials. France and Germany were in a similar mood. The Franco-Prussian war of 1870-1 had left France defeated and humiliated and Germany triumphant and arrogant. Overseas empires would help to console the former and further glorify the latter. Another factor was the impulse to spread Christianity and civilisation among the pagan and barbarous natives.

LAND-GRABBING

Actually there had been some grabbing long before this. During the nineteenth century the Turkish or Ottoman Empire was breaking up and many of the major European powers were seizing their opportunities and greedily picking up the pieces. One of the Turks' North African possessions, Algiers, was captured by the French in 1830. Down in Cape Colony the Boers (Dutch farmers), chafing under British rule, trekked to the Transvaal and Orange Free State and also to Natal. The British followed them up and in 1843 annexed Natal. (We shall come to the other two States presently.)

It was a newcomer on the scene—King Leopold II of Belgium—who gave the carving-up process its acceleration. An international association formed under his guidance in 1876 to develop the Congo River basin, led to the region becoming the Belgian Congo Free State under the unscrupulous Leopold's personal sovereignty. In 1908, his inefficient administration and the scandalous ill-treatment of the natives resulted in the colony being taken over by the Belgian government. Meantime Portugal was asserting her ancient claims to the areas of Angola and Mozambique (Portuguese East Africa). France pursued a fixed aim of extending her previously acquired equatorial possessions in the direction of the lower Nile and of linking up her old settlements in the Senegal area with Tunis—another piece of the Turkish Empire, which she had begun to filch in the year 1881.

Thus her ambitions eventually made the greater part of north-west Africa her own. Besides this she established herself, during the 1880s, in a scrap of Somaliland, and in 1896 she annexed Madagascar.

Swashbuckling Germany, of course, demanded its share of the joint. In 1884 it sliced off German South-West Africa, Togoland and the Cameroons, and in 1885 began on German East Africa—now Tanganyika. Spain's part in the movement was a minor one, directed to secure her ancient rights over the Rio De Oro (the Gold River) territory on the north-west coast and the Rif opposite Gibraltar. Italy, however, displayed a growing appetite. Somaliland was created from the 1880s onward, and her Red Sea holdings became the colony of Eritrea in 1890. But, when the Italians tried to establish a protectorate over Abyssinia, they came sadly to grief. At Adowa, in 1896, they suffered a disastrous defeat that sent them limping homewards.

Britain's share of the feast was the choicest, though not the largest, of all. By the end of the century the territories she occupied stretched in an almost continuous chain from the Cape to Egypt, besides those in the west. Her intervention in Egypt (1882) and the Sudan (1884)—more pieces of the failing Turkish Empire—resulted in her occupation of both these territories. In other quarters, between 1884 and 1900, the British government gathered in, in one form or another, Southern and Northern Nigeria, Bechuanaland, British East Africa (now Kenya), Uganda, Rhodesia, Nyasaland, British Somaliland, Ashanti (attached to the old Gold Coast Colony) and—though the fighting here was not yet over—the Boer Transvaal and Orange Free State.

CECIL RHODES

The most enthusiastic of those who were painting the map of Southern Africa red was Cecil Rhodes. He was a man of almost fanatical ideas about British colonial expansion. He made it his mission in life to unite the British, Dutch and native peoples in South Africa in one powerful and prosperous federation. In 1889, he founded the British South Africa Company which developed the colony—Rhodesia—named after him. In 1890, he became Prime Minister of Cape Colony. Unfortunately the fervent empire-builder was rather overbold in his actions. His complicity in the planning of the rash—and unsuccessful—Jameson Raid of 1895 across the Transvaal border, in a plot to overthrow the Boer government in Johannesburg, was widely condemned and ruined his splendid career.

THE BOER WAR

Many of Britain's acquisitions were first secured by granting charters to trading companies, such as the British South Africa Company. Others had to be fought for. Of the native tribes engaged, none other earned such distinction as the Sudan "Fuzzy-Wuzzies", as the British soldiers nicknamed them from their "ayrick 'ead of 'air". For, as Rudyard Kipling admiringly recalls, they actually broke a British infantry square. The most wearing contest, however, was the Boer War of 1899-1902. The sturdy spirit and baffling tactics of the untrained Dutch farmers taxed Britain's military power to the utmost. At first the outnumbered British forces were repeatedly beaten. Others were closely besieged in Lady-smith, Kimberley and Mafeking. From February 1900, however, when heavy reinforcements had been sent out and Lord Roberts and Lord Kitchener arrived, the tide of failure began to turn. During the year the besieged towns were

A revolt of the Arab tribes against the Turks was engineered by Colonel Lawrence—" Lawrence of Arabia "—an outstanding man who understood the Arabs and their country.

relieved—Mafeking (under the gallant Colonel Baden-Powell, the future organiser of the Boy Scout and Girl Guide movements) after an investment of 217 days. The Boer capitals of Bloemfontein and Pretoria were taken and the two republics annexed. But it was not until May, 1902, that the Boers finally surrendered.

At the end of the nineteenth century Africa was so thoroughly carved up that only a few sizeable scraps remained and early in the twentieth century France and Italy began to wolf these. France secured a protectorate over most of Morocco in 1912. Italy, in 1911-12, snatched Tripoli (later to become part of Libya) from the Turks.

SELF-GOVERNMENT

In the south, however, changes of a different character had taken place. Britain granted self-government to the Transvaal and Orange Free State in 1906. Three years afterwards the districts were united with Cape Colony and Natal in the Union of South Africa, which thus became one of the Dominions later declared to be equal, self-governing communities of the British Commonwealth of Nations—a state of affairs which lasted until 1961 when South Africa became a republic.

The First World War of 1914-18 made short work of Germany's colonies. They were captured and handed over to the victorious Allies as trustees or guardians under the League of Nations. South-West Africa went to the South African Union, East Africa to Britain; Togoland and the Cameroons were shared by Britain and France.

In 1935-6 the wolfing started afresh. Mussolini, the braggart dictator of Italy, recalling the shame of Adowa, and ignoring completely the League of Nations, set upon Abyssinia. But his brutal conquest was short-lived. In the Second World War of 1939-45 the British helped to throw him out, while for good measure Italian Somaliland, Eritrea and Libya also were taken.

INDEPENDENT AFRICA

In modern times Africa's story has entered on a new and exciting phase. Many of the natives have become educated and familiar with European civilisation. They have learned

In the unprovoked invasion of Abyssinia, Italian troops, using their armour and modern weapons, mowed down the lightly-armed Ethiopian troops.

European ideas of freedom and self-government and they are eager to apply them to their own countries. This great upsurge of nationalism is a part of the general movement which has taken place since the Second World War. As a result, independence has been attained by many of the British colonies. These include Ghana (formerly the Gold Coast), Sierra Leone, Nigeria, Tanganyika (now together with Zanzibar named Tanzania) and Uganda. French Senegal, the Congo and numerous other French possessions, including Madagascar, have been made separate, though not independent, States. Morocco has become an independent kingdom, Tunisia, Algeria, Guinea, Madagascar, Togoland and Dahomey are among the republics. Of the former Italian possessions, Libya is now an independent republic, Eritrea has been added to Abyssinia, and "Somalia" (restored to Italy after the Second World War and now combined with British Somaliland) is now a free republic.

CONGO REPUBLIC

In June, 1960, too, the Belgian Congo became the independent Republic of the Congo—with startling consequences. The mass of the natives were ill-prepared for the responsibilities of self-rule and a state of violence and anarchy rapidly developed. There were savage tribal clashes, bitter struggles between rival political party leaders, anti-European riots and a widespread mutiny in the army. Thousands of Belgians and other Europeans fled for safety, while Belgian troops intervened to protect them. The provinces of Katanga and Kasai seceded.

APPEAL TO U.N.O.

In this chaotic state of affairs the new Congolese government appealed to the United Nations Organisation to intervene. Thereupon, during July, 1960, a body of U.N.O. civilian officials and an international army (comprising units from various African, Asian, neutral European and other States) began a valiant attempt to co-operate with the government in coping with a situation that was getting completely out of hand. It was a thankless task and the United Nations Organisation eventually found itself at loggerheads with all the conflicting African parties and personalities. At the same time, Communist Russia exploited the situation by posing as the champion of the oppressed natives against the "Imperialist" Western powers.

By September, the republican administration had broken down and for long two rival premiers competed for office. Then, to add to the mounting confusion, the undisciplined army stepped in and—with deplorable results—seized the reins of power.

After strenuous and desperate efforts, in the field and at the council table, a new central government was formed in August, 1961, under Cyrille Adoula, one of the more moderate nationalist leaders. In time, conditions became less nightmarish than they were; but the government's authority was for a while still challenged in Katanga and other districts, while immense obstacles remained to be overcome if the country was ever to be pacified and reunited under a strong administration. Katanga finally rejoined the Republic in January, 1963, and in 1964 United Nations forces left the country.

SOUTH AFRICA

South Africa remained a member of the British Commonwealth until 1961. In 1960 a vote was taken among the white population and by a narrow majority it was decided that the country should become a republic. And so on 31st May, 1961, the Union of South Africa declared itself completely independent.

The Government is composed of two Houses—the Senate and the House of Assembly and members of both must be of European descent. The coloured population which far outnumbers the white—notably the Bantu race and Asiatics—are thus not represented. But determination to uphold the supremacy of the white in conducting the country's affairs is strong. The doctrine of *Apartheid* first formulated in the 1940s, prevails to-day. *Apartheid* is an Afrikaans word meaning segregation or separateness, and the idea contained in the theory is that the races should be kept separate and each allowed to "develop along its own lines in its own area", leading where fitting to the creation of self-governing native states within the Republic. With this aim in view the Government has undertaken extensive housing, educational and other welfare projects. Although the Government policy has been criticised outwith the Republic, the protagonists of *Apartheid* are convinced that it will provide the long-term solution to the country's problems.

Tribal superstitions still prevail in parts of Africa, yet, since the Europeans—especially the French and British—took a hand in the continent's affairs, they have wrought wondrous changes. Education has spread. Railways, roads, electricity and great public works have been installed. Modern towns, with hospitals and universities, have arisen. Agriculture and industry have been developed.

MATERIAL WEALTH

Africa is rich in material resources. It is the world's leading producer of diamonds, and the Transvaal has the most productive of all goldfields. Other products are copper, cobalt and coal, tea, coffee and cocoa, cotton, rice and corn, tobacco and oil-palms, timber, rubber, wool, and ivory from elephants. Wines and fruits come from the north and south, and uranium from the Congo Republic. And recently rich strikes of oil and natural gas have been made in the Sahara, as well as some smaller quantities in the Niger delta area.

THE SOUTHERN CONTINENT
Australia and New Zealand

Australia is the smallest and loneliest and, as far as discovery is concerned (unless we count Antarctica), the newest of continents. Before the seventeenth century, various navigators claimed to have sighted its shores, but the first Europeans to land there were the Dutch. They entered the Gulf of Carpentaria in 1606, and later sailed along the northern and western coasts. In 1642, Tasman came upon the island now named Tasmania after him. Then, in 1699, the reformed English pirate, William Dampier, having hauled down the Jolly Roger, explored the north-west coast for 900 miles. But the reports of the new lands were discouraging. The savages were hostile and—so the sailors heard—there were giants in Tasmania. One interesting discovery, however, was the kangaroo.

In those days there was more speculation than real knowledge about the southern Pacific. Many people believed in the existence of a vast inhabited continent stretching right down to the Antarctic, of which the lately-discovered lands might, or might not, form part. But then came Captain Cook, the farm-labourer's talented son. Cook had started life as apprentice to a haberdasher, but afterwards ran away to sea and finally joined the Royal Navy. His outstanding abilities in sounding, surveying and charting unknown waters soon brought him distinction. He served on the St. Lawrence during Wolfe's famous attack on Quebec. Afterwards he was given the command of an expedition sent out, amongst other purposes, to clear up the Antarctic continent question. His voyages of 1769-70 in the *Endeavour* are classics of marine exploration. The fearless and hardy navigator sailed round New Zealand, painstakingly charted the coasts and annexed the islands for Britain. He then surveyed, for the first time, the entire eastern shore of Australia, with the perilous Great Barrier Reef—and nearly lost his ship when it struck a rock in shallow water. At Botany Bay—so named by his scientific shipmate Sir Joseph Banks because of its wealth of unknown plants—the party found the natives unfriendly and departed after hoisting the Union Jack in token of Britain's claim to possession of the country. The savages must have been enchanted with the brightly coloured emblem.

In 1772, Cook revisited New Zealand and scoured the southern Pacific, with its innumerable islands. Three years of arduous voyaging and systematic observation disposed of the myth of a habitable Antarctic continent.

CONVICT SETTLEMENTS

Some years later the British government, having lost the American colonies, was looking for somewhere else to dump convicts sentenced to transportation. In 1788, accordingly, the first party of some 750 culprits arrived in the flowery region of Botany Bay. The settlement was eventually made at the nearby Port Jackson, which was renamed Sydney. To-day it has grown into the magnificent city of that name, the capital of New South Wales. In 1803, another penal station was started at Hobart, the future capital of Tasmania. Such were the unpromising beginnings of the great enterprise of colonising an immense continent. In thinking of convicts, however, we need to bear in mind that those sent out from time to time were not necessarily grave criminal offenders. Under the harsh laws of the period a starving man might be transported for stealing a loaf of bread. Some of the prisoners were not criminals at all, but political offenders.

Abel Tasman, at the command of the Dutch government, made an extended exploration in search of Terra Australis. His first landfall, modern Tasmania, he called Van Diemen's Land. Thence he sailed round the eastern shore of New Zealand, thinking that all the islands were part of the one continent.

Burke and Wills were outstanding among the explorers of Australia. After successfully reaching the Gulf of Carpentaria from Melbourne, they perished on the return journey.

Transportation to the Australian continent ceased in 1867.

Free settlers and more felons followed the first arrivals. For long the way into the interior was blocked by the Blue Mountain range. But in 1813, an opening was found and the prospectors were rewarded with the vista of a vast expanse of grassy plains which included some of the world's finest pasture land. Australia's future as a great sheep-farming and wool-exporting country was already decided. Cattle and horses were to follow. During the ensuing years exploration went on steadily. There was plenty of room for it: the field was almost as large as the U.S.A. to-day. It was quite different, though, in its physical characteristics and native peoples.

THE ABORIGINES

Two-thirds of Australia is arid country suffering from a low rainfall and long droughts, or a dry surface in which the rain is rapidly lost. Over immense areas of the centre and west, desert conditions prevail. As a result, half the continent is still almost uninhabited. As for the natives, they were among the most backward races extant. The Australian aborigines—" the black fellows " as the white men call them, though they are actually chocolate-brown—have no agriculture, no real homes, no domestic animals except the dingo or native dog and, for the most part, no clothes. The ingenious boomerang is one of their weapons. They have given Australia some jolly place-names: Woolloomoollo, Warrangumby, Bungarribbee, and such like. Only about 70,000 full-blooded or half-blooded, of these undersized and not unintelligent folk now survive on the mainland, mostly in the northern coastal regions.

The explorers pushed their way boldly in all directions: to Encounter Bay, where Adelaide now stands; to Victoria; to the western lands and northern Queensland; into the central desert to plant the Union Jack in the very middle of Australia; across the continent from the south to north. By 1875, grit and perseverance had won their reward: almost the entire area had been penetrated. But many of the adventurers never returned. Hard on the trail of the pioneers went the squatters. The stream of immigration from Britain broadened. Plans for more systematic colonisation were

encouraged by a British enthusiast, Gibbon Wakefield. Needy emigrants were to be assisted out of the proceeds of land sales. A Company was formed, a settlement made in 1836 and Adelaide founded. So the colony of South Australia was born. Elsewhere, other towns arose, some of which—Brisbane, Perth, Melbourne and others—have now become great and populous cities. By the mid-years of the century the population of Australia had swelled to 400,000. With its increasing "wool clip" the country was becoming prosperous.

GOLD RUSH

But more sensational events than these were now happening, events far more exciting than mutton and wool. From Britain, from France, from Germany, even from North America and China, eager prospectors were flocking into Melbourne and the population soared. In Australia itself everyone was downing tools to join in the feverish scramble. For, in 1851, near Bathurst in New South Wales and at Ballarat and Bendigo in Victoria, fabulous strikes of gold had been made. Copper was already being mined in South Australia. Later on, rich deposits of silver, tin, lead, zinc and coal were worked. Australia had secured a second string to her bow: it was marked out to be an important mineral-producing country.

From a dumping ground for convicts, the southern continent had now become a new and spacious land of opportunity for Britain's free surplus population. By 1859, the separate colonies of New South Wales, Queensland, Victoria, South Australia and the Tasmanian island, which already possessed local parliaments, were granted self-government. Backward Western Australia had to wait till 1890 for the privilege. The sparsely populated "Northern Territory", which includes large barren and desert areas, has had a different history. It was adminstered by South Australia till 1911, when it was handed over to the Commonwealth.

ECONOMIC DEVELOPMENT

During the rest of the century, while far-away Europe was pursuing its habitual wars and rivalries, Australia peacefully developed its grazing, farming and mining industries. The first railway came in 1853, a submarine cable to Britain in

Lake Eucumbene, is part of the vast Snowy Mountain Scheme, the largest civil engineering project in the Commonwealth.

1871. The federation of the six colonies, or States, was long debated and on 1st January, 1901, the united Commonwealth of Australia came into being. The federal parliament comprised an elected senate and house of representatives, the Crown being represented by a governor-general. Each State retained its own parliament for local affairs. In 1913, the Commonwealth laid the first stones of a brand new federal capital at Canberra in New South Wales, and in 1927 the first federal parliament to sit there was opened by the Duke of York.

Australia's noble efforts in the First World War of 1914-18 are well known. With a population of less than six millions, the Commonwealth sent 330,000 troops overseas. Under the peace treaty, German New Guinea and many adjacent islands were handed over to it as trustees or guardians under the League of Nations. The country's war services and the growth of its feeling of distinct nationhood led to Australia becoming one of the equal, self-governing communities of the British Commonwealth of Nations.

The year 1933 brought a further increase of territory of sorts—over 2¼ million square miles of icy Antarctica, the only "continent" those regions have in the end produced.

In the Second World War of 1939-45, Japan's supremacy in the Pacific was a direct threat to Australia. During the fighting in New Guinea and other islands, the Commonwealth forces played a valiant part with the Americans in extinguishing the threat and the Japanese too. In the Mediterranean theatre of war, they also served with conspicuous gallantry.

To-day, Australia's economic welfare is based on sheep and cattle, agriculture, manufactures and minerals. Its exports include wool, hides and skins, meat, dairy produce, wheat, fruit and sugar. Its steel, cement, motor-vehicle, electronic equipment, textile, synthetic fibre and other manufacturing industries are being actively developed.

NEW DEVELOPMENTS

One of the star performances in the great industrial drive is the Snowy River hydro-electric undertaking in New South Wales, begun in 1949. It will cost 800 million Australian dollars and will generate three million kilowatts of electric power per hour.

A project of less peaceful character is the Long-Range Weapons Establishment at Woomera, South Australia. From there many a rocket has shot into space in the combined research operations of Britain and the Commonwealth.

The Australians—there are nearly eleven millions of them now—are well over 90 per cent. British. They have built up their country, overcoming daunting natural and climatic difficulties by sheer hard physical toil and enterprise, and their dogged exertions have made them a spirited, self-reliant and, in the main, strongly democratic people. The Labour party has long been a powerful force in the local and federal parliaments. The Commonwealth—together with New Zealand, to which we are now coming—has led the way, well in advance of the mother country, in the modern movements of political and social reform.

NEW ZEALAND

New Zealand—discovered by Tasman—lies 1,250 miles from Australia. It was too far off for Britain. She didn't want it. When Captain Cook claimed the islands for her the Government wouldn't have them.

In 1814, British missionaries, landed and did their best to convert and civilise the native Maoris. But earlier roving sailors and pirates had debauched them with spirits and sold them muskets. For some time the warring tribes were more interested in mutual slaughter with the new and fascinating weapon than in their own reformation, though the missionaries did make good progress later.

Meantime the enthusiastic Gibbon Wakefield, who had advanced the founding of South Australia, turned his attention to the as yet unsettled islands. He formed the New Zealand Company in 1837, and sent out his brother, Colonel Wakefield, with a thousand colonists. To the British Colonial Secretary, Lord Glenelg, the irrepressible coloniser was nothing but a nuisance. He just didn't want remote New Zealand. But circumstances were conspiring to make his lordship think again. News had arrived that a rival French expedition was being organised. Lord Glenelg, with a sigh, changed his mind. The country must be annexed. So, in 1840, Captain Hobson landed in the Bay of Islands and ran up the British flag. By this timely act the French were nicely forestalled.

THE MAORIS

Hobson's orders were to make peaceful terms with the Maoris. Now these people—of whom there were about 100,000 in the North Island but only a few in the South—were a very different proposition from the primitive " black fellows " of Australia. They were tough, intelligent and industrious. And they were trained warriors. They practised a little agriculture, lived in villages and wore clothes woven by their women. Their colour ranged from light to dark brown. Hobson concluded a treaty with their chiefs at Waitangi. The Maoris accepted the sovereignty of Queen Victoria and in return were guaranteed the possession of their lands. In the same year, 1840, in the North Island, Auckland was founded by Hobson, and Wellington (the present capital of New Zealand) by Colonel Wakefield. Next year the Colonel established Nelson in the South Island.

Meantime the New Zealand Company's settlers had come to blows with the Maoris over the ownership of certain tribal lands which the Company thought it had acquired. Conditions became very troubled. Fortunately, however, a strong-

The Maori warriors of New Zealand were tough, intelligent and warlike.

handed and tactful new Governor, Sir George Grey, arrived in 1845 to deal with the situation. Grey bought large areas of land from the natives for colonisation purposes, his purchases including the whole of the South Island, which soon became thoroughly British. There, Gibbon Wakefield established the Scottish Presbyterian settlement of Otago and the Anglican community of Canterbury. Grey's firm and sympathetic rule, which lasted till 1853, went far towards licking the struggling colony into shape. New Zealand soon ceased to be an unwanted possession. Grey showed himself a good friend to the Maoris. He safeguarded their remaining lands, taught them more agriculture and financed missionary schools. For all of which he won their undying gratitude.

SELF GOVERNMENT

In 1852, Britain granted the colony a constitution. Four years later self-government was established. (In 1907, New Zealand attained the rank of a Dominion.) The parliament to-day comprises a single elected chamber, the House of Representatives. The Maoris return four members and may vote in their election. As with Australia, a governor-general represents the Crown.

The period of 1860 to 1870 was a time of troubles for the North Island. The Maoris, who had gradually retreated to the mountainous interior, took up arms to preserve their lands from the ever-extending maw of the white men. In the guerrilla fighting that followed, the natives put up a gallant fight against the disciplined British soldiers and colonial riflemen, but in the end their powers of resistance were completely exhausted. The opponents gladly came to terms and learned to live peaceably side by side. Since then many of the Maoris have become doctors, lawyers, engineers and ministers in the government Cabinet, while several have received the honour of knighthood.

In many respects New Zealand's history has followed similar lines to that of her giant neighbour. Sheep-farming became the country's mainstay, in later times for meat—the well-known " Canterbury lamb "—as well as for wool. Cattle-raising followed. Gold, first discovered in 1853, brought considerable wealth and a rush of immigrants.

The Maoris came under the royal protection of Queen Victoria on 6th February, 1840, with the signing of the Treaty of Waitangi.

New Zealand's main source of income is from its rich pastures, with dairy produce and meat being the chief exports.

The Dominion's performances in the two World Wars were on the same high level of loyalty and sacrifice as Australia's. In the first war the superb fighting qualities of the " Anzacs " (the Australian and New Zealand Army Corps) won them imperishable fame on the blood-drenched beaches of Gallipoli. During the second war the Australian and New Zealand forces fought gloriously in Egypt, Greece, Crete, Libya and the Pacific.

SOCIAL SERVICES

After the first war, the German Western Samoa Islands were entrusted to New Zealand by the League of Nations. The Dominion administers a section—the Ross Dependency —of Antarctica. It has achieved the position of one of the self-governing communities of the British Commonwealth. Its marked democratic principles and practices early attracted world-wide attention. After Wyoming, U.S.A., it was the first country to grant (in 1893) the parliamentary vote to women. It was the first British country to introduce (in 1898) Old Age Pensions. In 1894, it instituted the world's first compulsory system of State arbitration for settling labour disputes—a system which involved the fixing of minimum standards of wages, and hours and conditions of work. The Labour governments which were in office in 1935-49 and 1957-60 made further striking advances in social security legislation, including a comprehensive scheme of increased pensions and family allowances and a national health service. New Zealand has risen in importance in the world with quite remarkable speed.

MAIN PRODUCTS

The Dominion, which, like Australia, is overwhelmingly British, is the most British of the Commonwealth countries in character. New Zealand proper (comprising the two large islands, together with Stewart, Chatham and other small islands, but excluding its other insular dependencies) is somewhat larger than the United Kingdom and has a population, including Maoris, approaching 2,500,000. The country's rich pastures furnish most of its exports: meat, wool, dairy produce and skins. Among its growing manufacturing industries are steel, paper and aluminium.

MODERN CHINA

The liberator of China from the Mongol tyranny of Jenghiz Khan and his descendants was Chu Yuan-chang. He was a peasant's son and had been shepherd boy, monk and bandit before he founded the Ming dynasty in 1368. The new dynasty applied itself to restoring the empire and its native institutions. Confucianism returned to favour together with the scholar-officials, or " Mandarins " as they came to be called by Europeans. Temples, palaces and city walls were everywhere rebuilt. When Peking, later the capital, was finished, no other city in the world could match its architectural splendour. The arts and crafts revived, notably pottery and porcelain. Stage-plays became the fashion. A massive output of " heavy " literature (including an encyclopedia of over 11,000 volumes) was balanced by many entertaining romantic novels.

TRADE WITH EUROPE

The outstanding feature of the period, however, is the beginning of continuous contact with Europeans. This was to change the course of China's history. The Ming emperors began by banging the door in the foreigners' faces. The outrageous conduct of the non-Chinese traders deepened the Chinese sense of superiority over the " barbarians ". This policy of isolation was to cost China dear. At that moment her civilisation was in advance of that of Europe. But, when the West came to develop its science and industry and culture, China, shut in and bound to her ancient ways, lost the lead.

The Portuguese were the pioneers in the European quest for the spices of the East. In 1516 they reached the South China coast, where they behaved more like pirates and hooligans than honest traders. The disdainful emperor would have nothing to do with them, though the Chinese merchants could not resist the lure of their profitable commerce.

The Dutch, who followed the Portuguese in 1607, behaved little better than their predecessors, and the English, who arrived in 1637, were quickly involved in fighting. None-the-less, the first trading stations were established by the Portuguese at Macao, near Canton, and by the Dutch in Formosa. The closed door was forced ajar; but the seeds of China's lasting hatred of "the foreign devils" had been sown.

In the north, however, the story was very different. The earliest of a succession of Roman Catholic priests arrived. In the forefront was the learned Jesuit, Matteo Ricci, who was admitted into Peking in 1601. The Jesuits won court favour by their tactful and accommodating manner. They were permitted to found churches and they won many distinguished converts. Their knowledge of European astronomy, mathematics, geography and other sciences (to say nothing of spectacles and mechanical clocks) aroused the interest of the mandarins. To some extent at least East and West exchanged ideas. A little later the foreigners were found useful as artillery experts.

MANCHU DYNASTY

But their cannon could not save the Ming dynasty. Weakened by rebellion and decay, it fell before the Manchus from Manchuria, descendants of the Nuchens who had conquered North China from the Sungs. The Manchus, who founded their Ch'ing dynasty in 1644, were aliens; but, as had so often happened before, the barbarian conquerors eventually became more Chinese than the Chinese themselves. They adopted the ancient culture and the Confucian scholar-system of government. Yet they ruled their new subjects as a con-

Jesuit missionaries were among the first Europeans after Marco Polo to have contact with the millions of China. Here Jesuit missionaries are preaching the gospel to the Chinese, winning over some converts to Christianity.

The first envoys from England seeking an imperial audience with the Sun of Heaven caught no glimpse of him behind a yellow curtain. They were treated with disdain, since the Chinese considered them to be barbarians.

quered people and even forced them to adopt their own "pigtail" style of head-dress. Their military record up to the close of the eighteenth century was brilliant. Their empire, including tributary States, reached from Manchuria and Mongolia to Annam and Burma and from Korea and the Pacific Ocean to Turkestan (Sinkiang) and Tibet. In more peaceful paths, they produced exquisite porcelain-ware which is still highly prized by collectors everywhere. The Roman Catholic and Protestant Churches, notwithstanding periods of persecution, gained in strength.

Meantime the European powers, with John Bull in the lead, were pushing themselves forward. Portuguese, Dutch, British, French, Russian, American and other nationals all took part in a general scramble for the empire's prolific trade, particularly in tea, silks, cottons, and handicrafts. The Chinese had their own ideas of how commerce should be conducted. As a consciously superior and self-sufficient people they would only treat with the foreigners as an inferior breed. Accordingly, the government imposed on them all manner of humiliating and galling restrictions. Only specified ports, such as Canton, were opened for trading and only prescribed areas for residence. The "barbarians" were subjected to the cruel Chinese laws and likewise to the whimsies of the corrupt Chinese officials. Friction was inevitable, and at long last it reached flash-point over the opium trade, which was largely in British hands.

Opium-smoking is a soothing habit, but dangerous when indulged in to excess. The Chinese rapidly became addicted to it and the empire was drained of immense quantities of silver to pay for the imports. Eventually the emperors banned the traffic, though corrupt officials still openly encouraged it. In 1839, the government violently confiscated the foreign merchants' cargoes in a determined attempt to suppress a traffic that was injurious to their country. Britain, concerned only about her trade, regarded the act as another, and even more blatant, demonstration of China's high-handed attitude: so she, too, became high-handed and struck back.

OPIUM WARS

The ensuing war showed that the once vigorous Manchu dynasty had become as feeble as it was arrogant. In 1842-3, it was compelled to cede Hong Kong to the British, to open several ports to foreign trade and residence and to promise that the Chinese officials would thenceforth mend their manners. Soon afterwards other foreign powers secured similar treaties for freer commerce.

But China couldn't shake off her old habits and in 1856 a second war, against Britain and France, flared up. Peking was entered in 1860 and the Manchus were finally brought to terms with the principal foreign powers. Additional ports were opened and the opium traffic was recognised. Foreign ambassadors were to be installed in Peking and Christianity was to be freely practised. Britain was given the Kowloon promontory opposite Hong Kong, while the Russian Bear, hungering after a port on the Pacific, set its paws on the site of the future Vladivostok. Another inroad on China's sovereignty resulted from the two wars. The foreign settlements in the trading ports were exempted from Chinese law and practically became independent colonies on Chinese soil. This privilege was ever hated by the Chinese as one of the most wounding provisions of what they indignantly called "the unequal treaties". During the succeeding years further pickings of Chinese territory were gobbled up; Annam by the French, Upper Burma by the British.

China, in fact, was in decay. The imperial court and administration had become incurably corrupt and incapable. The empire groaned restlessly under chronic misrule. Chinese civilisation had reached the point of stagnation. The degraded Manchu emperors still clung to the antiquated and impractical system of scholar-class government. They serenely shut their eyes to the immense scientific and industrial developments in Europe. With them progress was both impossible and undesirable. The more enlightened of their subjects, however, were waking up to the need for fundamental changes. And in 1894 the whole country received a jolt that made it rub its eyes in earnest.

Japan had forged ahead of her great neighbour in adopting Western ways. Now she fell on China, brought her to her knees and forced her out of Korea and Formosa. It looked as if the obsolete old empire was breaking up. The watching foreign powers made a grab for the fragments. Numerous railway and mining concessions and further grants of territory were secured. Germany got Kiaochow, Russia, Port Arthur, and Britain, Wei-Hai-Wei.

BOXER RISING

But now the ever-growing groups of reformers threw themselves determinedly into the struggle to save China. A start had, indeed, already been made. Western ideas, in philosophy, politics and economics, had been studied. The electric telegraph and a few miles of railway had been installed. For a time it seemed that the Manchus might be definitely won over to the new ideas; but the hope failed. Then, in 1900, a fanatical "Boxer" rising, clamouring for the total expulsion of the foreigners, convulsed the country. Its instigators were the members of an odd secret society who practised certain rites, including a show of boxing, which they fondly believed would make their bodies bulletproof. The Boxers turned against the Christians, European and Chinese, and thousands were slain, while others, together with many foreign diplomats, were besieged in Peking by howling mobs. The foreign powers marched hot-foot on the city, relieved the besieged and wreaked a fearful revenge. The terms of punishment they imposed showed that the country now lay practically at their mercy.

After massacring Europeans in the provinces, the Boxers concentrated on Tientsin. They besieged the Legation and the cathedral of Pe-tang. However, in spite of their numerical superiority, they failed to overcome the few defenders.

178

In their quest for land and sources of raw materials, the Japanese invaded Manchuria. Here they enter the capital city, Moukden (Shenyang). Thus began, in 1937, the long war that only ended in 1945.

Russia thought this a favourable opportunity for advancing her designs in Manchuria and Korea. But these encroachments aroused the ire of Japan who had a special interest in Korea. In 1904-5, she set about Russia and gave her a sound drubbing, gaining for herself, among other plums, Port Arthur and a free hand in Korea—which she later formally annexed.

By this time even the blinkered Manchus had come to realise that they must bow to the rising demand for " westernisation ". Accordingly, various reforms were introduced. There was even the promise of parliamentary government. Meantime, eager students were flocking to the new schools which had been opened, teaching Western as well as Chinese subjects. Thousands journeyed to Europe, America and Japan to study there. Translations of Western books flooded the country. The reform movement swept forward on a wave of patriotic ardour and hatred of the foreign aggressors— and of the Manchus. For the Manchus had removed their blinkers too late. The whole country had lost faith in them. The tottering dynasty was only maintained now by the foreign powers who profited from its weakness. So the cry went up. " The Manchus must go! " And go they did, at a remarkable pace.

FALL OF THE EMPIRE

In 1911, the great revolution began. A provisional republican government was set up under the presidency of Sun Yat-sen, China's national revolutionary hero. Next year the emperor abdicated. Thus fell the empire which had first been established more than 2,000 years before. But the day that had dawned so brightly for the country's hopes was soon overcast. There were too many leaders inflamed with conflicting ideas about the future. The first years of the republic plunged the country into chaos and civil strife. Outer Mongolia asserted its independence. During the First World War of 1914-18, Japan took the opportunity to resume her aggressions.

By 1930, two main parties were fighting for supremacy in the civil war. One was the moderate Kuomintang, " The National People's Party ", which had been started by Sun Yat-sen and, after his death, was led by General Chiang Kai-shek. Its aims included the welfare of the peasants and industrial town-workers and their training for ultimate self-government. The other was the Communist Party. This was fostered by the Russian Communists, who wished the Chinese workers to set up a government like the one they had established in their own country.

In 1931, Japan was on the prowl again and fixed her claws on Manchuria. Notwithstanding the common peril, the civil war went on. In 1934, the Nationalists looked like winning it, for the main Communist armies were being hard pressed in Kiangsi. They eluded encirclement by a memorable march. In the face of every extreme of hardship and suffering, they forced their way over snow-clad mountains, swollen rivers and treacherous swamps, continually fighting off the persistent attacks of the enemy as they drove forward. " The Long March " dragged on for a whole year and covered more than 6,000 miles. A hundred thousand men had set out from Kiangsi. Twenty thousand survived to reach safety in northern Shensi. But the heroic feat of endurance had hardened the soldiers and their leaders into a brotherhood in arms whose ardour and determination were to prove indestructible.

In 1937, as the Japanese threat became more alarming, the rival leaders managed to sink their differences sufficiently to form a united front against the national foe. But they could not stay his victorious progress. During 1937-8, the Japanese advanced into Mongolia and also seized a vast area of north-eastern China, together with the southern ports. Their war-lords were bent on dominating all China. After the defeat of Japan at the end of the Second World War, the Nationalists and Communists set on each other again with renewed gusto. So matters continued till, in 1949, the Communists under Mao Tse-tung triumphed. Chiang Kai-shek was driven off the mainland to Formosa, where he sat down to wait " until the times should alter ".

ECONOMIC REVOLUTION

On the 1st October, 1949, the People's Republic of China was proclaimed, with Mao Tse-tung as chairman. Pursuing their long-range policy of State control of property and industry, the Communists set out to transform the old China, with its 650 million people, into a great, modern, industrialised power. It was the boldest national adventure in history.

179

In Khruschev's early days of office there was a great deal of contact between Mao Tse-tung and himself, but relationships later became more strained. The Communism of China, although allied to that of Russia, is not dominated by it.

Much had been done during the revolutionary civil wars. What has since been accomplished is astonishing. Agriculture and industry—coal, iron, steel, cotton, electric power and manufactures—have been modernised and enormously expanded. New railways and roads and gigantic irrigation and other public works have been undertaken. Education has become the right of all.

At an early stage the land was taken from the landlords and distributed among the peasants. Collective farms were formed and, in 1958, an ambitious new plan was set on foot. The peasants were organised into a number of communes which took over their holdings and farmed them as single, and largely self-governing, units. The workers received money wages for their labours, together with subsistence benefits, such as free meals. The communes were also planned to develop local industries, manage schools and to perform other administrative duties. They were later extended to the towns. The communal system, as it spread over the country, was enthusiastically claimed to be the biggest advance ever towards practical Communism.

Religion is another sphere in which a revolutionary change of outlook has taken place. The three religions of China—Confucianism, Taoism and Buddhism—were already in decline, though Confucianism still commanded wide respect among the educated classes. The Communist autocrats frown on all creeds, Christian or otherwise. The ancient family system, with its ancestor worship, is being undermined, especially in the industrial towns.

By a friendly treaty with Russia, Mao's government completed the freeing of the country from the " unequal treaties " and foreign interference, save that Britain still retains Hong Kong and the Kowloon promontory and Portugal holds on to Macao. In its dealing with other foreign powers the government asserted itself vigorously. Chinese troops played a conspicuous part in the Korean War of 1950-3, in which most of the great powers were involved and which led to the peninsula, already partitioned in 1945, being divided between a Communist State in the north and a democratic State in the south. During the same period China successfully asserted its ancient sovereignty over Tibet. Later it went on to seize several border regions claimed by India.

The Communists are itching to recover Formosa (or Taiwan as it is called in Chinese) and to liquidate General Chiang Kai-shek and all his works, and only the influence of the anti-Communist U.S.A., which is backing him, restrains their ardour.

With Russia, from whom the republic first learned Communism, a fairly close alliance was forged, and the association of these two colossal powers became a dominant factor in world politics. Yet some jarring discords have broken their former harmony. China is too proud to be a mere satellite of Russia; and Russia may be getting a little uneasy about her pupil's growing power, which could challenge her own leadership of the Communist world. Chinese Communism does not slavishly follow the Russian model; in various ways it is adapting its practices to China's own national needs. It has not suppressed all other parties in the State, though it has made them toe the line. The Chinese communes mark a step in advance of Russian achievements. Nikita Khruschev, who was Russian Premier from 1958 to 1964, repeatedly proclaimed a new policy of peaceful co-existence with the Western capitalist countries, on the assumption that, in time, Communism will everywhere prevail by its own strength. China, however, deems this attitude a betrayal of the sacred Marxist dogma that Communism can only be spread by force. These differences are more than ripples on the surface of the water, and it will be most interesting to watch what really comes of them.

China's progressive modernisation seems certain; but whether it will be achieved on the present Communist lines is anyone's guess. There is, of course, much shaking of wise old heads. But the younger generation have flung themselves into the movement with boundless enthusiasm. The peasants, despite manifold discontents, find their living conditions materially bettered. The women rejoice in new liberties. As the people studiously absorb the science and technology of the West, or labour in the growing factories or on the land, their minds are inspired by the proud thought that they are creating a new nation.

Napoleon once said, " China—there lies a sleeping giant. Let him sleep, for when he wakes he shall shake the world ". The giant is awake now.

JAPAN
The Land of the Rising Sun

The mountainous islands of Japan are rather a disturbing country for those who like a quiet life. There are too many typhoons, volcanoes and earthquakes. Quite apart from serious upheavals, earth-tremors of variously disquieting degree are as frequent as meal-times.

Japan consists of the four large islands of Hokkaido, Honshu, Shikoku and Kyushu and hundreds of small islands. In area they are rather more than half as large again as Great Britain. Because of the steep mountains only about 15 per cent. of the land can be farmed. The Japanese, however, are very industrious folk and the farmers' harvests of rice, wheat and barley, plus the fishermens' harvests of the sea, are in themselves sufficient to feed, if rather meagrely, most of the population of 93 millions.

EARLIEST INHABITANTS

The Japanese are a mixed, largely Mongolian, people. The earliest known inhabitants, the Ainus, are a hairy breed—like Esau. The women have flowing locks and the men flowing beards and hairy chests. Their survivors are located in Hokkaido, where they were gradually driven by later invaders from Korea and from the south—perhaps Malaya and the South Sea Islands. The Japanese are shorter in stature than Europeans, though the rising generation—rising in more senses than one—are stretching their limbs and catching up. Their small bodies, however, house a highly distinctive character. As a nation they are intensely proud, and self-satisfied. Individually, they have shown themselves in the past as a very submissive people, extremely respectful to all in authority. "Orders are orders", seemed, indeed, to be their ruling motto. Whether the orders were good or bad did not trouble their consciences. Ages of

repression and servility had made them reserved, suspicious and wanting in self-reliance—" Yes-men " in fact. In the same way, they were slow to invent but quick to imitate. Modern conditions are producing a more self-reliant and independent spirit, especially among the younger generation. For the rest, the Japanese exhibit a puzzling combination of kindness and ceremonious politeness, fanatical bravery and savagery, intelligence and industry, fastidious personal cleanliness, and a deep love of beautiful things.

SHINTOISM

The native religion of Shinto, " the way of the gods ", goes far to explain their outlook on the world until, as we shall see presently, defeat in the Second World War gave them a new pair of spectacles. Shinto is primarily a Nature religion similar to those of ancient China, but the old ruling classes made it something much more. The creed boasts millions of gods: deceased ancestors, emperors, national heroes, and other distinguished persons have been deified. All these beings govern the fortunes of the living. The outstanding religious rites are those of purification, which must be performed on prescribed occasions to ensure the favour of the gods. The teachings of Shinto stoked the fires of patriotic pride. Until 1946, the emperors were revered as divine beings directly descended from the sun-goddess and destined to rule forever. And not only over the Land of the Rising Sun, but wherever the sun rose or set. For the Japanese, like the Hebrews, were a chosen people. Their divine mission was to encompass the earth. Hence their superior airs, their fanatical fighting spirit, their self-sacrificing devotion and unquestioning obedience to the sacred emperor and the commanders of his armies.

The Ainu race, confined to the northern islands of Hokkaido and Sakhalin, and the Kuriles, are distinguished by the growth of the beard and hair.

One of the little lakes which are found all over the Japanese countryside: these lakes, besides being of great scenic beauty, are an important source of food.

The anniversary of Buddha's birth is a children's festival celebrated with great solemnity. The lotus flower is consecrated to Buddha.

Alongside this arrogant creed is Buddhism which reached Japan from China, by way of Korea, in the mid-sixth century and for over a thousand years it more or less overshadowed the old faith. It was from China, too, that the teachings of Confucius, blending with those of the Shinto creed, strengthened and spread the principles of family loyalty and obedience and the worship of ancestors.

From early times the Japanese were divided into a number of rival, and usually wrangling, clans, each ardently devoted to its own noble chieftain. The empire is *supposed* to have been founded in 660 B.C. by Jimmu, the head of the most powerful clan. Reliable historical records, however, do not begin till about A.D. 400.

EFFECT OF CHINA

The supreme event in Japan's social and cultural history is the introduction of the rich civilisation of China. The untutored islanders had early made contacts, aggressive or peaceful, with Korea, the stepping-stone on the way, and it was there that they first, as it were, saw the light. They had no writing of their own and, about A.D. 400, they adopted the Chinese pictorial script. It was a momentous step in their education, for without writing, learning cannot flourish. When Buddhism arrived, Chinese culture accompanied it. By the seventh and eighth centuries, when the illustrious T'ang dynasty ruled China, Japanese society had enthusiastically surrendered itself to the spell of the new learning. Even in dress and social life Chinese customs were slavishly followed. In the beautiful new city of Nara, itself built on the Chinese plan in 710, the court gave itself up to the study and practice of Chinese religion, art and literature, philosophy and political institutions. The tuition continued for centuries, but in time the pupils left school and developed their own alphabetical system, arts and crafts and literature. Yet the original impulse, and the first models, came from China. We shall see presently in what manner the Japanese repaid the debt.

Much of Japan's early history is taken up with the struggles of the rival clan-chieftains to dominate the country. In the ninth century a remarkable situation set in. While the emperors continued to be revered as the heads of the State, the most powerful of the nobles for the time being became the real, and virtually hereditary, rulers. The emperors were mere figure-heads. Britain had " Warwick the king-maker " for a while in the time of the Wars of the Roses, but the Japanese dictators, or Shoguns (generals), wielded their power for centuries.

SAMURAI

From the tenth to the twelfth centuries Japan battled through some troubled times. The country was rent by the civil wars of the nobles. A new warrior class, the Samurai (" those who serve "), uprose and became a powerful and privileged element in the State. These rigidly self-disciplined fighting-men were like the knights of early feudal Europe. They developed a stern and elaborate code of duty and chivalry, in which faithfulness to their lord and contempt of death were the supreme principles. With his richly decorated plate armour, his two (or more) swords, his spear and other accoutrements and queer gadgets, the Samurai, astride his hardy mount, was a fearsome spectacle. The Shoguns themselves, supported by their Samurai followers, became military dictators. Japan lived under army rule and continued to do so till the nineteenth century. In these times, too, the feudal system was establishing itself. As for the common peasants, they continued, as of old, to live in a wretched state of serfdom.

One calamity the country escaped was that of being swallowed up by the Mongolian invasion which engulfed China in the thirteenth century. The plucky Japanese defied the all-powerful Kublai Khan and, in 1281, Nature backed them up with a typhoon that wiped out the invaders' mighty fleet. It reminds one of the Spanish Armada when the elements aided the English fleet.

The sixteenth century ushered in two notable events. Another weary spell of devastating civil wars between the feudal nobles virtually ended with the triumph of a single clan, the Tokugawa. Their Shoguns, established in the newly chosen capital of Yedo (now Tokyo), opened a new era. They unified the war-wracked country and held it together in unbroken peace for over 250 years.

The Samurai were the professional warrior class who fought for their masters, the Shoguns. The Samurai might be likened to the medieval knights.

The other experience was the coming of the first Europeans and their quest for the rich trade of the East. The first Portuguese ship dropped anchor off a Japanese island about 1542, and during the next seventy-odd years Dutch and British vessels followed. In 1549, the fiery-hearted Spanish Jesuit priest, Francis Xavier, one of the most renowned of Christian missionaries, arrived. Within half a century he and other devoted workers had gathered in 300,000 converts.

TOKUGAWA SHOGUNS

The Tokugawa Shoguns, however, mistrusted the foreigners. They suspected that missionary work and commerce might be only the preludes to attempts at conquest, or that their feudal chieftains, when equipped with the terrible new Western firearms might rise in rebellion. Accordingly, Christianity was ruthlessly and almost wholly suppressed and the foreign traders, except a handful of Dutchmen, were expelled. So it came about that, from about 1640, the island empire, with its doors banged, bolted and barred, remained for more than two hundred years secluded from the world. The West, with all its intense political, social and scientific activities and advancements, might do as it liked. Japan stood apart, aloof and inaccessible.

During this extraordinary period the Tokugawa Shoguns held the empire in the iron grip of their feudal, barrack-yard dictatorship. Time, however, brought the long tyranny to an end. The Samurai, having no more fighting to do, grew slack in loyalty and military qualities. The nobles lost prestige. Social barriers weakened. Though the empire's doors had been closed against the foreigners, there were cracks in them through which something could be seen of foreign doings, something learned of foreign ideas. The feeling spread that the Shoguns were wrongly usurping the powers of the divine emperors. General discontent and restlessness were intensified by economic distress. By the nineteenth century the leading elements of society were ready for drastic changes.

SOCIAL UNREST

The changes came; and, once begun, they tumbled over each other like a mill-race. In 1853, the American Commodore Perry, with four ships, came seeking trade. Soon commercial treaties were concluded with America, Britain and France.

The closed doors were flung open at last. Japanese missions were dispatched to America and Europe. In 1867, the last of the Shoguns retired, and the fifteen-year-old Emperor, Meiji, a famous figure in modern Japanese history, was restored to power. Presently feudalism was abolished and the order "*Dismiss!*" given to the Samurai. An all-out programme of modernisation was vigorously pursued. The electric telegraph, railways, parliamentary institutions (though not very democratic ones), a great mercantile marine, a powerful army and navy—all these ambitious projects, coupled with increase of trade and industry, were eagerly undertaken.

Western military science and technique received particular attention and the empire's ambitions rose as its armed power increased. In the wars with China in 1894-5, and Russia in 1904-5, Japan demonstrated that she had become a great world power. When the emperor died in 1912 his 45-year reign had witnessed an unparalleled transformation. Small wonder that the Japanese had come to regard themselves as the salt of the earth.

During the Second World War, the Chinese suffered a steady stream of defeats. They were frequently driven from their homes, carrying away as much as they could.

Japan joined the Western Allies in the First World War—and did well out of it. While the Allies occupied themselves with the war, Japan occupied herself with wringing possessions and sweeping privileges from China when that country was in the throes of its great revolutionary movement. Later, however, she relinquished most of these gains. From this time, and especially after 1930 when further sinister designs were being hatched against distracted China, Japan enormously expanded her industries, both those which would serve her warlike plans and those which would help to pay the cost and also support her increased population. The first group included coal, iron and steel, shipbuilding and engineering; the second embraced raw silk and textiles, tea, pottery, lacquer work, toys and other manufactures. Unscrupulous attacks on China followed and the seizure of the north-eastern provinces and southern ports took place from 1931 to 1938.

After the treacherous attack on Pearl Harbor, the U.S. forces had to wage a grim island-hopping campaign to win back the bases overrun by the Japanese.

The old and new Japan are to-day mingling together and giving rise to a confusion of customs.

This block of modern flats in Tokyo's Station Square is designed to withstand damage by earthquake.

In the Second World War Japan backed the wrong horse: she sided with Germany. The Empire of the Rising Sun set blood-red in defeat and ruin. Atom bombs blasted Hiroshima and Nagasaki. American and British troops occupied the country. All foreign conquests were lost. The mass of the people who had gone on believing in their country's divine mission of world domination must have thought that something had gone seriously wrong with it.

For six years Japan lived under American Occupation. It was a period in which, with American guidance and generous financial aid, a revolution in the social, political and economic life of the country was effected. In 1946, the reigning emperor renounced his preposterous claims to divinity. Next year a new constitution was created with a Diet, or parliament, based on Western principles. It consisted of a House of Councillors and a House of Representatives, each elected by adult suffrage, women being given the vote. The people were to enjoy freedom of thought and expression, fit standards of living, universal education and all other human rights. Education was remodelled on American lines. The economic system was extensively reorganised. Trade unions were fostered and the labour movement in general encouraged.

These were sweeping achievements; but, so far as democratic parliamentary government is concerned, the Japanese have much to learn. They have too often evinced a weakness, inside and outside the Diet, for settling differences of opinion with their muscles instead of their tongues. The rugger-scrum tactics resorted to in the fierce struggles for power waged by private interests and political parties—Liberals, Progressives, Socialists and Communists—have frequently led to tumult and confusion. The Communist party is relatively small at present; but its revolutionary doctrines have struck fire in the hearts of the students and teachers and gained influence among the workers. Settled government is further hindered by gross corruption and self-seeking, and there are signs of a revival of the old militaristic spirit.

From about 1948, the Americans took to encouraging Japan's rearmament. They were apprehensive about the spread of Russian and Chinese Communism in the Far East, and their aim was to make Japan a powerful bulwark against this menace. In 1951, the American Occupation came officially to an end. At the same time, however, a Security Treaty (revised in 1960) between the U.S.A. and Japan provided for the retention of American armed forces as a defence measure.

Since then America, as Japan's friend and ally, has continued to concern itself closely with the progress of the country towards military and industrial recovery as a step in the "Cold War" against the Red peril. Unhappily, the prolonged occupation of Japanese bases, and the re-armament policy generally, have provoked a wave of intense anti-Americanism. The Japanese fear that they may be involved in another war. And for the most part they have had enough of war for the present. So deeply was popular feeling stirred that on one occasion the U.S. ambassador and other officials were besieged in their car by a seething mob and had to be rescued by helicopter.

Japanese industry has made some giant strides since the war. Immense hydro-electric undertakings supply power for her factories and railways. She beats all other countries in the tonnage of merchant shipping launched. Between 1956 and 1960, she almost doubled her production of steel. In the manufacture of cotton textiles she is a serious threat to the British industry.

What of the future? Will Japan continue along the road to democracy? Or will she be captured by Communism, or yield to some reactionary system of government more akin to her historic tastes? Only time can tell.

The religious outlook is equally hazy. The great majority of the Japanese are Buddhists, yet they still cling, in varying degrees according to class and generation, to what survives of the old Shinto faith. The more primitive and bumptious doctrines, concerning the emperor's divinity and the empire's glorious destiny, received a shattering blow as the result of the Second World War; and with the progress of education the whole creed should tend to fade out. Yet Shinto is so inextricably bound up with Japan's proud past and traditional way of life that its influence cannot easily be wholly shaken off. As for Christianity, its converts are comparatively few —but its teachings appear to have made a spiritual impression quite out of proportion to the size of its following.

IMPORTANT DATES IN WORLD HISTORY

B.C.					
5000	Egyptian and Sumerian civilisations flourishing	871	Battle of Ashdown	1406-37	James I
		878	Battle of Edington—Alfred the Great	1413-22	Henry V
4000	Earliest traces of Minoan culture in Crete	919	Henry the Fowler	1415	Battle of Agincourt
		936	Otto I	1422-61	Henry VI
3000	Indus Valley civilisation well established; Chinese settlements established	960	Sung Dynasty founded	1437-60	James II
		962	Otto I crowned Holy Roman Emperor	1450	Jack Cade's rebellion
2100	Hammurabi			1453	End of Hundred Years' War; Fall of Constantinople
1523-1027	Shang Dynasty	987	Hugh, first Capetian King of France		
1400	Hebrews invade Canaan			1455	Outbreak of Wars of the Roses
1200	Assyrians overcome Hittites	988	Russian leader, Vladimir of Kiev	1460-88	James III
1027-256	Chou Dynasty	1016	Canute, King of England	1461-70	Edward IV
1025	Saul anointed King	1040	Macbeth, King of Scotland	1462-1505	Ivan III, first Tsar of Russia
660	Jimmu founds Japanese empire	1042	Edward the Confessor	1470-71	Henry VI
612	Chaldeans overthrow Assyrians	1066	Harold; Battle of Hastings; William I	1471	Battle of Barnet
586	Nebuchadnezzar captures Jerusalem			1471-83	Edward IV
		1085	Arabs driven out of Toledo	1476	Caxton sets up printing press in London
551-479	Confucius	1085-7	Domesday Book compiled		
539	Medes and Persians overthrow Chaldeans	1087-1100	William II	1479	Union of Aragon and Castile
		1096	First Crusade	1483	Edward V; Richard III (1483-5)
490	Battle of Marathon—Miltiades defeats Persians	1097-1107	Edgar, King of Scotland		
		1100-35	Henry I	1485	Battle of Bosworth; Henry VII (1485-1509)
480	Death of Gautama Buddha	1107-24	Alexander I		
256-207	Ch'in Dynasty	1124-53	David I—foundation of abbeys	1488-1513	James IV
431-404	Peloponnesian War	1135-54	Stephen/Matilda	1488	Bartholomew Diaz rounds Cape of Good Hope
336	Death of Philip of Macedon	1141	Rise of Chin Dynasty in N. China		
331	Alexander the Great defeats Persian Darius III			1492	Columbus reaches San Salvador
		1147	Second Crusade		
327	Alexander invades India	1154-89	Henry II, first Plantagenet	1498	Vasco da Gama reaches India
323	Death of Alexander	1164	Constitutions of Clarendon	1500	Cabral Discovers Brazil
264	Outbreak of First Carthaginian War	1181	Assize of Arms	1509-47	Henry VIII
		1187	Fall of Jerusalem	1513	Battle of Flodden; Balboa sights the Pacific Ocean
218	Outbreak of Second Carthaginian War—Hannibal and Fabius Cunctator	1189-99	Richard I, the Lion-Heart; Third Crusade; Saladin		
				1513-42	James V
		1199-1216	John	1515	Rise of Wolsey; Francis I of France
207 B.C.-A.D. 200	Han Dynasty	1202	Fourth Crusade; sack of Constantinople (1204)		
				1517	95 Theses of Wittenberg
146	Carthage destroyed	1215	Magna Carta	1519-22	Magellan circumnavigates the globe
55/54	Julius Caesar twice visits Britain	1216-72	Henry III		
		1258	Provisions of Oxford	1520	Charles V crowned Holy Roman Emperor
48	Defeat of Pompey	1264	Battle of Lewes		
44	Caesar murdered	1265	Montfort's "Parliament"; Battle of Evesham	1526	Battle of Mohacs; Fall of Hungary to Turks; Turks at walls of Vienna; Suliman The Magnificent
42	Battle of Philippi				
31	Battle of Actium	1272-1307	Edward I (Hammer of the Scots)		
0	Birth of Christ			1527	Charles V sacks Rome
		1273	Rudolph I, first Habsburg King	1540	Formation of the Society of Jesus (Jesuits)
A.D.		1279	Kublai Khan, Emperor of China		
43	Romans invade Britain			1542-67	Mary, Queen of Scots
330	Roman capital moved to Constantinople	1291	First Swiss confederation	1547-53	Edward VI
		1295	The Model Parliament; Marco Polo returns from China	1547	Ivan IV, "the Terrible," becomes Tsar
397	St. Ninian builds Candida Casa at Whithorn				
		1305	Death of William Wallace	1552	Somerset beheaded, Northumberland supreme
410	Sack of Rome by Alaric	1307-27	Edward II		
432	St. Patrick begins conversion of Ireland	1314	Battle of Bannockburn	1553-8	Mary I
		1327-77	Edward III; Treaty of Northampton	1556	Charles V abdicates; Emperor Ferdinand I of Austria; King Philip II of Spain
476	Last Western Emperor dethroned				
		1329	Death of Robert the Bruce		
563	St. Columba to Iona	1337	Outbreak of Hundred Years' War	1558-1603	Elizabeth I
589-618	Sui Dynasty			1567-1625	James VI
597	St. Augustine to Kent	1346	Battle of Crécy	1568	Netherlands revolt
618-907	T'ang Dynasty	1348	The Black Death	1571	Battle of Lepanto
622	Hegira (Mohammed's flight from Mecca to Medina)	1351	First Statute of Labourers	1572	St. Bartholomew's Eve
		1356	Battle of Poitiers; The Black Prince	1579	Dutch Union of Utrecht
632	Death of Mohammed			1587	Mary, Queen of Scots, executed
711	Arabs enter Spain	1368	Ming Dynasty	1588	The Armada
800	Charlemagne crowned Holy Roman Emperor	1377-99	Richard II; Peasants' Revolt	1589	Henry IV of France (Bourbon)
		1389	Battle of Kossovo	1598	Edict of Nantes; death of Philip II
843	Partition of Verdun (division of Charlemagne's Empire)	1399-1413	Henry IV		
				1600	Foundation of East India Company

1603-25 James VI of Scotland becomes James I of England

1605 Gunpowder Plot

1610 Louis XIII

1611 Authorised Version of Bible

1613 Michael Romanoff elected Tsar

1618 The Thirty Years' War

1620 Sailing of the *Mayflower*

1625-49 Charles I

1628 Petition of Right

1640 The Long Parliament

1640-88 Frederick William, the Great Elector of Brandenburg

1641 Grand Remonstrance presented to Charles I

1642 First Civil War

1643 Louis XIV

1644 Battle of Marston Moor; Ch'ing Dynasty founded

1645 Battle of Naseby

1648 Peace of Westphalia—Dutch independence confirmed

1648 Second Civil War

1649 Execution of Charles I

1650 Battle of Dunbar

1651 Battle of Worcester

1652-4 First Dutch War

1653 Rump Parliament sent home; Protectorate (1653-8)

1660 Restoration of Charles II

1661 The "Cavalier" Parliament summoned

1665-7 Second Dutch War

1665 Great Plague

1666 Great Fire of London

1670 Treaty of Dover

1672 Third Dutch War; Second Declaration of Indulgence

1673 Test Act

1685-8 James II

1685 Monmouth's Rebellion; The Bloody Assizes; Revocation of the Edict of Nantes

1687 Declaration of Indulgence

1688 James II deposed; Frederick I of Brandenburg (from 1701, Frederick I King of Prussia); Trial of the Seven Bishops

1689-1702 William III and Mary II (d. 1694); Bill of Rights; Tsar Peter the Great

1690 Battle of the Boyne

1701 The Grand Alliance (against Louis XIV) formed

1704 Battle of Blenheim

1706 Battle of Ramillies

1707 Union of Scots and English Parliaments

1708 Battle of Oudenarde

1709 Battle of Malplaquet

1713 Treaty of Utrecht; King Frederick William I of Prussia

1714 Treaty of Rastadt; George I (1714-27)

1715 Death of Louis XIV; Louis XV; the "Fifteen"

1719 The South Sea Bubble

1727-60 George II

1740 Accession of Maria Theresa; Accession of Frederick II of Prussia (the Great)

1740-8 War of the Austrian Succession

1745 "The Forty-Five"

1751 Clive captures Arcot

1756 Outbreak of the Seven Years' War

1757 Battle of Rossbach; Frederick the Great routs French; Battle of Leuthen, Frederick the Great routs Austrians; Battle of Plassey—Clive defeats French in India

1761-2 Tsar Peter III

1762-96 Empress Catherine II, the Great

1769-70 Captain Cook explores New Zealand and Eastern Australia

1775 Americans revolt at Lexington

1776 American Independence declared 4th July

1783 Britain acknowledges American independence

1788 First convicts land at Botany Bay

1789 French Revolution

1792 Victory of the Jacobins

1793 Death of Louis XVI

1795-9 Rule of the Directory

1797 Battle of Cape St. Vincent; Battle of Camperdown

1798 Battle of Aboukir Bay

1799 Napoleon elected First Consul

1800 Act of Union with Ireland

1804 Napoleon elected Emperor

1805 Battle of Trafalgar

1806 Death of Pitt the Younger

1810 Bolivar's rising in Venezuela

1812 The Retreat from Moscow

1813 Battle of the Nations

1814-15 Congress of Vienna

1815 Battle of Waterloo

1818 *Zollverein* (German Customs Union)

1820-30 George IV

1829 Greece wins independence

1830-7 William IV

1831 Belgium wins independence

1832 The Reform Bill

1834 Mazzini and Garibaldi lead revolt in Piedmont

1837-1901 Victoria

1837 Formation of New Zealand Company

1840 New Zealand annexed

1840-2 First China War

1848 Year of Revolutions

1852 Louis Napoleon overthrows 2nd Republic

1854-6 Crimean War

1857 Indian Mutiny

1860 Garibaldi's "Thousand" land in Sicily

1861 Italian monarchy created

1861-5 American Civil War

1862 Bismarck made Premier of Prussia

1863-4 Prussia gains Schleswig; Austria gains Holstein

1866 Austro-Prussian War; Battle of Sadowa; Prussia gains Holstein

1867 Disraeli's Reform Act; Dominion of Canada formed

1870 Franco-Prussian War; Education Act

1871 German Empire created

1875 Britain buys control of Suez Canal

1877-8 Russo-Turkish War

1877 Victoria created Empress of India

1878 Congress of Berlin

1885 Gordon dies in Khartoum

1894-5 Sino-Japanese War

1896-8 Kitchener in Egypt and Sudan

1899 Boer War

1900 Boxer Rising in China

1901 Commonwealth of Australia formed; death of Queen Victoria

1901-10 Edward VII

1904-5 Russo-Japanese War

1906 Liberal administration; first Labour Party M.P.s

1907 New Zealand becomes Dominion

1909 Union of South Africa formed

1910-36 George V

1914 Outbreak of First World War; Battle of the Marne (September); Battle of Ypres (October-November); Turkey joins Germany

1915-16 Gallipoli Campaign

1915 Italy joins the Allies

1916 Roumania joins the Allies; Battle of Verdun (February-September); Battle of Jutland (May)

1917 Russian Revolution (March); United States enters the War (April)

1919 Conference of Paris; Treaty of Versailles; Treaty of St. Germain-en-Laye

1922 Rise of Mussolini

1924 First Labour Government in Britain; Lenin dies and is replaced by Stalin; Stalin v. Trotsky—Stalin wins

1926 Imperial Conference in London; The General Strike in Britain

1931 Japanese invasion of Manchuria

1935 Italian invasion of Ethiopia

1936 Spanish Civil War; Edward VIII; Hitler remilitarises Rhineland; George VI (1936-52)

1938 Anschluss—Union of Germany and Austria (March); Chamberlain goes to Munich (September)

1939 German invasion of Czechoslovakia; outbreak of Second World War

1940 Dunkirk evacuation; France capitulates; Italy joins Axis powers; Battle of Britain

1941 Attack on Russia (June); U.S.A. enters war (December)

1942 Battle of El Alamein (23rd October)

1943 Russians recover Stalingrad

1944 "D" Day (6th June)

1945 Germany surrenders (May); Atom bombs dropped on Hiroshima and Nagasaki, Japan surrenders, (August); U.N.O. formed

1947 Indian independence granted

1949 Formation of N.A.T.O.

1950-3 Korean War

1952- Elizabeth II

1957 Suez Campaign

INDEX

Lloyd-George of Dwyfor, David, 1st Earl (1863-1945), Welsh statesman, 117, 144, 145

Locke, John (1632-1704), English philosopher, 102

Lollards, 50

Lombard League, 44; Lombards, 26, 27, 28; Lombardy, 59, 125, 127

London Missionary Society, 166

Longfellow, Henry Wadsworth (1807-1882), American poet, 141

Lorraine (See also Alsace), 124, 129, 142, 146

Lothian, Anglic Province in Scotland, 90

Louis, King of the Franks, 43

Louis IX (1214-70), King of France, 45

Louis XI (1423-83), King of France, 92

Louis XIII (1601-43), King of France, 76

Louis XIV (1638-1715), King of France, 72, 76, 77, 81-3, 94, 101, 103, 162, 163

Louis XV (1710-74), King of France, 103

Louis XVI (1754-93), King of France, 102, 103, 104, 105, 106, 122

Louis XVII (1785-c. 95), King of France in name only, 122

Louis XVIII (1755-1824), King of France, 122

Louis Napoleon. See Napoleon III

Louis Philippe (1773-1850), King of France, 122, 123

Louisiana, 77, 79, 134, 139, 140, 162, 163; Purchase, 140

Low Countries. See Netherlands

Loyola, Ignatius de (1491-1556), Spanish soldier and ecclesiastic, 75

Ludendorff, Erich von (1865-1937), German general, 145

Lusitania, U.S. liner, 144

Luther, Martin (1483-1546), German religious reformer, 65, 70, 71, 73, 75

Luxembourg, 146

M

McAdam, John Loudon (1756-1836), inventor, 111

Macalpin, Kenneth, High king of the Picts in 843, 90

Macaulay, Lord (1800-59), English historian, 116

Macbeth (d. 1057), Mormaer of Moray, 90

Macdonald, Flora (1722-1790), Scots heroine, 97

Macdonald, Sir John Alexander (1815-91), Canadian statesman, 165

Macedon, 19

Macedonia, 20, 26

Mackenzie, Sir Alexander (c. 1755-1820), explorer and Canadian furtrader, 165

Madagascar, 77, 169, 171, 172

Magellan, Ferdinand (c. 1480-1521), Portuguese sailor, 56, 72, 137, 162

Magna Carta (signed 1215), 41, 42, 47, 78

Maid of Orleans. See Joan of Arc

Malay States, 116; Malaya, 156, 181

Malcolm II, King of Scotland, 90

Malcolm III, called Canmore (1057-1093), 90, 91

Malta, 99, 108, 116, 121

Man: Aborigine, 9, 174; Ape-man, 9; Australopithecidae, 9; Cro-Magnon, 10; Homo Sapiens, 10; Homo Neanderthalensis, 9; Java (Pithecanthropus erectus), 9; Man-ape, 9; Modern (Swanscombe), 10; Neanderthal, 9; Palaeolithic,

10; Piltdown, 9; Pithecanthropus pekinensis, 9; Primates, 9

Manchuria, 14, 16, 136, 177, 178, 179

Manchus, The, 177, 178, 179; Dynasty, 177, 178, 179

Maoris, The, 175, 176

Mao Tse-tung (1893-), Chinese communist leader, 179, 180

Marathas, The, 97

Margaret, Saint (c. 1045-93), Queen of Scotland, 91

Margaret (1283-90), Queen of Scotland, 92

Margaret of Anjou (1430-1482), Queen of Henry VI, 51, 52

Margaret of Denmark, wife of James III of Scotland, 92

Margaret Tudor (1489-1541), Queen of Scotland, 64, 78, 92

Maria Theresa (1717-80), Empress of Austria, 85, 86, 96, 97, 98, 101, 102, 103

Marie Antoinette (1755-93), Queen of France, 102, 103, 105, 106

Marie Louise (1791-1847), Empress of France, 109

Mark Antony (83-30 B.C.), Roman statesman, 21

Marlborough, John Churchill, 1st Duke of (1650-1722), English general, 77, 83; Sarah, wife of above, 83

Marlowe, Christopher (1564-93), English dramatist, 69

Marx, Karl (1818-83), founder of Communism, 147

Mary I (1516-58), Queen of England, 56, 65, 66, 67, 68

Mary II (1662-94), Queen of England, 82-3

Mary (1542-87), Queen of Scots, 66, 68, 78, 93

Mary of Guise. See Guise

Matilda (1102-67), daughter of Henry I, 39

Matilda, wife of Henry I, 39

Maximilian I (1459-1519), Holy Roman Emperor, 56, 59

Mayas, The, 137

Mayflower, The, 79, 138

Mazarin, Jules (1602-61), Cardinal and minister of France, 76

Mazzini, Giuseppe (1805-72), Italian patriot, 125, 126, 127

Mecca, 29

Medes, The, 12

Meiji (1852-1912), Japanese Emperor, 183

Melville, Andrew (1545-c. 1622), Scottish theologian, 93

Memling, Hans (c. 1440-94), Flemish painter, 73

Mercia, 35, 36, 37

Merovingian dynasty, 27; peoples, 27

Mesopotamia, 11, 19, 143, 146

Metals, discovery of, 10

Methodism, 95

Metternich, Prince Clemans Lothar Wenzel (1773-1859), Austrian diplomat and statesman, 109, 128, 129

Mexico, 56, 133, 134, 138, 140, 144

Michelangelo (1475-1564), Italian artist, 60

Milton, John (1608-74), English poet, 83

Ming dynasty, 177

Minorca, 72, 83, 99

Minos, legendary king of Crete, 12

Mirabeau, Honore Gabriel Requetti, Comte de (1749-91), French Revolutionary, 103

Moffat, Robert, Dr. (1795-1883), Scottish missionary, 167

Mohamet. See Mohammed

Mohammed (c. 570-632), Founder of Mohammedanism, 29, 31, 158;

Mohammed II (1451-81), 57

Mona. See Anglesey

Monasteries, 27, 30, 35, 36, 65, 66, 91, 92, 93; dissolution of, 65, 93

Mongolia, 178, 179; Inner, 16

Mongols, 13, 15, 16, 53, 177, 181, 182

Monk, George, 1st Duke of Albemarle (1608-70), English general, 81

Monks, 27, 34, 35, 41,

Monmouth. James Scott, Duke of (1649-85), 82

Monroe, James (1758-1831), fifth President of the United States, 134, 141

Montcalm, Louis Joseph, Marquis de Montcalm Gezan de Saint Vëran, (1712-59), French general, 163

Montenegro, 129, 136

Montezuma II (1466-1520), last Aztec Emperor of Mexico, 138

Montfort, Simon de (c. 1206-1265), Earl of Leicester, 42, 47

Montgomery, Bernard Law, 1st Viscount Montgomery of Alamein (1887-), British field-marshal, 151, 152, 154

Montrose, James Graham, Marquis of (1612-50), 94

Moors, 31, 55, 62, 71, 72

Moots, 34, 39 64; folk-, 34, 37, 39; Hundred, 34, 36, 38, 39; tun-, 34, 39

More, Sir Thomas (1478-1535), English scholar and lawyer, 65

Moreau, Jean Victor (1761-1813), French general, 108

Morocco, 152, 171, 172

Moses (c. 15th cent. B.C.), Hebrew lawgiver and leader, 18

Motor car, 116

Mozambique, 166, 167, 170

Murat, Joachim (1767-1815), King of Naples and general, 109

Murray, Mungo, Scottish explorer, 167

Mussolini, Benito (1883-1945), Italian dictator, 148, 149, 150, 151, 152, 154, 171

Mutiny, Indian. See India

N

Naples, kingdom of, 59, 60, 72, 109, 127

Napoleon I, Bonaparte (1769-1821), Emperor of France, 99, 106, 107-9, 111, 122, 125, 128, 130, 133, 135, 140, 160, 180; retreat from Moscow (1812), 108, 109

Napoleon II (1811-32), King of Rome, Duke of Reichstadt, 123

Napoleon III, Charles Louis Napoleon Bonaparte (1808-73), Emperor of France, 112, 123, 124, 127, 128, 131, 132

Nash, John (1752-1835), English architect, 109

Nasser, Gamal Abdel (1918-), Egyptian political leader, 156

Natal, 115, 116, 170, 171

National (Constituent) Assembly, 103, 104, 123, 124

National Insurance Assistance and Health Service Acts, 117, 156

National Socialist Party (Nazi), 148, 149

Nebuchadnezzar II (c. 600 B.C.), 12, 18

Nehru, Jawaharal (1889-), " Pandit ", Indian statesman, 161

Nelson, Horatio, Viscount Nelson (1758-1805), British admiral, 99, 100, 107, 108, 133

Neolithic Age, 10

Netherlands, 24, 27, 30, 56, 59, 64, 68,

71, 72, 73, 75, 83, 85, 92, 94, 96; Austrian, 85, 106; Spanish, 73, 83, 101

Newfoundland, 69, 79, 83, 115, 116, 117, 137, 138, 139, 147, 162, 163

New Guinea, 153, 175

New South Wales, 99, 173, 174, 175

Newton, Sir Isaac (1642-1727), English mathematician, 83, 102

New Zealand, 73, 115, 116, 143, 147, 164, 173-6; discovery of, 73

Nicholas II (1868-1918), tsar of Russia, 135, 136

Nigeria, 156, 171, 172

Nightingale, Florence (1820-1910), English nurse, 113

Nineveh, 12

Nonconformists, 81, 82, 83, 95, 110

Norman Conquest, 37, 38, 40, 47, 91

Normandy, 30, 36, 38, 39, 41, 45, 153, 154

Normans, The, 30, 37, 38, 39, 40, 42, 47, 48, 90, 91, 92; cavalry, 90

Norsemen. See Vikings

North Atlantic Treaty Organisation, 155

North, Frederick, Lord (1732-92), British politician, 99

Northmen. See Vikings

Norway, 30, 36, 70, 89, 150, 153, 162

Novantae, British tribe, 89

Nova Scotia, 83, 139, 162, 163, 164, 165

Nyasaland, 168, 171

O

Oates, Titus (1649-1705), English conspirator, 81

Octavian. See Augustus

Odin, Scandinavian god, 30, 34, 35

Orange Free State, 115, 116, 170, 171

Oswell, William Cotton (1818-93), English explorer, 167

Otto I (912-973), Holy Roman Emperor, 43, 44

Otto III (980-1002), Holy Roman Emperor, 43

Ottoman Empire. See Empire

P

Pakistan, 156, 161

Palestine, 18, 145, 146

Palmerston, Henry John Temple, Viscount (1784-1865), English statesman, 111, 113, 114, 128

Panama, 63, 94, 134, 137; Canal, 63, 124, 141

Pankhurst, Emmeline (1857-1928), English suffragette, 147

Papal States, 27, 108, 126, 127

Park, Mungo (1771-1806), Scottish explorer, 170

Parliament, 34, 37, 42, 45, 47, 48, 50, 51, 52, 64, 65, 66, 67, 77, 79, 80, 81, 82, 83, 94, 95, 96, 99, 100, 103, 110, 111-2, 117, 118, 119, 120, 163, 164; Cavalier, 81; Commonwealth, 94; House of Commons, 50, 78, 79, 80, 81, 95, 96, 98, 100, 112, 117, 118, 119, 120; House of Lords, 50, 80, 81, 95, 112, 117, 120, 156; Long, 79, 81; Model, 47; Rump, 80; Scottish, 91, 92, 93, 94

Parr, Catherine (1512-48), English queen, 66

Pearl Harbor, Japanese attack on, 153, 183

Peasants' Revolt, The, (1381), 50

Pedro I (1798-1834), Emperor of Brazil, 134

Peel, Sir Robert (1788-1850), British statesman, 110, 113, 119

Pepin III, the Short (d. 768), younger son of Charles Martel, 27, 28